Women of Purpose Creating a Better World

By

Dr. Shyla Day

Table of Contents

Foreward

In a world often marked by challenges and adversity, it is the stories of resilience, compassion, and purpose that shine the brightest. *Women of Purpose: Creating a Better World* is more than just a collection of chapters; it is a testament to the indomitable spirit of women who dare to dream, strive, and make a difference.

This anthology brings together the voices of extraordinary women from diverse backgrounds, each with a unique story to tell. These are not just tales of personal triumph; they are narratives of collective empowerment, demonstrating how one person's actions can ripple out and create waves of positive change in their communities and beyond.

As you journey through these pages, you will encounter women who have overcome insurmountable odds, who have turned their pain into purpose, and who have dedicated their lives to lifting others. They are educators, entrepreneurs, activists, and healers. They are mothers, daughters, sisters, and friends. Yet, what unites them is a shared commitment to creating a better world—one act of kindness, one bold move, one unwavering stand at a time.

This book is a celebration of those who prioritize giving back, who use their platforms to amplify the voices of the marginalized, and who believe in the power of storytelling as a force for good. It is a call to action, a source of inspiration, and a beacon of hope. The women featured in this anthology remind us that no matter where we come from or what we have faced, we all have the power to make a difference.

As you immerse yourself in these stories, may you find not only inspiration but also the courage to pursue your own purpose with passion and dedication. Let these pages be a catalyst for reflection and action, encouraging you to recognize the impact you can make in the world.

To the readers: May this book ignite a spark within you, urging you to join the movement of women who are changing the world, one purposeful step at a time. And to the incredible women who have shared their journeys: Thank you for your courage, your vision, and your unwavering commitment to creating a better world.

I dedicate this collection of Women of Purpose wisdom to my Nieces, Big Sister, Mom, Aunt and both of my Grandmothers.

May we continue to teach, raise, and empower strong women for many generations to come.

Dr Shyla Day

Dr. Shyla Day-

Women of Purpose:
Creating a Better World

The Founder's Story

His guitar used to stare at me from the corner of the apartment. Well, the apartments would change, over the years, because my Mom was working several jobs as a single parent and we'd move too often to keep count. But, there was always a constant yearning, almost a knowing. A radiant beam of light, on display, his guitar- with the glittering dragonfly sticker on the top that my big sister gave him, and the leather case open and falling apart both from the time of touring, practices, late nights- and from the wear and tear from the night it all halted and the collection of years that had passed since. This guitar held his energy, and this indescribable connection to my Father, who passed from Cancer when I was One. Singing was already a huge part of life- Mom and Dad were touring in a Band while expecting me; but there was always something about that guitar. One day I picked it up, plucking the strings up and down for hours. Then, for days.

Surprise! Christmas rolled around- and I asked for a Piano! You know what they say, though? Momma knows best. The weekend after Christmas, when she could afford it, she took me to a hole-in-the-wall guitar shop in Pacific Beach, San Diego, California. She had already picked out a beautiful guitar with tiger-looking stripes on it. The smell of fresh wood, the gloss glistening off of the surface. She told me to si down and play. Reluctantly, as there definitely wasn't a single piano in this music shop, I sat down and strummed the strings. Well, Cynthia Rudy and I have been together ever since. She has her own dragonfly sticker, as do each of my instruments- and she's been with me through every trial and tribulation since I was 14. My medium, contributing to the most growth I've had personally and professionally, as well as a catalyst for how I create positive change in the world and will ultimately leave a legacy.

One of my friends was playing an open mic night, and he told me to come warmed up and bring my guitar. Little did I know, it was a bar- and being under 21, they hurried me in, let me play my set, and hurried me out. Waiting outside, was the promoter of a Television show; he was looking for guests and wanted me to play. Of course I took him up on the opportunity.

After the show, he asked me if I was looking for more gigs. He said the shows are for fundraising so I wouldn't get paid; but being a brand new music artist, I was just excited to get on a sage and share the love of music. After that Charitable Gala, watching the flashing lights on the red carpet, the stars talking about what was important to them, seeing how much we raised for Cancer research that night- was my turning point. It had me completely re-think how we, as humans, are able to give back.

Art, passion, business, media, time- we each have something to share that can truly make a difference.

I was touring with that charitable music group, when I won a songwriting competition. As a prize, I had the privilege of recording my single "Kiss Me", which charted #1 in Paris, France the City of Love in 2016. From there, a platform was created where I could give back in so many ways. I was partnering with organizations to spread their mission in Media, Radio, Television, Red Carpets, Social Media, my music events on tour, which turned into bestselling books and speaking— realizing the power is within us to share this message of impact, even when you are faced with a challenge.

The year of my TEDx talk, I got into a life altering car accident that changed my perspective forever. I woke up the day after the accident and my left leg wasn't listening to me the way that it used to, and this continued for 2 weeks. I was faced with a decision- keep going or let this be the thing to define me forever. It was my last semester of college, and as a first-generation graduate, I was determined to walk across that stage- I was determined to tell the story of how music can make such an astronomical positive impact on people's lives around the world. Championing the cause of music- because, music- is censored, banned, or downright illegal in some places of the world. I still walked for graduation, another luxury some Women in the world don't have. I was more fired up than ever, being a new graduate to make a difference in the best way that I know how.

Next thing you know, COVID hit, and in-person events were canceled. Art, Music Entertainment, were deemed not "essential," right when we needed the healing of art and community the most. Well, it's so funny to think about it looking back, because the majority of the world still expected night show hosts and entertainers to clock in from home, too. After all, artists are just as necessary as everybody else to make the world go round.

Music helped me heal in so many ways and provided me opportunities I never thought would be possible- which then turned into a medium for creating that same opportunity for others down the line. Growing up,

During this time, I turned to Social Media to find my community. Fast forward to now, this community is 1 Million+ strong, supported by Women of Purpose and Influencers Impact- where change makers have the opportunity and platform to share their stories of how they give back in the lives of others every day. From the bottom of my heart, thank you for supporting Women of Purpose, reading the book, embracing femininity, transformation, but most importantly believing in the movement.

As you reach the end of my chapter, and the beginning of the rest of this incredible collection of wisdom- I hope you've felt the rhythm of resilience, the melody of purpose, and the harmony of hope woven throughout my story. Life, much like music, has its high notes and its lows, but it's in the spaces in between—the quiet moments of reflection and the crescendos of courage—where we find our true strength. My journey is proof that even when the strings of life feel worn and fragile, you can still create something beautiful. Let this be a reminder that no matter where you begin, you have the power to rewrite your song and use it to make a lasting impact in the world. Just like a guitar string that vibrates strongest when pulled tight, our greatest moments of tension often lead to our most profound growth. Keep playing your melody; the world needs to hear it.

Bio

Shyla Day is an Award-Winning Music Artist, Best-Selling Author, Social Media Influencer with over 1 million followers. She is a Speaker, and International Humanitarian formerly recognized by a senior member of the Nobel Peace Prize Family. She has garnered global prestigious accolades in the fields of music, humanitarianism, social media, and entrepreneurship- winning Young Philanthropist of the Year at the 2024 Humanitarian Awards Global, and Winner of a 2024 Global Recognition Award, who says, "Shyla Day's ability to harness the power of art and media to address pressing global issues sets a new standard for influential figures in the 21st century [...] her work as a social media influencer, artist, and humanitarian has established her as a driving force for global betterment."

Overcoming Dyslexia, she evolved into a three-time bestselling author. Achieving distribution in 189 countries, in thousands of the largest retailers, libraries, and airports around the world- she founded Women of Purpose; a next-gen equal opportunity publishing company and international organization dedicated to empowering women to lead with purpose and create meaningful change. Through publications, workshops, and online communities, Women of Purpose provides a platform for women to share their stories, elevate their influence, and amplify their voices. Womens Journal States; *"Shyla Day's work with Women of Purpose amplifies the voices of women globally, empowering them to turn their experiences into catalysts for impactful change; [...] her leadership has ignited a movement where women are celebrated for their strength and ability to change the world."*

Shyla Day has dedicated her career to world betterment and positive impact on millions through thousands of charitable organizations globally. Though English is her second language, she has emerged as a powerful speaker, captivating audiences on prestigious global stages with her message of hope and perseverance. She led a passionate talk on the TED platform with over 30 million subscribers called "Music for Global Impact," where she sparked conversation on unconventional humanitarian efforts. Claes Nobel, of the Nobel Prize Family, stated "Shyla...represents our very best hope for the future".

www.Shyla-Speaks.com

www.ShylaDay.com

K. Crystal Griffith

Seasonal Purpose

To everything, there is a **season** and a time to every **purpose** under heaven. Ecclesiastes 3:1 NKJV

How many seasons are in a person's life?

It's easy from a human development point of view to see that we have childhood, young adulthood, adulthood, and then our golden years. But there are so many more seasons within each of those. There are seasons of great joy and great sorrow. There are seasons of great physical development and physical decline. And even within those, there are seasons of trials, traumas, grand adventures, and triumphs.

It is exceptionally easy to see the purpose and even the blessings that come with all the positive seasons of growth adventures and such; however, it could be difficult, if not impossible, to see the purpose in the tears, pain, debilitating illness, tragic traumas, and even death.

For me, my seasons included amazing things like my daughter's first steps, earning a master's degree, and traveling. But it also included more challenging things like our first deployment of my husband's military career, car accidents, and medical issues. I've also had to deal with seasons of heartbreak with the death of family members and even the death of my marriage. This current season includes trials with my child having multiple health issues that are life-altering for her and for me while being a nomad and adding a new real estate business.

Sometimes when we are so wrapped up in these challenges, in these seasons, that we cannot scrape together the purpose of it all. Sometimes wrapped up in our pain, in our worry, and our anxiety we skip over what beautiful blessings and purposes come from these trying seasons of life.

How does a season of pain by illness, trauma or an event have a purpose?

What happens when some of those unexpected seasons last months, years or decades? How does one remain thankful in the middle of those turbulent seasons?

Normally, seasons mark our lives through the weather, life changes, events, and more. They are time milestones with a baby's firsts and a teen's lasts, calendar countdowns for deployments, celebrations of school in and out, learning achievements, and cycles of life from support to independence and back to support. Seasons are eras of marriages, a diagnosis from start to finish, school years, sports seasons, plays, even caregiving.

The weather periods are marked by patterns we see over and over that also hold a purpose. For example, in winter, a barren bitter landscape is incubating the seeds that will spring to life in just a few short months. As humans, we have lived in seasons of our lives, some barren and bitter, while some are enjoying the fruit of those incubating seeds. Then others are living in parched summer desert seasons, while some are seeing fall life changes, whether they are expected or unexpected.

No matter the season, we all endure all four seasons throughout our lifetimes. But not everyone reaps the harvest of purpose during or after their experiences. They can miss the purpose of the season, perhaps being wrapped up in their disappointment, anger, guilt, shame, or pain. Some miss the purpose because they've been in the season so long, they forget any other seasons exist.

Some of us may have been taught we are created for <u>A</u> purpose, in a singular form. I was taught we have a gift and calling given by the one who created us.

Let me clarify a bit.

Our <u>gifts </u>are unique skills and talents.

Our <u>call</u> is the authority to use those gifts.

What was missed in the teaching was the <u>season</u> to use those gifts. Each season may require a different combination of those gifts. For example, I don't teach technology on a daily basis anymore but I use it daily. Teaching empty nesters technology is quite different than teaching millennials.

The season we are in requires the gifts in specific ways at particular times. The application of those gifts becomes the <u>purpose</u>.

What does this look like in real life?

When my sister recently sent her youngest off to college, everyone asked, "Where's Crystal to pack the car?" The running joke in the family is I like to play Tetris while packing things, a unique talent as a packing expert to pull out as needed. The season is moving to college, and the gift with purpose is being able to visualize where things should go for the best use of space. The talent is applying the gift, and the skill is learning when to use it.

What about you?

What gifts have been hidden within you that have a purpose? Yes, every single one of us has gifts, talents, and abilities that support a purpose in various seasons. Nope, you will not be able to convince me otherwise. Yes, every single one of us.

How do I know this?

Because of seasons.

The seasons change consistently, every year, one season into the next. The Creator set up those seasons for the success and consistency of our planet, weather, predictability, harvesting, and life cycles of what continues to provide food, oxygen, water, and more just for us.

Those seasons each have unique gifts, talents, and abilities. Winter can drop temperatures that freeze the ground, setting it to thaw for the next season. Spring offers new life in plants, trees, rain and wind for germination, with new life for creations. Summer allows animals to feast, plants to grow, and foliage abundance to prep for those who will need to hibernate in the fall into the winter. Each season has a specific talent that repeats its intended design year after year.

You have these special qualities as well. Those talents show up and repeat when the season returns. The talents may mature and grow as you learn more, grow more, and gain wisdom. The application of the talents may also look different as you gain wisdom about when and how to use them.

What does this look like in the real world?

There was not a caregiver gene that was genetically included in my DNA. And yet, I was considered the "mother hen" of my friend group. I always looked out for them, helped them, was the one who went with anyone who passed out in band competitions, basically the leader who took care of others. Today, I care give for my adult daughter with medical complexities. The innate gift of caregiving was fine-tuned as a talent and increased in skill over the years as a lifeguard trainer, CPR and first aid trainer, and medical advocate. The season of caregiving has been almost two decades for my daughter and decades for being a "mother hen". This gift has also become a foundational cornerstone for an organization I started for Medical Mom Warriors.

This caregiving gift has also shaped me into an intercessor prayer warrior. Another talent I discovered along the way, honed by the essential need to stay in constant prayer for my friends, daughter, and others encountered along the way. I wouldn't have called myself a prayer warrior to begin with though. In multiple seasons, continued communication taught me how to stay in an attitude of prayer, and constant communication with the One who has the solutions and the shoulders to bear the weight for what was being faced.

As you reflect on your life, your gifts, and your talents, what patterns are you seeing in your seasons? What has been replicated throughout your life? Have you been taking care of others your whole life? Have you been called out as a leader over and over again? Do you find yourself teaching in many situations? Do kids flock to you? What do you have a knack for? Take a moment to jot down what is coming to you.

Perhaps you've been avoiding or dismissing the gifts and talents? Have you ended up in similar situations again and again but haven't wanted to see the purpose in them? There's no shame here, only awareness. We have to be aware of what we are avoiding to see the purpose in it. And keep in mind, I haven't mentioned purpose is only for good. I spent over two decades in a marriage I couldn't see purpose in. Today, God connects me with women all over the globe with an instant kinship for those who have been in marriages fueled with pornography and affairs.

Have you noticed some of my seasons have spanned decades?

One, two, and even four decades of a season, some of which were droughts like the ten years of infertility, some were learning to medically advocate during my recovery and my daughter's ongoing medical journey for over thirty years, and learning how to live life amid chaos. Our seasons in life are not neatly packaged in just four-month journeys like the weather seasons. Oh, how I do wish some of them were but the reality is the purpose in those seasons is longer than four months.

Consider your longest struggle.

What is the root cause? Why has it stayed active in your life? Sometimes our struggles are from ourselves, such as a lack of true financial wealth understanding. Sometimes from bad incorrect teaching or theology, we learn along the way, such as staying in an abusive marriage because of a vow. Sometimes it's from a lack of application about what we've heard that could change things but we don't or can't apply it. There is no condemnation or shame here. Without awareness, we cannot make change. No matter how it came to be, it can be changed, shifted, and leveraged for a purpose you may not have seen before. Here are three incredible examples of leveraging pain for the purpose.

Augusto Odone took a horrible diagnosis for his son and fought to find a treatment that had not been discovered yet, leading to Lorenzo's Oil. This medical miracle extended his son's life by over twenty years. Many will have hope for Adrenoleukodystrophy, ALD, because of a father's purpose in a season of hopelessness.

Amanda Ferrin was diagnosed a few years ago with a terminal illness. Every day since that news was delivered has been a miracle, leading her to start It's A Miracle as a global movement. The purpose of her season is being a light to help others in hard dark places and to have them partner in her journey with her, learning how to walk with someone in their hardest moments.

Dr. Lynnette Simm shared a heart-wrenching story of sexual abuse redemption in her book, And the Day Came, which is now a documentary, Tear Stained Forgiveness, being shared around the world. People are coming forward, healing, and helping others move from the darkness of sexual abuse to the light in this arena. The dark barren season of winter in my friend's life became a beacon of hope and life for many.

What about you?

Your season may not lead to a discovery, movement, or book but it does have a purpose. What is God showing you about what you've been living through? What gifts, talents, and abilities are showing through this season? Take time right now to jot them down. Please give yourself a gift right now. Do not dismiss anything that comes to your heart or mind as you are reading this chapter. Sometimes the most random thing becomes the most innovative purpose. One client had an image of a star come to mind and by the end of the heart healing session, God had reminded her that her dad called her his little star. It was a sweet unexpected gift.

Perhaps your season is a moment instead of a long duration of time. How many times you have been perfectly placed in what you thought was a coincidence, running into someone you had been thinking about? Or perhaps you've had someone on your mind or heart? Or you sat beside someone on a plane you connected with? I was walking through an airport and saw a sticker that said Splankna on someone's laptop. That random chance encounter led me on a path for a heart healing certification plus a deeper relationship with the Lord while being a part of hundreds of people and their generations being healed from pain they never thought possible to break free from. Random, I don't think so, part of a purpose in a season that was unfolding - absolutely!

Our season could be as short as a smile and a kind word to the barista as you pick up your morning cup of chai. That one smile leads that barista to reconsider taking her life after her shift. Yes, this is a true story. You have no idea what your kindness, patience, and generosity can offer others. I spent the better part of a morning recently chatting over breakfast with a gentleman from the streets. I was late leaving the house, I wasn't planning to go to this location, and yet God knew and had it ready for a divine encounter. That morning, this young man received confirmation about the book he needed to write about his near-death experience.

Your purpose is there, in your season whether it is a moment, a month, a year, or even a decade or more.

Let's take a moment to define Seasonal Purpose. We know each part individually, season and purpose, and how they connect. But how do they apply as we live through the season, especially when it is longer than we anticipate or longer than we want it to be? What if the purpose is hidden amid the chaos the season may be causing? The reality is a blizzard has an afterglow beauty but during it, your life is at stake, the stress is high, and that type of storm can have lasting effects.

How can we fortify ourselves emotionally, physically, and spiritually as we live through the seasons with the ups and downs? Seasonal Purpose reflects the dynamic nature of purpose, showing how it can evolve and remain strong despite the changing circumstances in life. Become more capable and influential as you pursue your purpose, focusing on the importance of being flexible, resilient, and growth-oriented as you navigate the various seasons of life. Most of all finding the things to be thankful for during the season you are maneuvering through.

As you read below through the active words that comprise Seasonal Purpose, take a few moments to ask yourself how you have incorporated that specific action into your seasons. What can you identify you are thankful for in the season?

Seasonal Purpose

S - Shift: The ability to change direction or focus as new seasons of life emerge.

The realization of a new season may come abruptly or you may be eased into it. Perhaps you see it coming but there may be some denial. In 2020, we all had an abrupt new season to contend with globally. But for my daughter, a different reason for a new medical season came. She collapsed on the floor unable to feel from the waist down. Fortunately, her season of physical loss was only 9 months before she regained feeling and movement in her legs. The season had been an unexpected thrust into a medical arena I didn't even know existed. As a result, I have now spoken on global panels and researched connections to a diagnosis she was given later with how it interacts with the body. It took years and putting together several diagnoses before we determined the cause. The season had a purpose. The purpose leveraged those speaking gifts and skills learned over the years, which have become part of coaching other medical mom warriors.

E - Endurance: The strength to persist through the various challenges that each season may bring.

The reality of seasons is they are much longer than desired. The quick-moment versions do happen, especially if you are looking for them. But the majority of seasons are often longer than a typical 4-month season. Our endurance is stretched beyond what we even think we can stand during some of these seasons. My infertility season was 10 long years with 2 failed adoptions. In fact, scientifically I should not have nor could I bear a child. Those tubes were blocked with scar tissue that special X-rays showed. It was truly a miracle through prayer I became pregnant. And even then there were several high-risk factors from family history, a traumatic brain injury, my age, and my weight. The challenges in that season were emotional and physical. The purpose is still being shown. I have no doubt my miracle child has purposes like no other. Each of us has a unique purpose only we can fulfill because of what we have survived, learned, and applied in our season.

A - Adaptability: The capacity to adjust to new circumstances and embrace change with grace.

Of course, we always have a choice to adapt, overcome, or shift, but the reality is these seasons tend to force it upon us. Divorce for example is never something we want to choose but may have to for safety, sanity, or health reasons. Having children in the picture while you walk through a divorce requires finesse and grace. Those interactions have spoken to our daughter and taught her how to adapt in incredibly difficult situations.

S - Solitude: The understanding and acceptance of times of quiet reflection, which are often necessary in all seasons of life.

This concept of solitude is so important in every season we encounter. Even Jesus took moments of reflective solitude, some for a moment and others for 40 days. Especially as a caregiver, you have to take moments for yourself to recharge. It wasn't on purpose but this year has had a season of travel. Some quick weekends, others a week while each of them has a unique purpose in reflection, renewal, or redirection. It's been an unexpected, appreciated, and well-needed gift this season. I teach clients to take a solo vacation quarterly. Be in charge of no one else, nothing else, and make decisions quickly for yourself only. No, this is not selfish. It is vital to put your oxygen mask on first, just like on a plane, so you can pour out to others from a place of health.

O - Openness: A willingness to embrace new experiences, ideas, and growth that come with different seasons.

As each season unfolds for you, there have been new experiences that have brought new skills, talents, or ways to use your gifts. As a public speaking teacher, I did not expect to use those skills by interviewing speakers at summits or hosting conferences. Those honed skills led me to speak on global platforms teaching others about medical advocacy, hope, and healing. The topics came from seasons in my life experiences. The gift to speak was given to me, with the talent to practice it, but the purpose was a way to share the hard seasons and how to come through them well.

N - Nurture: The act of caring for and developing oneself and others during each season, allowing for growth and renewal.

By nature, caregiving has nurture within it. To help the one you are caring for identify ways for more independence is not always easy. There is a protective mode to not only keep them safe but also to reduce collateral damage you may have to clean up. My daughter is spreading her wings more and I see the pitfalls I want to protect her from. In some areas, she could bounce back, although more slowly than other people, but in other areas I don't know that she could bounce back. It's a hard season of letting go, praying, and spreading as many nets as possible as she steps out and I find new ways to nurture her and me.

A - Awareness: The keen recognition and understanding of the distinct qualities and opportunities present in each season of life. It involves being attuned to the shifts and changes around you, allowing you to respond with intention and purpose, and making the most of each season as it unfolds.

How we respond to each season in our lives will determine the purpose initially. As we work out that purpose we do make adjustments. Our initial responses to a life-altering event may look radically different in a few months or even years later. Only four months into my marriage, I was in a car accident that rendered me useless. My initial outlook was "Why?" for a long time. It was destroying my marriage with lies coming to the surface and abuse starting. I thought my brain injury stole my life's dream of obtaining a Ph.D.. I didn't even know my name on many days. And the head pain was excruciating. How could there be purpose in any of this? Leaning on God was my saving grace in these moments. My awareness of Him taught me more about purpose even when I did not understand it in that season. Holding on, and adapting to the season, while learning how to shift, taught me to go deeper with Him, seeking healing, leading to opportunities for physical healing later. The years of medical advocacy I had to learn for myself became foundational in supporting my daughter during her health crises a decade later.

L - Learning: The continuous process of gaining knowledge, insights, and wisdom from the experiences that each season of life offers.

As you've seen through the life seasons I have shared, learning is a constant in every season. To surrender or give up is not an option, even in grief. Learning how to leverage those emotions of pain allows us faster processing, teachable moments, and healing. Each season holds a layer and depth of learning. The wisdom gained can be applied to another season in the future. And even if the seasons look similar, they are not because you are not the same. You have learned. You have grown. You have matured. You are encountering a similar season with more wisdom. Even if you think you messed up, went backward, or failed, I guarantee you did not. We are an ever-changing work in progress that is never complete because we are innate lifelong learners. I have started over ten businesses. Some never got off the ground. A hurricane took out a classroom the week before we started one business. My ex was in a horrible car accident a week before I started another one. Every business taught me something new to be used later. Failure is never a failure, it is an opportunity to learn something. Today, Medical Mom Warriors is a conglomeration of everything I have learned and continue to learn, and has helped me in coaching in ways I never expected.

PURPOSE:

P - Perseverance: The ability to continue striving toward your goals despite challenges and obstacles.

As each season comes upon us, we have a choice to give up or press through. It is not always mind over matter. YOU! It is sometimes just putting one foot in front of the other because there is no other way. Someone is depending on you. Just this past week, my daughter was diagnosed with yet another supposedly lifelong ailment, one we had already beat into remission. Faced with another variant of it, we both knew it could be beat. Using what we had learned in the first round, we immediately pulled out our tools to get to work. The purpose of the earlier season has led to what we know will be a success in this season.

U - Understanding: A deep comprehension of oneself, others, and the purpose that guides your actions.

Learning who you are in the process of walking through the seasons, can be valuable in the crisis and the lulls. It may be easy to find something to help you escape those moments of crisis or dark valleys. We can easily be tempted to check out of the situations by addiction, sleep, social media, work, or other vice. Who is the escape helping? Self-care is essential to include as part of your seasonal routine, even as a caregiver. Schedule it in. Teach it to your loved ones. The solitude mentioned earlier affords the time to get to know yourself, understand yourself, and choose how to interact with what the season may be throwing at you. Combining reflective solitude and understanding yourself will strengthen you. For me, the water is my healing space. There is something about the beach waves lapping the shore, the sun reflecting on the waves, and the smell of salt in the air that grounds me. A twenty-minute walk with my feet on sand can cure just about anything for me. It brings me a clarified understanding of many things I may be wrestling with in that season.

R - Resilience: The capacity to recover quickly from difficulties and stay focused on your purpose.

We would like to think we all bounce back quickly from a crisis or long hard season but reality says otherwise. Each hard season combined with a previous one does tend to make it harder to see hope as it wears us down. Notice I didn't say impossible though. Yes, you may have to persevere more, pushing through the muck and mire of the season, but it is possible. You can seek the hope that offers you peace in the middle of a turbulent time. You can have rest in it while it storms around you. Seeking that purpose in solitude and understanding while applying the learning helps you shift in the new season. These are all going to serve you well as you also leverage the wisdom you've gained.

P - Passion: The intense enthusiasm and dedication that drives you toward fulfilling your purpose.

Passion doesn't always feel like it's enough during certain seasons. I've been working on Medical Mom Warriors for four years. It's been a slow start-up process because kiddo's health crises tend to derail timeframes. Wanting to help others has never left but finding balance in supporting my daughter in her health journey has been challenging. Our passion can convert to purpose. I would never have considered Medical Mom Warriors without what my child has been through, even though I am a medical warrior myself. The passion to help other moms was activating for me and thus Medical Mom Warriors was birthed.

O - Optimism: A hopeful and positive outlook that fuels your journey, even in tough times.

Deployment seasons for military families tend to strain the single parent at home. The purpose to "get through" the deployment time becomes the focus. To keep a positive outlook, special visual calendars help the children stay focused on the purpose as a goal. Counting down the days gives a concrete time the season will be over and keeps the excitement going with the visual cues. I remember one deployment my kiddo had no problem with daddy being gone. She was getting an early birthday before he left, her normal birthday, and then extended family during our summer trip. For my child, who was only three at the time, the season wasn't as noticeable with the distractions of multiple birthdays that year.

S - Service: The act of helping others, which often aligns with and reinforces a sense of purpose.

Seeking others in the seasons is so pivotal to gaining wisdom. Realizing others are going through similar journeys as yours is reassuring to you and can offer you the value of what they have learned along the way. Sharing lessens a burden. Helping others really is helping yourself in many ways. It can also shape what the purpose may look like for you. How many moms have created a million-dollar product at their kitchen table because there was a need? I know a mom whose daughter needed a weighted blanket on her at all times for anxiety. The mom made a weighted vest and now is introducing it into the medical arena. Her act of service for her daughter led to an unexpected season that will support them financially and help thousands around the globe.

E - Empowerment: The process of gaining strength and confidence, aligning with a sense of purpose that fuels both personal growth and the ability to uplift others.

Overall seasons of hills and valleys empower how you live your life. Realizing you can work through the unexpected, you can find new answers and solutions, and you can create a purpose from the pain that will help others. The skin cancer mentioned earlier led to a sizeable melanoma on my head, resulting in a bald bodacious look for many months. It also empowered me to talk to hairdressers for them to say something if they see something while cutting hair. My melanoma season of purpose has actually saved lives!

I choose to share every Seasonal Purpose with others. If even one thing I have lived through can help someone else, saving them pain, time, and energy, I want to share it.

S - Shift

E - Endurance

A - Adaptability

S - Solitude

O - Openness

N - Nurture

A - Awareness

L - Learning

P - Perseverance

U - Understanding

R - Resilience

P - Passion

O - Optimism

S - Service

E - Empowerment

As you reflect on your Seasonal Purpose, what stands out the most? What patterns do you see? What do you see now you did not see before? How do you want to use your Seasonal Purpose moving forward?

SEASONAL PURPOSE encapsulates the idea that each season of life offers unique opportunities for growth, learning, and transformation. Embracing these changes with an open heart and mind can lead to a richer, more fulfilling purpose activated life. I have found people are receptive to sharing Seasonal Purposes. In fact, the season you may be in right now, multiple people are walking the same journey. People have been diagnosed, received healing, learned about tools, saved from a lifetime of pain, received healing, empowerment, and hope just because I am willing to share what came out of my Seasonal Purposes.

How are you willing to share your Seasonal Purposes?

Without question, you can and will excel in your Seasonal Purpose as you live your best life physically, emotionally, spiritually, and professionally. Want a beautiful visual reminder for Season Purposes? Bring your tea and visit with me at https://linktr.ee/kcrystalgriffith.com.

RESOURCES FOR THIS CHAPTER:

Lorenzo's oil:

https://adrenoleukodystrophy.info/treatment-options/lorenzos-oil

And the Day Came: by Dr Lynnette Simm (Author), Michelle Hoffman: https://www.drlynnette.com/

Terminal ain't Terrible: https://amandaferrin.com/

Bio

https://linktr.ee/kcrystalgriffith.com

K Crystal Griffith is a Jesus-loving, sweet tea-drinking, renaissance woman empowering Medical Mom Warriors with health, healing, and hope advocating for them and their medically complex kiddos to thrive.

Crystal walks with clients through deployments, life-threatening allergies, autoimmune diseases, cancer, traumatic brain injuries, concussions, marriage difficulties, abuse, PTSD, reactive attachment disorders, generational traumas, spectrum disorders, and all the things that go bump in the night. These and many more have influenced Crystal's life directly as well She is a Certified Heart Healing Practitioner, Business Coach, and Medical Advocate supporting medical mommas to advance their reach through their personal experiences.

Crystal, her beautifully creative, humorous, horse-loving daughter, and her service dog Otter, make their home in the Rockies.

Ana Sneeringer-

Women with purpose make a difference in people's lives

The sun hung low in the sky, casting a golden hue over the dusty streets of the escalating city of Hyderabad. I stood in my art studio on the third floor of our house, watching past the fence of our community, observing the city coming alive in the waning light. The town never really slept, but observing its movement later in the day was charming. There was a window in my studio, the only window that had this faraway view of the part of the city, where I found myself staring a lot of times to find myself reflecting resilience in my thoughts. India has been my home for almost five years. It became a land where I could lose myself in the vibrant chaos and rediscover who I was beneath the layers of a past that had stuck with me for years.

My journey to this moment had been anything but linear. It began with dark shades of light in the shadowed corners of my childhood, where chaos reigned and uncertainty was my constant companion. I learned early on to build walls, to protect the fragile parts of myself that still longed for safety, for love. I learned early on to become a tough woman. But these walls of my childhood home, once a refuge, soon became a prison, trapping me in a cycle of fear and self-doubt. When I turned nineteen, I left home to study. I was studying life instead of being assigned college.

In the quiet hours of the night, behind the walls of my tiny room in my parents' house, I would dream of being an artist. The thoughts were a simple act of rebellion. Were they? My parents wanted me to be a nurse and then a doctor. But all I wanted to be was to be someone else. I did not understand how I could be a doctor if I couldn't stand the blood, and I projected everyone's pain onto myself. Being an artist in my head was a way to carve out a space that was mine alone.

But life wanted a different me. I tucked away the thought of being an artist for years and became a TV director. Until I was twenty-nine, when I left my home country, Slovenia, forever. I started my life journey of exploring myself as a woman. It wasn't intentional. It all happened because I took a leap of faith and said, "It's this or better."

As the years passed, and I changed countries in between, I realized that I started painting. At first, making art was a release, but as the years passed, I realized that painting was my lifeline. Each brushstroke was a whisper of strength, a reminder that there was something within me that could not be broken. My art became my voice, telling the stories I was too afraid to speak aloud.

But it wasn't until I set foot in India that I began to understand the true power of storytelling, not just as an artist but as a woman. The women I met here were a revelation. In their eyes, I saw the reflection of my struggles, but I also saw something more—a quiet, unyielding strength that defied their hardships. They carried their stories with grace, their scars woven into the fabric of their identity, not as wounds but as marks of resilience.

One woman in particular, Jamuna, became a significant source of inspiration. She was young, in her early 20s, but had lived through a life that would have shattered many, yet she spoke of her past with a calm acceptance that astonished me. She was my friend, yet I was seventeen years older than her. She loved to cook, so every time she came to my house, we went to my kitchen, where she wanted to make me her Indian dish. The kitchen would fill with the thick scent of spices as she shared her stories. Her rich and full laughter would fill the room, and I was drawn to her warmth and unbreakable spirit. We had difficulty communicating initially, but she spoke English well as time passed. Through her, I began to see my story differently—not as a series of unfortunate events but as a testament to my survival. And it was through me that I saw her bloom in her independence.

As the months turned into years of being in India, my art began to change. The stories and strengths of the women I met in India started to bleed into my work. My paintings became a celebration of resilience and the quiet power within every woman. Each canvas was a tribute to those who had touched my life, a visual narrative of strength and identity.

But more than that, my art became a way to connect with others and build bridges across cultures and experiences. I conversed with women from all walks of life, sharing our stories and finding common ground. There was a solidarity in these exchanges, recognizing that while our struggles may differ, the strength we draw from them is universal.

During my time in India, I have deepened my appreciation for the world's rich culture. The vibrant colors, the intricate patterns, the rhythms of daily life—all of it found its way into my art. I began to see my work not just as an expression of my journey but as a reflection of the connections I had made and the beauty I had witnessed in the diversity of human experience.

And so, as I stood that day in my studio, watching the sunset over Hyderabad, I felt a sense of peace that had long eluded me. My journey was far from over, but I had found something invaluable: a sense of purpose, belonging, and a renewed strength that would carry me forward.

I want to share this story with you to encourage you to seek your passion and find strength in your stories. No matter whether the night is dark, the sunrise is always waiting on the horizon. In that light, we can see the power to heal, grow, and become the women we were always meant to be. **But this only comes with the statement that you want a change in your life.**

This story is not just mine—it belongs to every woman who has ever felt lost and struggled to find her way. It is a testament to the power of resilience, the beauty of cultural connection, and the transformative nature of art. It is an invitation to all who read it to find their path to strength and fulfillment, to know that they are not alone, and to know that within them lies a well of untapped power waiting to be discovered.

Bio

Ana Sneeringer is a Slovenian artist residing in Montgomery AL, USA. Having started her career in documentary journalism as a director of an environmental television station, Ana's experiences across Jordan, France, Russia, the USA, The Dominican Republic, The Netherlands, and India, led her to express her observations & learnings in her contemporary artworks. Women or the female presence form the epicenter of her artistic exploration and stories. Living around the world and engaging with women from different cultures, Ana's encounters resonated with the similarities of emotions and experiences everywhere, rather than the disparities of race or color. As a result, her artistic canvas is a vivid, kaleidoscopic world of thoughts, emotions, and experiences shared by the modern woman. Entirely self-taught, Ana finds liberation in employing free will and speaking from her heart, unconfined by a learned discipline. Whether in watercolor, acrylic, or digital media, she gives herself the freedom to experiment based on her subject matter.

Ana's art has been exhibited internationally in the United Arab Emirates, Italy, the United States, the United Kingdom, Canada, India, and Switzerland. Sneeringer has been exhibited in many arts and interior world recognized magazines as Beautiful Bizarre, Harper's Bazaar Interiors etc.

In 2020 one of her artworks was exhibited and is now part of their private collection in one of three National museums in India, Salar Jung Museum. Hyderabad, India.

Linda Thùy Le-

Releasing Hidden Blocks

Chào (hello in Vietnamese)! My name is Linda Thùy Le, I'm a healer, coach, hypnotist and spiritual teacher. My journey has been one of deep exploration into the ways our minds and spirits work— understanding how our conscious and unconscious minds interact, how our thoughts and emotions shape our realities, and how healing energy flows through our bodies. This knowledge allows me to guide others in their own healing, helping them uncover hidden wounds, break free from limiting beliefs, and transform their lives in profound ways.

My approach is not only about healing; it's about *integrative* healing and empowerment. Imagine your spiritual, mental, emotional, and physical health as the four wheels of a car. If one wheel is flat, the car can't move forward smoothly. In the same way, if any part of your being is out of balance, it affects your entire life. My work helps people address these imbalances at the deepest, unconscious level— places within them that they may not even realize exist. By releasing these hidden blocks, my clients experience transformation across all aspects of their lives. It's a holistic process that honors the complexity of the human experience and leads to lasting change.

My own journey into this work began unexpectedly when I became a mother at 33. I wasn't ready— emotionally, mentally, or spiritually. I was still grappling with my own childhood wounds, and suddenly, I was responsible for another life. Motherhood thrust me into what felt like an endless darkness, a time when I was forced to confront the deepest parts of myself. But it was also the catalyst that led me to discover my true purpose. Through the struggle, I found a path to healing, empowerment, and fulfillment, transforming from a lost and broken soul into a woman who now lives each day with purpose and passion. My life's work is to help others find that same path.

I want to share with you the steps I took to get here. I went from a place of no self-worth, no confidence, and no direction, struggling with addiction and depression to a life that is rich with meaning and contribution. The secret is that true fulfillment comes when there is no divide between what you do and who you are. As Mark Twain wisely said, "Find a job you love, and you will never have to work a day in your life." This isn't just a saying; it's a truth I live by **When your work aligns with your soul's purpose, it doesn't drain you; it energizes you. And that's what I want for you. If I could rise from my darkest moments to create a life of joy, impact and fulfillment, so can you. Let me show you how.**

My purpose is to empower people—to help them realize that they are fully in control of their lives. This realization might sound simple, but it's profound: you possess all the potential and resources needed to create the life you desire. My own purpose crystallized the day I freed myself from the chains of my past. The stories that once haunted me began to transform. The pain that used to pierce my soul turned into powerful lessons and deep wisdom. Now, when I reflect on my life, I see that every experience, every challenge, was meticulously designed to prepare me for the role I am meant to fulfill in this world. If even one of those moments had been different, I might not be able to show up as fully as I do today.

Let's start with a simple but profound concept: CHOICE. In every moment, in every situation you encounter, you have a choice, and these choices shape your reality. Let me illustrate this with a common scenario. You're driving, and someone suddenly cuts you off or honks at you for no apparent reason while you're sticking to the speed limit. What do you do? Do you think, "What a jerk," flip them off, honk back, or speed up in retaliation? Or do you take a deep breath and think, "Maybe they're late for something important; I hope they get there safely," and then go on with your day? In that moment, you have several choices. The first choice is the meaning you assign to the event. The second choice is how you act or react. The third is what you do with the emotional state that follows.

If you choose to think, "What a jerk," you'll likely become irritated, which might lead you to retaliate by speeding up, cursing, or making a rude gesture. This irritation could then seep into the rest of your day, affecting your mood and productivity at work. On the other hand, if you choose to think, "Maybe they're in a hurry," you might feel compassion, say a quick prayer for their safety, and continue your day unaffected. This small incident illustrates the power of choice. Now, imagine the impact of these choices multiplied over years and decades. How many decisions have you made, and how have they shaped your life?

Each choice creates a different reality and outcome, and over time, these choices accumulate to form the life you live. When you fully understand the power of your choices, you reclaim your power and take charge of your life. That is true empowerment. You have the daily opportunity to transform your poison into medicine, your pain into purpose. You can choose to find wisdom instead of casting blame, to seek help to heal rather than continue to wallow in your stories. The choice is yours; therefore, the power is yours as well.

The beginning of my path to empowerment was not a grand awakening, but a desperate effort to stay alive. At that time, life felt tenuous, as if I were clinging to the last frayed thread of existence, one that seemed ready to snap at any moment. It was the morning of March 20, 2010—a Sunday like any other. The house was quiet, with everyone still asleep as the first light of day filtered through my window. I tried to steal a few more minutes of sleep, pulling the blanket over my head. Outside, I could hear the familiar sounds of my elderly neighbors tending to their garden, their morning routine as predictable as the sunrise. These sounds were my daily alarm clock, signalling the start of another day.

I was in my final year of college, and after a late-night shift, I decided to sleep in, a rare morning of rest. The phone rang, interrupting the stillness. It was our landline—an oddity even in 2010—and no one rushed to answer, assuming it was another marketing call. But the ringing persisted. Finally, my sister groggily picked up the phone. Her sleepy murmurs quickly turned to panic: "WHAT? WHAT? ARE YOU SURE? HANG ON, I'LL GO CHECK." The urgency in her voice jolted me awake. I could hear her frantic footsteps as she raced down the hall to our brother's room, the door crashing against the wall as she flung it open. Moments later, she was back on the phone, asking, "What's your address? Can I come look at the stuff now? Can you tell me what's inside the bag?" The words that followed etched into my memory forever, unbound by the passage of time. After hanging up the phone, my sister turned to me, her face ashen, and said, "Troy died. Troy died. I think Troy is gone. WAKE UP. We have to go now." Her voice was filled with shock, terror, and disbelief, and it reverberated through my mind like an echo I couldn't escape. I jumped out of bed, my heart racing, and asked her what had happened. She explained, her words tumbling out in a blur of confusion and fear. Our brother Troy had gone to the beach with a friend the day before. They got caught in a rip current. His friend, Jane, was rescued, but Troy was nowhere to be found. Jane's mother had called, asking us to come and identify his belongings—left behind on the shore like remnants of a life that had suddenly vanished.

When we arrived and opened the bag, I was met with the unmistakable reality of his absence: his wallet, t-shirt, towel, sandals, cell phone. My chest tightened with a pain so intense it felt like a hundred daggers piercing my heart. My mind couldn't accept it. I kept thinking, this can't be real. This isn't real. Wake up. This is not real. You're still sleeping, wake up. But no matter how many times I told myself it was just a nightmare, the truth remained. Days passed in a haze of disbelief. We waited at the beach, hoping his body would wash ashore. But as the days turned into weeks, I had to face the unthinkable: my baby brother was gone, not just for a day or a month, but forever.

Troy was barely 18, with his whole life ahead of him. We were seven years apart, and because our parents worked long hours, I had taken on the role of his caregiver. Losing him felt less like losing a brother and more like losing a child. He was the reason I pushed myself to finish college, to work hard, to save up—to be a role model for him. And now, with no warning, no goodbye, no closure, my purpose was ripped away. The grief consumed me. I cried for months, my body withering under the weight of sorrow. My hair turned grey, sleep eluded me, and the thought of joining him in death became a constant companion. But I held on only for the sake of my parents, knowing I couldn't put them through another loss.

In the depths of despair, I found solace in a Buddhist community called Soka Gakkai International, not out of faith but from a need for distraction. What began as a fragile glimmer of hope gradually grew as I volunteered and gave back, slowly rediscovering a sense of purpose. Healing didn't mean the pain vanished, but that it no longer cripples me. I learned to face grief without numbing myself, accepting that Troy's journey had ended while mine continued. Through this experience, I realized the vital importance of community and contribution—our true lifeline during life's darkest and brightest moments.

Life is not a smooth, straight path. It is filled with bumps, turns, and unexpected detours. We each experience different seasons, just like the plants and trees around us. Some of us might be in full bloom, while others are enduring the cold grip of winter. But through community and shared purpose, we can thrive in any season. Together, we create a collective strength that uplifts not just individuals, but entire communities, and indeed, the world. Empowerment is not just about personal success; it's about elevating others, fostering a world where everyone is supported, cultures are preserved, and progress is made possible. In giving to and receiving from our communities, we find our deepest sense of meaning and the potential to create a brighter, more compassionate future. It is in this interconnectedness that we truly thrive, and it is through this unity that we can face any challenge, knowing we are never alone.

When I first became part of a community and started participating in youth groups, I was incredibly shy and timid. I found comfort in the background, always hiding at the back of the room, where I could support without being seen or heard. The idea of stepping into the spotlight was terrifying to me—filled with insecurities and fears that kept me silent. I didn't want to share anything too personal. I was afraid that if people knew the real me, they would judge me harshly. I worried about sounding stupid, appearing weak, or drawing attention to myself because I didn't feel confident in my appearance. All these insecurities created a chorus of doubts in my mind. Who was I to share my story or offer encouragement? I thought of myself as a no body, convinced that any attention would only highlight my flaws.

But as I became more involved in the community and attended personal growth workshops, something began to change. My confidence started to grow, and with it, I found my voice. I began to listen to the stories of others—stories of struggle and victory, vulnerability and strength—and I realized something profound: we are all the same. We all carry the same inner chatter, rooted in past trauma, wounds, and insecurities. Beneath the surface, we all long for the same things: to be happy, fulfilled, to do purposeful work, to feel loved, to belong, to be accepted, heard, seen, supported, and valued.

Here's a little secret I wish my younger self had known: no one cares nearly as much about the things you're worried or insecure about as you do. They probably don't even notice them because they're too caught up in their own thoughts, battling their own insecurities. Everyone is living in their own reality—a reality constructed in their minds. Once I understood this, it was like a weight lifted off my shoulders. The noise in my head, the self-criticism, began to quiet down. I realized that I had been my own harshest critic. The things I saw as flaws were often seen by others as strengths. This realization marked a turning point for me, transforming me from a shell of a human being into an empowered woman who had found her voice, courage and purpose.

From that point on, I didn't just show up to community events—I began mentoring youths, guiding them through their own journeys of self-discovery and empowerment. Bryant McGill once said, "To alter the universe, alter your thoughts, because the only universe you will ever know is in your mind." If the only universe you will ever know exists in your mind, then the script you run is crucial. Is your internal dialogue loving, empowering, and uplifting? If not, it's time to change the narrative.

Tell your mind that its job is to support you in all ways, to be a loving parent to you. Then, practice being an observer of your thoughts. When a thought arises, ask yourself: Is this something a loving parent or a trusted mentor would say to me? If the answer is no, let the thought pass without internalizing it. Over time, this practice will become second nature, and both your internal world and external world will begin to shift. By altering the way you think, you can alter your reality.

After finding my voice, I realized its purpose extended beyond my own healing—I used it to help my family and friends navigate their grief and introduced hundreds to the Soka Gakkai International (SGI) community that had saved me. Knowing the transformative power of support, I wanted others to experience the same. Books became another way I gave back, offering wisdom and guidance. I always kept multiple copies in my trunk, ready to share with anyone in need, whether they were facing grief, mental health struggles, or personal challenges. For me, sharing knowledge and connection became my way of giving back.

It didn't stop there. I also shared daily encouragements on my social media platforms, hoping to reach people who might need a boost of positivity. I hosted holiday dinners for youths who couldn't be with their families, offering them a sense of belonging when they were far from home. I even started doing pro bono work for those who needed my help but couldn't afford to pay for my services—a practice I continue to this day. My only request in return is that they pay it forward when they're able, not necessarily in monetary terms, but by offering their skills, time, or even just a listening ear to someone in need. Value, after all, is measured by the heart, not by money or status. If you have something that could help someone, whether it's a skill set, your time, a shoulder to lean on, or even just a piece of advice, share it. Let your heart lead you in giving, because that's where true value lies.

My support network has been the foundation of my growth, made up of community groups, family, friends, coaches, and teachers. Community groups gave me encouragement when I needed it most, while my family supported me so I could attend personal growth workshops. My friends were my sounding board, offering space to vent and helping me see myself more clearly. My teachers provided the skills for my career, and my coach held me accountable, keeping me focused on my goals. Together, they played vital roles in shaping who I am today.

I'll never forget something my teacher once told me: "You know a lot, you can do a lot. So, until you fully believe in yourself, hold onto my belief in you." Those words still hang on the wall in my office today, a constant reminder of the power of belief and support. This is why having a community and a support network is essential. Be a part of your community—contribute when you can, and don't hesitate to receive help when you need it. If any one piece of my support system had been missing, I am certain I wouldn't be where I am today. I am able to show up and serve my purpose because others showed up and served me. It's the circle of life, and it's what makes everything possible.

A few significant milestones in my journey stand out to me today: becoming a Certified Trainer of NLP, helping neurodivergent children reduce their triggers, and creating a series of children's books that will be published in 2025. These three milestones are especially meaningful because they represent the tangible proof that anything is possible. Your past does not define you, nor does it limit your potential. Whatever you think you are capable of, I assure you, you are capable of so much more. The only limitations that exist are the ones you impose on yourself. Just as the sky is limitless, so too are your beliefs and words.

To say I've come a long way would be an understatement. I was the kid who was relentlessly picked on in school, bullied from kindergarten through 12th grade, with the torment peaking during my middle and early high school years. There were days when I would spend my lunch hiding in a bathroom stall just to avoid the girls who made my life miserable. Other days, I would skip school entirely to escape the dread that filled me at the thought of facing them. I sat in class paralyzed with fear, watching the clock and dreading the moment when the bell would ring, signalling the start of another round of torment in the hallways. This constant fear and anxiety led to severe depression and social anxiety that left me almost mute through much of my adolescence. Speaking to anyone was a monumental task—just saying, "Hi, my name is Linda," or "Hi, how are you?" felt impossible without stuttering. Public speaking was an unfathomable horror to me. Yet here I am today, not just speaking in public but thriving in it, excited by the very thing that once terrified me. Becoming a Trainer of NLP, mastering communication, and being able to stand in front of an audience to deliver presentations are achievements that still astonish me. Your mind is an incredibly powerful tool when you learn to understand it and rewire it to support your purpose.

The second milestone that fills me with pride is my work with neurodivergent children—those with Autism, ADD, ADHD. I've been able to help them minimize their triggers, improve their social skills, and regulate their emotions through alternative tools and techniques. Seeing these children grow and find ways to navigate their world more comfortably is one of the most rewarding aspects of my work.

Finally, the milestone that perhaps means the most to me is the completion of my series of children's books, which will be published in 2025. These books explore a range of universal spiritual concepts that resonate across all religions—principles like harmony, peace, integrity, kindness, courage, confidence, faith, forgiveness, humility, love, and empowerment. The unconscious mind of a child, often referred to as their blueprint, is formed between the ages of 0-7. During these formative years, everything they experience imprints on their unconscious mind, creating the programming that will guide them throughout life. That's why my books are specifically written for children aged 4-7, with the goal of planting seeds of positive values that will grow as they mature into adults.

These books were inspired by the deep love I have for my own children, Charles and Joseph. Many nights, I found myself searching online for meaningful books to read to them at bedtime. While I found many great ones, I also noticed gaps—topics that were missing. So, I decided to write them myself. Why not? Despite writing being my weakest skill in school, compounded by ADHD and dyslexia, I took on the challenge. This milestone, more than any other, is one I share often to inspire others to believe in themselves, regardless of the obstacles they face.

I wrote these books not just for my children, but for all children. We do not live in isolation; everything around us affects our happiness and well-being. We are like flowers in a garden, sharing the same soil, the same sky, the same rain. By uplifting as many children as possible, I hope to contribute to a better world— because those children will one day be my children's classmates, colleagues, friends, spouses, and neighbours. In nurturing them, we nurture the future, and that is a responsibility I take to heart.

In addition to my community contributions and pro bono work, I've made it a personal mission to extend a helping hand to those in need during the cold winter months in San Diego. I distribute care packages, blankets, and jackets to the homeless, knowing that a small act of kindness can bring warmth and comfort to those who need it most. Looking ahead, my goals for 2025 and 2026 are ambitious yet deeply rooted in my desire to give back. I plan to have my children's books printed and distributed to all non-public elementary schools, daycare centers, and local mommy groups throughout San Diego. This initiative stems from my belief that every child deserves access to resources that foster growth, joy, and empowerment.

Additionally, I am in the process of creating an online platform designed to make my services accessible and affordable to a broader audience. Having experienced a profound transformation through this work—both in myself and in the clients I serve—I am driven by a deep desire to share these benefits with as many people as possible. My heart yearns to help the world, but knowing that such a task is impossible, I have envisioned this platform as a way to reach far beyond the limitations of time and space. I believe that happiness, fulfillment, joy, and inner peace are not luxuries, but rights that everyone should have. My vision is that once this online platform launches in 2026, it will become a beacon of hope and healing for those who seek it.

The impact of my work is far-reaching, creating a ripple effect that continues long after my clients and I have completed our sessions together. My approach is not about merely addressing symptoms or surface-level issues. When clients come to me with a list of problems, I listen deeply, identifying the root causes, negative beliefs, ingrained behaviours, and wounds that lie beneath. By releasing and healing these foundational issues, we create a permanent internal shift across all levels: conscious and unconscious mind, spiritual body, mental body, emotional body, and physical body. This holistic transformation makes them brand new, as Confucius wisely said, "No matter where you go, there you are." When the shift happens at this internal level, it touches every aspect of their lives. They might come to me hoping to improve their marriage, but they'll find that their career, family life, and mental health all flourish as well. How we show up in one area is how we show up in every area.

Here are a few examples of the transformative results my clients have experienced: • One client, who suffered from severe arthritis for over 12 years, is now completely healed.

- Another client, who battled severe anxiety and depression for 17 years, is now happy, off medication, and has been free from relapse for two years, living a joyful, normal life.
- A client who relied on steroids for pain management for over a decade is now pain-free and no longer needs any medication.
- A single mother going through a divorce, who struggled for six months to find a job due to a lack of confidence, secured a position just days after our sessions began.
- Another single mom, who had put her personal life on hold for a decade to focus on her children, was stuck in a cycle of attracting the wrong partners. After working with me, she met the love of her life and is now happily married.
- A self-employed client, whose business had stagnated for 15 years, saw his income double within six months after we worked on his beliefs around abundance, self-worth, and deserving.
- A teenager who wanted to quit school is now motivated and determined to get into Ivy League universities, with aspirations of earning multiple PhDs.

- A teen with ADHD and dyslexia, who was barely passing with C's, now loves school and consistently earns straight A's.
- A client who was miserable in her marriage and sought my help to release the guilt around divorcing her husband ended up rediscovering the love she thought was lost. After clearing the mental clutter, she saw her husband in a new light and is now happy in her marriage.

These stories are a testament to the power of internal transformation. When we clear the mind and heal the heart, we not only improve our own lives but also positively impact those around us. This is the circle of life—the more we give, the more we grow, and the more we grow, the more we have to give.

My journey has honed my leadership, communication, and listening skills, making me more heart centered and open to different perspectives. This openness allows me to connect with others deeply and appreciate the diversity of human experience. Most importantly, it has strengthened my empowered mindset, deepened my love for humanity, and fueled my commitment to creating a brighter future. I believe everyone has unique gifts and potential, and my purpose is to guide others in unlocking their inner strength and creativity, helping them step into their most authentic selves and embrace limitless possibilities.

Doubt is an illusion, a belief we create about the outcome before even trying. I know this all too well, having convinced myself countless times that I wasn't smart, pretty, skinny, worthy or experienced enough. The list of "not enough" was endless—until one day I realized the only difference between someone who can and someone who can't is BELIEF. Excellence comes through practice and repetition, and the time spent overthinking often far outweighs the time it takes to complete a task. So, if you're stuck in doubt, remember it's an illusion—take the first step, the path to success is paved with action, not overthinking nor rumination.

Looking ahead to the next five years, my vision is to expand my work onto global online platforms, making it accessible and affordable to everyone, no matter where they are in the world. I also plan to publish my series of children's books, ensuring they reach all non-public schools, daycares, local mommy groups, and communities. Additionally, I will launch a YouTube channel to document and share the transformative power of my work. I intend to travel, offering my services to random people I encounter, those I feel called to help. Through these live demonstrations, I aim to show the world that it is possible to change your life in as little as two days of focused effort. My message is clear: **It is possible to have everything you desire. It is possible to become who you want to be, Do what you want to do, and have everything you dream of having.** You deserve all the health, wealth, and happiness in the world, and it starts with a shift in mindset—from a victim mentality to an empowered one. Heal yourself, break free from the constraints of your past, rewire your mindset to become an empowered being, set your goals, take action, and watch as your life transforms.

Here are the top five pieces of advice I offer to everyone:

1. **Your past does not define or limit who you are**, and it has no bearing on your potential. The power lies in the meaning you assign to it. Choose to see your past as a series of lessons rather than limitations.
2. **Become an empowered being to close the gap between where you are and where you want to be.** EVERYTHING begins with an empowered mindset. Clear out the baggage and beliefs that no longer serve you, and replace them with new beliefs and values that align with your purpose.
3. **Everything starts and ends with you.** It begins with you taking responsibility and ownership of your life, rather than pointing fingers or blaming external factors. It ends with you taking action—no one else can do it for you. To become who you are meant to be, to achieve what you're meant to achieve, you must take the reins.
4. **Contribution and community are vital.** These elements are essential for creating fulfilling lives and promoting world peace. We are all interconnected—what one person does affects another, and this interconnectedness stretches across generations. The impact of our actions ripples through time, influencing our children, grandchildren, and beyond.
5. **Adopt a Lesson and Resolution approach to challenges.** When faced with difficulties, focus on the lesson the universe is trying to teach you and seek out solutions. By approaching challenges with this mindset, you train your mind to shift into "solution" mode, helping you uncover the wisdom your unconscious mind and soul want you to learn.

Remember, "Knowledge is potential, action is power, and an empowered mindset is everything." This philosophy is the cornerstone of my work, and it can be the foundation of your success as well.

I've learned the importance of faith and flexibility. Faith is the absence of fear, a deep trust that persists even when everything seems to be falling apart. It's the unwavering belief that light will follow the darkness, just as we trust that dawn will come after night without question. "Faith is the bird that feels the light and sings when the dawn is still dark", as Rabindranath Tagore beautifully put it. It's "daring the soul to go beyond what the eyes can see", as William Newton Clarke said. This kind of faith allows us to move forward with confidence, knowing the universe always supports us, even when the path is unclear.

Flexibility, on the other hand, is essential for navigating the only constant in life: change. It means being open and adaptable in our thinking, beliefs, goals, and expectations. Just as businesses must adjust to survive in a changing market, we too must be flexible to withstand life's change and challenges. Consider the willow tree, whose branches bend with the wind but remain strong and rooted. By being flexible, we not only survive but grow and thrive, no matter the storm. Charles Darwin said, "It is not the strongest of the species that survives, nor the most intelligent, but the one most adaptable to change."

Collaboration has shaped every step of my journey. In workshops and trainings, teamwork was crucial for completing the course. And today, I work with healers, therapists, coaches, doctors, and business owners to provide the best care for my clients. When a client's needs fall outside my scope of expertise, I collaborate with specialists. For my children's book series, I'm partnering with a London-based illustrator, despite living in the U.S.

Collaboration fills in the gaps where our strengths may not lie. No one excels at everything. While we can be good at many things, we're only great at a few. For areas where I'm not as strong or tasks that don't bring me joy, I collaborate with those who can contribute their expertise and passion. Collaboration enriches resources, strengthens outcomes, and elevates everyone's work. It's a win win for all involved.

My mission is my life, and I don't see a separation between the two. We often talk about balancing work and personal life, but in reality, every area of our lives—relationships, family, career, health, and spirituality—is interconnected. What happens in one area inevitably impacts the others. For instance, when you're in a happy relationship, it elevates your mood and energy in all aspects of your life. Conversely, struggles in one area can bring imbalance to the rest.

Rather than striving for balance, I focus on maintaining harmony. This means creating congruence and alignment both internally and externally. Internal harmony is ensuring that your actions align with your values and priorities, that you feel harmonize and not conflicted. External harmony is keeping your environment organized and conducive to your well-being. For example, if I neglect housework, my home becomes cluttered, affecting my mood and disrupting the flow of my day.

To maintain harmony, I follow three key principles: know your values, manage your time impeccably, and set clear boundaries. Understanding what's important to you is crucial. For me, spending time with my children is non-negotiable, so I block out a full day on weekends for them. My mission is equally important, so I start each day by dedicating the first hour to it—whether it's reading, writing, or planning.

Time management is essential for harmony. Many people fail to schedule time for what truly matters in their personal lives. I plan my calendar around what's most important to me, ensuring that my "happy" and "fulfillment" cups are always full. Each October, I plan my calendar for the entire upcoming year, making sure everything important is on there. I also build in "bonus time"—a few hours each week for flexibility, allowing me to adapt to unexpected events without disrupting my schedule.

Lastly, setting boundaries is critical. Without them, it's easy to get distracted and lose focus. Boundaries teach others how to interact with you and help you stay committed to your priorities. It also tells people what works for you, what doesn't, how to win with you. A win-win for everyone. This applies to personal interactions as well as managing distractions like electronics. Clear boundaries prevent interruptions and keep you on track, preserving the harmony you've worked to create.

As we close this chapter together, I want to leave you with this: No matter where you are in your journey—whether you're in the depths of your winter season, standing on the edge of transformation, or seeking deeper purpose—know that you are not alone. My hope is that my story has ignited a flame of hope, a spark of empowerment, and a call to action within you. You have the power to rise, to close the gap between where you are and where your heart calls you to be. The path may not always be easy, but each step forward is a step toward a life of fulfillment and meaning.

Now, it's your turn. Take what you've learned, embrace your unique gifts, and step boldly into your future. Remember, true transformation happens not in isolation, but in community. When we come together—giving, receiving, and lifting one another—the impossible becomes possible. Regardless of your gender, skin colour, childhood, education, or economic background, none of these factors can limit you from creating the life you desire because true potential and resourcefulness come from within. So, I urge you: Contribute to your world, nurture the connections around you, and become a force for change. Your actions will ripple far beyond your own life, and together, we can create a brighter, more connected future for us all.

Bio

Linda Le is a passionate author, coach, healer, medium and spiritual teacher, dedicated to healing others and guiding them toward empowerment and spiritual awakening. After earning a bachelor's degree in Accounting from San Diego State University, she successfully owned and managed two restaurants for nearly a decade. However, despite her outward success, she felt unfulfilled and disconnected, prompting her to sell her businesses in search of deeper meaning and purpose.

This quest led her to personal growth seminars that transformed her life and sparked an intense fascination with the mind-body-spirit connection, the workings of the conscious and unconscious mind, and integrative holistic healing. Her insatiable curiosity propelled her through extensive training, earning certifications as a Master Practitioner and Trainer of Neurolinguistic Programming (NLP), Hypnotherapy, and Mental and Emotional Release. She also studied Eastern modalities like Reiki, Huna (an ancient Hawaiian spiritual teaching), past life regression, and Quantum Healing Hypnosis Technique. What sets her apart in the vast world of healers, coaches, and spiritual teachers is her deeply integrative approach. She works with both the conscious and unconscious mind, uncovering and releasing hidden blocks, wounds, and limiting beliefs that clients may not even be aware of. Her release work encompasses all four bodies—spiritual, mental, emotional, and physical—allowing for a holistic and integrative transformation that leads to lasting healing and empowerment.

Having transformed the lives of thousands, she continues her work from San Diego, California, where she lives with her loving husband and twin boys, who inspire her vision of creating a better world. Her life's mission is to heal, help others tap into their full potential, and spread spiritual enlightenment across the globe.

Jody Steinhauer-

Giving Back Makes Great Business Sense

Founder/CEO of The Bargains Group Ltd., Engage and Change and Kits For A Cause. I am definitely one of those women whose later success in life was paved by my upbringing and business experiences VERY early on.

For as long as I can remember, two qualities have defined me: 1) an exceptional drive to succeed, and 2) a natural ability to make people happy by giving them exactly what they're looking for—at just the right price. From being the top Brownie sale girl in Toronto for Girl Guide Cookies, to becoming the leading salesperson in Ontario for (now-defunct) Regal Catalogues, to achieving the highest sales despite working only part-time in retail fast-fashion, I've always had an innate hunger for achievement.

But my entrepreneurial mindset didn't just develop by chance—it was shaped by these early experiences. Being in sales from such a young age taught me the importance of persistence, adaptability, and most importantly, how to create authentic demand where none seemed to exist. I quickly learned the art of using recommendations to spark curiosity and interest in products that people didn't even know they needed—until I showed them how it could benefit their lives. This was where the concept of "working smarter, not harder" truly began to resonate with me. Rather than just pushing products, I focused on connecting with people, understanding their needs, and showing them how what I offered could solve their problems or enhance their day-to-day lives. This approach made sales easier and ensured that customers felt valued, understood, and special.

My very first denim jacket pin design business at age 10 was more than just a way to earn extra pocket money. It taught me how to handle failure and refine my approach. There were days when sales didn't go as planned, and I realized I had to pivot—changing designs or adjusting my pricing. I used word-of-mouth recommendations from my earliest buyers to create a buzz that made others feel like they *had* to have one of my pins. It was a priceless lesson in how the power of 'word of mouth' can drive demand. Every obstacle I encountered reinforced that success comes from working smart.

For example, when I sold Girl Guide cookies, I would say: 'Don't just buy one box. Why don't you buy a box for everyone in your family?' It was obvious that I had a natural sales ability, and people trusted me at a very, very young age.

I also recognized that I was very creative, and I learned the laws of supply and demand at a young age. When the owner of the store where I sold my pins, Joel, said: 'Jody, your stuff's selling out. Just keep bringing me more.' At the time, I was making everything from rainbows to Sesame Street characters. I said, 'Joel, I want us to sell a lot of these. What do you think is best?' Now this was before we had UPC codes to track inventory. Since I was very in tune to working smarter, not harder, Joel suggested that I speak to the cashiers and ask about their experience with customers and my assortment of pins. My first foray into market research!

And I'll never forget…Joel looked at me and said, 'Wow, are you ever going to be a great salesperson when you're older!' I would go downtown every Saturday, bring him a new load of pins, and collect my money because we had a consignment deal. And I also realized that real estate equals profits. That meant there was a glass display case at the cash desk where they kept my pins next to the free jube jubes! By one month's end, I owned 50% of the display case with my pins because they were out selling everything else by the cash!

I realized then and there that if everybody's happy, business will be fine. For most, that meant focusing on the end consumer. But I also focused on my relationships. So, if it was a buyer, it wasn't just the customer who bought it; it was the people I was dealing with. And I was really honed in on having to ensure that relationship was good, too.

One year, I pre-sold so many Girl Guide cookies that I couldn't fulfill all the orders. As I had already collected all the money, it never dawned on me that there'd be a problem. I learned a valuable lesson from that: I had to give people their money back; from then on, I made sure I sold the number I was told was my maximum and not a box more.

As a pre-teen, I didn't drive; I did what everybody did. I knocked on the doors of neighbors, called relatives and my parents' closest friends, but where I really leveraged 'my' network was when I told my father on a

PD day that I was coming to work with him at his factory. I went to work with him at 6:00 am and set up a little cookie stand in the lunchroom. They had over 300 employees, and I promoted the offer: Buy 10 boxes, get one free. Oh, my God...I was sold out in an hour! I realized, if you make something exciting...people want excitement, right? And everyone loves a bargain!

That is also an example of a valuable insight I gained early on - sometimes people just want to talk to somebody.

With Regal catalogues, the whole premise was you drop a catalog off with a few recommendations as to what to buy for the season. I went one step further and dropped off my catalogues at my neighbor's houses with sticky notes on several pages. I'd call it Jody's Picks (sound familiar?). I sold more as people trusted me and knew that I wouldn't take advantage of them.

Growing up, I loved watching people make deals. I would always ask: 'How did that work out?' I was always trying to figure out the main business/item/product, and where was the money?' Nothing was easy, but where was the easier money? And I realized through the businesses that I've mentioned above, there was no risk for me. I didn't own the Girl Guide cookies, so if I didn't sell them, I could have given them back. Concerning Regal, all I had to invest in was buying some monthly catalogs. Nothing in the catalogs cost me any money until someone would choose an item and pay me for it upfront.

Even though I always had to invest a little bit in materials, my profit margin was huge. My father was an accountant, and he showed me early on that you have to charge at least a certain amount to make sure you pay yourself back. That was a great accounting lesson; at the age of 12 I learned early about cost of goods sold and profit margins.

I also learned the value of testimonials and word-of-mouth. When I delivered a purchase, I would always ask, 'Did this make you happy?' And when they said, 'yes,' I would then ask, 'Can you please tell your friends about my products so I can make them happy too?' I wasn't afraid to ask for referrals and testimonials. My entire business today is built 100% on referrals and testimonials, predominantly online.

I have no salespeople.

I do no advertising.

Of course, none of this would have been possible without the strong foundation of support from my family. My parents always encouraged my entrepreneurial spark, even when my ventures didn't take off as I had hoped. I remember my mom driving me to the craft store to buy materials and always reminding me that tomorrow is a new day to make it happen. My dad's wisdom, though quieter, was equally impactful.

He taught me to see every interaction as an opportunity to build a relationship. Those lessons stuck with me and have been instrumental in shaping the way I approach business today.

These early influences helped mold my drive and built the confidence I needed to take risks and push forward. With strong people skills, a love for fashion, and a keen eye for style, I pursued my passion at The International Academy of Fashion Merchandising (Toronto) right after high school. I completed a two-year program and graduated at the top of my class at the age of 18—ready to take on the world.

After 3 roles in high end fashion, my boss in the discount wholesale industry opened my eyes to a different side of the business. I almost had to unlearn everything I learned at school! Thanks to his teaching, I grew his wholesale business into a multimillion-dollar operation, but he was forced into bankruptcy due to problems in another division. He was ready to set me up in a new company, but as news of his bankruptcy spread, my phone began ringing off the hook with offers due to my reputation for being a rarity in the fashion world - a hard-working straight shooter. I resigned on a Friday in 1988; the Bargains Group (BG) was born the next day, on a Saturday, in my living room.

When it came time to start my own business, I took a leap of faith. But it didn't feel like a huge risk at the time. I had worked on 100% commission for several years, so I wasn't used to a steady paycheck. My attitude was, "Well, let's give it a try for a month or two. If I don't sell anything, I can always go get a job." That's the mindset I had at the age of 22.

My leap of faith wasn't just about starting a business—it was about believing in myself. I knew I'd have to answer the phones, manage the orders, and do everything in between, but I also knew I could handle it. I was young, with no children, no mortgage, no student debt, and only a few financial responsibilities besides rent and car payments. That made the risk feel manageable to me, even though people around me thought I was taking a huge gamble. What they didn't realize was that working on full commission had already prepared me for uncertainty.

The advantage of launching my own business at such a young age was the trust I had already built with industry suppliers. Because of my reputation, they were willing to back me from day one, sending me products on credit without hesitation. I didn't need a bank loan or outside investors, which gave me the freedom to build the business my way. While others saw risk, I saw an opportunity to turn my passion and determination into something bigger.

Seeing a gap in the discount wholesale market for basic clothing item in Canada, BG quickly found a niche selling to then-large Canadian retailers such as Eaton's, Bargain Harold's and Bi-Way, in addition to many often-remote, small-town mom-and-pop stores. Given my natural sales skills and outgoing personality, I found it easy to build a pipeline of manufacturers and importers looking to clean out remnant inventory; the network I nurtured then is still the base of my always-growing network now.

I was really, nimble and did not spend any money until I had to. Therefore, I had to do most things myself the first few years. And I was okay with this. For example, I didn't have a van; I had a Honda Civic. Getting all these clothes and samples into my car was funny sometimes, but I couldn't afford a bigger car. I had to pack it all in using large hockey bags. When I got my first office, I shared it with a friend who had leased the office, but he went bankrupt. One day he walked in and said, 'I'm going bankrupt, get your stuff out of here, or else the bailiffs are coming in.' I didn't even know what a bailiff was back then! I was lucky that the next-door neighbor offered me some of her extra warehouse space. I moved into the person's warehouse and used that for almost a year, and then they went bankrupt. I had to keep finding people that trusted me to give me the keys to their offices, because I didn't see the need to rent my own standalone office. I also needed to be close to home because I worked a lot. I wanted to ensure that if I was working until 11:00 pm, I would be safe going home.

Being lean and learning how to do everything yourself definitely helped shape my company. Even to this day, we're very lean. We don't hire people for whom we don't have a full-time role, and we only scale when we need to. Otherwise, we job share and cross-train.

I am thrilled that BG is now in its 36th year of profitable growth as I continue the original discount sales model the company was founded on. However, the bulk of my financial success traces to a specific area of business I am even prouder of – I am known Canada-wide as a top resource for charities, non-profits and donors. Giving back has made tremendous business sense for me and plays a significant role in guiding my plans personally and professionally.

I think that's really what has kept BG alive while many of our competitors are no longer.

I quickly outgrew my apartment, and after moving six times to and from friends' offices over 15 years, I bought my first building in 2003 – 20,000 square feet of primarily warehouse space. I expanded my product offerings and started a promotional products division; word spread quickly that Bargain Jody was who you should contact to buy $2 t-shirts…a sign that remains, to this day, outside the building.

I'm an accountant's daughter, and I realized I was in a safe business focusing on the everyday basics of t-shirts, underwear, socks, gloves etc. I remember when the brand Ed Hardy was popular, and I got a deal on Ed Hardy running shoes. I couldn't sell them - even though they sold for $100 in the store, and I was selling them for $20. This was not my customer. Today the joke in my business is that if I think something's gorgeous and I'd love to buy it personally, I can't buy it for my company; I'm not my customer.

This perspective has always helped shape my business decisions.

Awards and accolades started to pour in recognizing my business acumen and success at such an early age, *Canada's Top 40 Under 40,* and *Canadian Women's Entrepreneur of the Year,* to name just two. Invitations to join groups such as EO (Entrepreneurs' Organization), WPO (Women's Presidents Organization), and IWF (International Women's Forum) followed, as did speaking requests coast-to-coast.

In case you haven't figured it out yet, I don't believe there is such a thing as a work-life balance. I believe you CAN do everything – just not all at the same time. When I first started the company, I wasn't married, I didn't have children, but one thing I always was very big on was planning. Even when I got married, I planned the wedding around the least busy month of the year. This way, when I took a honeymoon, I wouldn't be neglecting my clients or my business. When I bought my first building, I also knew that wherever I lived, it had to be within 15 minutes of the office. I loved working and I knew I was in store for long hours. I also had the foresight to be honest with myself and I knew that once I had a family, my lack of balance could be more of an issue.

I also decided that children would have to wait until I could afford a nanny to come to work with me. I had to be able to afford that, and I did not have my first child until eight years after I was married. (Most people thought that was because I couldn't have children, but they didn't realize this was a life choice.) I realized, if I could be at work and do what I love the best - which is working while my baby was sleeping - then when my daughter woke up, I could be the one who could feed her and take her for a quick walk. For the first year of her life, I would worry about the 'eating', but someone else could deal with the sleeping, etc. My maternity leave actually lasted only three days; after that I was back at work because my assistant, who was my third employee at the time, quit right before I gave birth. I didn't mind because I loved working, and I was of the philosophy: "A happy wife is a happy life." I was lucky that my husband supported what I thought was important.

Over the next 20 years, I've learned to delegate and only do what I'm good at. I don't cook, I don't clean, I don't buy groceries. I outsource everything I can, allowing me to work longer. If I didn't have that ability, then I wouldn't be able to do what I do. Even being a hockey mom to my son, I made sure that my nanny had a driver's license so that she could drive my son to hockey an hour or two before the game started. I could then work an extra hour and a half and show up one minute before puck-drop and never miss a game. My son doesn't remember that I didn't drive him to his hockey games and sit in the parking lot like the other parents; he remembers that I never missed a game. I was the type of parent who became very passionate about anything that was important to my kids. I've always been there - as long as they've given me notice to block my calendar.

I've often had to explain to family and friends that I do not do 'spontaneous'. Every minute of my day is planned to do my best. I would never go to Starbucks with one of the other mothers unless it was already on my calendar.

As BG grew, I started to notice a change in the wholesale industry in Canada…especially when it came to clothing basics such as socks, underwear, etc. Manufacturers and importers started embracing the just-in-time production model, resulting in less inventory at each season's end. This remnant inventory was typically sold at a deep discount or donated to charity.

I saw an opportunity for a win-win when I decided to grow my customer base from retailers and for-profit companies to also include charities and NFP's. I realized that I needed to be seen as more than just a cheaper alternative to Walmart – I needed charities to view me as a donor and partner, not just a vendor. That's when the *Bargains Group Full Circle Donation Program* was born. We started offering goods at below-retail prices and added donations to sweeten the deal. This has become a cornerstone of our business model and continues to set us apart.

I knew I could make more impact and really help by offering my services to charities and non-profits. The idea of making money off a charity was frowned upon in the '90s, but I saw it as the right time to put my (future) mantra of 'Giving Back Makes GREAT Business Sense' into practice. And I really did want to HELP! By slowly building relationships in the sector, I learned about the differences between fundraising for money and collecting donations of goods.

My heart has always been with helping people facing homelessness, so I began reaching out to charities that specialized in that space.

Twenty-five years ago, I started *Project Winter Survival* after hearing about a homeless man who died in a Toronto bus shelter on a freezing night. It began with volunteers packing kits to distribute to the homeless through 200+ service providers; this continues until today with 3500+ kits packed in January 2024. The concept of matching corporations with charities has been the secret sauce behind its success. *Project Water* followed shortly after, addressing the needs of those struggling in the heat and humidity, providing summer survival kits and free bottles of water. These semi-annual kit packing events are the cornerstone of the charity I launched in 1999, *Engage and Change*.

I've always believed in supporting those doing good work, which has created lasting business partnerships. For example, when I started *Engage and Change*, my bank immediately became the largest supporter. They continue to support us until today because they see not only how much we're helping the community but also witness the incredible impression packing survival kits for the homeless has on their own employees.

Looking back, I realize the impact of these initiatives has been greater than I ever hoped. I'm proud of how far we've come and excited for what the future holds. Whether it's *Engage and Change* or *Kits For A Cause* - the social enterprise I launched almost ten years ago - my goal is simple: to keep helping, to keep growing, and to keep making a difference.

My purpose is rooted in helping, and that's how I define success. In the beginning, some charities were hesitant to introduce us to potential donors. They were concerned we might steal their connections. But once they realized we were in it for the right reasons, trust was built, and everything changed. Now, they reach out to us regularly for help, and that's been a huge win for both sides. Due to their tremendous financial disarray, charities have repeatedly told us that they wouldn't have the resources to support their clients with the necessities of life without the help from *Kits For a Cause*. Most charities also face the challenge of turning down large volunteer groups and donors as many of them do not have the capacity, physical space, time etc. to engage them.

On the other hand, corporations love the idea of getting involved and making a difference, but many times, didn't know how. I often had to explain the difference between a charity and a social enterprise as some companies assumed they could only work with us if we were a registered charity. Once we cleared up those misconceptions, the partnerships flourished.

Companies and charities alike have shared amazing stories about how our partnerships have made a difference. For example, a large Canadian bank heard me speak at a conference and loved the idea of engaging their employees coast-to-coast through *Kits For a Cause*. We introduced the program nationally and empowered each employee at branch level to select a local charity to help. *Kits For a Cause* facilitated the entire event and massive local impact was made. Upon reviewing their 12-month *Kits For a Cause* partnership, the bank saw their highest employee engagement scores.

These stories are so common now that they can be overwhelming at times. I've had non-profit employees in tears upon hearing from us about a new donor group or donation. I've even heard, 'Are you kidding me? You really are a fairy godmother!'

As we continue to scale, we're getting calls from all over the world (currently, *Kits For a Cause* operates in Canada, the US, and the UK). To grow without compromising our values, we've decided to run everything from a central office while using local providers in different countries for the supply chain. This way, we stay flexible, reduce shipping costs, and keep making an impact globally.

I see the future of *Kits For a Cause* expanding into a year-round employee engagement and local impact initiative for all companies – large and small - globally. The beauty of our model is that every event can focus on a different charity, which keeps things fresh, inclusive and relevant. One month, a company may support a refugee agency; the next, it's mental health. The global landscape is always shifting, and our model allows companies to stay in tune with these societal changes. There is no shortage of charities of all types that are in desperate need.

Additionally, looking ahead, I see younger generations being key drivers of change. As they demand authenticity from the companies they work for more and more, social impact is becoming a must-have. Environmental, Social, and Governance (ESG) factors are gaining more attention, but helping people in need – whether it's those facing homelessness, food scarcity, or illness – is timeless. Companies are eager to do more but also navigating the financial realities of balancing giving back with staying profitable. I know the answer lies in a mix of strategies: employees raising funds, companies contributing/matching and everyone getting involved in the ACTIVE PHILANTHROPY espoused by both my charity and social enterprise.

This model is here to stay.

Kits For a Cause has grown exponentially since the end of the pandemic. First, it was seen as a fun way to help charities with their needs in real time by remotely engaging groups of volunteers or teams. Then, it was seen as a fun way to give back while building employee engagement among in-person and remote groups. Now, *Kits For A Cause* is seen most often as a turnkey, fun way to engage employees during the workday while making a local impact in light of the increasing needs in the community; from an organizational perspective, *Kits For A Cause* is viewed as an aid in attracting/retaining top prospects, cutting down on turnover and adding to an organization's reputation compared to its competitors, overall.

Another important shift I recognized early was regarding the role of volunteers. Many women had the time to volunteer in the past because they weren't working full-time jobs, but that's no longer the case. To sustain the volunteer sector, employers need to give people – not just women – time, money, and resources during business hours to volunteer. If they don't, the sector will collapse. No one talks about this enough, but it's critical.

More recognition has come my way, such as the RBC SME (small/medium enterprise) Business Award, which I was awarded just last year. The team has grown from just me to five full-time 'Kits Champions'. Feedback via surveys after the fact has been outstanding. I'm lucky to include international leaders such as Amazon, Starbucks, Deloitte Global and Zurich Insurance as just some participants.

The 1,000+ companies globally that have made *Kits For a Cause* an integral part of their employee engagement experience programs have – to date - engaged: over 125,000 employees and delivered 750,000+ 'kits,' to over 5,000 charities globally.

Aside from profitable growth year-over-year, I am also immensely proud to share that *Kits For a Cause* has a 97% return/retention rate!

You see, for me it all comes back to kindness. I was raised in a world where people were kind, but businesses weren't necessarily part of that conversation. Now, things have changed. I want workplaces to reflect the core values that people hold in their personal lives. If we can achieve that, I believe society will become kinder overall.

On a personal level, I'm incredibly lucky to have a supportive family, but it's not always easy to switch off from work. I love what I do and finding that balance is tough. But I make time for myself and my loved ones by scheduling it. Whether it's a massage, a manicure, or time with my family, I block it out on my calendar, and it's non-negotiable.

My hope for making the world a better place includes companies of all types, shapes, or forms harnessing their employees to provide all the goods and supplies needed by the world's charities and non-profits via *Kits For a Cause*. That way, working dollars can be focused on other areas of operational budgets to finance talent and more infrastructure-based needs such as low rent/subsidized housing, healthcare, etc.

That means continuing my quest to educate and mentor as many companies as possible and teach them my belief that *Giving Back makes GREAT Business Sense!*

I see the change every day, one kit at a time.

This is my purpose for the last third of my life.

Bio

As President and CBO (Chief Bargain Officer) of the *Bargains Group*, Jody has mobilized her award-winning discount wholesale and promotional products company to revolutionize the business landscape.

A winner of the Canadian Woman Entrepreneur of the Year Award, Canada's Top 40 Under 40, and a PROFIT W100 Recipient, Jody Steinhauer uses her network of resources and leveraged buying power to aid every company and not-for-profit agency/charity that she touches to maximize their buying dollar. Since 1988, Jody has grown Bargains Group from her apartment living room to a multi-million dollar-a-year business.

Pioneering her belief of "giving back makes good business sense", Jody is a tireless not-for-profit advocate, and the founder of the national charity, *Engage and Change*, and its two annual initiatives, *Project Winter Survival* and *Project Water*. Through these projects, *Engage and Change* helps thousands of homeless throughout Toronto survive the extreme weather conditions while engaging and enabling citizens of all ages to donate their time to their local community through sponsored group engagement events.

Jody's most recent impact initiative is *Kits for a Cause*, a social enterprise dedicated to providing purposeful engagement to groups by matching them with charities through kit-packing events. To date, *Kits For a Cause* has engaged:

Over 120,000 employees,

To deliver 750,000+ 'kits',

To more than 5,000 charities globally,

Reinvesting $11MM in communities worldwide.

Jody resides in Toronto with her husband, their 5 children and dog, Jewels.

Aloma Loren-

The Transformative Power of Kindness

How simple acts of kindness can propel us forward, ignite a sense of purpose, and create a ripple effect of positive impact on ourselves, those who receive the kindness, and our communities.

I had just left my abusive husband in Las Vegas, driving north for 15 hours to Eugene, Oregon, with my two little ones and only what could fit in my car. I was fiercely determined to create a better life than what we had been living. Though I didn't know what that better life would look like, I was certain I had to escape the suffocating chaos and violence that had nearly crushed my spirit. That certainty alone was enough to propel me forward.

We slept on a mattress on the floor at my mom's house. She wasn't in a position to support us—barely getting by herself—but it was all we had. I started cleaning houses with a friend, scrubbing floors and toilets just to make ends meet, all the while trying to figure out what to do next. When I found a *Parenting in Crisis* class at the local domestic violence center, I signed up immediately. I was desperate to make sense of what I'd been through, to understand the patterns I was trapped in, and to find a way out for good. The fact that they provided dinner and childcare felt like a miracle—a free meal and a safe place for the kids to play was a lifeline during those hard days.

I'll never forget the moment it hit me—if I went back to my abusive husband, I would be passing the same trauma to my children. It happened during one of the classes. A grandmother was there, now raising her grandchildren because her daughter had been caught in a violent, dysfunctional relationship. She was determined to stop the cycle, to give her grandchildren a different future. I saw myself in her story. In that instant, I knew I had to break the pattern—for my kids and for myself. I had to learn how to build healthy, loving relationships, no matter how difficult it seemed.

It was a brutal time. We were barely scraping by, and I was emotionally exhausted, juggling the challenges of being a single mom to two kids under three. My husband, still not divorced, harassed me constantly, trying to wear me down and convince me to come back. On top of that, I had my own emotional baggage to unpack. I knew I had to figure out how to avoid falling into another abusive relationship—this wasn't the first one, after all. But I was determined that it would be the last.

There was something stirring deep inside me. I could feel that I was ready for change, determined to create something different for myself and my kids. Though I was exhausted, I pushed forward, driven by the life I envisioned for us. I kept reminding myself to stay open, to keep my heart soft.

There's a quote by Brené Brown I didn't know at the time, but now, looking back, it perfectly captures what I was striving for: *"Keep a strong back, soft front, wild heart."* I knew I had to keep my boundaries firm, to stay strong, but I didn't want to let the pain harden me. I wanted to believe that kindness and love still existed, even after an experience that had shown me the opposite.

Through this time, I was continuously amazed by the generosity of others. So many people reached out, offering support, and it meant the world to me. I'd always been interested in giving back but struggled to find volunteer opportunities that aligned with my life—especially as a single working mom and college student. I had volunteered at a shelter for homeless teens back in Las Vegas, and I loved it, but now, with my packed schedule and wandering mind (later diagnosed as ADHD), it felt impossible to commit to regular hours.

Then one day, while sitting at my computer, I had a moment that changed everything. I was looking through family photos we'd had done by a professional photographer. It was a trade: we couldn't afford professional pictures, so we offered to let the photographer use our photos in his portfolio and sell them as stock images. As I looked at those beautiful shots—me laughing with my young children—I felt such gratitude for having those moments captured. It struck me then: I wanted every family, no matter their situation, to have the same gift.

That's when it happened—an idea that was so much more than just an idea. It felt like a calling, a clear knowing: I was going to figure out how to provide free family photos to homeless and low-income families who couldn't afford them.

And so, I did. It changed the entire trajectory of my life in the most powerful and beautiful way.

The Birth of the Free Photo Project

My first event was at a nonprofit called Centro Latino. It was around the holidays, and a friend who worked there helped me spread the word. I didn't have any fancy equipment—just a simple point-and-shoot digital camera and a determination to make this happen. That day, I photographed five families. Since I didn't have a printer, I promised to return with their photos the next day. I took the images to a local department store, used their instant photo printer, and made a few copies of each family's pictures. Then I found a pack of photo-frame greeting cards at a thrift store for 99 cents, put the prints in the frames, and presented them to the families.

The smiles on their faces assured me I needed to continue this project. It was incredible to realize that something so simple could bring such joy.

I named it the *Free Photo Project*. I reached out to friends and family for donations—materials for backdrops, a photo printer, paper, and ink. My second event was at a family shelter, where I photographed a few more families. I worried people might be disappointed that I wasn't a professional photographer and didn't have high-end equipment, but they didn't care about that. They were simply grateful to have a special family photo, something they could hold onto. It was such a beautiful experience, and the families were so happy.

Not long after, I heard about a large homeless resource event at the local fairgrounds, where over 1,500 people were expected. I was determined to be there. With only two weeks to prepare, it seemed like a huge challenge, but people were eager to help. We pulled together enough supplies and volunteers to offer photos to anyone who wanted them. That day, we photographed over 120 families and gave out more than 300 prints. It was absolutely incredible.

The Power of Aligned Giving

Giving from a place of joy and alignment with your values, desires, skills, and resources has a unique power. There's something deeply meaningful about giving in this way. The energy and excitement of giving from the heart, of doing something you genuinely care about, is entirely different from giving out of obligation. When we look within ourselves and discover what we can give—and, more importantly, what we want to give—our contributions become much more impactful.

Take the *Free Photo Project*, for example. It allowed me to provide a service I was passionate about. I loved doing it, and it brought joy and hope to people going through difficult times. By offering portraits, we made people feel seen and valued. Many even used the photos to reconnect with loved ones they hadn't seen in years by mailing them, using the stamps and envelopes we provided.

Another example is the *Bless a Mom* project. I created this project during the early months of the COVID-19 pandemic, as Mother's Day approached. With kids out of school and many families isolated, I thought about the moms who didn't have partners—or whose partners wouldn't ensure they felt celebrated. For some moms, the only thing they receive on Mother's Day is a card or gift made at school. But with schools closed, that wouldn't be possible.

Though it seemed small in the scheme of things, I knew this would mean so much to those moms. Delivering gifts would spread joy during a challenging time, and it felt like a simple, safe way to make a difference. The project became so popular that we've continued it every year since, delivering gifts to hundreds of unappreciated, overwhelmed, exhausted—and deserving—moms.

This is an example of finding the gaps, noticing where light and joy are missing, and filling them. These Giving Projects often use resources and skills I already have, or can easily gather from friends and family. This makes the projects feel manageable, aligned with my energy and capacity, and more likely to get done.

There's something incredibly powerful about these simple, aligned giving projects. People want to contribute. The more specific and tangible the giving, the more it resonates with others. Often, those who contribute have a personal connection to the cause. For example, with the *Bless a Mom Project*, the majority of contributors are other moms who understand what it feels like to be unappreciated. Some of them even end up being nominated for a gift themselves, which is wonderful to see—the giving cycle coming full circle.

Giving as a Powerful Energizer

Finding a meaningful way to give back can lift us out of darkness, depression, or our own personal struggles. Shifting our focus from our problems to helping someone else offers a mental break from trying to solve everything ourselves. It gives us new perspectives, refreshes our gratitude, and re-energizes our positive outlook.

Kindness has been scientifically proven to benefit both the giver and the receiver. For example, research from the University of California, Berkeley, found that older adults who volunteer regularly tend to live longer. The study, published in *Psychological Science*, showed that the positive health effects were especially strong among those who volunteered for altruistic reasons, which suggests that the motivation behind kindness matters. This is another reason why it's so important to give from the heart.

We all have different skills, resources, and abilities—meaning we all have a unique way to give. There have been times in my life when I felt incredibly low, uncertain of how to fix my own problems. But when I shifted my focus to helping someone else, something amazing happened: my own life was blessed. My energy returned, my perspective shifted, and I could see a way forward. Not only did I help someone else, but it helped me too.

A 2010 study published in the *Journal of Social Psychology* examined the effects of performing acts of kindness on individual well-being. It concluded that participants who engaged in kind acts experienced significant increases in happiness and mental health over a six-week period. Collectively, these studies show that kindness doesn't just benefit the recipient—it also improves the mental and physical health of the giver. Acts of kindness reduce stress, boost happiness, promote longevity, improve heart health, and strengthen social connections. By incorporating kindness into our daily lives, we create a positive feedback loop that benefits everyone involved.

David R. Hamilton, PhD, explains in his book *The Five Side Effects of Kindness* that kindness makes us happier, benefits our hearts, slows aging, improves relationships, and can even be contagious. This means that by practicing kindness, we multiply these benefits for ourselves and everyone around us.

Conclusion: The Ripple Effect of Kindness

As you can see, there are countless reasons to cultivate a habit of kindness and giving that aligns with your skills and passions. Not only will it improve your own well-being, but it can also help make the world a better place. As the saying goes, *"In a world where you can be anything, be kind."*

References:

Kogan, A., et al. (2013). *Health Psychology.*Oman, D., et al. (1999). *Psychological Science.*Hamilton, D. (2017). *The Five Effects of Kindness.*

Bio

Aloma Loren, the founder of Build Your Dream Life and Empowered by Kindness, is a visionary, heart-led entrepreneur whose success is deeply rooted in acts of kindness and giving.

Her leadership and entrepreneurial spirit have not only inspired countless individuals but also built thriving communities. Through her work as founding director of the Sprout Children's Business Expo and Eugene Mindworks, Oregon's largest locally owned coworking space, Aloma has demonstrated that genuine care and compassion are the keys to lasting success. A devoted mother of four, she now shares her transformative journey and insights, guiding others to achieve their dreams with heart and purpose.

Alicia Pozsony-

Embracing Resilience - Overcoming & Beating the Odds to Live My Legacy

Hello, I am Alicia Pozsony, a Transformational Speaker, Author, Speaking Coach, former Radio show host, Podcast host, international society writer and even an award-winning scriptwriter. I am still amazed that I have started three businesses- a career coaching firm, a motivational speaking agency, and a podcast production company - and worked over 50,000 hours helping over 5,000 people with personal and professional growth. But it was not always this way! You see, I basically raised myself and I didn't go to college out of high school like most other kids. I didn't have a child until 35. How did I get to live my life spending time with my kids, focusing on effecting change in the world while helping people? How did I do it? My journey is rooted in resilience and the power of transformation, a testament to overcoming life's myriads of challenges. Through this chapter, I aim to inspire and empower women to align with their authentic selves and embrace a life of abundance using Resilience.

I am a woman of purpose, driven by a deep-seeded passion to help others unlock their potential and live fulfilling lives using their voice. My background is a tapestry of experiences that have shaped me into who I am today—a beacon of hope and a catalyst for change.

My story is one of resilience, a journey marked by trials and triumphs. I beat the odds and I am telling you, you can make it against the odds, too. Born in the 6th month weighing at just 1 pound 11.25 ounces, I had low chances of surviving. Doctors told my mother I would be sickly and not live to the age I am living now. I was so underweight that I could fit in the palm of my grandfather's hand and my lungs were underdeveloped. To top it off, growing up, I faced unthinkable obstacles that further tested my strength and resolve. I faced things that a child never should have seen, things that made this child grow up far too soon. To top that off, my resilience was tested yet again in my youth when I was faced with the unthinkable: abandoned by one parent and then left to give up my youth way too early when my mother became mentally ill. My struggle didn't stop there. Once I got out from under the dysfunction of living with a person having mental illness, in young adulthood, I faced depression and anxiety. When I began my professional career without a college degree, I had to climb the career ladder against all odds. However, it was through these adversities that I discovered my true purpose. You would not know it by looking at me now, but I was strong. Not only did I survive, but I learned to thrive by finding solace in books, seeking education, and making conscious decisions to improve my situation. All because I had resilience. And it worked!

When I was a child, I found solace in the library, a comforting place away from the dysfunction only abandonment and mental illness can bring. I survived the streets by going to the library. There, I read books to escape the real world. This allowed me a healthy activity instead of being in a situation that would hurt me.

Going to a safe place where I could learn and grow helped me realize that I could stand on my story, not in my story and not in my situation.

Choosing how I spent my time was a pivotal realization even at such a young age. It led to better things and taught me that even without adult power, I could still make decisions and shape my own outcome. This is one of the pillars that I share with the world. People can use what they have and get better at things as they apply themselves. With attempts comes failure, and failure is something that can make or break a person. Resilience helps us define what happens after failure. It's about the power of choice, the power to shape our lives, and the power to bounce back from failure.

The experiences that defined my journey started as a child – I got good at making choices that would help me throughout my life and bring meaning and purpose to myself and the world around me. I grew up in an urban jungle in the eastern part of the United States. I was a white girl in my school. I have always struggled to fit in. I went to seventeen different schools before I finished high school. I was a high school dropout and stricken with depression, anxiety, and panic, making my young adulthood a nightmare.

As a young adult, without a degree, depression creeping in, and no family to fall back on, I had a tough life ahead of me. But I learned the importance of embracing change. It's another thing I challenge you to do. I say this because the only thing that is constant is change. Change will scare you and cause you to fight, freeze, or flee unless you learn to embrace, adapt, and move forward with it. Embracing change is not just about survival, it's about thriving in the face of uncertainty.

Change will scare you and cause you to fight, freeze, or flee unless you learn to embrace it, adapt to it, and *move forward- move with it.*

I got support from my friends and reluctantly agreed to take medicine for the depression that led to anxiety and, worse, panic. Anyone who knows depression knows it can hold you down and make you a different person. Anyone with anxiety knows it can shake you at your very core, but anyone with panic knows it is like being in the death scene of a movie over and over and over again. Mine stemmed from unresolved issues and a lifetime of pain that was not dealt with. Despite the personal struggles, I persevered, and with the help of a stable boyfriend, structured routine, and counseling, my life started to become more regular. I knew every day this was how normal everyday life was and even though I knew this was just me doing what I needed, it was still a struggle. I struggled with the difference I lived from what my homeless sometimes missing mother must have been going through. I used resilience to keep going, stay true to myself, and make a better life. I eventually proved myself and climbed the corporate ladder with a career in technology as an independent consultant. I was making over $100,000 by 1999, and I was physically fit, engaged, and on my way to all my dreams coming true. I knew I had to remain focused on my strengths and not become deterred by negative thoughts, people, or patterns that would otherwise hold me down. The same focus that held me within my safety net as a child would now help me keep going, staying out of trouble, out of toxic situations, and moving forward even through life's most challenging times. This meant using tough love for my mother, who would not comply with society's norms due to her mental illness. It meant continuous learning and creating balance in every area of my life. This was not always easy, especially with people telling me what to do, me looking at what others had or did and what was going on in the world.

It is said that "If you do not choose your path in life, life will choose it for you." This is the essence of one thing that defines my journey to purpose.

Challenges continued to come in ways of personal and professional struggles like a constant current. You know, the ones that keep you up at night, make you stress, eat, and want to binge, well, anything and do things other than what you need to do. The personal and professional adversities I faced and how I dealt with them became the foundation of my resilience. When I finished a contract assignment at work, I worked to identify what was needed and then, went for another job. When a relationship ended, I did my best to learn from it not to be held down with self-pity or guilt and I tempered logic with emotion, forging a solid emotional core. Each time my homeless mother went missing, I tapped into support and did what

I could to stay strong in the love that she had for me growing up. I could not give up on her and, in turn, built the emotional strength to not give up on me.

Each challenge was a stepping stone, teaching me valuable lessons and shaping my outlook on life.

Remember that we are all imperfect and shaped by our own experiences and beliefs; however, if you can keep an open mind, you can start to be more emotionally strong and more resilient.

After writing my memoir when I was in my 40's, I reached a point in my life when someone asked me how I "turned out so good." Looking back, I should not have been surprised. I did overcome and make it despite the odds. I was humble and often used my lessons learned as an explanation. It was a proven formula to remain emotionally intense and focused, and it was a path I took whenever I faced challenges or something difficult.

Simply put, I started with emotional strength. I would look at myself, be open to knowing it was okay to change, and then take the steps to change. Inspired by something my mother told me: "You don't have to go through it; you can grow through it." I later put those steps into a self-help workbook so I could help others. As busy women, we do not have time to read a 300-page self-help book and then take action. We need something that will help us NOW.

In my life, I continued with strategies of asking for help when needed and keeping a balance. Without balance, we can become overwhelmed, and we know that everything starts to slip with overwhelm. I looked to people I admire in different areas and began connecting with them, practicing what they do. Les Brown says, "If you want success, look at successful people and do what they do. Look at unsuccessful people and do not do what they do." It is that simple. Do not be distracted and misled; stay true to yourself on your proper course to live your calling and purpose to find your authentic self and pure joy.

Transitioning from an IT consultant to becoming a motivational speaker and coach was a pivotal moment in my life. Here, I found my calling as a "a natural storyteller" to inspire and guide others on their paths to success. Founding my career coaching practice started me on my journey. My journey continued to life coaching, being a behavioral specialist helping people who faced trauma. That led to my book, my Radio-show-turned-podcast "Resilient YOU with Alicia Pozsony". Now, as a Certified Legendary Les Brown Speaker engaging in motivational speaking, I have reached countless individuals, sharing my story and empowering them to overcome their challenges.

Part of learning Resilience is being authentically you, accepting failures and challenges, and agreeing to get up again!

Resilience has been a caveat and turning point in my life more times than I can count. I want to share with you what you need to be a Purpose-Driven Woman. There are four things that you need to be a purpose-driven woman.

1. **The Power of Resilience**: Harness inner strength and resilience to overcome obstacles and achieve personal and professional goals.
2. **Embracing Authenticity**: The importance of aligning with one's true self and living a life that reflects personal values and aspirations.
3. **Transformative Growth**: Use strategies and insights to transform challenges into opportunities for growth and self-improvement.
4. **Inspiration and Empowerment**: Let real-life examples and motivational insights inspire you so you can take charge of your life and pursue your dreams with confidence and determination.

I hope that the pivotal moments of my journey, sharing personal anecdotes and insights that illustrate the power of resilience and the beauty of living a purposeful life, urge you to make a change in your life.

My story will resonate with women, encouraging them to embrace their journeys with courage and conviction.

The Power of Resilience requires Harnessing Inner Strength and Resilience to Overcome Obstacles and Achieve Goals. Inner strength is the core of our being, an intrinsic quality that empowers us to face challenges head-on. It is the unwavering belief in our capabilities and the steadfast determination to persevere, regardless of the circumstances.

Cultivating inner strength involves nurturing a positive mindset, embracing self-compassion, and developing a resilient spirit. In those moments of do or die, flee, fight, run, or be run over, is when we find our inner strength.

The best part is that we have it with us daily and can choose to focus on it and, like a muscle, grow that strength so it serves us. However, the only way to get more emotional strength and resilience is by acting, staying open, and getting up again.

I learned strategies to Harness Inner Strength and Resilience throughout my early life. This was done through Self-Awareness and Reflection. My advice is to Practice Mindfulness - Engage in daily mindfulness practices, such as meditation or journaling, to cultivate self-awareness. Understanding your thoughts, emotions, and reactions helps build a solid foundation for resilience. It's essential to Identify Strengths and Weaknesses - Take time to reflect on your strengths and areas for improvement. Acknowledging your capabilities boosts confidence, while recognizing areas for growth fosters a proactive mindset.

Once you accomplish this, **Setting Realistic Goals is another pillar to master. Define Clear Objectives -** Though an old concept, it is essential! Set specific, measurable, achievable, relevant, and time-bound (SMART) goals for personal and professional endeavors, but do it to align with your passions and authentic self. Clear objectives provide direction and motivation. Today's world is challenging because we have our old paper ways and technology that overcomplicates things with too many options. Be open, and remember, you should write down your daily goals – it does not matter where, but as much as it matters that you are active every day. Then, **Break Down Goals into smaller parts -** Divide larger goals into smaller, manageable tasks. This approach reduces overwhelm and allows you to celebrate small victories. Take time in the bathroom if needed – or at the library, so you have that time, not between making dinner and dropping the kids off. This time should be real-time. You are worthy and important enough for your own goals. Set an example for others around you.

Building a Support System to Seek Support helps you when you need it most. Surround yourself with positive, supportive individuals who uplift and encourage you. A robust support system provides emotional strength and valuable perspectives during challenging times. Make a list of people who are with you through thick and thin. The people who support you. If you do not have any right now, keep going. You will find your tribe! It's also essential to **offer support -** Being there for others fosters community and reinforces your resilience. Kindness and support strengthen emotional bonds and create a positive feedback loop. When you seek a club or group, you will find like-minded people and get support. As Lisa Nichols shared in a recent training, YANA, You are not alone.

Spirituality has helped me through some dark times. Your creator is there, and if you connect through prayer, writing, journaling, or prayer, you will find peace. One way to use this is by Developing a Growth Mindset. Embrace Challenges—View challenges as opportunities for growth rather than obstacles. Adopting a growth mindset encourages continuous learning and adaptability. Some of our challenges are things that are there to help us grow.

"Remember – Life is a Journey. Make yours on Purpose!"

-Alicia Pozsony

Learning from Failure is another critical pillar of resilience. Understand that failures are part of the journey to success. Each setback offers valuable lessons and insights, contributing to personal and professional development. Failure is inevitable. Your choice to act is up to you. Les Brown, my mentor, says, "As long as you can look up, you can get up." We have heard some of the most successful leaders say, "Fail Fast." Let these two things motivate you.

Cultivating Self-Compassion by being Kind to Yourself means treating yourself with the same compassion and understanding that you would offer a friend. Self-compassion fosters emotional resilience and reduces self-criticism. We all have the words of self-doubt. Realize what you want and what you are capable of.

Look at your past challenges, and you can keep going because you will see what you can accomplish when you thought you could not.

Practice Gratitude - Regularly reflect on and express gratitude for the positive aspects of your life. Gratitude shifts focus from challenges to blessings, enhancing overall well-being.

Maintaining Physical and Mental Well-Being is an ongoing goal to maintain resilience - Prioritize Health as I did throughout my later adult years- Engage in regular physical activity, maintain a balanced diet, and ensure adequate sleep. Physical health significantly impacts mental and emotional resilience. Put the phone in the other room at night to prioritize your health and wellness.

Practice stress management, though it may not be easy—especially when we are busiest—by incorporating stress-reducing activities, such as yoga, deep breathing exercises, or hobbies, into your routine. Effective stress management enhances your ability to cope with adversity. The balance can be hourly, daily, or weekly. The important thing is that you spend time realizing the things that help you relax, decompress, and feel lighter. Then, do those!

Everything will flow better when you have a balance in place.

I practiced Adapting and Learning Continuously to remain resilient. Stay Open to Change—Embrace change as a constant and inevitable part of life. Being adaptable and open to new experiences strengthens resilience. If you cannot move, you will stay stagnant. People and life will pass you by. We live our best lives by moving toward progress.

"By changing nothing, nothing changes." — *Tony Robbins.*

Seek Knowledge and Skills: Continuously seek opportunities to learn and grow. Expanding your knowledge and skills enhances your ability to navigate challenges and seize opportunities. This is one of the most important things I can share with you. Wisdom comes from not just knowing information but also taking what you have learned and applying it.

Your Legacy

When you believe in who you are like I did, you overcome the worst things like poverty, famine, and limiting self-doubt built from beliefs shaped by our experiences, our past and prior generations. When you believe in who you are like I did, you begin to break generational curses and lose those unhealthy habits you don't want in your life anymore. Some people think legacy is your children and their children's children. I am here to tell you something else.

Your legacy is the mark YOU leave on those around you.

It is how you will be remembered, the mark you make on the world, and the stories about you. If you can live with a legacy mindset, you will succumb to the belief that your circumstances will ebb and flow based on your idea of eternity, not something you want to happen or some state or dollar value. This will enrich your life and create a lasting legacy beyond your time on earth.

We can choose to keep ourselves focused. Because your legacy is your life's work, you know this requires you to stay positive, keep giving of yourself, and keep uplifting others. I have been motivated by people who have overcome—the people who had the odds stacked against them. Those who, if their lives were a movie, there would be that one scene where they come back and make everyone gasp in awe. I was that person in real life, and you can be, too.

The hardest thing about developing a Legacy mindset is that we have lived through the information age, the technology age, and now the experience age

So, of all the things you have experienced, can you take some of them and **remove** them? It's easier to adapt a new idea or skill by choosing to do it and acting on it because our minds like the idea, the synapses are firing, and it causes dopamine to be released, making you feel pleasure. Simply, it's new and exciting because it has promise. But would it be as easy to remove a behavior or belief that does not serve you? That would require a different series of events and other skill sets altogether. Sometimes, it would mean disagreeing with loved ones, previous mentors, or important people. It might even mean making ethical choices that separate you from family and friends. Changing to improve and evolve will require things that are not called of you and are often not easy to do. You can learn how others have done this and made changes, and from this, you will gain something far greater than what you believed was right because your parents did it or what your Aunt Martha told you back in 2004.

Achieving Personal and Professional Goals

Harnessing inner strength and resilience is pivotal in achieving personal and professional goals. By cultivating a resilient mindset, setting clear objectives, and building a robust support system, you create a strong foundation for success. Embracing challenges, practicing self-compassion, and maintaining overall well-being further empower you to overcome obstacles and thrive in both personal and professional realms.

Remember, resilience is not about avoiding difficulties but facing them with courage, determination, and an unwavering belief in overcoming them.

Your journey, defined by resilience and inner strength, is an inspiring testament to the transformative power of perseverance and self-belief. Through this journey, you achieve your goals and inspire others to harness their inner strength and resilience, creating a ripple effect of empowerment and positive change.

The Impact of My Life's Purpose

I have learned that if we level up, live our purpose, and be our best, starting with our why, we can influence and persuade others with power and impact to keep moving, bring the best out in others, and cause world change for a happy world.

The effect I have made spans generations, from volunteering in inner cities, giving skills to elementary school children, and supporting adolescent girls in my role as a Girl Scout leader. Hence, they make a difference in the world around them and can grow to be purpose-driven women, as well as the people I speak to in leadership and motivation, including being a speaker for AARP helping older Americans. I have talked to people in underprivileged countries using my inspiring words, dynamic presence, and articulate delivery to illuminate the stage, captivate minds, and stir hearts as an International Speaker at a Women's Empowerment International Conference and I continue to speak on motivational themes. In the future, I will connect and collaborate with causes that give back to the human spirit and return people to live whole lives.

Remember, *resilience is not about avoiding difficulties* but facing them with courage, determination, and an unwavering belief in overcoming them. I challenge you to embrace your journey, defined by resilience and inner strength, and let it serve as an inspiring testament to the transformative power of perseverance and self-belief. Through this journey, you will achieve your goals and inspire others to harness their inner strength and resilience, creating a ripple effect of empowerment and positive change for the world to come. I challenge you to overcome adversity and live your legacy!

Despite my "low chance of survival," lack of biological family, and inherent imperfection, I continue to live my legacy by helping others find their greatness. From inspiring and motivating audiences worldwide to assisting others in going from stage fright to the spotlight, teaching them confidence on stage and camera, clarity in their message, and power in their presentations as a speaker coach, my mission will help heal the ever-changing world. Visit https://alicia-pozsony.mykajabi.com/ for more information, and connect with me today!

Bio

Alicia is a beacon of transformation, a guiding light in the world of personal and professional development. With a passion for helping individuals break free from confusion and reclaim their authentic selves, she has become a renowned Les Brown Certified Legendary Motivational Speaker and Coach.

Empowering Authenticity: Alicia's mission is clear: to empower those who find themselves trapped in soulless, unfulfilling situations. She specializes in guiding individuals through the maze of uncertainty, helping them find inner peace and discover their true potential, whether in their career or personal life.

Motivational Speaker Extraordinaire: As a dynamic motivational speaker, Alicia has graced stages in businesses, schools, resorts, and communities worldwide. Her talks resonate deeply with audiences, touching on the keys to success and the importance of maintaining a mentally healthy lifestyle. She draws inspiration from Les Brown as a Certified Legendary Les Brown Speaker and from her groundbreaking "Power My Life" Program, which is at the core of her revolutionary "Impact Influence Income Academy."

Multi-Talented Influencer: Alicia's impact goes far beyond the podium. She is a Radio Journalist and Radio Show turned Podcast Host, a published Award-Winning Author, a compassionate Life Coach, and a dedicated Career Coach. Her expertise in resilience and mental health advocacy has touched countless lives, providing a roadmap to triumph over life's challenges.

Global Perspective: Alicia's words also reach an international audience through her role as a Society Writer for the esteemed Transatlantic Today magazine. Her insightful articles and interviews delve into the heart of societal issues and human experiences, fostering connections and understanding across borders.

Alicia's dedication to personal growth, mental health, and societal progress is an inspiration to all who have the privilege of hearing her speak, reading her work, or seeking her guidance. With her unwavering commitment to helping individuals and communities thrive, Alicia truly embodies the essence of transformational wellness and empowerment.

Alicia Pozsony is a Transformational Wellness Coach and host of **Resilient YOU with Alicia Pozsony**. Providing Solutions for decades, Alicia experienced underachievement, failed relationships, abuse, and worse. Once she put her 'Power Your Life' Practice to work, she developed her own behavior-based Empowerment strategies. A featured presenter at conferences in the U.S. and abroad, she is the #1 best-selling author of *Emotional Strength Explained*. **Get Alicia's free self evaluation,** at www.aliciapozsony.com.

For more info: info.aliciapozsony.com Alicia pozsony (mykajabi.com)

Christine Knight-

It's Not For Nothing

Trauma is not your fault. Take all the time you need for that to sink in. Over several years, "Trauma is not your fault - but healing is your responsibility" has made its rounds. For many trauma survivors, this phrase can feel dismissive, piling on pressure when what is needed most is understanding and support. Trauma is not your fault. Period.

This full stop creates a space where healing can begin, free from the dismissive "but" that often follows. It makes survivors feel heard and understood, a crucial step in the healing journey. This chapter is my story—how I transformed my pain into purpose, found my true Self, and dedicated my life to helping others do the same.

Early Life and Childhood Trauma

My childhood was marked by chaos and emotional pain. Growing up in a household with an abusive alcoholic father and a mother who was often the target of his violence left deep scars. Witnessing domestic violence, experiencing physical and sexual abuse, and living in an environment of constant fear took a heavy toll on my young mind. The ACE (Adverse Childhood Experiences) score, which measures childhood trauma, stood at a staggering seven for me. The effects of such a high score can be devastating, leading to long-term physical, emotional, and psychological issues.

Despite the turmoil, I tried to find ways to cope. I developed survival strategies to protect myself from the overwhelming pain. While necessary for survival at the time, these strategies became maladaptive as I grew older, impacting my relationships, self-esteem, and overall well-being.

The Journey through Relationships

My early experiences set the stage for a series of tumultuous romantic relationships. By age 47, I had been married and divorced five times. Each marriage mirrored my childhood trauma in different ways, and I found myself repeatedly drawn to partners who were emotionally unavailable, abusive, or manipulative.

Marriage #1: Escaping the Chaos

At age 16, I married an older man, hoping to escape the chaos at home. This marriage was marked by domestic violence, mirroring the abuse I had witnessed and experienced as a child. My husband's controlling and abusive behavior was painfully familiar, but I didn't recognize it for what it was. I was young and desperate to leave my family home, and I mistook control for care. This marriage ended disastrously, reinforcing my belief that I was unworthy of love.

The early days of this marriage were filled with naive hope. I remember thinking, "This is my chance for a fresh start." But the honeymoon phase was short-lived. Soon, the controlling behavior began to surface. He isolated me from friends and family, monitoring my every move. I was trapped, much like I had been in my childhood home. The fear was paralyzing, and the realization that I had merely swapped one form of captivity for another was devastating.

Marriage #2: Seeking Shelter

Seeking shelter rather than love, I married a man who turned out to be gay. This relationship was fraught with deception and emotional turmoil. I was looking for security and stability but found myself entangled in another complicated and emotionally draining situation. The stillbirth of our child added a layer of grief that compounded my existing trauma, leaving me feeling utterly alone and disconnected.

Our relationship was built on mutual desperation rather than genuine connection. We were two wounded souls seeking solace in each other but couldn't provide the healing the other needed. The revelation of his sexuality was a blow, but even more painful was the loss of our child. The stillbirth felt like the final nail in the coffin of my hope. I remember standing in the hospital, holding our lifeless baby, feeling a grief so profound it seemed to swallow me whole.

Marriage #3: The Miracle Baby

After several miscarriages, I finally had my "miracle baby," only to face infidelity and another painful divorce. This marriage initially seemed like a sanctuary; I felt cherished and hopeful. However, the eventual betrayal and divorce shattered my sense of self and trust. I had invested so much in this relationship; its collapse left me feeling broken and unworthy.

My husband in this marriage was charming and fun, a stark contrast to my previous partners. For a while, it seemed like I had finally found happiness. The birth of our child was a miracle, a beacon of hope in my otherwise tumultuous life. But beneath the surface, cracks were forming. His infidelity was a betrayal that cut deep. I remember finding out about his affair and feeling as if the ground had been ripped from beneath me. The pain was visceral, and the sense of betrayal was overwhelming.

Marriage #4: Repeating Patterns

A blast from the past, this relationship repeated old patterns of mental abuse and manipulation. This marriage was another attempt to find stability but based on the same faulty foundations. The cycle of abuse and manipulation continued, highlighting my unresolved trauma and my tendency to fall into familiar patterns, even when they were harmful.

I reconnected with an old flame, believing our shared history would provide a stable foundation. But history has a way of repeating itself. The manipulation and mental abuse began subtly, gradually escalating until I was once again trapped in a toxic relationship. The familiarity of the abuse was both comforting and terrifying. It was a pattern I knew well, a cycle that felt inescapable.

Marriage #5: The Love Bomber

What seemed like a knight in shining armor was another manipulative partner. This marriage was marked by "love bombing," a tactic often used by narcissists to control their partners. The intense attention and affection were intoxicating initially, but they quickly gave way to prevention and manipulation. This relationship, like the others, ended painfully, leaving me to confront the depth of my unresolved trauma.

The love bombing was a whirlwind. He showered me with affection and gifts, making me feel adored and special. But the intensity of his attention soon became suffocating. He was possessive, constantly needing to know where and who I was with. The control was stifling, and the realization that I had fallen for another manipulative partner was crushing. On the sidelines, he was involved in behaving in a completely different way with women he chased on the internet, secret texting and meetups, and even prostitutes.

Each marriage was a painful reminder of my unresolved trauma and the survival strategies that no longer served me. I was stuck in a cycle of victimhood, unable to break free from the patterns that had been ingrained in me since childhood. These experiences compounded my trauma, reinforcing the belief that I was unworthy of love and destined for pain.

The Turning Point: Finding Hypnotherapy

Desperate for change, I discovered hypnotherapy, a technique that allowed me to access and heal my subconscious mind. Hypnotherapy provided the breakthrough I needed, helping me uncover the root causes of my pain and begin the process of healing. It was the first step in a long journey towards self-awareness and inner peace.

Hypnotherapy: Accessing the Subconscious

Hypnotherapy works by inducing deep relaxation, allowing access to the subconscious mind where our most profound memories and beliefs are stored. Through guided visualization and suggestion, I was able to confront and reframe traumatic memories, release suppressed emotions, and replace negative beliefs with positive ones. This process helped me understand the underlying causes of my behaviors and provided a foundation for lasting change.

During hypnotherapy sessions, I explored my past experiences and the beliefs that had formed around them. I realized that many of my survival strategies were based on outdated and erroneous assumptions about myself and the world. For example, I had internalized the belief that I was unworthy of love and destined to be abandoned. Through hypnotherapy, I was able to challenge and change these beliefs, creating new, healthier narratives that supported my healing.

In those sessions, I delved into the darkest corners of my mind. I revisited my childhood, reliving moments of fear and pain that I had long buried. It was excruciating but also liberating. I cried for the little girl who had to endure so much and felt compassion for her struggle. The process was transformative. I remember one particular session where I visualized my childhood self holding her hand and telling her she was loved and safe. That moment of connection was decisive, a pivotal step in my healing journey.

Embracing Internal Family Systems (IFS)

While hypnotherapy was a significant milestone in helping heal the survival strategies of the powerful protector parts, the discovery of Internal Family Systems (IFS) truly transformed my life. IFS, a non-pathological psychotherapy model, focuses on understanding and healing the different parts of our subconscious that drive our behaviors and emotions. This approach resonated deeply with me, validating my experiences and providing a clear path to healing.

Internal Family Systems: Healing the Inner Parts

IFS posits that the mind is naturally made up of multiple aspects (multiplicity of mind) and that we all have different parts (sub-personalities), each with its perspective and qualities — that can become disconnected from our Core Essence early in childhood when emotionally overwhelmed. These parts often conflict, leading to internal strife and emotional instability. IFS therapy aims to help individuals access their core Self—a state of compassion, curiosity, and calm—and use this Self-energy to heal and integrate their parts.

Internal Family Systems (IFS): Healing the Inner Parts

IFS is based on the idea that the mind comprises multiple parts, each with its perspective and function. These parts can be categorized into three main types: Managers, Exiles, and Firefighters.

1. **Managers:** These parts try to maintain control over our inner and outer worlds to protect us from pain. They often take on roles such as perfectionism, people-pleasing, or hyper-vigilance.

2. **Exiles:** These are parts that hold our deepest wounds and painful emotions. They are often hidden away or "exiled" because their pain is too overwhelming to face.

3. **Firefighters:** These parts respond to the pain of the Exiles with impulsive actions to distract or numb us. They might engage in behaviors like overeating, substance abuse, or self-harm.

IFS therapy aims to help individuals access their core Self, a state characterized by calm, curiosity, compassion, and confidence. They can engage with their parts from this place, understand their roles, and facilitate healing.

In my IFS sessions, I learned to identify and connect with my various parts. I discovered that many of my behaviors and emotions were driven by parts trying to protect me from pain. By acknowledging and appreciating these parts, I could begin to heal the underlying wounds they were trying to protect.

For example, one of my managerial traits was perfectionism, which involved constantly striving to achieve and avoid criticism; I could find a less extreme role, allowing me to embrace imperfection and self-compassion.

IFS therapy also involves a lot of inner dialogue. I spent time getting to know each part and understanding their fears and motivations. It was like meeting different aspects of myself for the first time. This process was profoundly healing, allowing me to integrate these parts into a cohesive and balanced sense of self. I learned to lead my life from my core Self, making decisions from a place of calm and confidence rather than fear and reactivity.

In my healing journey, I discovered parts of myself that had taken on extreme roles to protect me from pain. Some parts were angry, fearful, and were driven to achieve at all costs. Through IFS, I learned to appreciate these parts for their efforts to keep me safe, and I worked with them to find new, healthier ways of functioning.

For example, I had a fiercely independent part of me, a protector who believed the only way to avoid pain was to rely on no one but myself. While this part had helped me survive, it also kept me isolated and prevented me from forming healthy relationships. Through IFS, I was able to thank this part for its service and help it find a less extreme role in my life, allowing me to connect more deeply with others.

IFS therapy was like peeling back the layers of an onion. Each session brought new insights and revelations. I learned to identify my various parts—the manager who kept everything in check, the exile who held the deepest pain, and the firefighter who tried to numb the hurt. Understanding these parts and their roles in my life was enlightening. I began to see how they had shaped my behaviors and relationships. By building a compassionate relationship with these parts, I started the process of integration and healing – and a new practice of self-reflection and attentiveness that has continued to the present day.

Nervous System Regulation and Somatic Embodiment

Another crucial aspect of my healing journey was learning to regulate my nervous system and engage in somatic embodiment practices. Trauma often leaves the nervous system in a state of dysregulation, leading to chronic stress, anxiety, and emotional reactivity. Understanding how to calm and regulate my nervous system was vital to achieving lasting peace and stability.

Trauma can leave the nervous system in a state of chronic dysregulation, often stuck in a heightened state of arousal (SNS dominance) or a state of shutdown (PNS dominance). Learning to regulate the nervous system is essential for healing, as it helps create a sense of safety and stability.

Several techniques can support nervous system regulation:

1. **Breath work:** Conscious breathing exercises activate the PNS and promote relaxation. Techniques such as diaphragmatic, box, and 4-7-8 breath can help calm the nervous system.

2. **Mindfulness Meditation:** Practicing mindfulness helps increase awareness of the present moment, reduce the impact of stressors, and promote a sense of calm. Techniques such as body scan meditation and loving-kindness meditation can be particularly beneficial.

3. **Yoga:** Combining physical movement with breath awareness, yoga helps release tension and promotes nervous system balance. Poses such as child's pose, legs up-the-wall, and savasana are incredibly calming.

4. **Progressive Muscle Relaxation (PMR):** This technique involves tensing and relaxing different muscle groups, promoting physical and mental relaxation. PMR can help release stored tension and reduce anxiety.

Engaging in these practices was transformative. I began to understand the intricate connection between my mind and body, learning how to listen to and care for myself in ways I had never done before. Each breathwork session and yoga pose brought me closer to a state of balance and calm. I felt more in control of my emotions, grounded in my body, and connected to my true self.

Somatic Embodiment: Reconnecting with the Body

Somatic embodiment involves becoming aware of and inhabiting one's body. Trauma often leads to a disconnection from the body, as individuals dissociate to escape the physical sensations of pain. Reconnecting with the body is crucial for healing, as it releases stored tension and trauma.

Several somatic practices can support embodiment:

1. **Body Scanning:** This practice involves bringing awareness to different body parts and noticing sensations without judgment. It helps increase body awareness and release tension.

2. **Movement Practices:** Gentle, mindful movements such as yoga, tai chi, and qigong can help release stored tension and promote a sense of embodiment. These practices encourage a deeper connection with the body and its sensations.

3. **Touch and Self-Massage:** Gentle touch and self-massage can help release tension and promote relaxation. Techniques such as acupressure, myofascial release, and simple self-massage can be effective.

4. **Grounding Techniques:** Grounding involves connecting with the earth and the present moment. Walking barefoot on natural surfaces, standing firmly on the ground, and visualizing roots extending from the feet into the world can help increase stability and connection.

Somatic practices became a cornerstone of my daily routine. I started each day with a body scan, checking in with myself and acknowledging any areas of tension or discomfort. This simple practice helped me start the day with awareness and intention. I incorporated yoga and qigong into my exercise routine, finding that these gentle, mindful movements helped me feel more connected to my body and grounded in the present moment.

Healing and Empowerment: A Lifelong Journey

The healing process is ongoing and requires dedication, self-compassion, and support. As I worked through my trauma, I began to see myself in a new light. No longer defined by my past, I embraced my true self—my essence that had been buried under layers of pain and survival strategies. This newfound self-awareness allowed me to break free from the patterns that had dominated my life for so long.

My journey is a testament to the power of healing and the resilience of the human spirit. By embracing hypnotherapy, IFS, nervous system regulation, and somatic embodiment, I transformed my pain into purpose and found my true Self. This journey has healed me and empowered me to help others on their healing paths.

Transforming Pain into Purpose

My journey from trauma to healing transformed my pain into a powerful purpose. I founded my practice to help others reconnect with their true selves, heal their inner parts, and create lives filled with peace and fulfillment. My work is not just a profession; it is a calling, born from my own experiences and driven by a deep desire to make a difference in the lives of others.

I have had the privilege of working with many clients, helping them uncover and heal the hidden beliefs and survival strategies holding them back. Creating a safe and supportive environment empowers my clients to explore their subconscious minds, heal their inner parts, and transform their lives.

One of the most rewarding aspects of my work is witnessing my clients' transformation. Many come to me feeling stuck, overwhelmed, and disconnected from themselves. Through hypnotherapy and IFS, they begin to uncover their true selves and experience profound healing. It is incredibly fulfilling to see clients move from a state of survival to one of thriving, creating lives rich with meaning and connection.

The Power of Connection

Healing is not a journey we take alone. Throughout my journey, the support of compassionate practitioners and the connections I made along the way were crucial. I learned the importance of co-regulation—the ability to feel safe and connected in the presence of another. This principle is central to my practice, where I strive to create a therapeutic alliance based on trust, empathy, and mutual respect.

Co-regulation involves using the presence of another person to help regulate one's nervous system. In a therapeutic context, this means providing a calm, supportive environment where clients can feel. Through IFS, I learned that this trait developed in response to my childhood environment, where perfection was necessary for survival. By working with this trail, I knew exploring their emotions and experiences was safe. This sense of safety is essential for healing, as it allows clients to access and process traumatic memories without becoming overwhelmed.

Creating a safe and trusting therapeutic relationship is fundamental to the healing process. I ensure that my clients feel seen, heard, and understood, fostering a sense of safety and connection. This relational safety allows clients to explore their inner worlds with courage and curiosity, knowing they are not alone.

Moving Forward

Today, I am living proof that trauma does not define us. It is an event that happens to us, but it does not have to control our lives. Through dedication, self-awareness, and the support of therapeutic practices like hypnotherapy and IFS, healing is possible and within reach.

My mission is to continue my healing journey and help as many people as possible move from a state of survival to one of thriving. By sharing my story, I inspire others to look at their lives, recognize their patterns, and take the courageous steps necessary to heal. Together, we can create a world where everyone has the opportunity to reconnect with their true selves and live fulfilling, empowered lives.

As part of my ongoing commitment to healing, I continue to engage in professional development and personal growth. I regularly participate in workshops, trainings, and supervision to deepen my understanding of trauma and enhance my therapeutic skills. This commitment to learning ensures I can offer my clients the most effective and compassionate support possible.

"It's Not For Nothing" is not just the title of this chapter; it is a testament to the transformative power of healing. My journey from a traumatic childhood through a series of painful relationships to a place of inner peace and purpose has taught me that our struggles are not in vain. They shape, teach, and ultimately lead us to our true purpose.

As you read my story, I invite you to reflect on your journey. Know that healing is possible, that you are not alone, and that your pain can be transformed into purpose. Embrace your inner parts, connect with your true self, and take the courageous steps towards healing. You are worth it.

Passion for Bringing Healing to Clients

As I continued to deepen my understanding and practice of these healing techniques, my passion for helping others grew. I became dedicated to making these transformative tools accessible to many people. Recognizing that trauma and emotional struggles do not discriminate, I wanted to provide support to individuals from all walks of life, regardless of their financial situation.

I developed a range of services at different price levels to ensure everyone could get the help they needed. From one-on-one sessions to group workshops and online resources, I aimed to create a comprehensive support system that catered to various needs and budgets. My goal was to remove barriers to healing and empower individuals to take control of their emotional well-being.

Creating My Dream Life

Through this journey of healing and transformation, I began to see the possibilities of a life filled with joy, purpose, and connection. I envisioned a life where I could live by the beach, which had always brought me peace and tranquility. This dream became a guiding light, motivating me to continue healing and build a life that resonated with my essence.

Today, I am grateful to live near the beach of my dreams. The soothing sound of the waves, the feeling of sand beneath my feet, and the endless horizon are daily reminders of my journey and the resilience of the human spirit. This environment nurtures my soul and enhances my ability to support my clients.

My relationships have also transformed. Through my healing work, I have developed deeper connections with others, built on trust, empathy, and mutual respect. I have learned to set healthy boundaries, communicate openly, and nurture relationships that support my well-being. The sense of connection and community I have cultivated enriches my life in ways I never imagined possible.

Passion for IFS Coaching Practice

I studied, trained in, and got certified in every technique along my healing journey that gave me traction in my healing. I became certified in clinical hypnotherapy and completed a master's degree in counseling. I also trained with the IFS Institute in Internal Family Systems. If I had to name only one technique that I would recommend to people to heal from trauma, anxiety, or depression, it would be Internal Family Systems. It was the "bow on top" of all of the techniques.

My passion for Internal Family Systems (IFS) coaching continues to grow as I witness its profound impact on my clients. Each person's journey is unique, and I am honored to be a part of their healing process. Whether working with individuals, couples, or groups, IFS provides a framework for deep and lasting transformation.

In my practice, I strive to create a safe and supportive space where clients can explore their inner worlds with curiosity and compassion. I guide them in connecting with their core Self, helping them understand and heal their parts and empowering them to create their desired lives. The work is deeply fulfilling, and I am continually inspired by the courage and resilience of those I have the privilege to work with.

Empowering Clients to Achieve Their Dreams

One of the most rewarding aspects of my work is seeing clients achieve emotional regulation and go on to create their dream lives. The techniques and practices that have transformed my life are equally powerful for others. By helping clients reconnect with their true selves and develop emotional stability, they can break free from old patterns and embrace new possibilities.

Clients often share stories of profound change—finding healthier relationships, pursuing fulfilling careers, and discovering a sense of inner peace. These transformations are a testament to the power of healing and the potential within each of us. My dedication to turning my pain into purpose fuels

I am committed to this work and passionate about helping others realize their potential.

Conclusion

"It's Not For Nothing" is not just the title of this chapter; it is a testament to the transformative power of healing. My journey from a traumatic childhood through a series of painful relationships to a place of inner peace and purpose has taught me that our struggles are not in vain. They shape, teach, and ultimately lead us to our true purpose.

As you read my story, I invite you to reflect on your journey. Know that healing is possible, that you are not alone, and that your pain can be transformed into purpose. Embrace your inner parts, connect with your true self, and take the courageous steps towards healing. You are worth it.

I'm Christine Knight. Stay curious.

Bio

It took me 16 years to travel through my own healing journey from childhood trauma, after being told by a PhD psychologist that there was no cure for the PTSD spirals and rage fits that I was tortured by. I got trained, certified, or licensed in every technique that brought me traction and momentum forward in my own healing journey. And then I created a new method of healing triggers, reactive behaviors, and repeated harmful patterns by combining Hypnotherapy and Internal Family Systems. I call it the Emotional Freedom Method, and I teach it in a 90-day online program that is self-paced, includes weekly live office hours with me, and a community forum where you can tag me and ask me questions at any time & also connect with like-minded people who are also on their healing journey. See my contact info in my bio to join this life-changing program today. Your Future Self will deeply appreciate it. Start now, where you are, it's the best time to start.

Elizabeth Meigs-

Equipped for Victory: Unleashing Resilience and Overcoming Life's Challenges

Imagine being 14 years old, full of life, and then, in a blink, everything changes. My name is Elizabeth Meigs, and my story began on a day that changed my life forever. A devastating car accident left me clinging to life, and with it, I lost the person I once knew. Grief, pain, anger, and the question of "Why me?" consumed me. But I didn't know then that this tragedy was the seed of something greater that would transform my life.

In those darkest moments, I was forced to develop strategies to survive—not just physically but emotionally and spiritually. These strategies became the foundation of my Pathway to Peace Method™— a journey that took me from hopelessness to becoming the unstoppable, confident person I am today. I turned my impossible into "I'm possible." Now, as an inspirational speaker, transformational coach, and author at Elizabeth Inspires, my mission is to share this journey with you, helping you believe in the possibilities and realize that you, too, have the power within you to overcome the unimaginable.

This chapter of my life isn't just a story of survival; it's a survival guide—a shortcut to help you navigate your challenges. It took me over two decades to fully harness the power within me, but you don't have to wait that long. Through Elizabeth Inspires, I'm here to show you how you can find that same strength, peace, and resilience in every aspect of your life.

You're reading this for a reason. Every struggle has a purpose; I'm here to help you discover yours. When you learn to embrace life's uncertainties, believe in a greater good, and trust in the journey, you tap into your inner spirit of resilience that will carry you through any storm. My mission is to guide you on your Pathway to PEACE™, offering you H.O.P.E: Healing that Opens Pathways to Empowerment.

Some moments define who we are and force us to search for meaning. My purpose became crystal clear months after I awoke from a coma due to a car accident one week into my first year of high school, leaving me with a traumatic brain injury. Before that night, my life was on a fast track to success—I was popular, played every sport, and was a cheerleader. My voice had been my ticket to a bright future, with years of singing and performing. My voice teacher, who believed in me, had arranged for me to go to a recording studio because she saw my abilities. I was set to pursue a career in country music. Everything was moving full speed ahead, and life felt easy.

But then, life threw me an unexpected curveball. After the car accident, where I was given less than a 25% chance of survival, I woke to a world where that confident girl chasing her dreams was gone. My life became one of relearning the simplest tasks, struggling through three months of hospitals and rehab before finally returning home. It was then that I realized something profound—the girl I once was had died in that car accident, and with her, the dreams she held.

Returning to school, I found myself in a world that had moved on without me. My friends continued with their lives—while I was left behind, feeling invisible, judged, and rejected by those who didn't know the person I once was. The isolation was devastating. For years, I would come home from school, broken and defeated, telling my parents, "I should have died in that car accident. I wish I were dead; I want to kill myself." The thought consumed me.

Have you ever felt like that? So, lost that the pain feels unbearable? I would collapse on my bedroom floor, crying out to God, asking, "Why did you do this to me?" And in those moments of deepest despair, I would feel a voice in my heart—a voice of calm and reassurance. "I have a plan for you. You can't stop. You have to keep going."

This was the voice of God, bringing me a peace and comfort I had never known. It became my lifeline. At that moment, I realized He didn't do this to me—it was a worldly circumstance. I knew then that I couldn't give up. I had to keep fighting because I would someday need to be for someone else, exactly what I needed in that moment. The pain wasn't just for me—it was to shape me for my purpose, my calling.

I began turning to God every night without fail, thanking Him for my life and blessings and asking Him to help me make the right choices so that I could do His will with my life. This was my first step—believing in the unseen, trusting His plan, and surrendering to Him. His promise was my hope, rooted in Jeremiah

29:11: "For I know the plans I have for you… plans to prosper you and not to harm you plans to give you hope and a future."

By God's grace, I made it through high school, graduating with my class. I went on to college, changing my major four times, continuing to fall and fail. But each failure was a step closer to understanding my purpose. I learned that when you are faithful to God, He is faithful to you. The choice is always yours—I had to learn how to fail forward.

In 2012, I graduated with an associate degree in Occupational Therapy. When I walked into the rooms of patients who had suffered strokes, I began to see the power of my story. These patients were discouraged and lacked hope, but I could sit with them, sharing my journey and offering hope. That was the confirmation I needed—that my struggles and challenges were meant to mold me into someone who could turn pain into purpose. There is hope in the breaking.

My mission is to guide you on your Pathway to PEACE™ and offer you H.O.P.E—Healing that Opens Pathways to Empowerment. Through my story, struggles, and faith, I became an expert problem solver. I'm here to help you discover your purpose and show you that even in your darkest moments, there is a light waiting to guide you forward. You are not alone, and you are stronger than you know. Together, we will find that strength and build a life filled with peace, purpose, and hope.

By this point in my life, I had faced enough judgment to realize it no longer held the power it once did. I learned to let go of others' opinions, knowing that those who judged me weren't worth my time or peace. Holding on to their negativity would only rob me of the joy and serenity I had fought so hard to attain. Instead, I focused on what truly mattered: pursuing my passions. This connection to what sets your soul on fire fuels you through the most challenging times, making moving forward possible.

In high school, even when I was drowning in despair, my passion pulled me through. For me, that passion was singing. Though my voice wasn't the same after the accident, being on stage still felt like a sanctuary. When I sang, the judgments faded, and people saw beyond my physical deficits—they saw me as I could be. This was a true gift from God.

I'll never forget when my voice teacher, who had stopped giving lessons, called my mom after I returned home from the hospital and said, "I want to work with Beth when she's ready and stronger, to help her get her singing voice back, to help her do what she loves." It was like a ray of light breaking through the clouds. Has there ever been a moment when something beautiful and unexpected came as a gift? Hold that memory close and reflect on it whenever life punches you in the gut. Know that this situation won't last forever. Be grateful for that gift, and remember, once you find your way out of the struggle, many more gifts await you.

What are you passionate about? My passions have always aligned with my purpose. Before the accident, singing was my passion. Afterward, helping others became my number one passion. I still used singing to carry me through until I reached a better place, where I had evolved through my struggles and could see my next steps more clearly, growing my confidence.

You might not see how your passion can work in your life right now, but I promise, it's there for a reason. You have everything within you to make your dreams a reality. It won't be easy—but nothing worth doing ever is. You are meant for so much more than your current circumstances. You deserve to achieve your dreams and are enough to make them happen. The struggles guide you toward your purpose, even when it feels bleak. Believe that.

Early on, I let negativity consume me. I let the anger and heartache take over. But it was God's voice that assured me my life wouldn't always be like this. That's when I developed an attitude of gratitude. Each night, I thanked God for my life and for knowing He had a plan for me. His voice was a promise in my heart that I knew He wouldn't break. Now, He's using my voice to reach you, to remind you He has a plan for you—a plan bigger and better than anything you could have imagined.

Think about the challenges you're currently facing. Every time I've felt burnt out or ready to give up, it was because God was preparing me to move. With the strategies I've developed, I now live open to possibilities. When you reach a point where you can't continue as you are, you'll know it's time to move. Release your burdens to Him, and the path forward will reveal itself. As it says in 1 Corinthians 10:13, "He will not allow you to be tested beyond your means, but with your testing, He will make a way out." I'm living proof of this promise. Time and time again, God has cleared the way for me, but it takes breaking free from the cycle of chaos and stepping forward in faith and trust in His will for your life.

I discovered the true power of my story when I began working as an Occupational Therapist, helping patients face their battles. Sitting across from those struggling, I realized the hope my story could give. But my journey of finding my voice didn't end there.

After moving to Waco in 2015, I felt something was missing—a companion to share my life with. I ventured into online dating and learned that God will use any means necessary to get you where you need to be, even online dating. In July 2016, I went on a lunch date with a man who invited me to his church. Little did I know that invitation would be the beginning of something much bigger. I didn't attend the church right away, but months later, I moved to that same suburb and passed by the church regularly without realizing the significance. Then, one morning in January 2017, I ran into the man at Walmart at 6:30 a.m.—a seemingly random encounter that was anything but random. It was God giving me a sign.

I reached out to him through the dating app and attended his church that Sunday. There, I found a community that became like family. For the first time in 17 years, I felt like I belonged. I also found Celebrate Recovery (CR), and while I didn't know much about it, I trusted that if I could help my patients, I could help those in CR, too. I stepped out in faith, became a leader, completed the 12 steps, and began sharing my testimony in the spring of 2017. God took my mess and made it His message of Hope! Through me, His message of love could reach others.

The impact was immediate. People approached me, telling me how much hope my story gave them. One woman said, "I wasn't going to come to church tonight, but something told me I needed to be here, and now I know it was God. Your story gives me so much hope. Thank you." In those moments, I realized the difference my voice and message could make when shared from a stage. I began to see all the possibilities and the positive impact I could make in this world.

Every time I stepped out in faith, trusting God's plan, He made a way. Even when I faced setbacks—wrong choices, financial struggles, imposter syndrome—God placed the right people in my life to lift me. It is the same for you. Surround yourself with a community that lifts you and helps you grow into who you are meant to be.

For me, my friend John was that blessing. He was the one who initially invited me to church, and in March 2017, God spoke to me, revealing that He had brought us together to bring us both closer to Him. John became a constant source of encouragement, reminding me of my worth and purpose. I now see God used him to help build my confidence, showing me the power of someone believing in you. That belief is a priceless gift, and I want you to know—I believe in you. You have everything within you to overcome the struggles and pain to come out on top. You can turn your "impossible" into "I'm possible." Don't stop chasing those dreams—they were placed in your heart for a reason.

By the end of 2018, John and I had grown distant, but the lessons I learned during that time stayed with me, preparing me for what was to come. Each person in your life serves a purpose. Some teach you lessons, some build you up, but each strengthens you. Everything happens for a reason, and as the song says, "There's hope in the breaking, there's hope in the sorrow, there's hope." You can't ever lose that hope.

In May 2019, I met someone new, and by the fall of 2020, we were married. I believed he would support my calling, but soon after the marriage, I was manipulated, verbally and emotionally abused. As I founded and tried to grow Elizabeth Inspires, his words became a constant source of pain: "No one will ever pay you to tell your story. Your only financial security is with your degree." But I knew that was a lie. God's voice in my heart remained a promise with overwhelming peace and comfort. My husband's voice brought only chaos and confusion. Despite the heartache, I kept going, trusting that God would make a way, as He had always done.

So, I pressed on. I had to continue putting one foot in front of the other, trusting and believing that God would make a way for me to do what He has called me to do. Just over two years into my marriage, I invested in a speaking seminar called "Take the Stage Dallas," not being fully supported by my husband, where I gained the tools I needed to elevate my message. During the seminar, I received a standing ovation, with audience members encouraging me to share my story nationwide. This was God's confirmation that I was on the right path, even though the challenges persisted daily. Clearly, God was moving mountains to get me where He needed me to be to fulfill my calling.

But the challenges weren't over. When I received a scholarship for a four-month coaching program from the seminar coach on April 3, 2023, my husband immediately opposed it. He said, "Until I see in writing that there are no fees involved, you are not allowed to do this." His words cut deeply, but I knew I couldn't let him stop me. When I cried in response, he coldly asked, looking at me with a look of pure hatred, "Why are you crying?" I replied, "Because this is who I am, this is what I've been called to do, and now that God is making a way for me to do it, you're telling me I can't."

After that conversation, I understood why God had spoken to me about John almost exactly six years earlier. He knew I would make a choice that would require His protection. Through this experience, I've been made stronger, and now I can help other women who've endured narcissistic abuse. God opened my eyes, and through this, He allowed me to recognize what was necessary for my survival.

John had contacted a mutual friend, inquiring about me just before the "Take the Stage" seminar on March 27-28. The timing was significant—he'd been on my heart since January, and although I didn't know why, I could feel his pain. After the argument with my husband, I realized he had never truly seen me. He saw only someone he thought he could control, manipulate, and never fully support. It became clear why God had brought John into my life when He did. So, I prayed, asking God for confirmation that I was on the right path. The days following brought clarity: God was leading me back to Waco, where I had first found my voice and purpose, speaking from a stage.

I contacted the rehab director at my previous workplace and, within days, secured a transfer from Dallas to Waco, along with affordable housing. I had no fear—I knew in my heart that God had me. By that Saturday, the night before Easter, I was ready to escape. I realized the only thing I could control was myself and what I allowed into my life. I left my marriage and returned to Waco, reclaiming the peace I hadn't realized I'd lost when I got married. Once again, God paved the way, aligning me with the right people to grow my business and transform my testimony into my mission of H.O.P.E. My business network had been crucial during my marriage, as they were the ones who lifted me while my husband tried to break me down.

As 1 Corinthians 10:13 says, "I will not allow you to be tested beyond your means, but with your testing, I will make a way out." This is how God moves mountains. But to see His hand at work, you must keep moving forward, refusing to stay stuck in the cycle of others dragging you down. It takes trust and faith to build the courage and confidence to continue, especially during difficult times.

Through podcasts, virtual, and in-person summits, I've continued to share how God turned my mess into a message of truth and resilience. This is what fuels me. I've come to understand that the power to rise above chaos and confusion lies within each of us. It's not just something we possess—it's a gift placed within us by a higher power. In our moments of weakness, when we turn to Him in faith and surrender to His will, He makes us strong. That same power resides within you, waiting to awaken and guide you toward a strength you never knew you had. After escaping my marriage, I started receiving divine clarity about the strategies I had developed since my car accident—strategies that not only helped me survive but thrive through the challenges.

As we conclude this chapter, let's reflect on the strategies woven throughout my story—strategies you can adopt to overcome your challenges and rise above the obstacles in your life.

The first key is to believe in something greater than your current circumstances. When life knocks you down, it's easy to feel overwhelmed, but in those moments, your faith becomes your anchor. Keeping your faith alive and trusting in a higher purpose opens the door to possibilities beyond what you can see. Embrace the uncertainty of your journey, and if you stumble, commit to failing forward—pick yourself back up and push toward the dreams in your heart; after all, they were placed there for a reason.

Next, adopt an attitude of gratitude. Just as I did after the car accident, begin and end each day by going to God in prayer, thanking Him for your blessings, and asking for guidance. This act of surrender and acceptance is the first step to discovering your true power. It wasn't easy for me, and it won't always be easy for you, but if I can do it with everything I've endured, I have no doubt you can, too.

Believing in a greater purpose and practicing gratitude are the foundations of inner strength. This is why God chose me to share His message of truth—to bring comfort, peace, and hope to your heart, just as His voice was my lifeline after my brain injury.

I invite you to view your challenges as stepping stones—tools that help you evolve and grow into the person you're meant to be. Find a supportive community that lifts you and enables you to move forward. Surround yourself with those who believe in you, and remember to set boundaries to protect your peace. After all, awareness is key to survival.

Above all, never underestimate the power of belief. There is someone who knows you have what it takes to succeed and believes in your strength and potential—and she's writing this chapter. I believe in you and know you can rise above and overcome any odds.

Your journey may be challenging, but it will be deeply rewarding. Trust the process, embrace the uncertainty, lean into your resilience, and keep moving forward with courage. You are stronger than you know, and your purpose is waiting for you to claim it. Always remember, the challenges make the victory so much sweeter once you finally break through.

To show my appreciation for reading how God has worked miracles in my life—and to demonstrate how He can do the same in yours—I'd like to offer you a **FREE VIP 1:1 Pathway to P.E.A.C.E Method™ Discovery Call.** When you book today, you'll also receive the "Guide to Double Your P.E.A.C.E and Joy with the Pathway to Peace Method™ in 12 Weeks, Guaranteed!*" Just visit my website to get started. I'm here to prove that believing in a higher power and purpose can take you from merely surviving to truly thriving. The only reason I am still here today is to give you a shortcut to your Pathway to P.E.A.C.E™ because that is what you deserve!

Bio

Elizabeth Meigs is a passionate Transformational Coach, Inspirational Speaker, Author, and Founder of Elizabeth Inspires, dedicated to helping others overcome life's challenges through faith, resilience, and actionable strategies. Creator of the Pathway to P.E.A.C.E Method™, Elizabeth draws from her personal experiences, including recovering from a traumatic brain injury and navigating complex life transitions, to offer practical guidance for those seeking clarity, protection, and inner strength. Her unique coaching approach empowers individuals to break free from cycles of confusion and chaos, enabling them to live with purpose and embrace their God-given calling.

Guided by the transformative power of hope, Elizabeth's mission is to empower individuals on their unique wellness journey, fostering Healing that Opens Pathways to Empowerment (H.O.P.E). Her courses and speaking engagements inspire audiences to rise above adversity, build the foundation they need to thrive and protect their mental and emotional well-being. By teaching strategies that build confidence, Elizabeth helps individuals chase their dreams and achieve success both personally and professionally. She believes everyone has the potential to create the life they dream of and is committed to equipping others with the tools and encouragement to make it happen.

If you are ready to find your Peace, Freedom and Joy, book a **FREE VIP 1:1 Pathway to P.E.A.C.E Method™ Discovery Call.** When you book today, you'll also receive the "Guide to Double Your P.E.A.C.E and Joy with the Pathway to Peace Method™ in 12 Weeks, Guaranteed!*" Just visit my https://elizabethinspires.com/ to get started. Elizabeth is only here today for one reason: to give you a shortcut to your Pathway to P.E.A.C.E™ because that is what you deserve!

Contact Elizabeth Today!

https://elizabethinspires.com/

Tina K Kailea-

"Becoming Unapologetic - From Corporate Coma to Wild Reawakening"

Meet the Wild Executive. My name is Tina K Kailea, and becoming a Woman of Purpose wasn't linear or straightforward. I am a woman who has walked the path from corporate burnout through the fire to reclaim the wild, untamed essence within me — unapologetically.

Born in Germany, my early life was marked by a desire to fit in despite feeling different for as long as I can remember. I always felt a deep, wild yearning for something more — a feeling that stayed well into my adult years. When I moved to New Zealand at age twenty-five, my journey unfolded as a rebel pushing against the status quo.

I was once a woman who climbed the corporate ladder with determination and grit, only to find myself suffocating under the weight of expectations, deadlines, and a relentless drive for success. I felt confined by society's rigid expectations, lost in pursuing a career I thought I wanted, but that left me hollow and disconnected.

Today, I am an international speaker, bestselling and award-winning author, feminine embodiment coach, and book doula living in New Zealand. I am devoted to helping women reclaim their wild essence, rediscover their inner power, and live authentically. I empower women worldwide to break free from the chains of not feeling good enough and guide them to step boldly into their true selves and to be wild, woo-woo, and wonderful. I wish for every woman to embrace her untamed womanhood and live a rich life with purpose, fulfillment, and joy.

My journey is one of rediscovery, resilience, and the relentless pursuit of a deeper purpose. It is a story of awakening — a woman who dared to break free from the chains of her conditioning and the norms she inherited and who forged a path uniquely her own.

In this chapter, I will share the path that shaped my journey, the challenges I faced, and the lessons I learned along the way. My story will inspire you to embark on your journey of self-discovery and empowerment, regardless of where you are. I want to show you how embracing your true self can lead to the life you were truly meant to live.

For me success was defined by titles, salaries, and the approval of others. I pursued a career in the corporate world with relentless ambition and I thought I had it all. A successful job as a General Manager in an international publishing company, earning a six-figure salary, traveling the world, and living what many consider the career dream. But beneath the surface, I was crumbling. With all its demands and pressures, the stress in the corporate world was slowly killing my zest for life.

The turning point came after anxiety, depression and adrenal fatigue set off a series of personal tragedies — five miscarriages that left me emotionally and physically shattered. These losses forced me to confront the reality of my life: I was living a lie. The lie that I could have my cake and eat it, too. How wrong I was The life I had built and sacrificed so much for, with all its trappings of success, was hollow.

My body was sending me clear signals that something was seriously out of order, but I was too caught up in the whirlwind of corporate life to listen. I wore my busyness like a treasured batch of honor, and I had lost my joy, my spark, and most tragically, my sense of self. I realized something had to change when I was on the brink of complete burnout. In the depths of this long darkness, I began to see the faint glimmer of light — an awakening that would lead me to rediscover my purpose in life.

This realization didn't come quickly. I had spent years building a career that, on the surface, looked impressive, but that was sucking the life out of me. The first steps on my new path were tentative. I began by exploring my identity, reconnecting with the parts of myself I had suppressed by pursuing success. This journey wasn't easy, but the more I leaned into my true self, the more determined I became to make a change.

My Purpose - A Journey of Self-Reclamation

The discovery of my purpose was like finding a hidden treasure buried deep within my soul. It wasn't a sudden revelation but a gradual unveiling — a process of peeling back the layers of conditioning and expectations that had smothered my true self. The turning point came during a particularly harrowing business trip when my narcissistic boss's cruel words pierced through the veil of my subconscious mind. At that moment, I realized that I could no longer continue living like that. He was toxic, and so was the environment I had been in for far too long. I needed to get out and pursue something that felt more authentic. Enough was enough.

I began to slowly reconnect with my feminine essence — a force that I had long subconsciously suppressed in my efforts to succeed in a male-dominated world. Back then, I didn't even know what that truly meant, but somewhere deep inside me, an ember was lit again. It started a fire that kept smoldering until it burst into full force. This reconnection wasn't easy; it required deep introspection, vulnerability, and a willingness to let go of everything that no longer served me. But as I delved deeper, I began to feel a powerful sense of alignment.

I was no longer chasing after external validations; instead, I was guided by an inner knowing that my purpose was to help other women awaken to their power. I wanted to share my story, vulnerably, to help other women avoid the same pitfalls I had fallen into. I wanted to guide them toward a life aligned with their true selves, where they could embrace their feminine power without fear or shame. Be a whole lot of women. This purpose became my guiding light, pulling me out of the darkness and setting me on a new path.

Challenges and Roadblocks

This journey wasn't easy. The road to purpose is rarely smooth, and mine was no exception. I faced significant challenges, both external and internal. Externally, I faced skepticism from those around me, and financial constraints loomed large as I considered leaving my stable job and a toxic work environment where I was constantly undervalued and pushed to the brink. Internally, I battled with deep-rooted beliefs of inadequacy — beliefs that told me I wasn't good enough and that I didn't deserve to live a life of joy and fulfillment.

But I refused to let these challenges define me. Instead, I saw them as opportunities for growth and transformation. I sought out somatic modalities, found women's circles, and built a strong support network — I began to practice radical self-care. I learned to say "no" to anything that did not align with my truth and "yes" to the things that nourished my soul. Each obstacle became a stepping stone, leading me closer to the woman I was meant to be — a woman of purpose, living her truth unapologetically.

One of the biggest fears I faced was leaving behind the security of my corporate job. I had built my identity around my career and title for years. The thought of stepping into the unknown was terrifying.

Who was I without the safety of my corporate armor? How would I support myself and my family? What if I failed?

The uncertainty of the global financial crisis unfolding compounded this fear. Many of my family members, friends, and colleagues couldn't understand why I would want to leave a stable, well-paying job to pursue something as nebulous as "finding my true self." They questioned my decision, and their doubts only amplified my own.

Overcoming Obstacles and Doubts

I sought out other women who had successfully transitioned out of the corporate world. I began to network in more authentic spaces, found confidantes, attended workshops focused on personal development, read books on empowerment, and sought mentorship from those who had walked the path before me. These experiences helped me overcome my fears and showed me that I wasn't alone in my struggles. I found a whole community of women who had faced similar challenges and come out stronger on the other side. Their stories gave me the courage to leap. They were shining a light for me when I felt lost.

With the support of this community, I began to take small steps toward my new life. I started by setting aside time each day for self-reflection and creative exploration. I began journaling, meditating, and reconnecting with nature — activities that helped me quiet the noise of the external world and tune into my inner voice. These practices became the foundation of my journey, giving me the strength and clarity I needed to move forward.

I need to tell you that self-doubt has been a constant companion on my journey, and there have been many times when I've questioned my ability to keep going, lead, and inspire others. These doubts have often been fueled by the voices of the past — voices that told me I wasn't enough, that I didn't deserve to succeed. Overcoming these doubts has been one of the most significant challenges on my journey, and I have accepted that this inner work never quite feels finished. I call it 'stepping out of the box and onto the spiral' — this is no linear path; it's full of twists and turns, ego deaths and rebirths, it feels much like a chrysalis.

One of the strategies I've used to overcome self-doubt is focusing on small, achievable goals. For example, when I set out to write my book, I didn't think about the entire project at once. Instead, I broke it down into smaller tasks — writing one chapter at a time, one page at a time. I allowed time to let the words flow instead of setting rigid writing goals. This approach helped my creative flow to build momentum instead of overwhelming me or sending my nervous system into high alert. I gained confidence and trust as I went along.

I also re-learned to seek feedback and support from others — to ask for help, which can be challenging for most of us as we are conditioned for perfectionism. When uncertain about a decision, I turn to my mentors and support network for guidance, allow myself to crack open in circles, and be uncomfortable with not having all the answers. Others have provided valuable perspectives and often helped me to see things in a new light. Their belief in me has been a powerful antidote to self-doubt. Please try that on for size — immediately.

Finally, I've learned to reframe self-doubt as a sign that I'm stepping out of my comfort zone and growing. Instead of seeing it as a weakness, I now recognize it as a natural part of pursuing something meaningful. Keep going, keep growing. This shift in perspective has helped me to embrace self-doubt and use it as a tool for growth rather than a barrier to success. Fear is where the growth is, so lean in and surrender.

Finding My Voice

Finding my voice was one of the most liberating aspects of my journey. For too long, I had been silent, allowing the demands and expectations of others to drown out my true desires and stifle my creativity. But as I began reconnecting with my truth and values, I found I had a message to share — one deeply rooted in my own experiences and the lessons I had learned. I cultivated awareness of where I was holding myself back by simply not speaking up and tuned into how that suppression showed up for me in unhealthy ways.

I started expressing my thoughts in daily journaling and self-inquiry, and I formed my mission through writing and later speaking. My first foray into sharing my story was through blog posts. These posts were raw and honest, detailing the challenges I had faced in the corporate world, the devastating effects that stress had on my body, and how the suppressed grief of losing five pregnancies had caused me trauma, both physically and emotionally. I was openly sharing the steps I was taking to reclaim my life and move through the trauma. To my surprise, these posts resonated with a broad audience. Women from all over the world reached out to me, sharing their own stories and expressing their gratitude for my honesty.

I also became aware of my body's responses to specific situations, learned about somatic practices that help move emotions, and have been diving into trauma-informed space holding. We associate trauma with very drastic events, but we often don't acknowledge that there are less significant situations or simply things that were said to us that can cause trauma.

The responses from others gave me the confidence to take my message further. I began to write more extensively, eventually leading to the publication of my book, *Corporate Rewilding: A Wild Woman's Guide to Reclaiming Your Feminine Power*. Writing my book was a cathartic experience, allowing me to process the pain and struggles I had endured and turn them into a message of empowerment for other women. It was healing; it gave me closure, but it was also a portal for me. I realized that my story had become more significant than myself and that I couldn't stop sharing.

In addition to writing, I strengthened my voice through public speaking, something that a few years ago would have been at the top of my list of things that terrified me the most. I started speaking at online summits, making guest appearances on podcasts, radio and at women's empowerment events. When sharing my experiences, I encourage other women to reclaim the power of their own voices.

By showing up vulnerable like that, I was able to connect with women on a deeper level, and the feedback I received was overwhelmingly positive. Women told me that my story had given them the courage to change their lives, fueling my passion to continue sharing my message.

My keynote, "The Revolution of Showing Up Fully and Becoming Unapologetic," is something I want to take to the world so I can continue to light the long-forgotten spark in women, join forces, and rise into our power — wild and unapologetic. Watch out, TEDx stage. I'm coming for you.

Making a Difference in the World

The more I stepped into my true purpose; I began to see the ripple effects of my transformation, not just in my life but in the lives of those around me. I founded Femmepreneur Pathfinder, a platform where I guide women to reconnect with their wild feminine essence and birth their personal stories into bestselling books. I mentor them to design businesses in complete alignment and I hold safe space to unpack subconscious limiting beliefs. Through my book *Corporate Rewilding* and the embodiment circles I facilitate, I've empowered many women to break free from the corporate grind and embrace lives that are vibrant, authentic, and aligned with their true selves.

One of my proudest contributions has been creating safe spaces for women to gather, share, and heal. These *Sacred Circle* events are more than just gatherings — they are powerful catalysts for transformation, where women are encouraged to explore and express their desires. In these circles, I have witnessed the profound impact of sisterhood and the incredible power unleashed when women come together to support and uplift one another rather than compare and tear each other down.

These circles have become a haven and have sparked a ripple effect of empowerment and change in my community. I am passionate about taking this powerful movement to women worldwide. It is time for us to join forces. When the tide rises, all ships rise.

Personal Growth beyond My Wildest Dreams

Throughout this journey, I have experienced immense personal growth. I've developed skills and qualities I never knew I had and become more resilient, conquer desires, release old wounds, and step boldly in areas for growth, determination, and empathy. One of the most significant growth areas has been my leadership qualities. Leading safe spaces with the ability to show up vulnerably has allowed me to mentor others compassionately and taught me the importance of authenticity and connection. I step into a space as a woman first — leader, coach, and mentor second.

I've also grown on a personal level. This journey has forced me to confront my insecurities and limiting beliefs, and in doing so, I've become more self-aware and grounded. I've learned to embrace my flaws and vulnerabilities, understanding that they are a part of what makes me human. This growth has made me a better human and a more compassionate and understanding person.

I love that my work and mission have had a profound impact on others, and it's something for which I am deeply grateful. I've accepted my superpowers fully. Every time I hold space, mentor, or coach, I grow alongside others, too. We are meant to nurture and connect — the days of Wonder Woman and Alpha Females are over. You can exhale, take a deep breath, and take a seat in the circle and just be you. Period.

Collaboration, authentic connection from the heart, and vulnerable sharing are the new paradigm — the new age of leadership, the female way.

I've had the honor of witnessing the transformation of women who have embraced their feminine power and stepped into their true selves in all areas of their life. These women have made significant contributions to their communities, starting businesses, speaking, writing books, and leading initiatives that create positive change. I wish for you to be next.

Lessons Learned, Wisdom Gained

The journey to purpose has taught me many invaluable lessons, but perhaps the most important is the power of authenticity. I've learned that true fulfillment comes from living a life aligned with who you are at your core, not who the world expects you to be. When you honor your true self, you create a rich, meaningful, and deeply satisfying life.

Another vital lesson is the importance of community. We are meant to walk this path with others. The support, wisdom, and encouragement of other women have been instrumental in my growth, and I now prioritize them in my personal and professional life. Together, we are stronger, braver, and more capable of achieving our highest potential. Find your wild ones and howl together.

I've also learned the importance of resilience and adaptability. Life is unpredictable, and the ability to navigate change with grace and flexibility is essential. There have been many times when my plans didn't unfold as expected. Still, by staying open to new possibilities and trusting the process, I've found solutions and opportunities I hadn't anticipated.

I've genuinely understood the power of alignment — living an authentic life aligned with who you are at your core. I've learned that when you suppress your true self, it manifests in every area of your life, often as physical and emotional pain. Embracing my wild feminine essence has taught me the importance of self-care, setting boundaries, and trusting my intuition.

Balance and Self-Care

Maintaining balance has been one of the biggest challenges on my journey as someone passionate about her work; getting caught up in the demands of running a business and helping others is easy. But I've learned that to be effective in my work, I need to prioritize my well-being. I honed in on the feminine and masculine energies and learned to draw on both. It's easy to default into go-go-go, hustle, and push, being in your masculine energy — so I consciously make time to simply be. I'm a beekeeper, so learning to slow down and 'bee-ing' is a valuable lesson they taught me.

One of the ways I maintain my balance is by setting clear boundaries. I've learned to say "no" to things that don't align with my values, or that would overextend me. This lesson has been difficult, as I naturally want to help others and take on new opportunities. But I've realized that to be truly effective, I need to protect my time and energy. I also studied Human Design and Gene Keys; understanding both has been a revelation. I encourage you to look into it — it's been a game-changer for me.

Self-care is also a non-negotiable part of my routine. I make time for regular exercise, mindfulness practices, and time in nature. These activities help me stay grounded and connected to myself, allowing me to be more present and effective in my work. I've also committed to prioritizing rest, recognizing that burnout is counterproductive to my mission. Yoga, breath work, crafting, gardening, sauna, spa, and ice plunging are just a few things I do that keep me well.

Encouragement and Advice

To every woman searching for the "why" in her life and her purpose, my advice is simple: trust yourself. Your body, intuition, and inner voice are your most excellent guides. Don't be afraid to break away from the norms, question the status quo, and carve out a path that is uniquely yours. Your purpose is not something you need to chase after — it's something you uncover as you break your shell and unravel the path to return to your true self.

Surround yourself with people who uplift and inspire you, challenge you to grow, and believe in your vision even when you doubt it. Most importantly, permit yourself to be wild and free and live a life that lights up your soul.

Remember that the journey to purpose is a personal one. Please don't fall for comparison to others; remember, we're done with that. Each of us has our own way. There will be detours, obstacles, and moments of doubt. But these challenges are not signs that you're on the wrong path — they are opportunities for growth and transformation. Embrace them, learn from them, and keep moving forward. Trust your intuition. Your body and instincts try to communicate with you, so be still, tune in, and listen.

Finally, don't be afraid to ask for help. None of us are meant to do this alone. Seek out women you trust, those you 'vibe' with — you'll know who they are when you meet them. Allow yourself to be mentored, build a support network, find a woman's circle, and be open to receiving guidance from others. The wisdom and support of others can be invaluable as you navigate your journey.

My Wild Vision - Looking Ahead

As I look to the future and reflect on my journey, my heart is filled with excitement and anticipation. I am deeply grateful for the experiences that have shaped me and those who have supported me. My mission is to continue expanding my impact, reaching even more women across the globe, and helping them reclaim their wild feminine essence. I plan to write more books, create transformative courses, and host retreats that give women the tools and support they need to live their purpose.

In the coming years, I envision Femmepreneur Pathfinder growing into a global movement of wild women and executives — connecting women from all walks of life and empowering them to create positive change in their communities. I also plan to launch online programs that make my teachings more accessible to women who cannot attend in-person events. These programs will cover various topics, from personal development and self-care to business strategy and feminine leadership, with a big dose of woo-woo in it.

Beyond my professional goals, I am committed to living a life of joy, connection, and abundance. I want to deepen my relationship with the mysteries of life, spend time with my family, immerse myself in the beauty of nature every day, ride horses on wild beaches, and continue to grow and evolve as a woman of purpose. I believe that the more aligned I am with my truth, the more significant my impact on the world will be.

This journey has been one of my life's most challenging and rewarding experiences. It has taught me the power of authenticity, the importance of community, and the incredible potential within each of us when we live in alignment with our true selves.

My advice to any woman searching for her purpose is simple: Listen to your body and intuition. These are your most excellent guides. Don't be afraid to step away from what no longer serves you, even if it's all you've known. Your purpose is not something you find; it's something you uncover as you peel back the layers of conditioning and reconnect with your soul.

My story serves to inspire you to embark on your journey of self-discovery and embrace the wild, beautiful essence within you. Life is too short to live anything less than your fullest expression. Remember, you are the creator of your own path, and it's never too late to change it. Step boldly into your purpose and let your light shine brightly for the world to see. Come and join me in circle, seek me out and connect with me. I'd love to hear your story. Surround yourself with a community supporting your growth and challenging you to be your best self. Most importantly, permit yourself to be wild and free.

Go Forth, Wild One!

Bio

Tina K Kailea is an award-winning feminine embodiment coach, bestselling author, international speaker and book doula. She is a Sacred Circle facilitator, unapologetic wild woman, a rebel, and fiercely devoted to helping female leaders break free from their limiting beliefs, reclaim their voice, and escape the not-good-enough loop that holds them back.

Tina specializes in supporting women to overcome subconscious conditioning, gain self-confidence, and be more assertive, empowering them to take up space and make a more significant impact in their lives and businesses.

She creates a safe space for women to explore and redefine womanhood, encouraging a deeper embodiment of femininity and soul purpose. Drawing on her decade of experience in publishing, Tina, an author herself, guides women to birth their personal stories into bestselling books as an extension of their brand. Her passion is to inspire women to be bold and reignite their zest for life on their own terms, in alignment with their values.

As the founder and CEO of The Femmepreneur Pathfinder, Tina is on a mission to inspire women to sign their own permission slips, confidently ask for what they truly desire, say NO without hesitation, and embrace prioritizing themselves without guilt.

Tina is the author of the bestselling book "*CORPORATE REWILDING – A Wild Woman's Guide to Reclaiming Your Feminine Power*," available worldwide on Amazon.

Website: www.femmepreneurpathfinder.com

LinkTree: www.femmepreneurpathfinder.com/linktree

Read Tina's Book: www.amazon.com/Corporate-Rewilding

LinkedIn: tinakkailea

Instagram: the_femmepreneur

Facebook: tinakkailea

Dr Rani Thanacoody-

A Journey from Disconnection to Wholeness

I am Dr Rani Thanacoody, born and raised in Mauritius. I have been living in the UK for the past fifteen years. I hold a PhD in Management specializing in work-family research from La Trobe University, Australia. I am an experienced educator with over two decades of teaching and research on work-family and workplace stress. I have published peer-reviewed academic articles in reputable international journals and presented at international management conferences. I have worked in academia in Mauritius, Australia, China, Spain, and the UK. I was nominated in 2020 by Griffith University Business School as the Outstanding International Alumnus for my contribution to teaching and research. In addition to working full-time as an academic in the UK, after my working hours, I am the Founder and Host of AmazingYou Podcast and Therapy. I am a clinical hypnotherapist using the rapid transformational therapy method, Mars Venus Life and Relationship Coach, Tarot Reader, Astrologer, Lifeforce Compassion Practitioner, Energy Healer, Breathwork Coach, and Past Regression Practitioner.

For this book chapter, my journey started when, at four years old, I began to disconnect from myself from feeling my feelings with the sudden loss of my grandmother. Soon after that, I was sexually abused at kindergarten, and at six years old, I was bullied by authority (school teacher) and later bullied by supervisors in several workplaces in the UK. In this chapter, I will share my journey from a child who had lost connection with myself to gaining the connection with myself and others. Since 2021, I founded The Amazing You Podcast, YouTube channels, and AmazingYou Community on Facebook to empower women who experienced deep childhood traumas and abuse to develop self-love and confidence.

Journey

This journey led me to empower myself through self-love and forgiveness. Finding my voice was not an easy one. On that life journey, I experienced a lot of anger, sadness, grief, pain, loneliness, and confusion. It all started when, at the age 4, my parents and I moved to a new home near the beach. After a few months, my beloved grandmother, whom I loved dearly and who deeply loved me, suddenly passed away. She was my safety net, my best friend, and my confidant. She would always find the time to listen to me. She was my fairy who made all my wishes come true.

After she passed away, I was sexually abused at kindergarten. After a few years, I was bullied by a schoolteacher at primary school. He was so scary, that I did not dare to tell my parents as I was unsure how my parents would respond. He did not appreciate my behavior of standing up for a classmate. He threatened me for a few years at the school gate until I moved to another school.

My grandmother's absence was deeply felt in challenging times as I had no one to understand me or to listen to me. To cope with life, I pushed down and numb my emotions as it was too painful to feel them at home and school. I became very withdrawn and shy. I missed her presence a lot growing up. As a child and adolescent, I had no self-esteem or confidence. I felt empty and lonely even when people surrounded me. Life seemed meaningless. I struggled to connect with friends and people. I never knew where it came from. I attended a girls 'school that was very strict and was run by Irish nuns. I did not feel safe to express myself anywhere. I was living on a day-to-day basis. I was living as a victim and blaming everybody for bullying me and ignoring me.

At school, I never raised my hands in class to avoid the fear of being ridiculed. I was known to be the quietest girl in my classes. I always felt anxious in class whenever I was asked a question. I dreaded that moment and felt uncomfortable. My teachers often mentioned in my report book that I was always polite and quiet but never questioned my behavior. I thought it was a good thing, I was proud of myself, and thought I was a good girl to my parents and teachers. But I did not know that I was hurting myself more in trying to please everyone around me.

When I joined academia, which is a very competitive place, I experienced bullying from my superiors. I moved jobs and home every year to the UK. That was very exhausting. In 2014, I started asking myself some questions and told myself I needed to find out where this issue originated. I thought it might come from within me. It must be something that I was not doing right. I blamed myself and others for years. I found a government therapist at the medical center, but she was not of great help to me, and she did not want to go to the root cause of my issue.

I was searching for the right course to help me get those answers. In 2017, the workplace bullying got so severe that I decided to leave the job. I was exhausted from the bullying pattern that was being repeated and getting worse every time. I packed everything and went to my home country, Mauritius, for a year. I had no idea what I would do from that moment. I have always had a strong faith in a higher power and have been praying and asking for help. One day, I heard that voice telling me to apply for another job in academia in the UK, and there was more for me to do. I did not understand, but I listened to that voice, applied for jobs, and returned to the UK in another academic post in 2018. The people around me did not always support my idea of getting another academic career, but I followed that inner voice and returned to the UK.

From childhood to my mid-forties, I held all these emotions that were mine and those of my caregivers inside me. I did not know how to process the sadness, fear, grief, hurt, anger, unworthiness, unloved, and loneliness. I found it challenging to connect with people around me. I gradually became shy and developed low self-esteem. I always felt alone, lost, unsafe, tired, with no energy, and an emptiness inside of me. I never knew where it came from. I did not feel safe to express myself anywhere.

Once I returned to the UK, I still felt there was something more for me than my day job. In 2020, while scrolling my Facebook page, I found a hypnotherapist. With faith and resilience, I started that healing work on myself. When the pandemic hit in 2020, I found the lifesaver hypnotherapy course while looking at my Facebook page, which brought the answers to my search. I knew that the course would help me to find the cause of the bullying issue. The hypnotherapy helped me to go to the root cause and understand my problems and myself. I cried so much in every hypnotherapy session that I participated.

I studied a lot during the pandemic. I received and delivered sessions to students on that course and gained more understanding and healing.

Purpose

I used most of my financial savings and invested massively in many courses I could afford from 2020 to 2023. I also studied several modalities that helped me feel my emotions by undertaking many self-development courses, webinars, and training.

I aim to empower women to develop greater love for themselves and grow their self-esteem and confidence. My purpose became apparent in 2023 when I spent those three intensive years going within myself, healing my inner past lives and childhood wounds, and releasing my limiting beliefs from being my true self. I did not look for my purpose, as I know many people are looking for their purpose outside of them. My purpose found me when I found myself through the healing of the inner wounds inside of me.

I felt grateful and happy as I acquired a sense of youth in my forties that gave me joy, peace, and purpose. In finding my purpose I am now on a mission to empower as many women around the world as possible to heal themselves by finding the love, happiness, and peace within themselves to achieve their dreams and feel alive.

Finding your Voice

I found my voice through public speaking in 2020 during my healing journey when I was recommended by a friend to listen to Les Brown, a well-known motivational speaker in the United States. His speeches inspired me to attend his Power of Voice training for six months. Under his mentorship, I was allowed to share part of my story live with 180 students worldwide and receive personal live feedback from Les Brown and his team. This was something I had never done before. It took me out of my comfort zone. I remember shaking when I delivered my 3-minute talk to Les Brown and 180 students. This course motivated me to start my podcast and YouTube channel, AmazingYou, in July 2021. My channels aim to inspire and give hope to people facing tough times and help them become more resilient. It also allows speakers to share their stories and have a voice. These channels have helped me build a wider audience worldwide to encourage more people to heal themselves.

Overcoming initial obstacles

One of the significant challenges on my journey was overcoming the pattern of workplace bullying and leaving jobs every year due to it. Leaving jobs every year also meant I had to move home. I was so; adapting to a new way of organizing the transfer of addresses to all the utility companies was costly.

"Everyone has been made for some particular work, and the desire for that work has been put in every heart." – Rumi.

Since starting the workplace and moving to a new home environment, I have been hassled in my current job for six years for the first time in my life, and I have not experienced any workplace bullying. However, it is still present in the organization. I have built my self-esteem and self-love, responded more calmly, have not taken anyone personally, and focused on others. I have learned not to react to people but to respond more creepily, including the network.

My supporters have been critical to my healing and growth journey. My key supporters include my coach, friends, and therapist, who believed in and supported me. They were a listening ear, offered me a space to express myself and celebrate my achievements, and motivated me to look ahead and try new things. They accepted me for who I was and who I was becoming. They created a safe space where I felt safe to express myself.

Key Milestones

The most significant achievement on my journey has been completing my PhD in Management from La Trobe University. I obtained an international scholarship from the university. It took work, as I needed supportive supervisors, and I struggled to find the right company to enable the data collection. During my studies, I changed supervisors a few times and thankfully, the final supervisor was beneficial, and with his help I successfully completed my studies. The PhD has allowed me to relocate to the UK and finance my growth journey.

Since 2020, I trained in several modalities and I become a clinical hypnotherapist using the rapid transformational therapy method, astrologer, tarot reader, compassion practitioner, and speaker. Practicing those modalities on myself helped me heal the different layers of traumas and help others. I also trained with the well-known Mr Les Brown, and his course encouraged me to host my podcast and YouTube channel called AmazingYou by Dr Rani. I have co-authored books Love and Coachin and have provided online sessions to clients worldwide since 2021. In March 2024, Global Woman Magazine nominated me among the top 100 women entrepreneurs. I have co-authored two books: namely: Love and Coaching and Bare, Naked and Beautiful. I speak regularly in the UK at local libraries, international podcasts, local, and international summits, conferences and TV shows.

Most of my clients have suffered severe emotional and physical traumas. By applying those modalities, they can quickly transform their lives and those around them. Today, I want to remind you to put yourself first and that 'you are the treasure you seek. 'When you heal yourself, you heal others around you, and Life becomes much more peaceful, and happy.

Challenges and Triumphs

Another challenge I faced was attracting toxic people and love partners around me, as I had no boundaries. It was tough to deal with their manipulative tactics and behaviors. I worked intensively on myself to clear those beliefs and traumas and read a lot on that topic. Now, I can spot such people easily without letting them into my life. I also created my social media channels in 2021, where I daily provide materials to support people experiencing trauma and abuse. I also financially support charities like Save the Children and Compassion UK. I sponsor a child from a developing country. I created a private Facebook book where I help individuals, primarily women, facing narcissistic abuse and childhood traumas and we meet online each month to watch a movie that will help in their growth and healing.

Impact on Others

Receiving testimonials from past clients after the sessions is very rewarding and motivating. Knowing their lives and families have been transformed through their healing is a great feeling. My website has many testimonials: https://drranithanacoody.com.

Client 1 shared the following message on my phone: Day by day, I am feeling better in my mind and soul. There are many things to learn, and you are a great help. There are so many things to learn and put into practice in our daily lives. Thank you again. Hugs and love to you.

Client 2 wrote: I am so grateful for you, Rani. Words cannot justify how blessed I feel to have you in my life.

Client 3: Your voice is so healing to me, giving me another perspective on the situation. Thank you for being my guide, mentor, and coach.

Personal Growth

I have developed a greater connection with myself and people. I also feel a deeper sense of belonging to the planet. I feel more alive and energetic in my body than I never felt in my youth. I speak my truth and express myself easily to people around me. I have gained a great love, appreciation and acceptance for myself and others. I feel like a new-born person who has so many dreams to achieve. I have discovered my hidden talents, such as painting, intuition, playing music, and enjoying being present. There are more things for me to find out on my self-discovery journey. I feel each day deep gratitude for being alive and healthy on earth. I am more open to receiving and giving the love of people and the universe.

Inspirational moments

I often receive this feedback from people I meet on how I made them feel safe to express themselves. One of my students at university told me that she was in a panic mode as she felt stuck in her thesis, but just talking to me, her worries flew away instantly. She felt calm, and she did not feel the need to contact the therapist that she was allocated. She told me she feels inspired by the quote I wrote in my email and in the class. She found them very useful. I often hear people and clients say they feel safe around me. This shows me that my challenges and healing journey have been worth it and contributed to my wellbeing and the people around me.

Overcoming Self-Doubts

Many times on my journey, I encountered self-doubt when making crucial decisions. I overcome them by first going within myself through meditation and asking for guidance from my angels and God. I also learned to listen to the cues my body gave me. I learned to trust my body, which always gives me messages about what suits me.

Vision for the Future

I plan to expand my business internationally through my online hypnotherapy and coaching business, grow my private Facebook community, co-author more books, and speak on international stages to inspire and help more women worldwide. I will also continue to grow my podcast and YouTube channels by inviting guest speakers worldwide to share their stories to build hope and resilience. I will also grow the monthly private online community so that more people can access the knowledge to help them to heal their inner wounds.

Advice to Others

To every remarkable woman reading my chapter, I advise you not to look for a purpose outside of you as you will feel stressed and confused. Your purpose does not come from the external world but within you. As the Book of Life says: ''The Kingdom of God is within you'' Luke 17:21.

Work on loving yourself and building your self-esteem and confidence by becoming a better version of yourself each day. You are lovable, and you matter. Always love first and put yourself first. The most beautiful romance you will ever have starts with yourself, as Oscar Wilde said. When you love yourself, others will love you too. Do little things that make you happy, such as treating yourself to a nice walk in nature, smiling at yourself each day, and finding the time to breathe and exercise daily.

Many of us were not valued and loved for who we are, so now you must build your self-esteem and confidence by praising yourself daily. Use affirmations to grow your self-worth, self-image, and self-value.

Make yourself a priority and let go of the people pleaser, blamer, carer, or perfectionist role you acquired. It was helpful when you were young, but not anymore. The roles are only hurting you now to achieve your dreams. You can only please others if you are happy with yourself first. Start to invest in your personal growth. Remember that you are a divine goddess and you are here to create your story. The power is in your hands and not in anyone's hands. Invest your emotions, time, and finances in you first. Reclaim your energy and heal your inner wounds and blocks. Create time for you, love and praise who you are, as you are. You do not need anyone's approval, as your opinion is the most critical approval and opinion.

"Why are you knocking at every other door? Go, knock at the door of your own heart." —Rumi.

Ask for help from the universe or God and find people who can help you heal yourself and take by take action daily. When you clear those inner wounds and release all the beliefs, people, and emotions that are not yours, your gifts will appear effortlessly to you. You will find your creativity and purpose in life. You create your reality. This life is your story; you can decide what and how you want to write it. You have only one chance, as you cannot edit it. Make it one that you are happy and fulfilled.

When you take your infinite power back, you become a superpower. Remember that you are powerful and that you are on earth for a reason, no matter your journey: 'You are the treasure you have been seeking.'

Lessons Learned

I have gained many valuable life lessons on that journey, and some of the lessons are: The primary lesson for me was to understand that the experiences of abuse, the loss of my grandmother, and years of being bullied have left a deep imprint on my body. I stored a lot of emotions in mostly my belly. For my whole life until 2020, I suffered from irritable bowel syndrome (IBS). Once I started the healing journey, the IBS disappeared.

I also understood that my shyness and low self-esteem were acquired from my environmental conditioning. Session after session with my hypnotherapist, I kept peeling those layers of the fear of being heard and seen, self-doubt, guilt, shame, betrayal, unworthiness, and unloved; I felt freer to express my feelings after each session to my therapist, to my friends and people around me. I managed to release these stuck emotions in my body by daily adopting several self-care practices. I learned to develop love, acceptance, compassion, forgiveness, and patience with myself and others.

Peeling away those layers of conditioning was vital for me to feel alive and joyful again. I feel like a new me. My transformation has been life-changing. I now enjoy life and connecting with people.

I have learned to develop greater compassion and love myself first and for others each day. I maintain my balance by engaging in self-care practices. I give myself the love and approval I have been searching for in other people daily. I practice gratitude, energy clearing, affirmations, meditation, and reading self-development books to keep my frequency high and not be affected by people and situations in my environment. I also attract people who are more loving towards me. I realized that we are the treasure that we are seeking. I used to blame others for things that happened to me until I understood it all started with me. I learned that everything starts with me, and when I change my thoughts, I change my life.

I also learned to forgive myself and others to find peace within myself. Forgiveness was an essential exercise that helped me forgive myself for the guilt I felt and the pain I held. I also forgave others, as I now know they did their best with what they learned.

The fourth lesson I learned is to cultivate gratitude daily. I live with a deeper appreciation for each moment, situation, and every person I encounter on my journey, whether good or bad. I know there is something for me to learn from each person or situation. I am more daring to get involved in new activities that give me joy. I also do not take anything personally and have more acceptance for others. My transformation has been life-changing. I thoroughly enjoy each day and develop a stronger connection with my family and the people around me.

The fifth lesson I learned is that life is about constantly growing and evolving. I am on an endless journey of self-discovery and growth through my relationships with others, and personal development is a lifestyle. I continually read self-development books, attend online and in-person courses and seminars. You heal others around you when you heal yourself, and life becomes much smoother.

Collaboration and Networking

I have never enjoyed networking in person in my professional field, as people are not friendly and are very competitive. I always felt isolated and rugged. When I started to network online during the pandemic in 2021 with people from the business world, I gained a profound appreciation for networking with like-minded people. I understood that collaboration is critical for anyone's success and that no man is an island. We need each other to grow and thrive. We cannot succeed alone. Behind the success of any great person is a team of people. Life is not about competing but about sharing and supporting each other. Collaboration has been hugely helpful in meeting authentic guests for my podcast from around the world and developing new, lasting, genuine, loving friendships. Some of those friends invited me to be part of their communities. These friends have offered opportunities to collaborate on podcasts, TV shows, conferences, and book projects such as Bare, Naked and Beautiful book, and Love and Coaching book, and develop further connections while enlarging my network. So, never underestimate the power of networking. I am here today based on the network I joined, which has brought so many unimaginable opportunities my way.

Balance and Self-Care

Self-care has become a lifestyle for me. It is how I care for my body, thoughts, emotions, and actions. I practice balance and self-care daily, even on holidays, by working on myself for more than an hour each morning before meditating, affirmations, self-praise, reading positive self-help books, and breath work. I also walk in nature often during the week for one hour to ground myself. I do my best to eat a healthy plant-based diet complemented by organic supplements. In addition, I am mindful of what I watch and listen to on TV by consciously avoiding polluting my mind with the news around me.

Power of Community

Since starting my self-development journey, being part of several communities has given me a sense of belonging, providing a safe place to express myself and connect and build friendships with like-minded individuals. These communities have offered me opportunities to write books, attend and participate in meetings, and networking opportunities. We can grow and heal with each other. We need others to thrive because we are born for connection and community. We are not born to be alone.

Conclusion

Whether your past circumstance has created a disconnection of your true self, it is never too late to heal, and feel a deep connection with yourself and others. The greatest gift you can give yourself is loving yourself and building that connection with yourself by peeling off those layers of conditioning, letting go of the past, and growing your self-esteem and confidence. As you invest in yourself emotionally, financially, and timely, your life and those around you will improve massively. You heal past, current, and future generations and the world when you heal yourself. If I have reached where I am today, you can do it. It is difficult, but everything is possible if you believe in your divine power and listen to your heart murmurs. It all starts from within you and is about being your best self on that return journey home daily. Remember that you are powerful beyond measure and are here for a great purpose, no matter your family or childhood circumstances. So, make an incredible, great journey as you are the alchemist and heroine of your life.

Bio

Dr Rani Thanacoody is a visionary entrepreneur based in the United Kingdom. As the esteemed Founder of AmazingYou, she has carved an indelible mark in the field of holistic wellness. Armed with a diverse array of qualifications, Dr Rani is an international clinical hypnotherapist, a certified Mars Venus Life and Relationship Coach, a skilled Breath work Coach, a compassionate Chakra Healer, a proficient Lifeforce Compassion Practitioner, a seasoned Past Life Regression Practitioner, a perceptive Tarot Reader, and an insightful Astrologer.

Driven by an unwavering passion for empowering women, Dr Rani adeptly employs various modalities to guide individuals through their transformative journeys towards self-discovery and healing. Her podcast and YouTube channels, under the banner 'AmazingYou by Dr Rani Thanacoody', serve as beacons of inspiration, offering solace and enlightenment to those navigating through life's tumultuous waters.

An esteemed co-author alongside Dr John Gray in the Amazon No. 1 Best Seller, 'Love and Coaching', Dr Rani's chapter, 'The Best Investment You Will Ever Make', stands as a testament to her profound insights into relationships and personal growth. Her contribution to 'Bare, Naked and Beautiful' further underscores her commitment to uplifting others through her words.

As an international inspirational speaker mentored by the legendary Les Brown, Rani's eloquence and compelling presence have graced platforms such as e360Tv, where she continues to touch hearts and inspire positive change.

Rani has been nominated among the 100 women entrepreneurs globally and is featured in the Global Woman Magazine in the March 2024 edition.

She regularly writes articles on various topics for the Diamond Moments Magazine.

Dr Rani champions the importance of holistic health, emphasizing the transformative power of nutrition. Her partnership with JuicePlus underscores her dedication to spreading awareness about the profound benefits of a well-balanced diet for overall well-being.

Rani can be contacted by email:

ranithanacoody@marsvenuscoaching.com

Social media links are:

Instangram:thanacoodyrani and ranithanacoody

Twitter:ranithanacoody

- Instagram: https://www.instagram.com/thanacoodyrani/

- Podbean: https://ranithanacoody.podbean.com

Buzzsprout: https://amazingyoubyrani.buzzsprout.com

Spotify: https://podcasters.spotify.com/pod/show/dr-rani-thanacoody

YouTube channel: @amazingyoudrranithanacoody

Websites:

https://drranithanacoody.com

https://marsvenuscoachrani.com

https://drranithanacoody.com/amazing-you-astrology

Kimberly Clement-

Lighting the Path: My Journey of Advocacy, Empowerment, and Change.

I have dedicated over 45 years to the non-profit sector, and upon retirement, I became a successful author of 12 mystery novels. I own and operate Travel by Destiny, a world travel business, and I continue to work part-time, coordinating my local community's sexual violence resource center. I'm also deeply involved in establishing a community youth center and cherish my role as a great-grandmother. My journey is a testament to pursuing passions and positively impacting the community.

Of course, you're wondering what experience or lesson inspired me to live a life of service to others and purpose. Well, let me take you back to my teenage years in the late '60s and early '70s, a time when I was what you might call a rebellious teen. Picture this: I had a knack for trouble, so much so that the public school system decided they didn't want me back after I accidentally set the school on fire. In their wisdom, my parents sent me to a private Christian school with a police officer escort to and from school daily. This officer was a friend of my father's, adding a layer of embarrassment to my already tumultuous teenage life.

Fast forward to my senior year at seventeen. I had been on relatively good behavior for most of the school year, so my parents allowed me to go on my high school's senior class trip to New Orleans. I was over the moon! But let me tell you, those Christian schoolkids knew how to party. Believe it or not, alcohol wasn't my choice of poison, but I still got caught up in the excitement.

One day, we were touring on a boat and checking out famous pirate gravesites when nature called. Growing up in Minnesota, in an all-white, middle-class community, I was blissfully ignorant of certain harsh realities.

So, I rushed into the nearest bathroom to return to my group quickly. I nodded hello to an elderly Black woman sitting in a chair and continued my business.

As I came out, a man in his fifties grabbed my arm and slapped me across the face, knocking me to the ground. He was yelling at me, but all I could focus on was the shock and pain. That elderly Black woman emerged from the bathroom, quickly leading me to the back of the boat. She sat me down, put ice on my swelling face, and asked me where I was from. When I told her, she patiently explained that by using a "colored" bathroom, I had not only put my life in jeopardy but hers as well. I was clueless about the segregation of toilets and water fountains.

Angry and confused, I bolted as soon as the boat docked. I ran into an old public school friend whose dad owned a tugboat. He was originally from Mississippi and offered to give me a ride home to Saint Paul. Three weeks later, I arrived home, ready for the conversation of a lifetime with my dad.

That incident was a turning point. From that day on, I swore I would make a difference. It opened my eyes to the injustices others faced and fueled my commitment to living a life of service and purpose. The catalyst set me on a path to advocate for change, support the vulnerable, and ensure that everyone, regardless of their background, is treated with dignity and respect.

And that, dear reader, is how a rebellious teen from Minnesota found her calling most unexpectedly. Life has a funny way of teaching us the most profound lessons, often when we least expect it.

When I stepped into the world of non-profit work, I knew my life would be dedicated to making a difference. Over four decades later, my journey has been marked by triumphs, challenges, and an unwavering commitment to improving the lives of others. This chapter reflects on my experiences, the changes I've helped bring about, and heartfelt encouragement to all women to pursue their paths of purpose.

A Journey Begins: The Domestic Violence Field

When I stepped into the world of non-profit work, I knew my life would be dedicated to making a difference. Over four decades later, my journey has been marked by triumphs, challenges, and an unwavering commitment to improving the lives of others. This chapter reflects on my experiences, the changes I've helped bring about, and heartfelt encouragement to all women to pursue their paths of purpose.

My career in the non-profit sector began in the Domestic Violence field. This wasn't just a profession; it was a calling. I witnessed firsthand the devastating effects of domestic violence on women, their children, and communities, and I knew I had to be part of the solution. My years in this field were filled with heartbreaking and heartwarming moments.

One of the most significant periods of my career was when I served as a lobbyist for the women's movement in Minnesota. For five years, I dedicated myself to advocating for stronger legal protections for victims of domestic violence. My proudest achievement during this time was lobbying a bill through the Minnesota Legislature in honor of two children whose father tragically murdered them, mainly for the reason that if he couldn't have them, then their mother couldn't either. This bill, now a law, stands as a testament to the resilience of women and their rights to keep their children safe and the power of advocacy. It was a difficult journey, filled with long hours, emotional testimonies, and relentless determination. Still, the success of this legislation remains a beacon of hope and a reminder of what can be achieved through collective effort.

Advocating for domestic violence victims was an eye-opening experience. I encountered countless stories of resilience and strength from survivors who had endured unimaginable hardships. These stories fueled my determination to push for legislative change, knowing that stronger laws could provide better protection and support for those in need. I worked closely with other advocates, survivors, and legislators as part of a coalition dedicated to creating a safer environment for victims of domestic violence. Together, we navigated the complex political landscape, overcoming obstacles and resistance and ultimately achieving our goal. This experience taught me the importance of perseverance, collaboration, and the power of a unified voice.

Raising Funds for Native American Elders

After my tenure as a lobbyist, I joined the AmeriCorps program as a VISTA (Volunteers in Service to America). My mission was to raise funds for Native American Elders, focusing on health and wellness initiatives. This role opened my eyes to Indigenous communities' unique challenges and the critical importance of preserving their health and cultural heritage.

Working with Native American Elders was a profoundly enriching experience. I learned about their traditions, listened to their stories, and understood the importance of their wisdom in guiding younger generations. Fundraising in this context was not just about securing financial support but building relationships, fostering trust, and ensuring that the programs we developed were culturally sensitive and sustainable. The success of these initiatives demonstrated the power of collaboration and the importance of respecting and honoring the voices of the communities we serve.

One particular initiative that stands out involved a health and wellness program aimed at addressing the high rates of diabetes and heart disease among Native American Elders. We organized health fairs, educational workshops, and fitness programs, incorporating traditional practices and holistic approaches to wellness. By integrating cultural elements into these programs, we created a sense of ownership and pride among the participants. The positive impact on their health and well-being was evident, and it was enriching to see the Elders reclaiming their health and vitality. This experience reinforced my belief in the importance of culturally competent approaches to community health and the need to empower communities to take charge of their well-being.

Empowering At-Risk Youth

The next decade of my career was spent working with at-risk youth, an incredibly fulfilling role for someone who believes in the potential of every individual. I served as the executive director for a rural community youth program. Our youth are the bridge to our community's future, and this work allowed me to help them realize their potential.

Empowering at-risk youth through this program was transformative. We provided them with training and opportunities that fostered a sense of purpose and hope for their futures. These young people, often from marginalized communities, discovered their ability to contribute positively to society. Witnessing their growth and success was one of the most rewarding aspects of my career. It reaffirmed my belief that given the right opportunities and support, every young person can thrive and make meaningful contributions to their communities.

Over the years, I have had the honor of taking these youth to yearly events where they can interact with Nobel Peace Laureates from around the globe, including Argentina, Guatemala, Iran, and Liberia. These interactions are invaluable, broadening their perspectives and inspiring them to share their stories and wisdom.

Together, we created service projects both locally and worldwide. One of our most impactful projects was raising enough funds by recycling color crayons to build and implement a community clean water fountain in Haiti. This initiative provided a vital resource for the Haitian community and showed the incredible power of resourcefulness and collective effort. The joy and pride on the faces of the youth as they saw the tangible impact of their efforts were unforgettable moments that underscored the importance of giving back and making a difference.

Through these experiences, I learned that genuine service goes beyond providing aid; it involves empowering communities, respecting their unique cultures, and working together towards common goals. This journey with at-risk youth was a testament to community strength, cultural heritage richness, and collaboration's transformative power.

Empowering Communities through Renewable Energy and Social Justice

My journey in renewable energy advocacy has been one of the most fulfilling aspects of my career, especially the work I've done with indigenous communities. Renewable energy isn't just about harnessing the power of the sun, wind, and water; it's about creating sustainable solutions that respect and enhance people's lives and our planet's health. Let me take you to one of the most memorable projects I worked on, which took place on the Big Island of Hawaii—a place of breathtaking beauty and stark contrasts.

The Big Island Project: Wind Turbines and Water Irrigation

We found ourselves in Kona, known for its lush, green beef ranches. But on the other side of the volcano, it was a different story—rocky, dry, and not nearly as verdant. This site was home to Indigenous farmers struggling to raise crops due to insufficient water. Our mission? To bridge this environmental gap and provide a sustainable solution for these farmers.

Picture this: eight wind turbines standing tall on the ranch side of the volcano, catching the mighty trade winds that swept across the island. The energy generated by these turbines powered an irrigation system, transporting much-needed water over the volcano to the arid farmland. This innovative solution provided the essential water to sustain crops and ensured the energy used was clean and sustainable.

The impact on the Indigenous community was unforgettable. For the first time, farmers had a reliable water source for their crops, significantly improving their agricultural output and livelihoods. The project fostered a sense of pride and empowerment among the community members. They weren't just beneficiaries but active participants in implementing and maintaining this initiative. That sense of ownership was crucial for the project's long-term success and sustainability.

The Importance of Renewable Energy

Renewable energy is essential for many reasons, but let me share why it matters so much to me. Firstly, it addresses the urgent need to reduce our reliance on finite fossil fuels, which have significant environmental impacts. Burning fossil fuels releases greenhouse gases, contributing to global warming and climate change. Renewable energy sources like wind, solar, and hydroelectric power produce little to no greenhouse gases, helping mitigate the effects of climate change and protecting our planet for future generations.

Secondly, renewable energy promotes energy security. Unlike fossil fuels, which are often concentrated in specific regions, renewable energy resources are more evenly distributed globally. This means communities can generate energy locally, reducing dependence on imported fuels and enhancing energy independence. This is particularly important for indigenous communities, as it allows them to harness their natural resources and take control of their energy future.

Impact on Tribal Communities

The impact of renewable energy projects on tribal communities extends beyond environmental benefits. These projects often bring significant social and economic advantages. They support local infrastructure development by providing reliable and sustainable energy sources, such as schools, hospitals, and businesses. This, in turn, creates jobs and stimulates economic growth within the community.

Moreover, renewable energy projects can help preserve cultural heritage. Many indigenous communities have a deep spiritual connection to their land and natural resources. By utilizing renewable energy, they can protect their environment and maintain their traditional ways of life. In the case of the Kona project, using wind turbines to support agriculture enhanced food security and upheld the community's agricultural traditions.

The Betterment of Our Planet

Shifting to renewable energy benefits individual communities and improves our planet as a whole. Climate change is a global challenge requiring an international response. By transitioning to renewable energy, we can reduce our carbon footprint, slow the rate of climate change, and protect the natural world.

Renewable energy also plays a crucial role in conserving Earth's resources. Fossil fuels are non-renewable, meaning they will eventually run out. In contrast, renewable energy sources are abundant and, as the name suggests, renewable. The sun will continue to shine, the wind will continue to blow, and water will continue to flow. By tapping into these resources, we can ensure a sustainable energy supply for future generations.

Through my journey in renewable energy advocacy, I've seen firsthand how sustainable solutions can empower communities, protect the environment, and create a better future for all. This work has reinforced my belief in the power of collaboration, respect for cultural heritage, and the urgent need to transition to renewable energy for the health of our planet.

Retirement at Last

Retirement was a challenge for me. I have trouble sitting still, and working on flower beds was not helping the situation. So, I found Pinterest. Sitting on my deck painting rocks one day, I sobbed, wondering, "What do I do now?" It hit me—I liked to write, so why not bring joy into others' lives through storytelling? Today, I keep cookies in the freezer just in case the FBI shows up because my browser history is filled with research on how to make pipe bombs, create the perfect murder using herbs, and hide a body.

Parallel to my non-profit work, I pursued a passion for writing. Over the years, I authored a dozen mystery books. Writing became a way to channel my experiences and insights into stories that could engage and inspire readers. Each book was a labor of love, reflecting the complexities of human nature and the resilience of the human spirit.

My journey as an author has been incredibly fulfilling. It has allowed me to reach a broader audience and share the themes of justice, perseverance, and hope that have defined my career. Writing has been a way to process my experiences, reflect on the lessons learned, and contribute to the broader discourse on social issues. It has also provided me with a creative outlet and a means of connecting with readers who share my passion for stories that make a difference.

Through my writing, I have explored various social issues, drawing from my experiences in the non-profit sector. My mystery novels often feature strong, resilient characters who navigate challenging circumstances, mirroring the real-life stories I have encountered. These narratives serve as a platform to raise awareness about important issues and inspire readers to take action in their communities. Writing has also been a form of self-care, allowing me to process the emotional weight of my work and find solace in storytelling. It has been a journey of growth and self-discovery, and I am grateful for the opportunity to share my stories with others.

So, while retirement initially had me questioning my next steps, it ultimately led me to a new and exciting chapter in my life. Through storytelling, I've found a way to continue advocating for change, one mystery novel at a time. And if the FBI ever does show up, I'll have some cookies ready for them!

Current Endeavors: Continuing the Fight Against Sexual Violence

One day, while I was deep into plotting my next mystery novel, our community's local sexual violence resource center called. They asked how I was enjoying retirement and then asked me to return part-time to coordinate our local office. How could I say no? So, today, I continue to work part-time as the coordinator for our local sexual violence resource center. This role continues my lifelong commitment to supporting survivors and advocating for their rights. Each day brings new challenges and opportunities to make a difference in the lives of those affected by sexual violence.

Our work at the resource center is multifaceted, encompassing advocacy, education, and direct support services. We strive to create a safe and supportive environment for survivors, offering counseling, legal assistance, and advocacy services. We also work to raise awareness about sexual violence and promote prevention strategies within our community. This work is essential, and I am honored to be part of a team dedicated to making a difference.

One of the initiatives we have launched is a comprehensive Community Action Plan, a program aimed at preventing sexual violence through awareness and education. We conduct workshops and seminars in schools, workplaces, and community centers, providing information about consent, healthy relationships, and bystander intervention. These programs are designed to empower individuals with the knowledge and skills to prevent sexual violence and support survivors. The response from the community has been overwhelmingly positive, and it is heartening to see the impact of our efforts. This work is a testament to the importance of education in driving social change and creating safer communities for everyone.

Empowering Dreams: Crafting Success and Inspiring Change

One day, while plotting a murder and convincing my sister to travel to Oregon to scope out a new location for my book, I had an epiphany. Amidst our laughter and excitement, it hit me like a lightning bolt—I could help people create lifelong memories! The idea was electrifying. Why not combine my love for travel with my desire to make a difference? Thus, Travel By Destiny was born. It was my destiny to continue helping others, hence the name.

Today, I proudly own Travel By Destiny, a travel business that helps people create lifelong memories. Travel has always been a passion of mine, and through this venture, I get to share that passion with others. I organize group cruises and tours worldwide, providing my clients with unforgettable experiences.

To me personally, Travel By Destiny is more than just a business; it's a way to bring people together, foster a sense of adventure and discovery, and create lasting memories. I take pride in offering personalized service and creating unique itineraries that cater to my client's interests and preferences. Seeing the joy and excitement on their faces as they explore new destinations is incredibly rewarding and reinforces the importance of creating opportunities for connection and discovery.

One of the highlights of my offerings is group cruises. These trips provide a unique opportunity for people to bond, relax, and explore new cultures. I have organized cruises to various destinations with distinct charm and appeal. From the pristine beaches of the Caribbean to the historic cities of Europe, my clients have had the chance to experience the world meaningfully and meaningfully.

Imagine standing on the deck of a cruise ship, the wind in your hair and the sun setting on the horizon, surrounded by new friends who feel like old companions. That's the magic of our group cruises. We've seen strangers become lifelong friends and families grow closer as they share these incredible journeys.

Travel By Destiny is not just about travel; it's about creating experiences that enrich lives and foster connections. This business has allowed me to combine my passion for travel with my commitment to helping others, and it has been an incredibly fulfilling journey. So, while retirement initially had me questioning my next steps, it ultimately led me to a new and exciting chapter in my life. Through Travel By Destiny, I get to craft stories of adventure, joy, and discovery for my clients, and in doing so, I continue to write my own story of purpose and fulfillment.

Conclusion: Inspiring the Next Generation of Women

Reflecting on my journey, I am deeply grateful for the opportunities I have had to make a difference. My work in the non-profit sector, my experiences as an author, and my endeavors with Travel By Destiny have all been driven by a passion for helping others and a commitment to creating positive change.

From the rebellious teen who accidentally set her school on fire to a seasoned advocate, author, and entrepreneur, my life has been a testament to the power of resilience and the importance of following one's passions. Every step of the way, I have been guided by a desire to lift others, provide support where needed, and inspire those around me.

Imagine a young girl reading one of my mystery novels, her eyes wide with wonder as she follows the twists and turns of the plot. She may not know it yet, but she is being introduced to the themes of justice, perseverance, and hope—values I hold dear. Or think of a woman on one of our Travel By Destiny tours, standing at the edge of a pristine beach, feeling the warmth of the sun and the promise of new adventures. She is creating memories that will last a lifetime, inspiring her to embrace life with open arms.

Through my various roles, I have seen the incredible impact that one person can have on their community and the world. The joy of seeing at-risk youth find their footing, the pride of watching a community project come to life, and the satisfaction of knowing a survivor feels seen and supported are the moments that define my journey.

But this journey is not just about me but the next generation of women. It's about you. Yes, you—the woman reading this now. You have the power to make a difference, to follow your passions, to overcome obstacles, and to create a life filled with purpose and joy. Whether you're advocating for change, telling your own stories, or exploring the world, know that every step you take is significant.

As I continue my advocacy work and through Travel By Destiny, I am committed to inspiring and supporting women everywhere. We are the architects of our futures, the storytellers of our lives, and the creators of lasting change. Let's embrace our destinies with courage and enthusiasm, knowing we can build a brighter, more inclusive world together.

So, here's to the next chapter—a chapter filled with adventure, love, and purpose. Keep pushing boundaries, keep dreaming big, and never forget the power you hold to shape your destiny.

Bio

Kimberly Clement has dedicated over 45 years to the non-profit sector, beginning as a Minnesota women's movement lobbyist. She spent a decade empowering at-risk youth and continues her advocacy as a coordinator for a local sexual violence resource center.

An accomplished author of twelve mystery novels, Kimberly also owns Travel By Destiny, a travel business creating unforgettable group cruises and tours worldwide. Through her diverse roles, Kimberly embodies a life of purpose and fulfillment, inspiring and supporting others every step of the way.

Explore unforgettable experiences with Travel by Destiny at www.travelbydestiny.com

Micaela El Fattal-

Success

We are born into a world where we strive for perfection and success. I was born, like anyone else, to a mom and dad, but my perfection story ended as I arrived at Tri-City Hospital in Oceanside, CA. The weekend I was born, there was an attempted kidnapping by a mentally ill mother of a stillborn, who pretended and disguised herself as a nurse. While wheeling me out of the room, my grandmother noticed she didn't have the standard nurse attire. She wore ripped-up old tennis shoes. Thankfully, my family understood the seriousness of having fresh white tennis shoes as a nurse in the 80s so this woman did not get too far.

As you already know, my story is different. Some might argue that it looks like anything but success. After experiencing traumatic developmental years, I was forced to live with a neighbor. which became extremely toxic. I even had to flee for my safety, moving in full-time with my father, 45 minutes away. I started my life over, even leaving my cell phone and pager behind to buy myself some time to get out of harm's way.

In high school, I was faced with starting to understand my heritage and ethnicity, at one point even interviewing my paternal grandfather about his migration to America. Even a few years ago, he remembered his journey to becoming an American citizen and his home country and nationality, so well. I remember that I am privileged, lucky, and so grateful for the opportunity, due to his perseverance. I know that perseverance, resilience, and determination live on me. Facing my circumstances, I was kicked out of high school but continued to develop my cultural identity and what success and purpose looked like.

I was even on educational probation in my graduate program, due to questioning systematic ethics. As an American, I was raised knowing my voice matters, yet, even now, my Lebanese roots fight to be heard, seen, and acknowledged. As I age, I recognize how much purpose I hold in continuing toward individual and community success. My bloodline serves as a daily reminder of the importance of speaking up, even when you may be alone.

There is so much to consider when you think of success and purpose. Was my idea of success more shaped by my travels worldwide or how I co-parented two incredible children? Do I mention how I successfully avoided being abducted by Russian Hooligans in Russia as a high schooler or when I did get abducted in a carjacking while visiting San Francisco many years ago? Or maybe I should mention how I was the first American known to interact with Indigenous tribes in the jungle of Boracay Island in the Philippines? I could also mention how my family lost everything we owned in the Lilac Fire. Regardless, as adults that success is identified by everyone individually.

My idea of success is acceptance, striving for greatness, determination, and resilience. It can be having a laser-sharp focus on something you believe in or simply getting through something that could have broken you. As a small child, success became making friends and being accepted into society.

As a high schooler in America, the bar is raised on what success means and how to achieve it. Success becomes having a good core of friends, enrolling in AP classes, and thinking about what four-year university to attend. Success becomes having a direct pathway to a purpose; it becomes being able to leave the house successfully in the future. This obsession with success is exacerbated in the media, with newspapers pointing out what celebrity is divorcing which week and who gets to keep the mansion.

As a teen, just stepping on my own full of ambition, I decided on a community college. This was unacceptable to my family, which was full of teachers, nurses, superintendents, and lawyers. The pressure was on when I was encouraged to apply to CSUSM. At the time, I was working full-time with an adult couple with Down syndrome, and I was also a part-time caregiver and hospice aide for my close friend's grandmother, who was passing.

I remember the looks I received when I told my family I didn't want to go college "right now," every single family member pressing a different reason why I should give it a shot. After getting accepted, I felt a significant cloud on me. I had two incredibly meaningful jobs with incredible families, where I was learning more about who I was daily. I continued pouting as my mom, and I walked up the many, many stairs to the college's office to pay for my acceptance.

The office attendant didn't make eye contact when she told us we missed the payment deadline by one day. My mother was devastated, though I was relieved. A few months later, my friend's grandmother passed a few weeks after I had stopped working with her. I continued to do the right thing by following my heart and being available if needed.

The following summer, while stopping by my parents' house, I picked up their house phone. This was around the last year when house phones were the norm. I never, ever answered their phone. "Is there a lot of confusion? I realized this was a call from CSUSM. "You were accepted into our Master's Program. As Micaela?" a woman softly asked. Are you excited?!" I was elated.

A few moments later, confusion settled in. I hadn't applied for college. I decided to give the number a callback. The same woman answered the phone. "Excuse me, I hope I am not being rude….and I am very excited and grateful…but you must be mistaken, I didn't apply." She responded right away, "You are right. This is a brand new program for Social Work, so we were hoping you would be interested. We waived your application fee. You must have applied to Sociology or Psychology last year."

As I started my Master's Program, I learned about my family's mental health background. Because of the perfect timing of my schooling, I was able to help my Uncle through many drug-induced psychotic episodes, as well as counsel my family members individually on how we could best help him with the love he still deserved. I had quality time with him at a time when he was still in and out of consciousness. When he died late last year, I looked back on that year when I gave my all to help him, even staying late crying to my professor one day.

As a young adult, my idea of success turned into having a purposeful life. I traveled to Thailand and Cambodia, where my life would never be the same. I saw individuals with less than $50 a month living more happily than I was, some satisfied. I made friends who used their last dollars to buy me a birthday cake, even as I showed up an hour late, completely oblivious. I volunteered to teach English at Feeding Dreams in Cambodia. I had students showing up 2 hours early to have a chance to learn or have a conversation to practice their English skills.

I threw out the idea of what success looks like to others and focused on what it looks like to me. After the Lilac Fire destroyed our house, success was escaping the fire alive. Suddenly, possessions became meaningless, but we continued to feel rich by having each other. When your life is aligned with purpose, God will continue to help you follow your heart, whether you live in a house, trailer, or even off the grid. Keep showing up for yourself and be grateful that everything you work hard towards will come to you at the right moment.

Bio

Micaela El Fattal, also known as "Love," is a CSUSM graduate, with a Master in Social Work. She is a published author on The Mighty, an advocacy website for mental health. She has worked as an Individual and Family Therapist, and a caregiver, and recently opened Lovely Hearts Nonprofit in 2023. She enjoys traveling to her second home, Cambodia, and volunteering with children at hospitals, schools, and orphanages. She is a mother to two teens, Raiden and Zoey. She enjoys helping the homeless, advancing policy change for minorities, and standing up for refugees, deportees, and asylum seekers. She has volunteered with the United Nations, HeadCount, Cambodian Buddhist Association for Vulnerable Children, SEARAC, and Tiny Toones. In May 2023, she also co-founded Lovely Hearts NGO, which is located in Siem Reap, Cambodia.

This Chapter is Dedicated to Her Mother, Erin English, who has been facing breast cancer. Keep Fighting.

Sam Ballington-

From Learning to Liberation: Empowering Lives through Education

This chapter is dedicated to the women of purpose in my life: my friends Lauran, Rebecca, Donna, Jade, and every other woman who has made a positive impact in my journey; my friends, colleagues, and students. It is also dedicated to the girls who give me purpose: my daughters Eva and Ella.

From Education to Empowerment

School. I suppose I liked going to school. I can't say it was because I enjoyed learning; in reality, I found my early years in school insufferable and difficult. It was not until I reached the age of fourteen or fifteen, when the really important exams were approaching- you know, the ones that define our future selves- that I pulled my socks up and surprised everyone with some good grades.

The reason I liked school was that it was always my safe space. For several hours a day, five days a week, I was in a sanctuary away from the abuse I suffered at home. Nevertheless, this story is not about that part of my life. The cover photo of this story won't depict an abused girl. No. This story is about the transformative power of education. I embraced it, and I encourage everyone I can to do the same. For themselves. For their loved ones. This narrative will not only show how education can change lives for the better but will also highlight how I continue to challenge policy and practice to ensure meaningful and accessible education for all.

After the shock of achieving the desired grades in school, it took me a little while to find out what I wanted to do next. I hadn't really thought about it too much. My childish dreams of being a volcanologist were crushed by an abuser's "no." A vocation like that would mean leaving him—out of the question. I initially tried studying English at University, but that didn't last long. Eventually, I took a job in a local primary school and began my career in early years and childcare. From there, I returned to university to study Early Years and Primary teaching for four years. However, my love for the classroom and working with children was tainted by strict regimes and government policies that suffocated the creativity and expression of both teachers and the children. Just a few years into primary teaching, I took the opportunity to work with adult learners, supporting individuals who were unemployed in obtaining qualifications to help them return to the workplace. Had I finally found my happy place? I found a sense of purpose not only for myself but also in helping others to do the same. It was here that I discovered the transformative power of education. Let's come back to that later.

My self-education journey paused for a while as I focused on building a career helping others. It wasn't long before I realised I needed to keep updating my skills and knowledge to stay abreast of an ever-changing world. I returned part-time to complete my first Master's degree at the University of Manchester, studying Education and Digital Technology. I thoroughly enjoyed the experience, discovering that 'zest' for learning, which has since turned into a bit of an addiction!

Since graduating with my first MA in 2018, I have undertaken two further Master's degree in Early Years Education, and Montessori Education. I returned to Manchester for my PhD in Education and am currently working through my second doctoral programme at Edgewood College in the United States. In the interim, I've been invited to study for my fourth MA in Creative Writing and Publishing, which will be underway by the time you read this chapter. In addition, I've been working on vocational qualifications such as my Leadership Fellowship, Chartered Teacher Status, and Digital Learning Designer Apprenticeship. I say this not to boast, but to demonstrate that once you start, it can be very difficult to stop learning new things and empowering yourself with knowledge. The more knowledge you have, the more you can help and advocate for others. Personally, while school had been my physical safe space, continued learning as an adult has become a sanctuary for my mind. It keeps my brain active and safe from falling into the memories I try so hard to repress.

Identifying the Developmental Gap for Early Years Educators

Empowering people through education is not simply an interest or passion of mine; it is a cause I actively advocate for with the resources at my disposal. I have been fortunate to build strong relationships with awarding and accrediting organizations here in the UK as a part of my career choices and job roles. My experience in external quality assurance and qualification development has given me an inside look into Ofqual and Department for Education procedures and policies, as well as the processes for apprenticeship and qualification approvals. I have harnessed this insider knowledge and the network I have built in the sector to continue developing educational programmes and qualifications for our ambitious and caring workforce in the Early Childhood Education sector.

In 2022, I began researching the crisis impacting the early years workforce, particularly the issues of staffing recruitment and retention. As a highly regulated profession governed by official bodies such as Ofsted (the Inspectorate for Education and Care Provision) and the Department for Education (DfE). Early years professionals in England must meet ratio requirements based on the qualifications held by workforce practitioners. These qualifications, in turn, must be approved by Ofqual (the inspectorate for qualifications, assessment, and awarding) and the DfE as what is known as 'Full and Relevant' Early Years Educator qualifications.

Until recently, these qualifications have been available vocationally at levels 2, 3, and 5. Academic routes are also available, which include work placements and, upon completion of a degree at level 6, can lead to entry into teacher training qualifications. Unfortunately, this halt in learning at level 5 has prevented vacational learners from moving on to Level 6 qualifications unless they opt to attend university to complete a degree pathway. Most instances found via empirical research indicate that the 'top-up' degree (the level 6 element of a full degree programme, which is one year of a three-year degree programme) often does not accept level 5 vocational graduates. Vocational learners interviewed during the research shared that universities told them their level 5 vocational qualification didn't hold enough academic value, or that the number of credits on their chosen course had was too low. It seemed critically unfair that learners who undertook so much training, learning, and development could not progress to future opportunities, including teacher training, due to the lack of a vocational level 6.

The consequences of this gap are dire: continued low pay, high staff turnover, limited progression opportunities, and generally low morale for the job. It is well documented through research and lived experiences that the role of the year educator is not valued as highly as that of their school-based educator colleagues, who enjoy better pay, enhanced progression opportunities, benefits, and a more favourable work-life balance. Faced with the absence of a vocational Level 6 in Early Years, I took action and created it!

Creating the First Level 6 Vocational Diploma for Early Years Professionals

As an experienced qualification product developer and manager, I set to work using my skill set to develop a level 6 qualification for early years professionals. Drawing on my extensive knowledge of the early childhood sector, I began to design the qualification. I collaborated with an Ofqual-approved awarding organisation to ensure the qualification became recognised, and designed to include 120 credits, meeting the QAA (the official body for higher education) requirements for Early Childhood Studies degrees. The DfE also approved the qualification with that all important 'Full and Relevant' status. This means that the qualification can welcome those who have achieved a level 5 qualification in an allied profession, such as education or social care, and wish to transition into Early Years education while obtaining the Full and Relevant Early Years Educator status.

With my awarding team by my side and the support of my workforce research participants, I developed a qualification aimed at empowering those in the sector. They can now use this qualification to develop their careers without having to pause their professional journey to head back to vocational study. This qualification allows them to avoid the difficult choice between leaving a sector they love and pursuing better wages.

While I am immensely proud of this achievement and look forward to its growth and wider recognition, it is important to note that the intellectual property rights of the qualification now belong to the awarding body. This was a crucial step in ensuring that the qualification gained the relevant statuses and recognitions. As a result, I make no profit from this qualification; it is my gift to the sector. Any training provider or college can apply to offer and deliver the qualification via the awarding body, and any potential learner who meets the entry requirements can register to undertake the programme of learning to achieve the qualification.

The key indicator of success is, of course, the participant testimonials. One such testimonial reads: "Having completed my Level 5 Diploma for the Senior Early Years Practitioner, I was disappointed to find that I could not join a Top-up BA Degree with the number of credits I received from the Level 5, and was looking at having to start the entire degree from the beginning. While researching my options for further education, I came across the Level 6 Diploma, which would allow me to continue studying alongside full-time employment. This was the perfect option for me, and I really enjoyed completing the course in a way that was flexible for my role as deputy manager of an early years setting. It has improved my everyday practice and knowledge of childcare and development. After completing the Level 6 Diploma, I plan to continue my studies by completing a Masters Degree in Infant Mental Health and Wellbeing, which the Level 6 Diploma will prepare me for, both through the learning and the credits I will receive. I am incredibly grateful to Sam and the team for developing this Diploma!" Emilia H. Current Early Childhood Pedagogy Level 6 Student.

Expanding Empowerment beyond Traditional Education

So far, I have shared an example of how I have used my own experience to create an opportunity for empowerment through education for others. This example covers a large sector workforce and allows individuals therein to progress and develop. In turn, staff retention and morale improve, which positively impacts the babies and young children they care for.

However, there is a much larger group of people I am working to empower through education: parents and careers.

I began developing internationally accredited training programmes in Therapeutic Coaching in 2021. The areas of focus include Parent Coaching Practice, Therapeutic Creative Arts Coaching, Child and Young Person Therapeutic Wellbeing, and Therapeutic Play Coaching. These programmes are certified by UK awarding organisations and accredited by an international professional coaching and counselling body based in the UK.

But how do they empower?

These accredited therapeutic coaching certifications provide comprehensive training opportunities pitched at levels 3 to 5 on the UK qualification's framework. All participants in the programmes learn essential knowledge and practical implementation skills across various areas, such as child psychology, communication in coaching, therapeutic techniques in arts and play, and coaching strategies. Learners are able to choose the direction of their education; for example, a student in the Therapeutic Arts Coaching Diploma may specialise in musical arts or dance. I have one student who solely uses pop punk and rock music in his practical work, reaching out to the alternative music scene to support young people experiencing mental health difficulties. In addition, those completing the programme benefit from business and management training, preparing them to establish their own therapeutic coaching practice. My students engage in marketing, accounting and finance skills, and other relevant business strategies, including securing insurance.

By undertaking these programmes, my learners empower themselves by achieving the confidence and knowledge necessary to set up their own coaching practices, allowing them to establish their own work and life goals. My successful candidates seize the opportunity to use education to take control of their professional careers, enabling them to be more present for their families.

Furthermore, the topics that graduates explore empower others through their coaching practices.

Empowered parents

Empowered children

Empowered young people

Empowered teachers

Parents become empowered to refocus their parenting direction. Families who have experienced loss or separation need to navigate new horizons in light of a changed family structure. Often, parents need support to understand the behaviours their children exhibit and the power of co-regulation in the parent-child relationship.

Children become empowered to express themselves through play, to express what they are unable to communicate or comprehend through the use of metaphors and stories.

Young people become empowered to stand up to their traumas and gain the courage to take a stand for themselves through the power of creative arts as their confident voice.

Teachers and other professionals who work with coaches become empowered with knowledge that can support children, young people, or families who have been through traumatic experiences in their classrooms or workplaces.

Here, we see how education, with the programmes developed through a professional educator and coach, leads to the empowerment of more than just oneself. The 'one' takes control of their own lives, empowering themselves to set up their business. They then use the knowledge and skills gained from their education to empower those in their community: the parents, the children, the young people, and the teachers, and other professionals. This creates a positive riffle effect, demonstrating the true power of education.

It's our children that drive us, isn't it?

I have often wondered if it took me so long to find my purpose because I didn't have one until 'children'. I found a role working with children that led me on a lifelong journey in education and a career as an educationalist. When I had my first daughter in 2014, I knew it was the time to empower myself to ensure I could be there for her, to care for her, and to watch her develop and grow. I realized instantly that I didn't want to miss those key milestones by placing her in daycare five days a week all year round. It was then that I decided I needed to become self-employed.

Just weeks after Eva, my eldest child, was born and during early stages of my maternity leave, I registered as a self-employed worker and began to market myself. I already had set what I wanted from any roles given and what I would accept. At the time, it was less about money (minimum wage would cover what we needed if necessary) and more about the situation. My non-negotiables were: flexible hours and remote working.

With my experience and qualifications, it didn't take too long to secure regular, flexible, part-time work that I could fit around my child. It did not replace my full-time salary, but income was coming in, and frugal practices kept us covered without losing out. As it worked out, I became pregnant with my daughter Ella when Eva was six months old (a classic case of Perfect First Baby syndrome… if you know, you know!). I decided not to return to traditional employment.

As my children, now aged 9 and 10 by the time this chapter is published, have grown, I have been able to attend their first days at school, Christmas plays, sports days, competitions, and other events. I did, however, ensure they had the opportunity to attend nursery (daycare) for two five-hour days per week when they were younger (from ages 2 and 3) to aid them in preparing for school and to have the opportunity to experience time spent with the amazing early years practitioners from the sector I train. This time was also valuable for me, as it allowed me to keep up with my business work. It's very different to have a baby who sleeps nine hours a day compared to two toddlers who require all your attention while trying to work!

Once again, I saw an opportunity to leverage my educational experiences and the knowledge I gained in the education sector to empower myself, market the services I offered, and grow a successful business as a tutor, assessor, coach, and quality assurer from home, around my children and our family's needs. The arrangement complimented my husband's role as a teacher, even though he sadly continues a (albeit amazing) career where his children's milestones were missed - but we have him home for longer holidays over Christmas, Easter, and Summer, just as the children are!

It took a long time to reach a point where my salary was fully replaced and to build a reputation that led to invitations to speak at conferences and requests to guest write in professional magazines. I accomplished it all myself. I have moved from being self-employed to setting up a limited company and employing myself and others. Through learning, I empowered myself. Now, I teach and empower others through my own experiences and through various learning and training opportunities. I will always advocate for parents to set up and work for themselves whenever possible, using the superpowers they already have and harnessing them to their advantage.

Superpowers… yes, parenting is a superpower, and each of us as parents has something amazing to share and coach to another parent. A parent can become a specialist in any number of areas—supporting other parents with new babies, home education, special educational needs and disabilities, behaviour and regulation, balancing parenting with a career, breastfeeding support, organisation, family life management, decluttering a home… absolutely anything! This is why the Therapeutic and Coaching business diplomas were born: to enable these superpowers to be shared safely and ethically with fellow parents, but parent coaches could empower themselves to take control of their businesses and lives, just as I did. As I share my own experiences, my coaching participants are, of course, much more equipped to do it at a faster pace than me, who started with no guidance and just a dream—what I thought at the time was a dream—to stay at home with my children. I am living this dream as my reality and helping others to do the same.

I have definitely found my drive through children. They ignited my career, and my own children made me who I am today. They fuel my desire to be there for them, and I want that for every other mother, father, and parent figure out there. Empowering them to choose how they want their careers to go and the direction they take.

Personal Reflections: Education as a Lifeline

Earlier in the chapter, I touched upon how I used school as an escape—a lifeline, so to speak— while suffering horrendous abuse at the hands of a parent. The very person who should have loved, protected, and cared for me took my later childhood from me. I refer to my later childhood because, looking back, my early childhood was filled with wonderful memories. My family—my mum, dad, and younger brother—lived in the South East of England. My mother worked a full-time 9-to-5 job, while my father worked shift work in children's social care and youth offending. We had au pairs from different countries who stayed with us to help my parents care for us around their busy lives. During that time, my parents were very sociable. They were members of a motorcycle group, and I have some positive memories of the events we attended across the country, often in huge camping fields and always a giant bouncy castle My parents also used to host a very well-attended summer barbecue each year. Sometimes, as is typical with the English summer, it rained—heavily. Sometimes, the weather was glorious. I remember during the hotter days, I would overeat watermelon and honeydew. On the wetter days, I generally remained inside, along with what seemed like hundreds of 'biker' men and women.

My sister was born just before I turned 11, and not long after, it became clear that we needed to start looking for a larger home. Leaving a home that had been pretty much your whole life gave me a mix of sad and excited feelings. It was a new adventure, but I was leaving behind what I knew. The family moved from a secure mortgage to the unpredictable landscape of private renting so that we could afford a larger home. The social events my family partook in seemed to dissipate, too.

When I was 12, my mother received a job offer that required relocation. She began this role around April of that year and would work and live away from home from Sunday afternoon until Friday evening each week. We followed her and relocated to the East Midlands of the UK at the start of the Summer Holidays. This was in the '90s, before the idea of 'working from home' became a reasonable concept.

The absence of my mother meant that the abuse could begin.

I used to think I was loved. He was lonely, and this was triggered by the lack of a woman in the house. I was 12, after all, and beginning to mature. However, this idea I had painted in my mind to protect myself was robbed when he once told me he had controlled himself when I was a lot younger. He recounted a time when he came in to wake me up for school one day, and my nightdress had ridden up. He had to leave the room and call my mother in to wake me instead. As time passed and I became older, I realised that there was no 'love' in the sense I wanted to believe, despite some part of my child's brain knowing it was not an appropriate situation to be in. No love— only pure abuse, control, manipulation. I endured physical, sexual, and mental trauma every single day.

Once, I had a boyfriend whom I defiantly decided to announce to my parents. With previous boyfriends, I had kept it a secret. I avoided sex with them because I was scared I would be found out. With this particular boyfriend, my father would drive around following us to see what we were doing. Once I came home he first pulled me down the stairs for walking through town holding his hand. Then, his anger turned to manipulation as he took the CD my boyfriend had bought for me that evening at a local Battle of the Bands event where his friends were playing. He snapped the CD in half and actioned the slicing of a piece of the CD across his throat and then slumped his whole body to the floor, lying still and silent as I watched in horror. It was all in pretence, of course, but what happened next revealed the true terror of the life I was living.

Fearfully, I ran upstairs to my mum, who was in bed with my twin sisters, who had been born a few years after we moved to the East Midlands. She was cross, trying to settle them, but saw my desperation as I begged her to come because "Dad's done something to himself." When we got downstairs, he was casually making himself a snack in the kitchen. I remember that was the first time I completely lost my mind away from the privacy of my own space, and it would begin a downward spiral in my mental health. I would run away, but I had nowhere to go. I would scream and growl loudly like a wild animal when inconvenienced by the slightest things as if all the trauma and torment of the past years came out all at once. The loss of my cool this first time lent me the courage to finally reveal my dark secrets.

"Mum", I said almost too calmly, my voice awash with tears and anguish from the evening's events. "I need to tell you what Dad's been doing to me all these years…". Then came the moment. The moment I knew I would never be saved. The moment I realised I was alone. The moment that changed who I was as a person, that made all the past years of putting up with the abuse because one day, I'll be an adult, in my own home, with my own family, and surely it would stop. Without asking for any further details, my mother grabbed me by the hair and shoved my face into the corner wall and doorframe, pushing me into the frame and speaking loudly into my ear in a tone of warning, "Whatever you say next, don't you dare say anything that will risk this family." And there I had it. My mother knew—probably all along. She allowed it to happen. For that, I don't know if I'll ever forgive her. She hasn't even reached out to ask for forgiveness. I will certainly never forget.

I cut ties with my family in 2006. I ran away and this time stayed away, although that wasn't without its events, and I injured my father quite badly in the process. It involved the police, who, although there to arrest me, actually ended up helping to free me. No charges were brought against me, and the battle to begin what might be considered a normal life would begin. I attempted to regain contact with my younger siblings some years later, and we had some nice times together, but in reality, I needed a clean break for my own family: my husband and my daughters. My siblings also had this complex view of my father as some superior being, a hero. And so they should. I wish he had been. He had died in 2009 when all my siblings were still children, and they loved and adored him. Any mention of negatively around him was simply rebuffed or met with anger. I did, however, hear that my mother is an entirely different person now, willing to do anything for her children, to the point where she is at their demand, despite them being adults now. It offers me some comfort that she is not harsh and cold towards them like she was with me. I am also assured by all of them that they were never touched inappropriately, although my brother, who is the oldest of my younger siblings, seems set on forgetting that he was beaten by my father regularly, both with hands and with objects.

While my brother and I didn't manage to rebuild our relationship at all—which is a great shame for many reasons, but I'm told we have the same humanist and socialist values and would make wonderful friends—I made the difficult decision to remove all links to the remaining members of my childhood family from my life in 2024. It was too painful to continue, and as a parent myself now, I recognise that my own mental well-being is required for adequately caring for my family. It's time to focus on myself and not walk on eggshells around my sisters, cousins, aunties, and uncles for fear of saying something 'wrong' about my "amazing" dad. It was also painful to read their social media celebrations of his heroic behaviours as a father or brother, and their monologues of sadness over key life events he's missing. I committed a selfish act by deciding to have no contact with any member of my childhood family, removing them from my social media accounts, and locking down any access they have to my life and the lives of my children, whom I will protect with all my being.

Education has been my lifeline. As a child, school provided a physical escape. Now, as an adult, education continues to serve me as a therapy as I come to terms with my past and balance this with the amazing life my husband and I have built for my family.

Despite the amazing life I have been able to build with the unwavering support of my husband, my past haunts me. I still have terrible nightmares— some that take me straight back to childhood, and some are where he is still alive, trying everything to roadblock any form of happiness in my life. The worst dream

I have, though, is of him being in Hell, burning, and reaching up, screaming for help to escape. I hate that nightmare. It makes me cry. It's almost like I harbor some guilt that I put him there. I used to have this nightmare all the time when he first died, but it has occurred less frequently as time has passed. The dream of Hell reflects the fears instilled in me by my Evangelical Christian family; "born again," they would call themselves. Personally, I would say I'm agnostic. I cannot fully remove my belief in God, the Devil, Heaven, and Hell, because of how instilled they were ingrained during my childhood years.

Occasionally, I experience night terrors. In the early days of living with my now-husband, I was convinced I saw one of his gargoyle statutes move from the back to the front of the shelf and that a demon was going to possess me. I was absolutely terrified, a symptom of being brought up in a God-fearing, abusive home. My ever-patient partner took the statue and threw it out of the window, but not being enough to calm me. We then got in the car, along with the gargoyle statue, and drove at 3 a.m. to the farthest point on the other side of town, where we placed the poor, most likely innocent (I am still convinced I saw that movement) statue in the bin. On the way home, we stopped at a 24-hour Tesco store because it was brightly lit, and I could buy my favourite remedy: chocolate.

I had another night terror in the early days of my escape when I opened my eyes to see a figure of a man standing at the foot of our bed, one hand on each of the bottom bed posts and shaking the bed. Eventually, I was able to scream, and my husband had to check the whole house. Coincidentally or not, the next morning the television news informed us that an earthquake had hit the UK, stemming from a couple of counties away.

Engaging in education helps me refocus my mind. It keeps me active and busy. Distracting me from the thoughts of the past and offering me the opportunity to look forward. My current studies include my qualifying training in Child and Adolescent Mental well-being, as I am now in a space of mind where I can use my experiences of trauma to help others. Building on my coaching practices, I work as a children's psychotherapist, focusing predominantly on working with children and young people who are survivors of abuse. Furthermore, my fourth Master's degree in Creative Writing and Publishing will allow me to hone my expertise in children's care and early years into textbooks and guides for others to use in their studies. There is potential for me to write on areas of trauma therapies if I become brave enough to face my past head-on.

If I hadn't had education as a child—a safe space to retreat to, even for a short time—I may not have survived the childhood I was given. How could anyone be expected to live in those conditions? I did try to hurt myself once as a child, but it's safe to say that drinking a small pot of TipEx liquid doesn't do much except make your tongue white and cause a call from the school to be made my home, making things seem much worse in that moment. If I hadn't have access to education now, I don't think my mind would survive my own mental torment and the terrible anxieties and paranoia I suffered. My husband, family, and friends remained as patient and empathetic as possible with my spiralling behaviours from the past. I wouldn't be in a position to work for myself, nor would have gained the skills and knowledge to help others—whether that means supporting a parent wanting to establish a therapeutic coaching practice, bridging career gaps for early years educators, or helping children express their traumatic experiences through the power of play.

Final Thoughts: A Call to Action

I am aware that there are some sensitive themes within this chapter. However, I hope that you, the reader, understand the importance of including these themes to provide background on where I have come from and what I have been able to achieve. It is essential to recognise that even the most huge obstacles can be overcome.

Everyone deserves the opportunity to feel empowered—whether in their work, personal life, parenting, or any other aspect. I have found my empowerment by continuously challenging and developing myself through education, which has, in turn, allowed me to help others feel empowered.

I have challenged educational barriers for the amazing Early Years sector workforce by creating resources that help them navigate policy challenges and build better futures for themselves. I have developed programmes to empower parents and others to take control of their careers and businesses, all built upon an ethos of helping and empowering others.

I now call all readers to action; harness the power of education in whatever capacity works for you to empower yourself or support your communities around you.

As I continue my work in research and development, I will explore further ways to ensure that empowering education is accessible to all. We all deserve the opportunity to empower ourselves through education.

Bio

Sam is an academic and professional researcher, author, educationalist, and qualification developer in the fields of Early Years Education, Playful Interventions, and Parent, Family, and Child Therapeutic Coaching and Wellbeing.

As the creator of the Level 6 Advanced Diploma in Early Childhood Pedagogy and Practice, as well as the play intervention programmes CalmPlay and PlaySense, Sam develops training and development opportunities for childcare professionals and those seeking to harness the power of play to change the lives of children and young people. She also offers Therapeutic Play Coaching and Parent Coaching training for individuals wishing to build their careers and businesses in these areas, empowering them to continue their positive work with children and families.

Sam possesses a solid academic and research background, demonstrating a commitment to her education and transformation, having undertaken a variety of Master's degrees and Postgraduate training at UK universities, including the University of Cambridge, and holds a PhD from the University of Manchester. She is currently pursuing an EdDoc programme and completing her postgraduate professional training in Child and Adolescent Mental wellbeing to further build her knowledge and skills in therapeutic play and wellbeing coaching in practice.

In addition to her academic pursuits, she runs a small training provision that offers the aforementioned services, private therapeutic play coaching, and parent coaching. She also provides freely available social media resources for childcare students focusing on early years qualifications and apprenticeship programmes.

Sam lives in Derbyshire, UK, with her husband, two daughters, a corn snake named Tom, a Tortoise named Flash, and a large family of Indian stick insects, all named Stickie, as there are too many of them to name individually!

To learn more about Sam, or collaborate on projects in the field of early years, childcare, play, or therapeutic child and family coaching, or learn more about undertaking accredited training with Sam, please visit www.SamBallington.co.uk

While the web address is based in the UK due to Sam's location, the accreditations are international. So, please don't hesitate to join the amazing community of Parent, Play, and Wellbeing Coaches, regardless of where you are located.

Jessica Erlendson van Remmen-

Jessica Erlendson van Remmen: Living a Purposeful Life

I dropped out of high school when I was 17 years old. I could not attend school without the foundation of music, band, choir, concerts, and rehearsals. I was not motivated to go to school. I tried being in choir in grade 11 but couldn't get through. I dropped out three times. I kept going back, and I kept dropping out. I didn't have any help for the dyslexia that I had been diagnosed with while I was in junior high, because none of my school records had come with me when I moved to a new province. My educational assessment just got dropped because I didn't have an active parent at home. My father was very passive about how he parented. He didn't even realize that I needed accommodations, and neither did I. Except I did need learning accommodations. When I asked for extra help, I was laughed at by my teacher, told I was just lazy, and eventually, I became depressed.

I was the victim of various degrees of abuse from people in my life over the years, and I could no longer function normally. At 18 years old, I was in a band with my boyfriend, who lived with me and my Dad. We made beautiful music, but I was depressed, and I couldn't even imagine living a purposeful life. At that point, I was still determined to be helpful. I was taking care of the household, planning shows, performing, singing in concerts, recording, and playing percussion in my Dad's jazz band, but I didn't make enough money to support myself. I didn't feel like I had any hope for my future.

One day, I was sitting at home with my boyfriend when we heard the door open. It was my dad who had brought a woman home. This is the only time that he ever showed up at home with a woman. He only brought people home if they were in a band, and my boyfriend and I thought that it was strange at the time. They came in, and she sat down.

She said "This is going to sound strange, and I don't care if you believe me, but I need to tell you that I came here to talk to you. I like your dad. He's a great guy, but I know you're depressed, and I have a message for you." At the time, I was disallusioned and feeling hopeless. She said, "The way that you feel about yourself now, well it's not the truth at all. It's just what's happening right now. The person you'll become is a teacher and a significant person to many women. You'll change a lot of women and children's lives. I don't know exactly how that will happen, but that is your future."

I remember thinking, "This is the weirdest thing ever. How could a woman who can't get through high school become a teacher? How could I become a teacher at all? They don't let high school dropouts teach classes at school." I felt I couldn't learn because of my broken brain and nobody is going to help me.

It was so weird that we all remembered it! I didn't think about it again until many years later. I was teaching music lessons, and had probably taught hundreds of kids by that time. I'd encouraged many women to leave bad relationships, and to go back to school because I had done that myself. I guided them to get the educational testing done, to get the learning accommodations they needed, to leave the destructive relationships behind, and to move forward with what was important to them.

I thought, "Oh, maybe that's it, you know? I mean, maybe I'm doing what I was supposed to do. Who knows? Right?" Maybe teaching music was what she was talking about. For every child I helped with music lessons, I felt I always helped their mother as well, with our conversations, the marriages that broke up while I was teaching, and the informal counseling sessions that I gave the moms many times. I was often helping them with a child who had an undiagnosed or diagnosed learning disability, or neurodivergence, and giving them the support that the mom needed to deal with that child to help them grow.

I've had several music students stay with me for many years, and I have also changed their lives. Then, one day in the CPMS Canadian Perimenopause and Menopause Support group, after it had gotten to about 3,000 people from all across Canada (as well as some in the States and elsewhere) I thought, maybe that's what this woman was talking about. Perhaps I would make the most significant difference by supporting the women in the group I had started online.

The question is, how on earth could she have known about a pandemic, everything being shut down and forcing everyone to go online? The timing also corresponded with my finishing the yoga therapy program at Mount Royal University, which taught me to design treatment plans to target specific human body, mind, and spirit conditions. So, it didn't matter to me if they had a diagnosis of perimenopause or post-menopause. I had the physical symptoms, and that's all I needed to design a care program for these women.

As the group grew, I continued designing classes and did the 2023 Fall Symposium. I was bringing in experts to speak on perimenopause and menopause to our group. We had 4,000 members when I got a CBC radio interview in Nov 2023, suddenly making the group explode again. I did a talk on Anxiety and Moods for Naomi Campbell, a naturopath from Australia, who hosted an international Menopause summit online, and the group exploded again. And now here it is 2024, a little more than three years after I started the group, and we're almost 10,000 members; all active members, profiles of real people. There are no fake profiles or bots in there. We screen everybody very carefully. I have four volunteers that help me run the group. Another volunteer helped me build the Canadian Perimeno website

(www.canadianperimeno.com).

Helping women in peri and post-menopause has given my life a greater purpose!

Living a life filled with purpose has meant that my decisions are based not only on what I want for now and today but also on a lesson that my parents taught me; the idea of making yourself useful. Idle time in my family was not considered dangerous but a waste of precious time. We only have one life to live, and this life that we're living is what we make of it. Being raised in the 1970's by an alcoholic mother and a jazz musician father meant that my learning disability went undiagnosed. As I wasn't creating problems in school, I didn't have behavior issues. They just considered me lazy, which didn't warrant testing.

I took care of our family dog. I started walking other people's dogs when I was ten. I decided not to participate in bullying. I wouldn't become a bully or let other people be bullied. I stood up for myself, not through violence but through telling on people when they were being bullies. You may think that made me less popular in school, but the opposite happened. The younger students loved me. By the time I was in Grade 6 because I would escort them home. I often carried the smaller students so that other older students wouldn't bully them. Whenever I saw people being bullied, I stepped in. This may be about my temperament, though. I never enjoyed watching or participating in fighting. I didn't enjoy being in the fight or made to fight.

As an adult, I became a single mom when I was 22 with a 10-month-old baby who learned to fight through words. Word fighting is much more sophisticated, and the winner might not be evident initially because there's no blood. I tried again, only to become a single mom when the relationship I had with the father of my second son became toxic. He was a gambler, and we were destitute. One advantage of being with people who kept me poor was that I was never afraid to leave. What did I have to lose? An inconsistent partner who was unwilling to work with me to solve problems and didn't want to live a purposeful life as much as I did. They thought it was terrific that I was always making myself useful. Unfortunately, human nature means that some people will take advantage of that, which I found repeatedly in many relationships. In my mid-20s, I focused on playing music, loving my kids as much as I possibly could, and spending time with them. I started having higher standards for how I would be treated and what I would put up with. I concentrated on learning as much as I could and being with my kids.

I became determined to live where I was safe at home and could pursue my dreams and interests, essentially writing songs and sharing them. My focus on learning had me returning to school repeatedly until eventually becoming a teacher myself.

By the time I was in my late 40s, my music lesson career had slowed, and I had gone back to school yet again to study Yoga and then further my studies to become a Yoga therapist. I was on the verge of graduating from my program but was feeling worse with symptoms of perimenopause myself. I had high hopes for my program at Mount Royal University, which had a world-class reputation as an excellent Yoga program. Like most established programs, it did leave out everything about women's health other than there might be some issues during menopause. This meant that I had to become very driven to learn everything I could.

I had an active Facebook profile with a lot of friends. I graduated from my yoga therapy program at MRU in the summer of 2019. Things had just started to pick up. I was actively looking for a contract with a clinic, but then 2020 happened, and we were all shut down. During that time, my symptoms got incredibly worse. My anxiety went through the roof. I started taking an antidepressant just before COVID hit. I had my gallbladder removed, and I did begin to feel better physically in some ways and worse in others.

I tried talking to all my friends about what I was going through, and unfortunately, because doctors don't say the word perimenopause to women, my friends didn't want to talk about it. They didn't think that it applied to them. I felt more frustrated and alone. I started to feel disillusioned, isolated, and scared for the future. I realized there must be many women in Canada going through that same thing in North America and other places in the world. So, I decided to start a Facebook group.

I began the CPMS group in the Spring of 2021. I put both perimenopause and menopause in the title of the group because perimenopause is a very confusing time in a woman's life. It is a time when it is almost impossible to be taken seriously and get treatment. Perimenopause means that, just like me, you can have perfect periods, perfect blood tests, and many troubling, disruptive symptoms.

For me the strange symptoms were: sudden increased anxiety, insomnia, strange itching, weird body sensations, joint pain, vision changes, dryness, sudden chronic UTI's, and more. Remember, I had perfect blood work, my doctor said to me that many women in my age range would love to have that blood work but what good does it do if you are struggling with those symptoms? I knew some women online who probably were in perimenopause or menopause and might want to talk about it, and I just asked them to invite people into my group who they thought were in the same boat. It didn't take long before we had a hundred people in that group.

Once the group reached one hundred people, we kept having new people, people that nobody knew in the group wanting to join. We debated whether we wanted to keep it small. The culture of support we had worked on could be lost if clueless or even cruel people would join.

I thought of the woman crying in her car because her doctor didn't find a problem with her tests and had sent her home as if she was fine. What if she had just seen the doctor with the horrible symptoms that I previously described, and I had been told, "Your blood work is perfect. There's nothing wrong with you?" Now, she feels like she's crazy and dying, and nobody cares. I decided to open the group for that woman and all women doing that right now because they're not alone and they are not crazy. They are having those symptoms, and they are perimenopause symptoms that can be treated. There is no magic pill, and of the options, the most readily available one is antidepressants. Many women object to that and don't want to go down that road. I felt that way for a long time until I was really struggling with anxiety. When I tried the antidepressants, I couldn't believe what a huge difference they made, and my doctor reassured me that I'm not stuck on it for the rest of my life. This is a temporary situation. Once I am through menopause, I likely won't need the antidepressants anymore.

I've been incredibly blessed and supported in getting this message out there because I have been able to help so many of the women who have no one to listen to them. Everyone who has been helped and has pitched in to help other women has enriched their own lives and ultimately lessened their own symptoms. When thinking of others and being busy helping others, you're less preoccupied with the conditions you're having yourself.

My long-term vision for this group is that it continues to grow so that I'm able to move over onto another platform and have a membership so that I can offer courses, classes, and workshops in a way that's much more streamlined than what I'm doing now. I want to have more of a relationship with the members than I do now on Facebook. A free group on Facebook means many people feel it's just a free group that happens magically out of thin air, which it's not. It's a lot of work. I'm often helping women online when I could spending that time with my husband and family. He's pretty understanding, and he's come a long way, but I have to have boundaries, and I need to earn a living providing this care.

At the time of this writing, I'm planning for the second Annual CPMS Symposium in Nov 2024. I have a naturopathic doctor from Ontario, Tanya McEachern. She's going to talk about all the alternatives to prescriptions and how naturopathic medicine looks at perimenopause and menopause from a holistic standpoint. Tanya will answer all kinds of questions about what type of supplementation you might try, all-natural remedies and lifestyle issues, and all those good things that make a massive difference to women's lives because what I've seen more and more is that when Mom takes care of herself, everything else takes care of itself. Some obligations will need to be postponed, and some things adjusted, or things won't happen because you don't do them, but eventually, the people around you will catch up. For other people to pick up something, you first must put down that obligation and allow others to pitch in. It is frustrating to accept limitations and adjust, but it's better than being exhausted by the demands of those around you when you can't continue the way you used to!

Another issue I hear all the time from the women in CPMS is bladder leaks, chronic or recurrent UTI, and sexual pain or dysfunction. The second speaker I have arranged for the fall symposium is Trish Gipson, a pelvic floor physiotherapist from BC. She works at the Cheerful Pelvis. She's going to talk about how pelvic floor treatment can help with incontinence, sexual pain, and even bowel issues. She will discuss exactly what a treatment might look like for a woman and how invasive it can be but usually there's less invasive ways she can use. It doesn't necessarily have to be as invasive as every woman is thinking and getting the word out to women that pelvic health is important, that treating their incontinence does matter, and even educating that it is treatable. I'm surprised how often a woman will share that she had no idea it was treatable and that you might have to work on it. It is worth working on because it affects the quality of your life. The number two reason for women being placed into long-term care facilities is that they have incontinence. Urinary incontinence is the reason that they can't live at home, and it's treatable. It's appalling. It's enraging. I can't believe that there's so much ignorance about women's health in midlife. The people attending the symposium will get a great bang for their buck!

When you look at the stats, we've estimated that approximately 1.6 million women in Canada who are likely to be in Peri or post-menopause, having symptoms and getting answers like, well, get some diapers and don't worry about it. Stop lifting heavy weights. Stop jumping on the trampoline. Stop working out and do Kegels, all of which are not correct advice for people living through and trying to figure out their incontinence issue. I'm excited about the message of hope that Trish can give to women who have been suffering, feeling inadequate, broken, and ashamed. They will be helped!

The last guest I am bringing in is a hormone specialist medical doctor, Shafeena Premji. This doctor is on the board of directors for the Menopause Foundation; she runs her practice, helping women to manage their peri and post-menopause journey and, as she said to me, getting to the other side of things and feeling fabulous. She helps women to get their lives back! The group needs to hear from a functional medicine or hormone specialist doctor because they can talk about the prescriptions. For us in Canada, it's easy to find people online talking about prescriptions, but they are usually in the UK or the US. Our healthcare system is different. We need to hear the doctor talk about HRT. We also need clarification about antidepressants, how they work, and why they work! Why they are a good option. Antidepressants are the number 2 option after HRT, but that doesn't mean that we should throw it out. It doesn't mean it isn't worth trying, and it doesn't mean it isn't a helpful treatment.

Hormone replacement therapy got a bad reputation because of something the press did, and it's a terrible problem. The Women's Health Initiative study looked into hormone replacement therapy, and it was supposed to be the Fountain of Youth. It was supposed to be a beautiful thing, and it turned into a cancer scare because they weren't conscientious about choosing the participants. They picked postmenopausal women, which we know now is not the right demographic to be tested on for this kind of treatment, and they gave them estrogen without progesterone. We now know this is dangerous for the uterus. But the whole study was flawed, so they threw it out! I think it was the New York Times that published an article that said HRT causes cancer, and that was it. From then on, everybody has felt this and there's still this paranoia that it has caused cancer. It has lasted this whole time, and it has damaged a lot of people's lives, and it is damaging a lot of people's lives right now, for example. I've heard this a lot in the CPMS group. A woman gets diagnosed with abnormal cells from a uterine biopsy, which means some cells are on the way to perhaps becoming cancer, and they would like to treat that. The treatment they're offered is progesterone-only pills, and then they don't want to take it because they think it's HRT and all hormone treatments are dangerous. They wrongly believe that all hormone therapy is going to cause cancer. This is not true at all! Just today in the group, a woman finally got her prescription filled. When the pharmacist gave her a lecture about taking hormones that scared the crap out of her, she became afraid to take her medication again! She's already learned all about it and honestly needs the medication because, without it, she is not functional.

As far as I know, progesterone has never been linked to causing cancer, and it is a viable treatment, especially if you're talking about the health of the tissues inside the uterus. The Nurse Practitioner Amanda Cameron, from our first Fall Symposium in 2023, described this by comparing it to being like the lawn. If you think of the lining of your uterus like a lawn, estrogen causes the lawn to grow. We need a nice, soft, squishy place for the ovum to implant and grow a fetus. When you get pregnant, progesterone comes in and trims the grass, keeping the environment optimal for your body to keep the pregnancy and controlling the growth of the lining of the uterus. Estrogen causes the grass to grow, and progesterone trims the grass or keeps the lawn from getting out of control.

So, progesterone, if you're growing abnormal cells, is potentially beneficial to keep the health of the lining of the uterus. But when women are prescribed this, it is not adequately explained. Doctors don't have enough time to describe it, and there isn't the literature on hand in the doctor's office to hand the patient with the progesterone-only prescription, saying, this is why this is what it will do, and it is safe. So, they come into the group, and they say my doctor's an idiot, and I got abnormal cells, and now they want me to take HRT. Then, when you ask them more questions, it turns out the prescription is only Progesterone. Well, that's like a modified version of HRT. It's not a traditional HRT at all because there's no estrogen involved. It is a safe, viable treatment option and much less invasive than having them remove the uterus from your body or leaving a thick uterine lining to develop into cancer. I see there's a massive gap in information for Canadians online. If you want to learn about perimenopause or menopause, you go on to Instagram or social media. Many people are talking about it, but anyone can say anything they want, and people will say whatever they want, but it's not necessarily true.

The other issue is that even when you find someone you like, who is knowledgeable enough to get clicks and likes, they're almost always American or UK-based, which means a lot of the information is a little different and does not translate for Canadians. What we can get for prescriptions, what it's called, how accessible it is, and other issues around insurance come up because we are in Canada. This is highly frustrating! It's part of why I wanted to start the CPMS Group. The mission is to create Canadian content with Canadian experts who can discuss navigating this challenging time of life with as much grace as possible, which is a big stretch for the lady who's sitting crying in her car right now. I've already helped several people directly with one-on-one coaching sessions and many more indirectly. Probably a lot more that I don't even know about have been helped from my videos, putting up quality content, providing files and documents as well as resources, clinic information, putting on workshops and classes. I am hosting on the Symposium and bringing in experts who are answering our questions, instead of pretending everything is beautiful when suffering isn't beautiful.

I often say, "Perimenopause is a jungle, don't go in there alone". It's much safer with a guide, especially when trying to go it alone is so frustrating. Always take a friend. That's what support is. It doesn't mean I'm going to agree with you on everything. Specific topics are off the table. We don't discuss politics, and we don't discuss COVID. The main reason is that everybody has an opinion on politics, and their opinion is firm and not necessarily based on science.

I will be hosting the CPMS Symposium and I will be speaking about how Yoga can be a valuable part of every woman's journey through Perimenopause into post menopause. As a Yoga therapist, it doesn't matter to me why you can't sleep. What matters is you can't sleep, so what can we do to address that? (I have a class available for this online called "21 Days to Fix Your Sleep".) Often, I find that the cause will present itself when you start treating what's happening, especially when you start treating yourself with yoga, which is what I do: lifestyle, movement, meditation, especially mindfulness, Yoga Nidra, talking, listening, and music. Then, the truth comes out, which is liberating in many ways. I will be explaining things in common language that makes understanding hormones, nutritional changes, body composition and other issues more accessible for everyone.

In the long run. I would love a fully functional website where people can find people in their community quickly and get the resources they need, close by or online. I have several classes that are already pre-recorded for women to access. I already have some and would love to have more resources available to help as many women as possible understand what is going on with their bodies and how they can help themselves to get back to living well.

At the symposium, I will also spend time explaining why setting healthy boundaries is important for our health journey. It's time for the men and partners in our lives to stop making excuses for themselves about how she's always done the cooking, or she's always done the cleaning, or she's always done all the planning, or she's always made sure that everybody was okay and start pitching in on that as well. There's a definite correlation between the amount of burnout and the burden placed on the mom, or the women in the family or that the women begin thinking that it's her job to take on the responsibility of everybody's wellness in the family. While often the male partner thinks his responsibility is only to make money. Most of us are working, and many of us are taking care of children, we're taking care of seniors, we're not sleeping, we're feeling uncomfortable in our bodies, and we're gaining weight. We're having trouble seeing. We're having issues with digestion and pain, etc   Women need more help, and we have been demanding more help, one person at a time. My services aim to end the confusion and help women find clarity and a path back to strength and resilience!

Bio

I am a second-generation musician and yogi; my parents studied Transcendental meditation and were award-winning musicians. I have a classical music degree, a jazz diploma, and a yoga therapy certificate. I have even written the "Music Theory Coloring Book," to aid divergent learners in achieving their musical goals. I have encouraged many women to return to school, leave unhealthy relationships, and pursue their life's purpose. I have extensive experience with event planning and doing interviews, and I started my support group, CPMS (Canadian Perimenopause and Menopause Support) in 2021. This group is growing at about 4%, mainly from women inviting other women. I have been coaching women in peri and post-menopause since 2019. I was raised in Toronto, where equity, diversity, and inclusion are necessary for survival. I am happily married and have been with the same partner since 1998. I have two grown sons, a daughter in law, three granddaughters, a dog, and two cats.

Sonia Rodrigues-

Resilient Paths: Guiding Women through Challenges to Embrace Post-Traumatic Growth

As a first-generation European-American woman, my journey has included diverse roles: I'm a daughter, a mother, a partner, a psychotherapist, an entrepreneur, and a passionate advocate. For over 22 years, I've immersed myself in the field of psychotherapy, working in a variety of settings—from school-based mental health programs and outpatient clinics to rape crisis centers and private practices. I have primarily focused on helping children, adolescents, and adults navigate the complexities of trauma, while also advocating for the rights and needs of families in underserved communities.

I have secured several grants aimed at enhancing mental health services in schools and developing innovative programs to expand behavioral health resources for those in need. My commitment to philanthropy has led me to serve on boards for educational institutions and nonprofit organizations dedicated to supporting underserved youth and survivors of domestic abuse.

Additionally, I have had the privilege of sharing my insights at conferences, addressing issues such as teen stress and anxiety, the integration of mindfulness in educational settings, and the unique challenges faced by immigrant and Latinx youth in our schools. My written work explores emotional health and wellness and have collaborated with organizations to revamp their organizations to better promote the emotional and physical well-being of their communities. Through each role I embrace, I strive to make a meaningful impact in the lives of those I serve. My work experience along with my own trauma narrative have led me to focus on helping others heal and embrace their own narratives as opportunities for post-traumatic growth.

We All Have a Journey

Being the daughter of an immigrant family has shaped a journey filled with personal growth, cultural insight, and a deep commitment to helping others in need. Growing up, I witnessed the challenges my parents faced as they adapted to a new culture, often working tirelessly to support us. Their sacrifices fueled my empathy and inspired me to seize the opportunities they fought so hard to create. From a young age, I felt a strong urge to follow a path that would honor their struggles and allow me to make a meaningful impact in the world around me.

As I progressed through school, my academic achievements became a source of pride for my family. However, balancing cultural expectations with personal aspirations was often challenging. My desire to pursue higher education and a career that could make a difference sometimes clashed with traditional expectation combined with a lack of financial resources. Despite these tensions, I remained focused on my goal of achieving more and finding a way to give back to others who were struggling and wanted more for their life.

During my college years, I became deeply involved in community service and volunteer work. These experiences were eye-opening, revealing the profound impact that support and compassion could have on individuals facing various struggles. I found myself drawn to roles where I could provide emotional support, guidance, and advocacy. This realization was a turning point, solidifying my decision to pursue a career in a field that would allow me to help others professionally. Driven by a passion for helping others, I pursued a career in psychotherapy. My academic and professional training provided the tools and theoretical framework to support clients through their struggles. However, it was also during this period that I began to confront my own unresolved issues which particularly showed up in my relationships. The more I learned about psychological theories and therapeutic techniques, the more I realized how one's personal trauma can be so impactful on their lives.

My journey into the professional world of helping others involved rigorous academic training and hands-on experience. As I immersed myself in my field, I encountered both the rewards and the challenges of this work. It was during this period that I began to really think about how I wanted to make an impact on the world through my professional work and learned that many people who become psychotherapists do so after learning how to heal themselves. My training and experiences taught me that balancing the demands of life and making sense of our personal experiences requires continuous self-reflection and growth. Learning how to weave the intricacies of our past with our future goals and making sense of the things that happen to us can help us all lead happier, healthier lives.

As I advanced in my career, I embraced my identity as a daughter of an immigrant family. I recognized that my unique perspective allowed me to connect with others who faced similar struggles, providing a bridge of understanding and support. I became committed to using my experiences to empower others, particularly those from marginalized backgrounds, and to advocate for systemic changes that could improve their lives.

I began to use my platform to raise awareness about the issues faced by immigrant communities and other marginalized groups. This included engaging in public speaking, writing articles, and collaborating with organizations focused on social justice and support services. By amplifying the voices of those who often went unheard, I aimed to create a broader impact to drive positive change.

The journey to finding my purpose has been one of continuous learning and evolution. Each client interaction, each community engagement, and each personal challenge has contributed to my understanding of what it means to make a meaningful difference. I have learned that purpose is not a fixed destination but an ongoing process of aligning my actions with my values and passions.

As I advanced in my career and also experienced my own trauma, I felt compelled to advocate for others who faced relational trauma. I began to engage in public speaking, write articles, and participate in workshops aimed at raising awareness about trauma and the importance of mental health. I also became very focused on teaching survivors of trauma about post-traumatic growth. This advocacy work became a way to channel my experiences into broader societal impact.

A significant turning point came when I faced a major relational trauma in my own life. This experience was a crucible that tested my emotional resilience and professional skills. It was a time of intense vulnerability and self-exploration. This period of pain was also a profound opportunity for growth. It pushed me to do my own internal healing and to connect with other women who had experienced similar trauma.

As I worked through my personal trauma, I found that my experiences made me an even more empathetic and effective therapist. I could understand and relate to my clients' pain in a more nuanced way This intersection of personal and professional growth became a cornerstone of my practice. My own healing journey informed my approach, blending compassion with insight and personal experience. Through this process, I began to redefine my sense of purpose. I realized that my journey was not just about helping others but also about integrating my own experiences into my professional identity. I became more committed to using my experiences to foster a therapeutic environment where clients could feel understood and supported.

Embracing my own vulnerability became a strength. It allowed me to connect with clients on a deeper level and to model resilience and growth. This shift was not without its challenges. It required continuous self-reflection and a commitment to personal growth. I learned to balance my professional role with self-care, ensuring that my work did not become an avenue for my own unresolved issues but rather a space for mutual healing.

My current work continues to be focused on expanding my impact, both professionally and personally. I aspire to mentor others who share similar backgrounds and dreams, helping them navigate their own paths and find their own purpose. My journey is not only about my own growth but also about paving the way for others to achieve their potential and contribute to the greater good.

In reflecting on my own journey, I learned that figuring out what one's purpose in life is often the result of a combination of personal experiences, cultural experiences, and professional training. Furthermore, it has been defined by the commitment to honoring my family's sacrifices, embracing my unique identity, and dedicating myself to helping others who are facing their own struggles. I see it as a tapestry woven with threads of pain, healing, and purpose. My experiences with relational trauma have profoundly shaped my approach to therapy and my commitment to helping others navigate their own journeys. This path has ultimately led me to a place of profound meaning and purpose both in my personal and professional life.

The journey of being a Woman of Purpose is ongoing. Each client interaction, each personal challenge, and each new development in the field of psychotherapy contributes to my evolving understanding of purpose. It is a continuous process of learning, growing, and re-evaluating my path. I am clear however, that my purpose is to help women heal from trauma and turn their experiences into opportunities for learning and growth as well as guiding them towards creating the life they desire.

Understanding Trauma and Its Impact

Trauma is a complex and deeply personal experience that profoundly affects individuals on emotional, psychological, and physiological levels. It arises as an emotional response to shocking or distressing events, which can range from physical violence and emotional abuse to accidents, natural disasters, or significant losses. What constitutes a traumatic event is highly subjective; for instance, two people may witness the same incident, yet one may find it traumatic while the other does not. The impact of trauma varies based on an individual's personal history, resilience, and coping mechanisms, often altering their worldview, self-esteem, and emotional well-being.

Consider someone who has experienced a severe car accident: the immediate aftermath may trigger acute trauma characterized by overwhelming fear and helplessness. Over time, this can evolve into chronic distress, manifesting as persistent flashbacks, nightmares, and anxiety. Such ongoing stress may lead to behavioral changes like avoiding driving or withdrawing from loved ones, straining relationships due to diminished trust. Physically, trauma can result in symptoms such as headaches and fatigue, reflecting the body's response to emotional stress. However, with appropriate therapy, support systems, and self-care, individuals can navigate the challenging path to recovery, gradually reclaiming their lives and discovering resilience and renewal.

There are three different types of trauma. Individuals can experience acute trauma which occurs as a result of experiencing a single distressing event. Chronic trauma arises from repeated or prolonged exposure to distressing events and complex trauma involves exposure to multiple, varied traumatic events, often occurring within the context of interpersonal relationships. Regardless of which type of trauma one experiences, it is essential to find ways to heal and recover from each traumatic experience. The impact of trauma can be profound and long-lasting, but with the right support and interventions, individuals can work through their traumatic experiences and go on to lead fulfilling lives. In fact, for many individuals, their traumatic experiences can at times, be the conduit needed for changing something instrumental in their lives that sets them on a more successful trajectory. Some individuals may experience positive change or personal growth as a result of their trauma, finding new meaning or strength. This concept is referred to as post-traumatic growth.

Post-traumatic growth (PTG) refers to the positive psychological change that can occur as a result of struggling with highly challenging life circumstances. While trauma is often associated with negative outcomes like post-traumatic stress disorder, PTG explains how people can grow and find new meaning or strength as a result of their traumatic experience or of struggling with a highly challenging life circumstance. While trauma is often associated with negative outcomes and symptoms, PTG suggests how people can grow and learn from their traumatic experience and find new meaning or strength in what happened to them. Understanding PTG in your own life can lead to greater appreciation for one's life and recognizing one's personal strength and resilience. Top of Form Bottom of Form

Self-Reflection and Purpose Discovery

When reflecting on the values that drive me and shape my approach to supporting others and facilitating their growth, I find that several core principles guide my work and interactions. Empathy and connection are the cornerstone of my approach. Understanding and genuinely feeling the experiences and emotions of others allows me to connect deeply and provide meaningful support. By putting myself in others' shoes, I can better appreciate their perspectives, validate their feelings, and tailor my support to meet their unique needs. This empathetic stance fosters trust and creates a safe space for growth and creates the path towards deeper connections with others.

Respect for individuals' backgrounds, choices, and experiences is fundamental. I believe in honoring each person's autonomy and valuing their contributions. This respect not only helps in building strong, trusting relationships but also empowers individuals to express themselves openly and engage more fully in their own development.

Having integrity and being consistent are also key values. Maintaining ethical standards and being transparent in my interactions is extremely important for me. Fostering trust and credibility, and ensuring the support I provide is dependable and rooted in sincere intentions, are integral parts of this process. Approaching others with compassion, kindness and understanding is also essential. My experience has compelled me to provide support that is not just professional but also heartfelt. By showing compassion, I aim to alleviate suffering, encourage resilience, and foster a nurturing environment where individuals feel valued and cared for.

Facilitating personal and professional growth is a major focus for me. I believe in empowering individuals by helping them identify their strengths, set goals, and overcome challenges. My approach focuses on fostering self-efficacy, encouraging continuous learning, and supporting people in realizing their full potential.

Inclusivity shapes how I approach support and interaction. I strive to create an environment where everyone feels welcome, valued, and heard. By embracing diversity and actively addressing biases, I aim to ensure that all voices are included and that everyone has equitable opportunities for growth and success.

Collaboration is essential in my approach to supporting others. I believe in working together to achieve common goals, drawing on collective strengths and insights. By fostering a collaborative spirit, I aim to build partnerships that enhance learning, problem-solving, and mutual support.

These values—empathy, respect, integrity, compassion, growth and empowerment, inclusivity, and collaboration—are the foundation of my approach. They guide how I interact with and support others, ensuring that my efforts are aligned with fostering meaningful, positive change in their lives.

My purpose is to empower women to achieve their full potential by offering compassionate support, providing valuable resources, and creating programs that foster personal and professional growth. This purpose aligns with my core values and addresses the needs of the women I aim to help. I am dedicated to providing empathetic and respectful support to women at various stages of their lives. This involves actively listening to their experiences, understanding their unique challenges, and offering guidance that is both validating and constructive. By creating a safe and nurturing environment, I help women navigate their struggles, celebrate their successes, and build confidence in their abilities. Access to the right resources can significantly impact a woman's ability to grow and succeed. I aim to connect women with relevant tools, information, and opportunities that can facilitate their development. This includes offering educational materials, professional networks, mentorship opportunities, and practical resources tailored to their individual needs and goals.

To address diverse needs and aspirations, I develop and implement programs designed to foster personal and professional growth. These programs may include workshops, training sessions, and support groups that focus on skill development, leadership, mental health, and self-care. By tailoring these programs to the specific needs of women, I ensure they are both relevant and impactful.

Understanding that each woman's journey is unique, my purpose involves being responsive to her specific needs and aspirations. By providing personalized support and creating adaptable programs, I address the diverse challenges women face and help them overcome barriers to success.

In summary, my purpose is to empower women through compassionate support, valuable resources, and growth-oriented programs. This purpose reflects my core values and is designed to meet the needs of the women I aim to help, fostering an environment where they can thrive and achieve their full potential.

Developing Support Strategies

My advice for women is to develop support strategies as well as build a strong support system. Building trusting relationships, whether in personal or professional contexts, is fundamental to effective interactions and successful outcomes. Developing support strategies for fostering these relationships involves a combination of empathy, communication, and consistency. Trust is built through consistent, respectful, and empathetic interactions, and maintaining it requires ongoing effort and attention.

In my experience working with women who have experienced trauma, heartache or despair, it is often difficult for them to trust others. Naturally their guard is up and they want to distance themselves from others because they do not want to get hurt again. Therefore it is crucial to find ways to surround oneself with compassionate and empathic individuals in an effort to create a safe and supportive environment for themselves. A sense of safety and trust is fundamental for effective healing. Exploring ways to connect with others who have experienced similar hardships can create a sense of connectedness and feeling like you are not alone in your healing journey. Asking one another what strategies have been helpful during one's healing process and sharing resources along with serving as a support system can be someone's sense of purpose. It surely helped lead to mine. I knew after my own traumatic experience that I wanted to create a process that would help other women who had experienced similar challenges, I wanted to come up with resources and strategies that would help them move through the healing process faster and stronger.

Empowerment through education, particularly in the context of trauma and post-traumatic growth (PTG), can be profoundly beneficial. Understanding what happened to them and making sense of their trauma can lead them towards post-traumatic growth. The process of post-traumatic growth helps move women away from a victim mentality and into a survivor and thriver mentality. Educating women about trauma and PTG not only fosters personal growth and resilience but also enhances their ability to support themselves and others. Furthermore, empowerment and understanding enhances emotional and psychology healing, supports the development of a growth mindset, empowers leadership and advocacy for causes that are important to them, facilitates access to resources and enhances overall well-being.

Setting realistic goals for oneself can aid in healing and growth. This process can be helpful in terms of healing, understanding why you experienced the challenges you experienced and in identifying your purpose. Using a structured and supportive approach that breaks down larger objectives into manageable steps can be a useful strategy. Start by identifying what you want to achieve by setting goals that are meaningful and relevant to your personal story.

Utilizing the SMART criteria to set goals that are Specific, Measurable, Achievable, Relevant, and Time-bound can be one approach. Focus on addressing immediate needs first before moving to long-term aspirations. Another approach could be to create an action plan that outlines specific steps to achieve each goal. Divide larger goals into smaller, manageable mini-goals. Mini-goals can act as stepping stones towards a larger goal and help build momentum. These are two examples one could try to implement:

- Mini-Goal 1: Read one article or watch a video about mindfulness each week.
- Mini-Goal 2: Practice mindfulness for 5 minutes, then gradually increase to 10 minutes.

Identifying resources and support systems, such as therapy, support groups, or local community organizations, can assist in achieving your goals. Networking can be another great resource that helps you foster connections with others who share similar goals or experiences. Support groups and peer networks can provide encouragement and accountability and make you feel like you are not alone. Scheduling regular check-ins to review progress, address challenges, and adjust goals as needed on a weekly, bi-weekly, or monthly basis can ensure momentum. Do not forget to reflect on what has been accomplished and how far you have come. Recognizing progress can help you staying motivated.

Be flexible and open to adjusting goals based on changing circumstances or new insights. It is important to make changes as necessary and adapt the goals as needed to stay relevant and achievable. New goals or areas for growth may emerge, and it's essential to integrate these into the overall plan. Lastly, promoting self-compassion and patience during the healing and self-discovery process is critical. It is important to recognize that healing and growth are gradual processes and that occasional setbacks are part of the process. Fostering resilience occurs when one can view challenges as opportunities for learning and growth rather than as failures.

Creating Opportunities for Growth

One major catalyst for healing can be creating opportunities for growth. Essentially you work on reconnecting with any parts of yourself that you have put aside which can include making time for things you used to enjoy or interests you did not have the time for. For example, this can include someone who grows up dancing their whole life but gave it up after starting their career or raising a family. Reconnecting with activities that brought us joy in earlier years can allow us reconnect with younger versions of ourselves and positive memories we once experienced. Life and its challenges sometimes has a way of causing us to focus on others while forgetting to take care of ourselves in the process. Learning new skills or strategies can also help us heal and move towards fostering resilience. Identifying new ways to cope with our challenges and taking care of ourselves helps us work through the healing process by allowing us to find strength in ourselves and our abilities to navigate tumultuous situations. When we have new information and strategies to use, we often feel confident about setting goals and moving forward with our lives. Utilizing techniques such as mindfulness, breathing techniques, and incorporating a mind/body approach to healing can give us the tools we need to navigate life's challenges. Adopting a mind/body approach to healing guides us towards making connections between how the things that happen to us impact us emotionally, physically, and spiritually. Therefore, when something traumatic occurs in our life, we need to take care of our mind, our body and our spiritual self.

The journey to self-discovery allows us to make sense of the things that happen to us and encourage us to find meaning in the trauma. Many will say things such as, "if this had not happened to me then I would not be where I am today," or "I'm stronger because of what I endured," or "I am so grateful that I was able to see how toxic that was for me because I have a peace in my life I could not have ever imagines" These phrases are from women who have made sense of their challenges and recognize that they needed to ensure their challenges in order to be where they are today. It is often hard to see that while in the midst of the trauma or shortly thereafter. This kind of insight comes later, after you have done the work. The work can include making sense of things by journaling and reflecting on what occurred and why and making connections to why things may have happened and what they mean to you. Asking how does this connect to my past and what does this mean for my future can be two prompts you use. Using creative ways to express yourself can also be very beneficial, such as through art, music or dance. Utilizing self-reflection exercises can help us explore our identities, values and beliefs post-trauma. These exercises can lead towards creating a clear vision of what you want in your future and how to get there.

Another approach to healing and creating opportunities for growth is to building strong support networks, many women call this their "tribe". Who do you want in your tribe? Who will support you and encourage your personal growth? Find them, connect with them and support each other. Connecting with others who have faced similar challenges can provide a sense of solidarity, validation, and additional perspectives on the healing journey. Everyone will have their own stories and strategies and sharing them with one another can foster a tremendous sense of connectedness. Connections with others is the antidote to loneliness, sadness, depression, anxiety and so many others. Find your tribe and grow together!

Celebrate Your Growth and Achievements

Acknowledging and celebrating important milestones and successes, no matter how small helps reinforce the belief in one's ability to overcome challenges and leaves us feeling accomplished. Have you ever looked back on something difficult you've accomplished or work through and said to yourself, "Wow, I can't believe I did it!" Create as many opportunities to say this to yourself. Each small achievement helps. We run marathons one mile at a time. We climb ladders one step at a time. Celebrate your wins!

Celebrating your wins allows you to reflect on your growth. Reflect on how your trauma or your challenges and adversities have led to your growth. Explore how your perspective has changed, and what personal growth or development occurred in the process. This reflection will help you understand the post-traumatic growth that occurred and explore ways to integrate these insights into your everyday life.

Sustaining Growth

Recognize that healing and growth are continuous processes and maintaining a support system helps sustain the progress made. Be prepared for obstacles or triggers because they will show up from time to time, this does not mean you have not done the work, it is just part of life and the healing journey. Remind yourself of the strategies that are most effective for you in navigating challenges and be prepared to use them from time to time.

Adapting to Change is also another key factor in ensuring you sustain your growth perspective. Recognize that as we grow and evolve, our needs and goals will change so its important to check in with ourselves and our goals from time to time to make sure we are always in alignment. Adaptability and flexibility are necessary for continuous growth. Throughout this process, help others along the way and help advocate for change when necessary to ensure other women do not suffer in the same ways you did. Whenever possible, advocate for change and be someone who breaks the cycle of trauma. This can be empowering and help us find additional meaning in our journey's. Our story and journey leads us to find our sense of purpose. I know mine did.

Conclusion

This chapter emphasizes the importance of creating robust support systems and developing effective strategies to foster trusting relationships, particularly for women who have experienced trauma. Building connections based on empathy, communication, and consistency, are crucial for healing and growth. Past trauma can make it difficult for women to trust others, underscoring the need for compassionate environments that facilitate emotional safety. Sharing experiences with those who have faced similar hardships can create a sense of solidarity and support, which is vital for healing.

Empowerment can be fostered through education as a pathway to post-traumatic growth (PTG), helping women shift from a victim mentality to one of survival and thriving. By setting realistic, structured goals—using the SMART criteria and breaking them into manageable mini-goals—women can navigate their healing journeys more effectively. We learned that the identification of resources, support groups, and networks that provide encouragement and accountability can aid in the process of healing and fostering PTG.

Reconnecting with personal interests and activities that bring joy, as well as adopting mind/body approaches to healing can be powerful for healing. Reflective practices, such as journaling and creative expression, can aid in making sense of our trauma and envisioning a fulfilling future.

Building a strong support network, or "tribe," will foster connection and help combat feelings of isolation. Remember to celebrate your achievements and that healing is an ongoing process. Your personal journey can lead to greater advocacy for change, fostering resilience and purpose.

I believe that one of the most powerful things we all hold onto is our story. Our story defines us and serves as a guide for our life. Quite often women feel lost, scared and confused after a traumatic event "Why me?" they ask. The reality is that we all deal with adversities, our power shows up when we explore why they happen to us and how can we grow from them. Finding our purpose and transforming trauma into growth involves a combination of empathy, education, empowerment, and ongoing support. It requires us to ask "How do I make sense of this? What is this teaching me?" instead of asking "Why me?" By understanding our trauma and adversities, reflecting on our personal values, tailoring strategies to overcome our challenges, and celebrating our growth, we go through a transformative process that turns our adversities into opportunities for profound learning and discovery. I wish you all luck in your journey's. You've got this!

Bio

Sonia Rodrigues has been a licensed psychotherapist for 20 years. She is the owner of a psychotherapy and coaching practice called Transition to Wellness. She has worked with people of all ages, helping them navigate various challenges in their life. She utilizes a holistic approach and provides a safe and supportive environment where her clients can feel supported on their path towards healing from their traumatic experiences and she guides them towards creating the life they desire. She provides individual therapy and coaching and also offers a variety of presentations and workshops on topics related to trauma, post-traumatic growth and fostering resilience.

References:

Block, P. (2008). *Community: The Structure of Belonging*. Berrett-Koehler Publishers.

Brown, B. (2018). *Dare to Lead: Brave Work. Tough Conversations. Whole Hearts*. Random House.

Covey, S. R. (1989). *The 7 Habits of Highly Effective People: Powerful Lessons in Personal Change*. Free Press.

Duckworth, A. (2016). *Grit: The Power of Passion and Perseverance*. Scribner.

Dweck, C. S. (2006). *Mindset: The New Psychology of Success*. Random House.

Goleman, D. (1995). *Emotional Intelligence: Why It Can Matter More Than IQ*. Bantam Books.

Rogers, C. (1961). *On Becoming a Person: A Therapist's View of Psychotherapy*. Houghton Mifflin.

Suzy Rawlins-

When Faith Leads the Way

Through every challenging situation as an adult, my faith and the grace of God have been my guiding lights. They have carried me through the darkest valleys and lifted me to new heights. My story is one of resilience, determination, and an unwavering belief in the power of faith. Overcoming the immense challenges of being a two-time cancer survivor and a single mom, with God's help, I transformed my life, ultimately becoming a holistic health and wellness coach dedicated to helping others find their paths to healing and fulfillment. Before we get to that, let's take a few steps back.

Growing up, I had influential mentors and unique, loving people who instilled deep values in me. My mom was a single mom and a teacher, and she gave us abundant love. My dad was not always around, but I watched him work hard all my life. My grandparents had a powerful presence in my life, and I have a tremendous amount of respect and admiration for them. I was even blessed to have a babysitter, her family was essential to growing up. Growing up in the country and with incredible mentors taught me the values of family, hard work, resilience, and finding joy in the small things.

As a kid, I developed an authoritarian personality on the outside. I was that skinny, kind of awkward girl. I was unpopular, although I had a small group of close friends. I am blessed to say that to this day, I am still friends with them almost forty years later. I was picked on a lot because I was the schoolteacher's daughter, or not great at sports, or not the smartest. My childhood experiences helped me find my resilience. I remember thinking in about third grade if they were going to make fun of me, I would give them something to make fun of. So, I chose to wear mismatched clothes or put my hair in piggy tails. Hey, if you cannot beat them, join them.

Growing up, I was not raised in church and did not understand what faith was. Sure, we had attainable studies with friends now and then. It was not until I was sixteen, attending church with a boyfriend, that I met a pastor who helped me understand what it meant to have a relationship with Jesus. I chose to be baptized and surrender my life to Him.

As a teen and young adult, I discovered the transformative power of exercise. It became my sanctuary, a few churches, and it had become a way to step outside my thoughts and find clarity in the rhythm of movement. In high school, I was introduced to weightlifting and running. These activities quickly became more than just physical workouts—they were an escape, a way to channel my energy and emotions into something positive. The gym became a place to push my limits and build physical strength and mental resilience—running offered a similar release, allowing me to clear my mind and reconnect with my inner self, one step at a time.

After high school, I felt the intense pressure of attending college, even though I was not drawn to it. I almost joined the military to get out of college. I moved out of the house while attending community college. I completed a year of classes before I chose to pause my education until I knew what I wanted to do. Not long after that, I decided to get married and move to Washington state, 1500 miles from everyone and everything I had ever known. As a newlywed to a U.S. Navy sailor, life quickly took on a new rhythm, vastly different from anything I had experienced. Leaving behind my familiar surroundings, support system, and the life I had built up to that point, I was stepping into a world of unknowns. The Pacific Northwest, with its misty mornings and lush green landscapes, became the backdrop for the next chapter of my life. I had to learn to adjust to the challenges of military life. This was my first giant leap of faith.

This marriage blessed me with two beautiful boys who have filled my life with immeasurable joy and purpose. However, the marriage itself was not all rainbows. Being in a marriage that was both mentally and emotionally toxic took a significant toll on my spirit. The constant negativity and emotional manipulation created an environment where it was difficult to lean into God, especially since my partner did not share my Christian faith. I struggled to find solace and support amidst the turmoil, often feeling isolated in my beliefs. Yet, through quiet, persistent prayer and seeking God's guidance, I gradually found the strength to recognize that I deserved a healthier, more supportive environment. Ultimately, through my unwavering faith and divine guidance, I gathered the courage to leave the marriage and begin a journey of healing and self-discovery. This was indeed my next giant leap of faith.

As a single mom, raising two boys alone presented its own set of challenges. I am eternally grateful for the abundant support and guidance that my mom gave me. I was juggling multiple jobs to keep us afloat, all while managing the physical and emotional toll of my health problems. There were countless nights of exhaustion, worry, and uncertainty about how I would make it through. But every time I looked into my sons 'eyes, I found the motivation to keep pushing forward.

My days were a delicate balance of work and parenting. Yet, I discovered a deep resilience during these challenging times. Each obstacle became a stepping stone toward a greater understanding of my strengths and capabilities. Leaning into God during tough times as a single mom gave me the strength and peace I needed to carry on. When the world's weight felt too heavy, I found solace in prayer, trusting God guided me through every challenge. In those quiet moments of faith, I discovered a source of resilience and hope that reminded me I was never truly alone on this journey.

After experiencing several unsettling symptoms, I knew something wasn't right and decided to visit the doctor for answers. It was through a series of tests and exams that the news came: cancerous cells had been found. When I was first diagnosed with cancer, my world turned upside down. The fear, uncertainty, and physical toll were overwhelming, yet I knew I had to fight not just for myself but for my two young boys who depended on me. I decided to keep this diagnosis private, confiding only in one close friend who prayed with me daily. Thankfully, I was fortunate enough to avoid chemotherapy, only needing several surgeries to remove the cancer cells. Faith became my anchor during the two years that I was under the care of my gynecologists, giving me the strength to face each day with courage.

I prayed for guidance in my career, seeking a path that aligned with my passions and purpose. This prayer led me to massage therapy school, where I felt a deep sense of belonging. As a natural human anatomy enthusiast, the coursework resonated with me profoundly, making me feel like I was exactly where I was meant to be. My education in massage therapy was a blessing, not only because it deepened my understanding of the body but also because it provided insights into my past and present health challenges. Just two weeks after graduation, I faced a life-changing surgery, which prevented me from obtaining my massage license as I focused on my health. Yet, I believe it was no accident that God led me to massage school; it was part of a more excellent plan, preparing me with the knowledge and tools I needed for my healing journey and the path ahead.

Little did I know that the battle wasn't over after the first diagnosis. After a second about of cancer, I tested my resolve even further. While attending massage therapy school, I became seriously ill, prompting doctors to run numerous tests to find a diagnosis. Just before graduation, they determined that my thyroid needed to be removed. After surgery, a biopsy revealed the growth was cancerous. I underwent two rounds of radiation and several more tests before being officially cleared as cancer-free. Yet, my faith grew more robust, as did my determination to survive and thrive.

Meeting my husband, Guy, during my time in massage school was like finding the missing piece that completed our family. From the moment we came into each other's lives, he embraced my boys with open arms and a whole heart, loving them as if they were his own. He never hesitated or questioned his role; he stepped in and became their needed father figure. His presence brought a sense of wholeness and stability that we had been missing, turning us from a small unit into a family full of love and connection. His unwavering support and genuine love transformed our lives in ways I could have only imagined, making us a true family. I believe God led him to us at the perfect time, knowing he would be the one to fill the gaps in our hearts and make our family whole. He was by my side through the second bout with cancer.

Shortly after we got married, several things changed. Guy supported my decision to become an entrepreneur, which I will discuss later. Life threw us an unexpected curveball when my husband was laid off from his job. It was challenging, but we trusted God had a plan for us. With limited options locally in Arizona, he made the difficult decision to take work out of state in Texas, where he is originally from. We both felt God leading us toward this move, sensing it was part of a bigger plan. During this time, I traveled back and forth between states, determined to support him and keep our connection strong despite the distance. The road was not always easy; God was with me through several flat tires and even a close call with a potential robbery. The separation was rigid on us, especially soon after starting our life together. We had to navigate the challenges of maintaining our marriage across the miles while balancing our daily life demands.

Despite the distance, his commitment to providing for our family never wavered, and our faith kept us connected and strong. This experience, though challenging, taught us the importance of resilience and trust in God's timing as we worked through this season with hope and determination. Despite the challenges, this period allowed us to spend precious time with his family, creating memories we wouldn't trade for anything. Although we ultimately couldn't move to Texas permanently, those trips were filled with moments of grace and growth. It was a season of learning about each other and trusting God's guidance, even when the path didn't unfold as planned.

Another trial that God brought our family through was losing our home; we had only been renting it for approximately eight months. Losing our home to a house fire was a challenging and frightening experience. It happened in the middle of the night, and I still remember the terrifying sound of the fire alarm jolting us awake and that awful smell of our burnt belongings. We had to act quickly, walking through flames to help our boys out of their bedrooms. Thankfully, we all made it out safely, including our pets, but the trauma of that night left us shaken and uncertain about the future. We will never forget standing outside in the cold in our pj's, watching the incredible firefighters do their jobs.

In the aftermath, we faced the overwhelming reality of losing everything we had worked so hard for. But what could have been a devastating low point was transformed by our community's outpouring of love and support. My sister, unsure how to help, posted on social media, highlighting how I was connected to some truly unique people through my Mary Kay business and networking. The response was nothing short of overwhelming. Friends, acquaintances, and even strangers rallied around us, offering help in ways we never expected. We received more than we could ever ask for: donations, essentials, and, most importantly, the reassurance that we were not alone. The experience was a powerful reminder of the strength of community and the impact of the relationships we had nurtured over the years. Though the fire took our home, it also revealed the depth of the support we had around us, turning what could have been a tragic loss into a profound testament to love, resilience, and the power of human connection.

After the house fire, we were blessed to have a dear friend help us find an incredible rental just down the street from her. It was a perfect fit for our family during a challenging time, and our boys quickly became friends with the kid next door. The neighborhood became a hub of joy and connection, with several get-togethers that filled our lives with laughter and cherished memories. Settling into our new home brought a wave of decisions and adjustments. One of our most significant choices was to homeschool our boys, a conclusion reached through prayer and reflection. As we navigated this new chapter, it became clear that homeschooling would offer us the flexibility we needed, allowing us to spend more quality family time together and tailor our children's education to our values and needs.

To enrich their experience, we also enrolled them in 4H, which opened doors to enriching activities and life lessons. 4H is a youth development program that aims to help kids learn new skills and have fun while contributing to their communities. Both of our boys decided to show hogs. This was a huge learning curve; I needed to learn about showing livestock. This program provided them with hands-on experiences and fostered a sense of community and responsibility. Showing hogs at the county fair was quite the experience, and both boys won several awards during their time in 4H. Homeschooling was one of our best decisions, as it allowed us to incorporate our faith into our daily learning and brought us closer as a family.

During this transformative period, I developed a morning routine that became a cornerstone of my day. Each morning, I would sit with my coffee and spend ten minutes reading my Bible, grounding myself in God's promises and seeking His direction for our lives. This daily ritual helped me stay centered and reminded me of the divine guidance shaping our journey.

We were fortunate to call this house our home for two years before the owner decided to sell, marking the end of a beautiful chapter. Initially, we thought our need to move across town to another county was driven by a lack of availability to fit our needs. This logistical necessity seemed more practical than inspired. However, as we reflected on the journey, it became clear that God's hand guided us. What we saw as a challenging relocation was part of a more excellent plan, leading us to a place where we could find a new home and a more profound sense of connection and purpose. This move brought us closer to family and opened doors for new opportunities, revealing that what we once perceived as a mere necessity was a divine orchestration aligning our lives with His greater purpose. This is when we landed in Maricopa, AZ.

About five months before our big move, my 89-year-old great-uncle came to live with us, allowing us to take on the role of his caregiver. This experience, while demanding, provided us with profound lessons in patience, compassion, and the importance of family. Caring for him was both a privilege and a challenge, and it brought us closer together as we navigated this new chapter of our lives. The responsibility of caregiving taught us to appreciate the small moments and to support each other with unwavering love, reinforcing the values that would guide us through the transition to our new home.

Our move to Maricopa, AZ, felt like a clear manifestation of God's divine plan unfolding in our lives. Okay, let's be honest. It took us about two years to realize this. Maricopa offered a fresh start, supportive community, and opportunities we hadn't anticipated. It was as if every step of the process was guided by a higher hand, orchestrating our path to ensure we were in the right place at the right time. This move reinforced our trust in God's plan, revealing how His guidance can lead us to unexpected blessings and new beginnings.

It was here in Maricopa that I had to build a new customer base. Shortly after marrying Guy, I joined Mary Kay and pursued a full-time career as an entrepreneur. This journey led me to forge incredible friendships and connections, and I was profoundly blessed by the support and faith of many remarkable women in the Mary Kay community. God's direction to join Mary Kay was pivotal to my divine purpose. It guided me toward a path where I could build a fulfilling career and connect with a community of like-minded, faith-driven women. This opportunity aligned perfectly with my calling, allowing me to grow personally and professionally while making a meaningful impact on the lives of others. I started this career about seven years before moving to Maricopa, so now I would have customers spread all over.

Another reason I know why God brought us to Maricopa is because That is where I met Dr. Yolanda Rodriguez, a Naturopathic Doctor. This is when my personal healing journey took a profound transformation. At a time when I felt as though my body was on the verge of quitting, this ND stepped into my life with a solution that would change everything. Her approach was a revelation. Instead of offering quick fixes or temporary relief, she emphasized the importance of addressing the root causes of my symptoms and fostering genuine healing.

My health issues presented as persistent fatigue, discomfort, and an overall sense of imbalance. It became clear that these symptoms were more than just minor inconveniences—they were signals that my body was struggling with underlying problems. The ND's guidance uncovered that my ailments were primarily related to significant lymphatic and digestive issues, all of which were intricately linked to food sensitivities. She encouraged me to focus on holistic wellness rather than merely masking symptoms. This approach was a game-changer for me. It required a shift in perspective, embracing the idea that true healing involves listening to my body's needs and making lifestyle adjustments to address them. Through her support, I learned the importance of not just managing symptoms but actively working towards a complete recovery. Our relationship blossomed into a deep and meaningful friendship, and I am eternally grateful for her guidance and the new path she helped me discover. This journey began a more profound and lasting healing process that continues to shape my approach to health and well-being.

By having more energy and feeling better, I could return to activities I love, weightlifting, and spending more time in nature. I also discovered new, like hiking, a passion for CrossFit, and paddle boarding Completing three 5K races and finishing with an average time for my age group felt a significant accomplishment, especially in my 40s. It was a reminder that age is just a number and that we can continue to achieve our goals at any stage with dedication and consistent effort. Crossing those finish lines was more than just a physical achievement; it was a testament to my resilience and commitment to staying active and healthy. These activities became more than exercise; they were integral to my healing journey. As I reconnected with my active self and felt my vitality return, I realized that this transformation was more than a personal victory—a testament to the power of living intentionally.

Taking control of my health through holistic practices was a pivotal moment in my journey, transforming my life in ways I never imagined. After discovering the root causes of my health issues and implementing a holistic approach under the guidance of my naturopathic doctor, I began to experience profound changes. Embracing a lifestyle centered on natural healing and mindful living allowed me to regain my vitality and energy. I found renewed joy in activities that had once seemed out of reach, such as hiking and working out. These activities were not just physical exercises; they became vital components of my healing process and a testament to the effectiveness of holistic health practices.

As I reconnected with my active self and felt the strength and wellness returning to my life, I realized how transformative this journey had been. The empowerment I felt from taking control of my health

It was profoundly motivating and inspired me to share what I had learned and experienced with others. This passion for holistic health and my personal success story led me to pursue a career as a holistic health and wellness coach. In this role, I am dedicated to guiding others on their paths to wellness, helping them live intentionally and embrace a balanced, healthy lifestyle.

My faith has bolstered my resilience, helping me not just to survive but to thrive. Faith has guided me in every significant event, leading me through triumphs and trials as I reflect on the journey that brought me here. From the uncertainty of leaving college and navigating the complexities of marriage and divorce to facing health crises and enduring a house fire, faith has been my constant companion and source of strength. Each chapter of my life has been marked by moments of doubt and challenge, but faith has illuminated the path, showing me that even in the darkest times, there is a more excellent plan at work.

Finally, community has been a cornerstone in my journey to become who I am today. The support, encouragement, and love from those around me have been invaluable, guiding me through challenges and celebrating my successes. A few critical people who know who they are stood by me when I needed it most, offering wisdom, strength, and unwavering belief in my potential. Their presence in my life has shaped my path, and I am deeply grateful for their role in helping me reach where I am now. It's a reminder that we don't walk our paths alone, and the people we surround ourselves with can profoundly impact our journey.

As you consider your path, I encourage you to allow faith to lead the way. Embrace the challenges and uncertainties with the assurance that there is a more excellent plan at work. Trust that the lessons you learn and the obstacles you overcome are part of a more extensive journey shaping you into the person you are meant to be. When you align your actions with your values and trust in divine guidance, you create a life that is not only purposeful but also deeply fulfilling.

Living intentionally requires a willingness to listen to your inner voice and follow the right direction for you, even if it diverges from the conventional path. It means taking control of your health, relationships, and career with a mindset guided by faith and committed to your well-being. By doing so, you empower yourself to live authentically and aligned with your deepest values and aspirations. One of the most profound lessons I've learned is that living intentionally involves more than just setting goals or making plans; it requires a deep alignment with our values and faith. It means recognizing that our choices, actions, and attitudes reflect our inner beliefs and aspirations. By living with intention, we create a fulfilling life that reflects the purpose we believe we are called to fulfill. Faith has been the compass that has guided me through every significant event in my life. It has led me to embrace holistic health, rediscover my passions, and find purpose in helping others live intentionally. I encourage you to let faith be your guide, to trust in the journey, and to embrace a life of purpose and fulfillment. When you allow faith to lead the way, you open yourself to the possibilities and blessings that await, creating a life rich in meaning and aligned with your highest aspirations.

Here are a few quick steps to help you let faith lead the way and live intentionally:

1. Trust in Divine Guidance: Start each day with a moment of reflection or prayer, asking for clarity and direction. Trust that faith will guide you through challenges and opportunities.

2. Set Clear Intentions: Define what living intentionally means for you. Set specific, meaningful goals that align with your values and purpose.

3. Align Actions with Beliefs: Ensure your daily actions reflect your core values and beliefs. Make choices that support your long-term vision and contribute to your well-being.

4. Embrace Challenges as Lessons: View obstacles as opportunities for growth. Approach difficulties with faith, knowing they can offer valuable lessons and lead to personal development.

5. Seek Support and Community: Surround yourself with a supportive community that shares your values. Connect with others who can offer encouragement and accountability on your journey.

6. Practice Gratitude and Mindfulness: Regularly reflect on your gratitude and stay present. This helps maintain a positive mindset and keeps you focused on what truly matters.

7. Be Flexible and Open: Stay open to unexpected changes and new opportunities. Trust that adjustments and detours can be part of a more excellent plan.

By incorporating these steps into your daily life, you can let faith guide you and create a more intentional, fulfilling path. As I write this today, I am leaning into my faith and trusting God's divine time for another major transition in my life. So, I encourage you to find peace and joy while letting "Faith Lead the Way."

Bio

Suzy Rawlins is a woman of faith, holistic health and wellness coach, best-selling author, international speaker, and Roots & Boots Intentional Living, LLC owner.

She is also a farm girl at heart.

Suzy's journey includes various careers and life-shaking moments (such as Cancer not once but twice), and her conversations with hundreds of people have reinforced a single truth: Live Intentional God's guidance; Suzy shares her process for intentional living. She guides people to set meaningful goals, develop actionable plans, and take inspired steps toward a fulfilling life. This is her mission and passion.

You can download her wellness tracker as well as other powerful resources at www.suzyrawlin.com

Katie Barnett-

Proof of Purpose

I'm here with you, in the pages of a book you're holding, or perhaps scrolling through on a device.

This connection between us might seem insignificant, but I've read and re-read this opening sentence a dozen times, marveling at its truth. Here I am, writing for you. And I pray that this time you've chosen to invest in yourself will be well worth it. I don't take this lightly.

I wish I could be sitting with you right now, learning about your life and hearing why you chose this book. I'd look into your eyes and do what comes naturally to me—really *see* you. I would listen to your stories, marvel at the resilience woven through them, resilience you've likely downplayed or perhaps never even recognized.

Yes, I've experienced my share of trials, both personal and professional, and I'm honored that you've deemed this book worthy of your time. But as we talked, I would undoubtedly think to myself, *This person has an incredible purpose. She is remarkable. She is so resilient.*

You can easily google "what it takes to be resilient" and find plenty of good advice:

- Maintain an internal locus of control.

- Give yourself grace.

- Surround yourself with strong, ambitious women who cheer you on.

- Approach situations rationally to respond rather than react.

This is all solid wisdom. But the problem is, we often don't acknowledge our own resilience until something forces us to—usually something big and catastrophic. Sometimes, it takes looking back years later to finally recognize and take ownership of our strength, growth, and survival.

But why wait for hindsight? My goal is to help you *own* your resilience now because, let's face it, hard times are ahead. Life throws curveballs. The fact that you're here, though, shows you already know that. You've got goals to achieve, and you're ready to face what comes.

Resilience is, by definition, "the capacity to withstand or recover quickly from difficulties." It's what gets us through tough times. But let me be real: there are things I survived by the skin of my teeth. I've experienced depression so deep that, while I could never leave my children, I begged a God whose existence I questioned to take me away.

I survived that depression. My business grew, and I had some incredible successes. If there were a badge for resilience, I might have earned it. But here's the thing—what I went through wasn't resilience. It was survival driven by defense mechanisms. Work was the only area where I felt any control or confidence, so I clung to it. Depression distorts everything, making it hard to see that my most important role—being a mother—was one I was still fulfilling, even if I couldn't feel it at the time.

Years later, when I looked back at videos of my children, I saw that I had been there, giving them more than I ever realized. At the time, I was separated from my husband, living with my parents, raising three young children, and dealing with the heartbreak of a life and marriage I desperately wanted to save. All while battling a professional crisis that left my business and reputation in tatters. I was just surviving.

True resilience however, isn't just about surviving; it's about purpose. It's different from survival, though both are noble. Resilience is proactive. It's a mindset and a purpose you hold onto before the storm hits. Survival is reactive—it's what we do when the storm is already upon us.

As a mother, for example, there's an innate resilience in loving and protecting your children, long before the sleepless nights and teething tantrums. That love is resolute, unwavering, and prepared for the challenges to come. It's the same with purpose. When you find and own your purpose, resilience becomes second nature.

Let me tell you a story about that—one morning, after a long night with my baby girl, who suffered from constant discomfort, I hit a breaking point. I was sleep-deprived, overwhelmed, and ready to throw in the towel—or, as I candidly admitted to my husband, I felt like throwing her across the room. I didn't, of course. But admitting how hard it was didn't make me less of a mother. It made me human.

Resilience means understanding that things will get hard—possibly harder than we can imagine—but never giving up on what matters most. Sometimes it means taking a break, stepping back, and realizing that we don't have all the answers. And that's okay. That's where growth happens.

I used to think that purpose had to be something tangible—something with a name, a title, or a door with a plaque on it. But one's purpose is far more divine. My purpose, I've learned, is in *to see* people, help them recognize their worth and potential. It took me years to realize that this is my gift. I used to apologize for qualities that are now my strengths, thanks to tools like the StrengthsFinder assessment. Understanding yourself allows you to offer grace, both inwardly and outwardly. It helps you embrace your purpose.

When I was separated from my husband for the second time, I found true resilience. It came to me through a newfound faith and realizing my greater purpose. I couldn't control whether my husband would fight for our family. But I knew my purpose was to help others recognize their strength and purpose, just as I had found mine.

Resilience, the kind that comes from knowing your purpose, gives you the strength to face any storm. And when you embrace it, challenges become invitations for growth, opportunities to serve, and moments of profound self-discovery.

I'm not writing this from a place of final victory. In fact, as I write, I'm awaiting a diagnosis that could drastically change my life. It's terrifying. But here's what I know: resilience comes from within, and it's powered by purpose. Whatever comes next, I will face it with the knowledge that my purpose is to continue growing, learning, and serving others.

If I were with you now, I'd grab your shoulders, look into your eyes, and say with conviction: *You are here. You ARE the proof of purpose.*

Now go. Do your thing. The resilience comes free.

Bio

Katie Barnett is an authentic, dynamic, and passionate leader recognized for her impact as an agent of change, dedicated researcher, and ethical leadership expert. She began her entrepreneurial journey with Chico Chalk & Calligraphy, which sparked her love for business. Balancing family life, Katie transitioned to running a successful online business, mentoring others worldwide to replicate her success. In a time when many chose to stay safe, she embraced bold, disruptive changes, earning her a reputation as a trailblazer.

Katie's leadership style is deeply rooted in her personal experiences. As the daughter of a fire chief who transformed Santa Monica's fire department through integrity and respect, she learned the value of strong leadership early on. Watching her father lead, Katie gained a profound understanding of what it takes to earn and maintain trust while driving positive change. Her inspiration also comes from her role as a fire wife and her deep admiration for her mother, who remains her best friend and role model as a parent.

A staunch advocate for mental health, women's rights, personal development, and authentic living, Katie's work extends beyond business. She holds a Master's of Education and works tirelessly to empower others to discover their purpose through her writing, business, and two successful podcasts: *Level After Next with Katie Barnett* and *If You Lead Them*. In her personal life, Katie finds immense joy in watching her sons play baseball and her daughter shine in theater productions. Whether at home or in her professional life, she remains committed to leading with integrity, doing the hard work first, and always striving for the "level after next."

The Importance of Choosing Yourself by Keisha Bloise

As I sit here, reflecting on my path of twists and turns that has led me to this moment, I can't help but smile at the beautiful irony of it all. My journey began in the world of science, where empirical evidence and logical reasoning reigned supreme. I thrived on logic and measurable outcomes. It got to the point where I would try to reason through every situation, instead of feeling through my feelings. Now, I guide others into the intangible realms of spirituality and financial transformation powered by life insurance. Life, in its infinite wisdom, has a way of leading us exactly where we need to be, even when we think we have it all figured out, or our minds trick us into feelings of doubt. Little did I know that the greatest experiment I would ever conduct would be on myself.

My name is Keisha Bloise, and I am The Love Scientist. But before we dive into how I earned that title, let me take you back to where it all began. My journey, like yours, has been anything but linear. I've lived many lives in this one body, each experience peeling back another layer, revealing a truer version of myself. From the challenging days of pharmaceutical research to the intimate spaces of sound bath healing, from serving clients by protecting their families through mortgage protection and sharing ways to build generational wealth as a life insurance broker to pouring my heart out in poetry, every twist and turn has been a lesson, a death and rebirth, propelling me towards my purpose.

We are put through trials and tribulations (what I like to call growing pains) to shed the old parts of ourselves to uncover other layers in search of who we truly are and our purpose in the world.

I was raised by two hardworking Jamaican parents who poured their hearts and souls into giving their children a better life. They were my example of being good hearted, amazing souls. I witnessed countless instances of my parents' vibrant personalities touching the lives of strangers. Their small acts of kindness—a well-timed joke or a humorous remark—could light up a room, leaving everyone smiling. Though we faced challenges like any family, my parents' lively spirits ensured there was never a dull moment. Whether we were teasing each other, exploring Palisades Mall, or dining at our favorite restaurants, their energy was irresistible.

When I think back to my childhood, our home was filled with the rhythm of my father's eclectic music collection and my mother's love for cooking. Their fashion sense gave me the courage to spread and explore my individuality. My parents didn't just encourage my dreams; they actively cultivated them. They got me involved in pageants and modeling. They saw it as a canvas for my self-expression and growth.

Later, I was crowned Miss Congeniality of Newark Preteen, won 2nd runner-up for Homecoming Queen, and graduated as valedictorian of East Orange Campus High School. My voice echoed across the football field as I delivered my speech, and I could feel the weight of my parents' love and sacrifices. Their support always made me feel invincible.

I would pay close attention to my parents' interactions with strangers. People watching has been one of my pastimes. I admired how my parents could transform a simple interaction into something memorable, and I aspired to emulate this quality as I grew into my own identity. Their impact extended beyond our family and trickled into the hearts of individuals with intellectual and developmental disabilities; my father rose to management in his career, while my mother was an influential counselor at her company. In both roles, their hearts shone through their dedication to service and love.

These formative experiences shaped my own superpower, which I later realized was the ability to uplift others and pour love into others effortlessly. The abundance of affection my parents poured into me became the foundation from which I now draw, enabling me to be authentically myself while nurturing those around me. Their legacy lives on in my commitment to leaving people better than I found them, a testament to the enduring power of love and kindness.

Growing up, I was that girl who had a plan and everything would have to go as planned. You know the type — overachiever, convinced that if I just worked hard enough, I could control every aspect of my life. Oh, how the universe must have laughed at my naivety.

My father, with his unwavering work ethic, always told me, "Go into the medical field. Every day a child is born, and every day someone takes their last breath. You'll always have a job." His words, practical and well-intentioned, set me on a path that would eventually lead me far from where I started, but exactly where I needed to be.

I chose the pharmaceutical industry. When I graduated from Montclair State University, I felt accomplished because I did what I set out to do. I received my bachelor's degree in biology with a minor in psychology and maintained my full academic scholarship. I learned at an early age that I was an executor. My parents would reframe my doubts into positive thinking and tell me often, "you can do anything you put your mind to".

For seven years, I was a Clinical Research Scientist in the field of Infectious Diseases. By then, I wanted to spoil my parents and take them around the world. I would daydream of the scenic views we would share in our world travels. But life, as it often does, had other plans.

I managed and executed clinical trials for drug development, leading a cross-functional team of brilliant experts. Together, we conducted clinical trials that could potentially change lives. In retrospect, I made things happen! During this time, I didn't see it as anything extraordinary. To me, it was just the career I chose and was dedicated to Monday through Friday.

My mother, though? Oh, she saw it differently. Her eyes would light up every time she'd proudly announce, "My daughter is a scientist!" Her dimples would deepen, etching joy onto her face as if she'd won the lottery. And in a way, she believed she had. I would bashfully tell her to keep it on the low, but she never listened. Every time she put me in the spotlight, I would feel a mix of shyness and secret pleasure. Did she listen? Of course not. Mothers never do when it comes to bragging about their children.

For the longest time, I thought being ambitious was common. Doesn't everyone want to reach for the stars? Don't we all have that fire of desire, pushing us to be more, do more?

But as I paid closer attention, I realized that my normal wasn't everyone's normal. My ambition wasn't just a trait; it was my hidden gift. A force that propelled me forward, even when I didn't fully appreciate its strength.

I understand why my parents' pride knew no bounds. I wasn't just doing a job. I was potentially changing the course of medical history, one clinical trial at a time. I really needed to sit with how powerful that was. This was the start of moving in the energy of embracing the complexity of my ambitions, the impact of my work, and knowing that I was different.

There's a projection that owning our achievements is a form of bragging. No, it's acknowledging the power we hold to make a difference. It's recognizing that our ambitions, our drive, our relentless pursuit of excellence, these are the things that move mountains and change lives.

As I excelled in my career, there was a persistent whisper in my heart, a longing for something more. I craved a creative outlet. I grew tired of betting on everyone else instead of taking a chance to bet on myself. My dreams became so loud that I couldn't ignore them, I decided to go all in and see what would happen. It led me to create, The Love Scientist, a space where I could explore the complexities of modern dating and self-love.

The scientist in me couldn't help but analyze the patterns I saw — the rise of ghosting, the lost art of fostering deeper connections, the dance of vulnerability and fear that seemed to dictate modern love. I pursued my dreams outside of work hours, part-time. I was willing to put in the hours to someday make my dream my reality. I was far from normal and never wanted to be average.

Little did I know, this was just the first step on a journey that would completely elevate my life and lead me to my true purpose.

Corporate America was where I got my first glimpse of real independence and started to understand what I was truly worth. I was the youngest, black woman in my department. There were plenty of times my heart raced, palms sweaty, but I found my voice in forcing myself to speak up in meetings full of seasoned executives. It wasn't easy, but it was necessary. My voice mattered and demanded to be heard, even when I felt nervous.

The pharmaceutical industry became my training ground, where I sharpened the art of salary negotiation by practicing in the mirror, learned the art of code switching, and how to conquer my fears while leveraging my diverse and extensive background. I honed skills that would serve me far beyond the clinical trials arena.

My professional metamorphosis coincided with a period of personal upheaval. My parents were separated when I graduated with my Master's degree in Clinical Trial Sciences from the University of Medicine and Dentistry of New Jersey. At a time, where I was supposed to feel my happiest, I was sad inside. My parents' separation played a heavy toll on me. My norm was no longer the same and my life was forever changed.

I yearned for a new kind of stability — one I could create for myself under my own terms. I wanted to live on my own. The new goal became to secure the means for true independence and self-reliance. I moved out of my father's house. It was bittersweet. It was terrifying and exhilarating all at once.

I was in the school of hard knocks, where lessons came fast without mercy. I learned through life and my career that sometimes, you've got to be your own biggest advocate. In a world that doesn't always recognize your worth immediately, self-belief becomes your most precious asset.

I discovered life doesn't come with a rewind button. Each action sets off a chain of reactions, making every decision pivotal. I learned to stand firm in my choices, knowing that second chances aren't guaranteed. This realization brought both weight and freedom—the weight of responsibility and the freedom that comes from owning your path.

The most crucial skill I developed was knowing when to pivot. In the ever-shifting landscapes of life and business, the ability to reassess, readjust, and redirect became my secret weapon. It's a survival skill, yes, but more than that, it's the key to thriving in a world of constant change.

Amidst the accolades and professional development courses, my intuition would remind me in an insistent voice, asking, "Is this the dream I fascinated about as I would step further into adulthood?" It was like an itch I couldn't scratch, a feeling that maybe, just maybe, my true calling was waiting for me outside of the constraints of Corporate America. I would look out the window and pray to God asking for guidance and a clear sign it was time to leave, even though I knew in my spirit that I wasn't completely satisfied.

The morning of September 1, 2017, my world shattered. I received a call that no one ever wants to receive — my mother, my best friend, my rock, had unexpectedly passed away. In that moment, everything I thought I knew about life, love, and purpose was turned upside down. And, I had no idea how to put it back together.

Grief is a peculiar thing. It doesn't just break your heart; it breaks you open. And in that breaking, if you're brave enough to look, you find pieces of yourself you never knew existed.

As I navigated this loss, I found myself turning inward. It came in cycles. I was angry and questioned why would the divine take my best friend away from me. It would be five years later talking to a client, where I had an epiphany looking at flashbacks of my healing journey. My client shared we don't own people, we experience them. This perspective would later change the trajectory of my story.

The logical, analytical scientist in me wanted to make sense of it all. But for the first time in my life, logic failed me. The depth of my pain was immeasurable. It was as if someone took my heart out of my chest and I didn't know when I would ever get it back. Losing a parent is never easy and my heart goes out to you, if your parent(s) are no longer here on this physical plane with us.

I was faced with a choice; I could let this loss destroy me, or I could use it as a catalyst for change. After the days turned into months, and months turned into years of crying my heart out, I woke up one day and told God I didn't want to be sad anymore. I wanted to be happy again. I was tired of sitting in the pain and hurt. It was in this darkest moment that my spiritual awakening began. It was in this darkness that I discovered the light of self-love.

Losing my mother forced me to confront parts of myself I'd long ignored. It made me question everything — my career, my relationships, my purpose. The logical, scientific mind that had served me so well in my career couldn't make sense of this intense pain. I had to learn a new way of being, a new way of understanding the world and my place in it.

In the stillness, I revealed uncomfortable truths about myself, about the ways I'd been seeking validation from others instead of cultivating self-love. I had to face the reality that I'd been chasing love in all the wrong places, trying to fill a void that could only be filled from within.

I would talk to my mother about my business ideas with The Love Scientist. She would inquire about the latest updates. Before she passed away, I shared I wanted to write my first book. As a little girl, getting my feelings out on paper or in the notes section of my phone was my way of reasoning. I would often sit with my emotions, allowing them to fully process. As a result, I would often intellectualize my emotions.

Writing became my lifeline, a way to process my grief and make sense of the transformation I was undergoing. With each poem, each affirmation, I was not only healing myself but creating a roadmap for others to ignite self-love, healing, spirituality who might find themselves lost in the darkness of self-doubt and pain.

As I poured my heart onto the pages, I realized that my journey wasn't just about personal healing — it was about stepping into my power and purpose. "Imperfect Self-Love" was created to let go of self-judgement, ascend to one's highest timeline, and step into transformative work. My vision was to show that true love and connection with others starts with self-awareness and truly loving ourselves as the foundation and the secret to understanding others.

One day I questioned the divine about my mission because I didn't feel qualified, and heard, "Why not you?" In this moment I knew I was given the green light to follow my heart.

This simple question became my mantra, pushing me to embrace my gifts and share them with the world. I began to see that everything I'd been through — the triumphs and the heartbreaks — had prepared me for this part of my story. My background in science, my experience with loss, my journey of self-discovery — all of it converged to create a unique perspective that could help others navigate their own paths to self-love and purpose.

But embracing this calling meant stepping out of my comfort zone. It meant trusting my intuition as much as my intellect and being willing to be naked as I learned and grew. I could hear the rumors, "Why would she leave behind her career as a Scientist"? My answer, I wanted and desired more, and I'm not stopping until I get it.

It meant facing my fears and insecurities head-on, challenging the limiting beliefs that had held me back for so long. It was a slow, often painful process of peeling back layers of conditioning, facing my fears, and learning to embrace every part of myself — even the parts I had long tried to hide or change.

One of the most profound lessons I've learned on this journey is the power of authenticity. For years, I'd hidden parts of myself, afraid that if people saw the real me — with all my flaws and quirks — they wouldn't accept me. But as I began to embrace my true self, flaws and all, I found that it was precisely these "imperfections" that allowed me to connect deeply with others.

This realization led me to expand my work in unexpected directions, even when I felt like I was freestyling. Later on, I found out I was operating in ebb and flow. I discovered the healing power of sound baths, using vibrations to help people relieve stress and tap into the hidden parts of their soul. I began to study spiritual practices and reprogram the subconscious mind with meditation and positive thinking.

Self-love isn't always pretty. Real self-love is about showing up for yourself, even when it's hard. Sometimes, self-love looks like choosing yourself over others It's about setting boundaries, making difficult choices, and sometimes, letting go of people and situations that no longer serve your highest good even when you don't want to let go.

On this ride, I've learned that self-love is a multifaceted practice. It includes:

Accepting yourself.

Forgiving yourself for past mistakes.

Setting healthy boundaries in relationships.

Pursuing your passions without apology.

Taking care of your physical and mental health.

Surrounding yourself with people who uplift you.

Letting go of the need for external validation.

Celebrating your achievements, big and small.

Being kind to yourself in moments of failure or setback.

Trusting your intuition and honoring your needs.

As I began to practice more principles in my own life, something magical happened. Not only did I feel more peaceful and fulfilled, but I also noticed that my relationships began to improve I attracted people who respected my boundaries and valued my truth. I found the courage to pursue my passions, including writing "Imperfect Self-Love" and exploring new avenues like sound bath healing and life insurance.

It's okay not to know how everything will pan out. I know I didn't. I thought I did, but I learned quickly that we are all trying to figure it out. I had a plan but gave myself grace when my reality didn't look like my plan. One of the bravest things I've ever had to do is bet on myself and step into entrepreneurship confident, yet scared. Although the road of entrepreneurship hasn't always been clear, it has been the most fulfilling and a rewarding experience.

And that's the beauty of it. I can vividly remember the prayers of the past that has shaped my reality of today. We don't know how everything will unfold but if we believe hard enough, show gratitude with tests of faith, we leap into our desired timelines by the grace of divinity.

I could be unconventional. I could use my background in science, my journey of self-discovery, and my passion for helping others to make a real difference in the world. This realization led me to expand my work beyond just writing about self-love. With the help of my father, I started a life insurance agency, Vivid Envisions, helping families prepare for life's unexpected turns and build generational wealth.

In essence, I became a bridge between the worlds of science and spirituality, logic and intuition, personal growth and practical financial planning. I recognize that true freedom comes not just from emotional and spiritual wellbeing, but from financial security as well.

Two years and counting, I strive to change the way people perceive life insurance. I'm working to change the narrative from a misunderstood, "boring" financial product into a powerful tool to close the racial wealth gap.

Another part of my mission is to share tools and resources with individuals and families to take control of their financial destinies by not leaving it up to chance, ensuring peace of mind while also benefiting from their policies during their lifetimes.

They say the divine has a sense of humor. Back in my clinical research days, I dived into exploring strategies to ensure I was on track for retirement, and the fastest ways to get rid of credit card debt. I was intrigued with saving money and how to make my money work for me. I started to educate myself on credit repair, sticking to a budget, reviewing my weekly finances, and buying stocks. I had no idea that later I would rely on this knowledge to draw parallels to the present. I read books and articles, listened to podcasts, and read through The Budgetnista group, because Tiffany Aliche made the financial education easily digestible. For a while, I realized how unprepared I was, then I grew curious about my circle of connections who possibly weren't privy to such information or didn't have accessibility to the same resources.

When I look back at certain points in my life, it's like I'm watching a movie reel, and all the highlights are replaying and I'm jumping back in time rewatching those scenes with corrective vision.

Sometimes you have to break your heart to find your soul.

I'm grateful for the power of self-love and healing, and mastering solitude. It saved my life. It instilled a confidence in me to walk in my purpose boldly because everything I've been through was not for me, but to be a shining light for others.

Life is a rollercoaster. It has its highs and lows. There may be longer durations of each depending on which season you're in. It's about pushing through, despite those highs and lows, and your attitude towards your circumstances. But they don't teach us how to transmute our power. Somehow, we just have to figure it out, which might look completely different from those around us. Everything works out the way it's supposed to.

It was more so trial and error for me with a strong support system. I recall when I learned how to really pray. A colleague at work became my confidant, lending his attentive ear to my troubles. During our lunchtime scrolls, we would engage in deep conversations about the complexities of my challenges. While I valued his opinion, I had yet to develop trust in my own discernment or patience to let situations unfold naturally. Our conversations often revolved around relationships and love, with him consistently reassuring me that better days were ahead. And I always wanted to believe with the same amount of conviction he possessed.

One day, he shared a few scriptures and suggested I undertake a fast. His advice would lead to one of the most beautiful experiences of my life, fundamentally altering my approach to prayer, my connection with the divine, and evolve with self-reflection.

I've learned the importance of choosing yourself, always and under all costs.

Every time, I abandoned myself, God was there to guide me back. My spiritual growth involved doing the work when no one was watching me. True prayer is not just about words, but about listening to your heart with a balance of mind and heart coherence, while paying attention to the gentle nudges of the divine.

This ongoing process of death and rebirth, of shedding old skins and growing new ones, is what makes life breathtaking and terrifying. It's what makes us human.

I'm filled with a sense of awe and gratitude. Awe at the incredible journey that has brought me here, and gratitude for every experience – good and bad – that has shaped me into who I am. Everything happens for a reason whether we understand its meaning or not. Nothing happens by coincidence.

Earlier this year, my most affirming moments came when I was invited to be the keynote speaker at my former school, Hart Middle School in East Orange, New Jersey. The invitation came from Mr. Willie Worley, my former high school history teacher who is now the principal.

In the beginning of the year, I told God I wanted to get more involved with the youth. Our desires come from a place letting us know that we can bring it into fruition. When I stood before those young graduates, sharing my story and encouraging them to follow their unique paths, the room vibrated with possibility and opportunity. I was exactly where I needed to be. And I know that the best is yet to come.

I'm a firm believer that everyone can achieve incredible things because abundance is our birthright. You are worthy of love, especially your own. Your purpose in this world is not something you find – it's something you create, day by day, choice by choice.

You may feel lost, broken, or unsure of your direction. That's okay. I've been where you are. And I want you to know that you are powerful beyond measure. Your struggles don't define you; they refine you. I invite you to embrace your imperfections, to love yourself fiercely, and to trust that your unique experiences and perspective are exactly what the world needs.

Self-love isn't about being perfect. It's about embracing all parts of yourself – the light and the shadow – with compassion and grace. It's about setting boundaries, honoring your energy, and recognizing your inherent worth. As you navigate your own path to purpose, I encourage you to:

Listen to your inner voice. That whisper in your heart, the one that calls you to something greater? Pay attention to it. It's your intuition guiding you towards your destiny.

Embrace your unique journey. Don't compare your path to anyone else's. Your experiences – good and bad – are shaping you for your unique purpose.

Practice radical self-acceptance. Love yourself fiercely, imperfections and all. It's from this place of self-love that you'll find the courage to step into your purpose.

Be open to unexpected opportunities. Sometimes our purpose reveals itself in surreal ways. Stay open and receptive to new possibilities.

Trust the process. Even when the path seems unclear, trust that you're exactly where you need to be. Every experience is preparing you for what's to come.

Surround yourself with support. Find your tribe – people who uplift you, challenge you, and believe in you even when you don't believe in yourself.

Take inspired action. Purpose without action remains unfulfilled potential. Take small steps every day towards your dreams. All you have to do is show up and be consistent.

Practice gratitude. Even in your darkest moments, there is always something to be grateful for. Gratitude opens your heart and aligns you with your highest purpose.

Serve others. Often, our greatest fulfillment comes from using our gifts to help others. Look for ways to make a positive impact in the world around you.

Keep growing. Your purpose will evolve as you do. Stay committed to personal growth and lifelong learning.

In the words of my parents, "You can do anything you put your mind to." But I'll add to that – you can do anything you put your heart and soul into.

So go forth, beautiful soul. Experiment boldly. Love yourself imperfectly. And watch as your purpose unfolds before you, more magnificent than you ever imagined. Because you, Goddess, are a Woman of Purpose. And the world is waiting for you to shine your radiant light.

Bio

Keisha Bloise, author of "Imperfect Self-Love," is a force of nature in the realms of personal growth, spiritual awakening, and financial empowerment. A published scientist turned dream architect and wealth strategist; Keisha's unconventional journey embodies the transformative power she ignites in others.

Known as The Love Scientist, Keisha blends her analytical background with intuitive wisdom, creating a unique approach to life's challenges. Her mission? To shake people awake to their own magnificence and guide them towards vibrating at their highest frequency.

Keisha's raw honesty about her own path - from navigating profound loss to discovering the healing power of self-love - resonates deeply with her ever-growing tribe. Through her electrifying speaking engagements, soul-stirring sound bath sessions, and no-nonsense coaching, she's helped countless individuals unpack their potential and step boldly into their power.

But Keisha's vision extends beyond personal transformation. As the dynamo behind Vivid Envisions, she's on a mission to revolutionize how we think about financial security and generational wealth. She's served over 300 families by creating lasting legacies through life insurance strategies, proving that financial planning is crucial, a form of self-love, and a gift of love.

Whether she's dropping truth bombs on her podcast, leading a heart-opening sound healing session, or strategizing a client's financial future, Keisha brings the same fierce love and unwavering belief in human potential to everything she touches.

Robbie Motter-

"A Life of Purpose: Empowering Women"

As I reflect on my 88 years of life, especially on my birthday coinciding with International Women's Day, March 8th, I'm reminded of the power of purpose,

My journey from a tumultuous childhood in Hawaii to becoming the founder and CEO of the Global Society for Female Entrepreneurs (GSFE) has been a tapestry woven with struggles, triumphs, and an unwavering dedication to elevating women. Every twist and turn has contributed to my mission to empower, inspire, mentor, educate, and connect women to become successful entrepreneurs.

Born in Hawaii in 1936, I was five and experienced the chaos of Pearl Harbor. Shortly after that, I was separated from my mother, and she placed me into a series of foster homes over the years. I often wondered what my life might have been like if I had grown up with a stable family. My mother's five marriages ensured that I never had the opportunity to meet or know my father, leaving me feeling like an only child trapped in a world of uncertainty.

At the tender age of 14, in CA., I made a bold decision. Feeling stifled in the children's home, I boarded a Greyhound bus to San Francisco, fueled by a desire for independence. In those days, employers didn't ask for proof of age, and since I looked older, it paved the way for my first office job; I embraced this opportunity, diligently learning new skills early each morning and ultimately ascending the corporate ladder in various cities with various companies. This journey was about more than just employment; it was about self-discovery and resilience.

A moment of rejection can spark purpose; I faced a defining moment in my quest to become a woman of purpose in Omaha, Nebraska. I approached a female colleague, eager to learn from her experience, only to be harshly refused: "I will not teach you or any woman." These words stuck a chord deep within me, igniting a lifelong commitment to empower other women. I vowed to spend the rest of my life sharing knowledge and helping others achieve their dreams.

The vow transformed into action, as I became a source of inspiration and guidance for women in my workplace and beyond. I recognized that empowerment is not just about personal success but creating a ripple effect that uplifts others- a fundamental belief that would shape my career.

My life took another turn when I married, became a mother of two, and later had my last child. Balancing corporate responsibilities with the demands of parenting was a significant challenge, especially as I transitioned through several states back to Hawaii, then onto Nebraska, Virginia, Texas, and New Jersey, then back to Virginia, then California. Each location marked a new chapter, often filled with uncertainty and change. After my first and second divorce, I found myself the sole breadwinner. It was a daunting prospect, but it also fueled my ambition. I dedicated myself to not only surviving but thriving. I worked harder than ever, using my corporate jobs as platforms to continue my mission of mentoring women. As a volunteer coordinator, I actively participated in the National Association of Female Executives (NAFE) and built nationwide networks for female executives.

These years have taught me the importance of community. I was never alone; I had my children, who now numbered three, and I was committed to showing them the value of hard work and purpose-filled living.

With a firm belief that every woman deserves support and mentorship. I founded the Global Society for Female Entrepreneurs in 2017. This non-profit organization became the manifestation of my passion, providing resources and a community for women to thrive in their entrepreneurial pursuits. It was a significant milestone, but the journey was beginning. I leveraged my corporate experience with my great nonprofit board and created structure programs within GSFE that focused on education, networking, and skill development. Each workshop and seminar offered women practical tools to navigate the often-challenging waters of entrepreneurship. Our monthly network meetings always have dynamic speakers with nuggets to help our members grow personally and professionally. The true satisfaction came from witnessing women blossom -overcoming fears to write or speak and enhancing their abilities to achieve their dreams.

Moreover, we utilized social media to expand our reach, share success stories, and build a vibrant online community. Platforms like Facebook, LinkedIn, and Instagram have allowed women to connect, share experiences, and form lasting relationships. These virtual spaces reflected the real-world networks we cultivated, allowing our mission to resonate globally.

The advent of the COVID-19 pandemic profoundly impacted all our lives, including the work we did at GSFE. With physical events on hold, we quickly pivoted to virtual platforms, ensuring our mission continued unabated. It was a challenging transition but presented a unique opportunity to innovate and reach an even wider audience.

We established online workshops and virtual networking events that connected women from diverse backgrounds and experiences. The challenges we faced highlighted the strength of our community. Women rallied together, sharing resources, advice, and encouragement in ways that transcended geographical boundaries. This experience reaffirmed my belief that we can discover new paths of empowerment through adversity.

As I celebrate my 88th year, I reflect on the legacy I wish to leave behind; over the years, I have often spoken to young women in schools and organizations, emphasizing the importance of believing in oneself and pursuing dreams relentlessly. I share my story not as a road map but as a testament to what is possible when passion drives purpose.

The next generation is full of potential, and I am committed to nurturing that potential. Through GSFE, I continue to mentor aspiring women entrepreneurs, guiding them as they navigate their unique journeys. Their stories inspire me and remind me that my purpose is more alive than ever.

I invite others to join this empowerment movement as I look to the future. Whether you are a woman seeking to unleash your potential, a mentor willing to share your expertise, or an ally supporting the cause, we all have a role to play. It is time to harness the power of community and social media to amplify our voices and support each other.

Share your journey, use platforms like Instagram to showcase your progress, and connect with others. Post stories of resilience, highlight the achievements of fellow women and celebrate the victories—big and small. Together, we can dismantle barriers and foster a culture of collaboration where women thrive

Bio

My life has been a testament to the strength of the human spirit and the potential of collective empowerment. Together, we can navigate challenges and rise above adversity. Today and every day, let us continue to empower, inspire, and uplift one another. The journey is far from over, and I am excited about all the possibilities for women everywhere.

As you continue your journey and inspire others, remember that every story can create change and ignite purpose in the hearts of many.

A gift that I will always cherish is this past summer. I was surprised by a book in which 99 individuals worldwide shared stories of how I impacted their lives. The book is called "A Leader with a Heart of Gold." It was compiled by Professor Caroline Makaka, the CEO and founder of Leaders of All Nations (LOANI), Dr. Angeline Benjamin, Dr. Angelica Benavides, and Dr. Randi Ward, who contacted the GSFE and LOANI families for their stories. They compiled the book and presented the published book to me at a celebration in Lake Arrowhead, CA, which was a total surprise. The stories touched my heart and brought back so many memories of the individuals sharing their stories of my impact on their lives. This book is part of my enduring legacy. The book is on Amazon US and UK, and it achieved the #1 US and International Best Seller. It shares my life of purpose.

Always remember that we don't compete; we complete each other. We are ONE, and together, we can do more.

Lady Ambassador Dr. h.c. Robbie Motter can be reached at

rmotter@aol.com her websites are gsfeus.com and robbiemotter.com. Her phone number is 951-255-9200, the same as WhatsApp, except for adding the US code. She is Robbie Motter, and she is on Facebook and LinkedIn.

Hege Sakseid-

Trust Your Intuition, Discover Your Calling

Imagine taking full responsibility for your life and shaping a proper future. How would it feel to break free from past patterns and emotions? How do you want to live, and what's holding you back? Your well-being directly impacts your ability to thrive in life, your self-worth, and your success.

"Vision is the art of seeing things invisible" – Jonathan Swift.

I have always known where I was headed, not where I would end up. I ended up trusting my intuition—trusted the journey and discovered my calling back in 2014. During a period of personal struggle, years of stress and overwhelming commitments, including a dissatisfying 9-to-5 job and two additional jobs, led me to hit rock bottom. During this time, I realized I was responsible for my health and well-being and that of my two boys. I began to create my reality!

Since then, my life has taken a transformative turn. I am now dedicated to mentoring others who, like me, understand the importance of taking ownership of their health and lives. I've discovered that healthy cells are the key to unlocking a life full of energy and fulfillment.

My passion is to inspire others to achieve success by believing in their strength and abilities, finding their truth, and building the life they want on their terms.

Seeing the smile on the lips and the willpower in the eyes of someone you've mentored as they continue working toward their goal truly melts your heart. It's proof enough that I found my purpose in life.

Trigger Warning

At 22, I knew for sure I was sexually abused as a child. That moment fueled my mission over the years towards becoming a mentor for those who've faced the toughest beginnings and I want to give hope to the younger generation with belief in their future. My purpose is to mentor does who are ready for change and from doubt to possibility. It is possible to create a life of purpose and success no matter where you are in life.

My body didn't remember what happened in my childhood, but my mind did. That's science; our bodies shut down trauma to survive. Mine did for years.

I started experiencing flashbacks at age 16 but it escalated from age of 20 - triggered by various stimuli, such as sounds, smells, words and other sensations – so I started to escape from my misery and mind. In the weekends I liked to hang out with friends, dance, and drink. This is a common behavior.

When I lived in Copenhagen Denmark, it hit me: I have been abused. I lived and felt alone with my thoughts and emotions. Felt lost, scared, sad, and confused. Everything felt like it was spinning out of control – the body and mind were separated.

In 2001, I was a student in Brisbane, Australia, and afterward, I spent 36 months in Copenhagen. Looking back, I realize it was an escape from reality and my family.

One day, I decided I needed to tell them, but first, I went to see a movie at the cinema—an intelligent move. Escape again. I didn't grasp any of it at all. When the film ended, I felt even more lost and alone. I found a payphone near the bus stop. I needed to take a bus to get back to my flat, so I finally dialed one of my sister's phone numbers. When she answered, I just said, 'Hi.' She immediately responded, 'It happened to you too, didn't it?'

I managed to say, 'Yes,' and then I cried. I hadn't spoken to my three sisters or mom for many days; they knew something was wrong. I got a phone call from my eldest sister one day at work after this. I sat at a Scandinavian Headquarters in a call center – she said: I've told mum, I told her your story. She understands and stand by you. The day after, I went to a doctor and got sick leave for a few days – that became weeks.

There were so many feelings and things to sort out and figure out what was next. I slept and cried for a few days and found my computer, an old note with a name and email address on it, and wrote a short message in an email to the man who would be my savor in the following years: "Hi, I got your name from my eldest sister through a friend who speaks nice of you, and I was wondering if you could help me. I've just found out that my father abused me as a child, and I need guides. What's next... Regards, Hege."

I also found our father's email address and wrote him a message I, of course, never got a response too: "Hello, dad. I just wanted to let you know I know what you did to me as a child. How could you?! Your daughter... If you have done the same to my sisters, too... I will never forgive you!"

A few days later, my eldest sister arrived in Copenhagen. She cared for me, and I could sense she felt relieved too. It seemed that her earlier fight against our father in court had strengthened her belief in the justice of her cause—she found our father in bed with our disabled stepsister, aged 11 back in 1995. We talked for many hours and spent time together (two lost, shocked souls in a million-inhabitant city) for a weekend.

"Dear Hege, I want to help you. When will you be in Stavanger again so we can meet? Until then, if you're open to it, we can keep in touch through emails and phone calls." Kind regards, Reimunn.

Relief! I cried, laughed - cried again, and I fell asleep. A new era was about to start.

Weeks later, I met my `savor 'in Stavanger at a church. He was a vicar who had dedicated his life to helping victims of trauma and sexual abuse and has helped hundreds.

I remember the first meeting well. I was sitting in a chair in a hall surrounded by yellow-brown brick walls, waiting for him, and I got nervous and anxious. I am going in that room—alone, with a man the same age as my dad!! I shook it off and followed him in —The meeting was in a small room with soft pink furniture, wooden shelves, and a desk.

"You can decide where you want to sit," I suddenly heard. I picked out the seat closest to the door. It was time to get to know each other and build trust.

Next question: "Is there anything about me you don't like? Like, what do you see? Anything that could remind you of your dad? I'm asking because you must trust me now that we will go deep into your hidden traumas, so you need to let go of the scares "

I found a few things that were like my dad...his age, eyeglasses, and necklace! I didn't like that one (funny enough, every time I came for a session, he had his necklace in front of his sweater) The sessions were tough! He talked with me, asked questions, and revealed many episodes hidden in my subconscious mind. He was brilliant and professional, and his methods worked!

"To move forward in your life and let your body and mind finally rest.... you must let the `garbage` leave your mind" (garbage=memories of trauma). Hours went to weeks and weeks to years. He was always available if I had bad days; I could text or call him, and he would be there. He knew how important trust was for us`. He was an angel.

As the years passed, I became more robust, precise, and confident, taking on new challenges. I know that if he hadn't shown up in my life, it would have been a totally different outcome! I don't know if I would have had my family, so I am so grateful he came into my life.

After twelve years of my first connection with Reimunn, I made my dream come true…

I asked if he would give me the honor of marrying my husband and me. He devoted us, proud and honored, in 2016, outdoors in our little city park where we come from. My best friend from my childhood (who also got help from him for the same reasons) was my bridesmaid. I can still feel the love, warmth, and gratefulness that day – towards him and for family members who were there with us.

Our family needed self-development and self-care, so some of us separated for some years. It was hard but necessary. It's about protecting yourself and become strong for living. We are all together again and more vital as individuals and as a family. We support each other and are close.

Going backward, I got help from Reimunn and a lawyer to press charges against my dad. The case was outdated and would put him in jail, but I could win and receive monetary compensation, and he got it on his record. I won.

1995 was the turning point.

My eldest sister, 22 years of age, was home with our grandpa on our father's side when she heard sounds from the bedroom to our parents when she walked in the hallway. Mom was away for the weekend… She became a witness of a horrible scene which she struggles with today ♡

The upcoming week felt like watching a surreal movie. On Monday, I came home from school to the news that my dad had been kicked out of the house. Drunk and locked out, he tried to get in that evening before driving away. We called the police, worried because not only was he drunk, but his military-issued gun was missing.

We sat in the living room, scared and in shock, with a police commander my eldest sister knew. My father called the house several times, and my sister spoke to him with guidance from the police. He eventually threatened to kill himself, and the night passed in uneasy silence. We slept on the floors in two bedrooms, the house surrounded by armed officers, in case he returned. The following day, he was found in Stavanger, two hours away, eating breakfast at a fancy hotel restaurant. He was jailed for three months but was free again after a trial where he inexplicably won.

The following months were spent in court. Despite clear evidence, he won. This outcome made us lose our family from our father's side and the community we grew up in. My sister appealed and finally won at the court of appeal. It took us years of emotional and financial struggle before people understood we were telling the truth.

The fact that my dad only served three months – and over the years we found out that he, of 20+ years total, abused three daughters of five (one adopted) and my friend - and who else...? This awakened my desire to combat child abuse, advocate for legal change, and fight against child sex trafficking.

While pregnant with my first child, I met with the local incest center, driven to help kids even without a professional background. Though I didn't get a job, I left with a clear sense of purpose, realizing my time to make a difference would come later.

A year later I became pregnant again and this time in my spare time, I wanted to start pushing for stricter laws against pedophiles; inspired by the high-profile 'Operation Dark Room' case in Norway at the time.

I was following through news and conversation with a police lady I knew from the neighborhood. However, I soon realized I didn't have the voice or influence to enact change.

Going for the dream.

In 2013, after growing tired of my technical drawer and interior designer job, I pursued my true calling as an entrepreneur. My first business—a short-lived interior design venture—was challenging and didn't generate much income. I took a temporary position at the university as an interior designer, but soon became overwhelmed by stress, juggling work, my business, and caring for my two young sons.

One day, the stress caught up with me. I collapsed in my office, only to be found by a colleague and rushed to the emergency room. It turned out to be stress and PTSD. That episode, though frightening, became a turning point in my life. I had ignored lots of symptoms like poor sleep, irregular heartbeat, mood swings, short of breath and muscle aces to mention some. This episode allowed me to rebuild my strength and step into the life I was meant to live.

A year later, I started school again to study Traditional Chinese Medicine, muscle Reflexology and ear acupuncture. This new path gave me valuable insights into the body's healing ability. The body is amazing; our job is to provide it with some tools to keep in balance. My new era had begun, and I believe everything happens for a reason, guiding us toward our purpose.

Over the years, I've learned that we can either let past pain ruin our future or choose to work through it, learn from it, and become stronger. I decided to learn from my experience.

It keeps me motivated and enthusiastic about being there for those who want a change—with over 20 years of personal growth myself.

I love to see the light in people's eyes when they start the journey towards the life they are meant to live. I guide and mentor people in health, self-development, and give them option to build a financial legacy. I want to encourage the younger generation to go on this path too, for a better future for themselves and independence.

Helping one person might not change the whole world - but it could change the world for one person. In this case, I believe both will get their world changed (the helper/the receiver)

Be there for others, give Hope and inspiration to their transformational journey, and let them find their true potential and live a fulfilled life. We all have different path of recovery.

As a therapist I helped clients who were experiencing many health issues. Clients with stress symptoms, mental issues, lack of confidence, muscle tension, kidney problems, problems sleeping, and low energy, amongst other symptoms. Whit great results.

Clients and colleagues describe me as confident in my work and I make them feel calm, peaceful and begin to believe in the importance of good health. Others have thanked me for helping their bodies fix their physical pain, and for the last five years, people have thanked me with gratitude for introducing them to a cellular innovation that has changed their lives completely. Without a strong cellular communication network, little else matters. Our cells are the key to a vibrant, fulfilled life.

My purpose isn't just to live my best life; it's to help others live theirs.

Power potential

We have powers within, such as the strength to overcome traumas and struggles energetically and self-healingly. If we set our mind to it, we can deal with ANYTHING. If we start to live IN the presence instead of the past and see the future as something that will happen. By setting goals and dreams, we have already done much.

Fear stops us from becoming who we are and achieving what we truly want. I've feared so many things—and still do fear a few—but I used to be the quiet girl who hated speaking in public. I would have preferred to skip class, but the 'nice-girl syndrome' kicked in whenever we had presentations at school. I always did what I was told because I believed there would be consequences if I didn't. I avoided everything that put me in the spotlight or led to conflicts.

Everything changed when my body and mind became balanced by strengthen the cells communication system within me (redox). They are vital to life, scientifically speaking. It was strange because, one day, I suddenly found myself speaking in front of people during a Zoom meeting. I thought, 'Hey, was that you, Hege?'

In just a few years, I've had one-on-one mentoring sessions, spoken in groups, and given online and in-person presentations. I've agreed to participate in events when that comes. I know I must continue my purpose in life, and if that means I need to speak up in public (even though I don't like it that much), so be it.

This is growth, and everyone can experience it – just decide to do so.

When you fear something, that's the moment you should dive into it with both hands. Please start with minor challenges, see how they go, and then tackle the next fear. The brain's automatic fight-or-flight responses can be retrained by consistently practicing new habits to overcome rooted reactions. When we overcome a fear, it's like deleting it from the brain, like clearing data from hardware. It's when we become too comfortable that's when we need a shift. It is our responsibility to create the life we want—meaning in health, achievements, economics, and dreams—not everyone else!

If you're sitting on a thought or dream of pursuing a cause that matters to you and will benefit others, please go for it! Follow your heart and intuition. Please don't listen to opinions— you will hear plenty of them. Follow your passion and purpose in life. Someone out there is waiting for YOU to come and help. Join us in bettering people's lives and being a force for good! If you remain open-minded and look for clues on your journey, you will find the answers and a way to achieve your mission.

I took charge of my journey and life. Why wouldn't I? I refused to continue living in misery.

I had been there for years, under the control of an abuser who stole my childhood and confidence, and it was not a place I wanted to stay. I wanted more; it was time to reclaim my life, and I encourage you to do the same!

That's why I'm sharing my personal story, because, unfortunately, I know many of you will recognize yourselves in it. Please, find your voice, your strength, and pursue your dreams! I'm here to offer advice and support. When I opened, both energetically and verbally, healing options began to emerge. I was introduced to affirmations, meditation, breathing exercises, coaching, nourishing food for the mind and body with natural ingredients, and the importance of maintaining healthy cells.

When we are open to options and opportunities, everything will fall into place—eventually. We encounter a lifetime when we let our fears and doubts fade away. It starts with saying, "Yes, I want it." Only you can decide how you welcome it by letting go of the past, releasing fears, and opening to who you are. That's right, YOU. A happy, fulfilled, and different world of opportunities with beautiful people. Some of our meetings will be a one-time experience and lesson; others will last a lifetime.

From birth, we're surrounded by voices telling us how to act, speak, learn, and live. We're part of a system that often hides our true identities. So, how can we be 100% ourselves?

Releasing stress and letting go of the 'have to,' 'need to,' and 'must do' attitudes. Instead, listen inwardly. Put down your phone, close your eyes, and breathe. Listen within, ask questions, and the answers will come. If this is new to you, it will take practice and patience. Try spending a few minutes daily in nature—by the forest, sea, or water. This is when change begins, leading to a happier, healthier, and kinder version of yourself – and talk nicely to yourself.

Over time, you'll notice changes in yourself and your surroundings, and you might even see signs guiding you in the right direction if you're open to them. I've experienced many signs and changes that have led me to the life and business I have today. Everything transformed when I finally dared to listen to my intuition. I wouldn't be where I am if I hadn't stopped and listened to my inner voice and dream.

What I do.

Working with US based Biotech Company and global entrepreneurs, we are committed to making a positive impact on lives with a groundbreaking technology in health no one else in the world has. We help people to become the best version of themselves starting with the health. Someone introduced me to this five years ago, and that is why I know it can help you too. The results amazed me so much that I purchased worldwide distribution rights. I recently started weekly webinars for survivors, where I talk about my journey and an easy way to fully recover and become independent much faster than I did.

The company´s moral and ethics is to bettering people's lives and being a force for good in the world and I´m proud to be a part of it. I finally found the missing link to achieving peace with myself, both physically and mentally. Everything fell to place, and I became a better version of myself—I discovered my truth, voice, and confidence. I finally felt peace after 20 years of healing, coaching, and self-development. Wow.

I became a more robust, prouder woman and a better mother with a heart full of goals. My boys see a different way to live a life; they have seen their mother tired, crying, and sad - to become a happy, stronger mum with a goal in mind.

Yes, it's taken a long time, but the dream, mission, and business model have led to my eldest son wanting to join me when he turns 18 next year. I´m proud to hear he wants to go in the same direction and pursue his dreams

Finally, a meaningful contribution on a bigger scale came before me when I partnered the company. Their foundation and their vision to be a force for good in the world where donations help:

https://advancinglife.net/child-trafficking/

Did you know that 1.2m children are trafficked each year? Sold! It must be stopped. Studies also show that approximately 1 in 4 women and 1 in 6 men experience sexual violence in their lifetime...

The day I work with many strong, beautiful women of all ages who have overcome their traumas and fears and started bettering others' lives too, I know my mission is complete. We need to work together to make the world a better place.

And in a world of confusion and worries, let us reach the younger generation and help them find their voice and maintain their health as they age. They need Hope, a Vision. They are the next generation with the power to improve the world.

Transformation.

One experience from a few months ago is exceptional. I was on a morning walk in the forest near my home, feeling frustrated and emotional, questioning whether I should finally quit my one-day-a-week therapist position. As I walked, I discovered a new path leading to the water.

Passing by some large trees, I noticed something hanging from a stem. It was an insect hanging upside down, seemingly lifeless, with another insect beneath it. But then I realized the hanging insect was a dragonfly undergoing its final transformation and opened her four wings. I felt incredibly fortunate and in awe. At that moment, all my frustration melted away. I knew it was a clear sign that my time as a reflexologist had ended. I had bigger vision.

Later, I learned that dragonflies undergo 15 transformations, with the final one preparing them to fly. I suddenly saw my own life mirrored in that dragonfly…

Last words.

We learn from bad experiences and take them with us. Dare to follow your heart, bring in humor and laughter too! Let the past be past and don't take life too serious anymore. You shape your future, which empowers you to emerge as a leader in your own life!

If everyone did this, the future looks brighter.

Bio

I am Hege, and I am from the west coast of Norway. A mother of two wonderful teenage boys, a wife, a holistic health and wellness entrepreneur, and a survivor of childhood trauma who found my inner power and strength to become a leader in my life. I □m living a happy life now with my lovely family and mentoring others who want a change in their lives too. I strive to connect with like-minded individuals who know we must embrace change to lead a fulfilling life. We are the creators of our destinies.

Claire Libré-

The Liberation Sanctuary: A Path of Healing the Inner Self to Transform the Outer World

My name is Claire Libré, I am an emotional healing coach and mentor. My journey has been made over the past 20 years, as I embodied and embraced my Being; stepping into my own authenticity and Soul purpose, and cleared the bondages that held me in old structures of manipulative energy and belief systems. You will discover my path from an invisible young girl, to thriving speaker and clairvoyant who supports women to transition into modes of *power -centered* living.

I am CEO of **The Liberation Sanctuary**, an organization that invites women to attune to their inner Soul nature, via tuning into the power of their subconscious minds for deep inner shifts and healing. I use a method called the **Emotional Resonance Code™**, to slowly attune to the emotional and energetic body, by utilizing the intuition, and visualization techniques.

By utilizing our inner faculties that derive from the feminine creative power, and trusting in the importance of our own intuition, we create miracles in our lives. It is my knowing that our watery element of the feminine divinity has tremendous power and potential, and when we apply techniques to our psyche to accentuate this watery element, we discover many hidden treasures in our subconscious that allow for deep shifts to be made in our consciousness.

My truth, is that we must shift and transform our inner selves, in order to make any level of impact in our outer world. Even to be wealthy, and to create a good quality of life for ourselves; it all begins within, by changing the energy of who we are on the inside.

In this way we will magnetically attract what we desire in our lives, when we become an energetic match for that on the inside. It begins with our inner selves. By changing our inner Selves, we will change the world.

We will align, step by step, with the true inner channel that is ultimately a clear channel of Light. When this channel of Light becomes cleaner and cleaner, then we can decide and vigorously manifest that which we most desire. This channel of Light is revealing our Soul truth – who we are at a Soul level, and that will reveal to us our Purpose, in this world.

My story inspires people who feel stuck in their lives; those who feel invisible, silent, small, and are doubtful of why they are here on earth at this time. My deepest prayer is that they are inspired by my message and by my work.

My mission in life is to re wild our sacred Mother Earth with biodiverse trees and species, and to support individuals in healing their own inner nature and the path of Inner Connection, so that we as a species can connect to the outer nature and wonder of life on this planet. I also aim to financially support rehabilitation projects of mangroves and coral reefs, essential assets to this subtle and vulnerable ecosystem we are a part of. For Communities to rise up again in the world, and for humans to remember the importance of Community in self-empowerment and self-actualization; the highest level in Maslow's hierarchy of needs.

I encourage people to get activated by The Liberation Sanctuary, and to tune into and tap into the Emotional Resonance field, which is the human language of our energetic field. Emotions are *Energy in Motion*. This energetic field enables us to explore the imprints that lay upon us from our past history: past lives, youth, childhood and school lives. The metaphysical world of manifestation draws much interest and intrigue for me. I have found that when we go into our subconscious psyche, and use our intuitive field, enhanced with a sense of curiosity and playfulness, then we discover very much about our history ~ and we truly discover the Spiritual Purpose that we have on this earth.

My journey began as a young woman. This is where the seeds of my growth were made clear and visible, and I had a very active mind and imagination, always recognizing that there was something greater for me on this earth; some deeper purpose I had to fulfil.

I grew up as a very independent young girl, a *'self-soother'*, taking care of my own inner emotional needs. The truth is that I felt emotionally neglected, yet I only lately discovered this truth. I grew up with the belief that *'I'm not good enough'*, and I felt scared of life and uncertain of my direction in life. I felt like there was a force that was holding me back, and holding me down. People didn't really see me; wouldn't be able to truly connect with me, and I saw myself as an invisible force, compared to others.

I found it difficult to move away from the emotional and physical constraints of my parents, who were very mollycoddling, and I later discovered this was to do with an inner merging of my reality with theirs, a lack of clear boundaries, and a lack of emotional support.

Little did I know at that time, that there was a divine reason that all of this was taking place, and a reason that I had chosen my parents at this time of my growth.

In my 20's, I was in a difficult place financially, feeling that I had not followed my true path and vocation in life, and I was living with my parents for a few years. I began getting repeated panic attacks as I would argue with my mum, and I noticed that I really wanted to escape, but I did not have the financial means to do so. I had a particular experience that truly shocked my system, and awakened me to the very sensitive empathic Being that I am. A meeting with an ex-boyfriend of mine made way to some rough love making. I later learned that the world of sexuality. Is one to be very careful with, for it contains a lot of power and access to different dimensions. Your power can be accessed by others through the means of sexuality. I remember thinking "is this what I really want at this time?" Why can I not set my boundaries and say "no"!? I remember feeling that I was not allowed to say "no", and that I had to go along with what others wanted of me, and I had to please others. After this experience my body went into shock because of trauma, and I found myself running over the Dorset fields and hills at 6am, trying to shake off the intense energy that had shaken my inner Being. At the time it felt like a demon had taken over my Being.

I prayed to the Universe for something to take me out of this feeling state and situation in my life. Gratefully, she answered, with a discovery to a weekend workshop of deep inner emotional healing. I went to this workshop called **The Journey™,** feeling hesitant but very curious, and at the end of the weekend I felt like another person. So much weight had lifted off me, and this depression I had lived with my whole life was released. At the workshop, I dove into a deep black void, which was terrifying, yet I had three trainers urging me on to let go and surrender, which I did, and I was awakened to the most incredible feeling of Love, Peace and Bliss. I understood that this is our true nature, and when we really welcome our emotions, and dive into them and really feel them, then that gives rise to deeper emotions, layers of emotion, which ultimately rest in pure truth, and freedom: the nature of our Soul, and expansion.

Learning this lesson, was simple yet very profound for me. When we really welcome our emotions, and dive into the deepest parts of them, and let them overtake us completely, we realise that WE ARE NOT our emotions, yet we are an awareness and consciousness that is far greater than this. I had also learnt this previously, in my 10 years of training with Tibetan Buddhist meditation, yet this learning of how to truly release emotional stagnancy, painful memories and old beliefs was truly astonishing for me, and took me energetically to another level.

I had always wanted to work in nature, because I wanted to be with Mother Nature and to heal the great Earth, bringing animals, humans and nature into alignment and harmony. However, my path organically led me to not follow the route of scientific studies, and something didn't quite fit. I had an underlying feeling that getting a job in the natural sciences would not have the worldly impact that I was desiring.

Then one day, it came to me. What if all of the world leaders would dive into work like The Journey? What the world needs, is a shift in consciousness in fact. So that ALL the people in the world, and especially those who *lead* us, can do so from a place of alignment with their inner Joy, harmony and Bliss. When people act from this place, rather than from a place of fear, it is understood that they will create a positive impact on the world around them, as they will originate from a place of deeper compassion and empathy for those around them- by welcoming and inviting their emotions, rather than pushing them away, which creates fear & separation.

This was a turning point for me in discovering my mission and purpose in life:

To create a deep shift in consciousness in the world, so that we are living deeply in harmony with our environment. The outer nature is a reflection of our inner nature.

I am very much aligned with a great Vision of humans living in community life, where many inner wounds and conditionings are healed, so that we are confident, powerful and assertive human beings, authoritative in our own right, and with momentum and incentives to make a positive change in our environments, for ourselves and for others.

I can see it happening, with a Vision so strong I can almost touch it! So, in this case, I deeply know that it will happen. I even have ideas of creating films to reveal the essence and elements that embody this aliveness and empowerment in physical form.

It also refers to the balancing of the inner masculine and feminine elements, which have been distorted in the times gone by. This also needs clearing, and bonds of trust, respect and honor are ready to be formed on both sides.

My own journey has been a road also paved with many obstacles, the greatest being those of my own Inner beliefs and emotional heaviness. My personal catchphrase for life is: 'Your greatest challenges in life are also your greatest gifts', which I discovered as I began transforming my inner shyness, lack of confidence and self-doubt into that of confidence, empowerment, steadfastness and resilience. It came at a cost though, of staying aligned with my inner truth, no matter what. Even if it meant stepping away from the beliefs and values of my blood family, moving away from my home country, and feeling lost for a while in my sense of belonging in life. Yet, I know for sure that these things are temporary, and as my own boundaries become firm, and my inner Woman becomes a Priestess, and then a Queen, that all of these challenges will have been deeply worth it. The obstacles of my own inner beliefs, I have been able to work on, day by day, bit by bit, to clear them and to accelerate the process of stepping into my own truth. I have three different techniques to do this, and also managed to manifest the time and space required to be able to dive into this deep processing. The emotional heaviness, is still a process for me, because of the wallowing in the feminine, which I know is a result of the emotional neglect I felt as a child, and lifetimes back, as well. The more I work and intend to clear the feminine pain and distortion that exists in my energy and auric field, the clearer my feminine channel becomes and the more aligned I become with that which I am creating.

Sometimes I had the worry, that my assertiveness cannot yet be carried by the world: what if I want to re wild 20 fields in the UK, but the farmers are still stuck in an old mindset of conservative officialdom that does not allow me to make my impression?!

To address these internal niggling doubts, I have worked with local places- with charities, nature reserves and individuals who are making a positive impact in the way I wanted to see, and I either financially supported them, or I physically helped them out. I went to Portugal to support a start-up couple in planting thousands of native tree species to their plot of purchased land, to cover the fire ravaged desert that had once been non-native eucalyptus forest, which was ready to regenerate into a healthy a biodiverse environment.

I also connected with my local town councilor in the UK, back in 2012, and got together 70 species of native trees from the woodland trust (a national nature conservation organization), and also a bunch of local volunteers, to plant these trees. It was received with great enthusiasm, people are today enjoying the meadow and young forest, and it has inspired a local tree planting Facebook group for this town, and gives encouragement for others to take initiative, and to believe that they can make a difference. I fully believe that when a group of people come together with an aligned intention, and aligned vision for how things will manifest, then there is no way that it cannot manifest.

Unified thought brings way to manifestation, much faster than an individual thought pattern. This is why it is fundamentally important for us now to come together with a communal vision for highest manifestation, and also to have group Visionary sessions where you come together with a group of like minded individuals, and decide what you want to create, and close your eyes and fully envision that coming into fruition, with all the steps, gratitude, and high vibration energy that can be summoned.

The work that I am offering in the world is really being formed now. I lately held a workshop in a community called 'Turning Fear into Power'. I assisted a group of women to be guided internally to an old memory, that held energies of fear in asserting oneself, expressing boundaries and activating their inner anger and rage. I helped them to transform these old memories, through the power of the subconscious mind. They also shifted an old belief that held much power over them. It felt so incredibly transformative and needed at this time, to offer this powerful work to women, so that they can step up into the true powerhouses that they wish to be. We will be stepping into a new consciousness in this world, when we can activate our inner potentials. This requires us to feel into our life force energy, which is activated through connection with our rage, and to say 'no' to the things we no longer agree with in our lives. To feel the gratitude at the end of the workshop from these women, who truly felt the transformational power of it, was very heartwarming.

In my work I use the three fundamental components to guide Oneself on the beginning to healing: Awareness, Intention, and Action. To have the awareness about what is happening in your life and your Being, via journaling or other means, is the first step to shedding light on that which needs to be healed. I know that intention and gratitude are two incredibly important steps in our lives, with which we manifest our greatest desires.

When we set an intention in our lives, and make it very specific, combined with gratitude, we are telling the UNIVERSE in advance that we are so thankful for what we *have already received* in our lives.

The application of stating that we have 'already received it', even though we haven't, and believing it fully, feeling it in our bones, and knowing it internally, is a magnificent practice of manifestation. This is the way I recently manifested my Soul partner in my life (after having never felt capable to fall in love), and also manifesting my gorgeous one bed apartment (after never having had a home to call my own). The trick is that the more you do this, and the more habitual you make it, along with continuously clearing the channel of Light that you are, the more that you will manifest. Because you trust in the whole process greater and more deeply, and this makes your magnetism very strong. The Universe is like a Magnetic Vacuum. I like to coin the term *'channel of Light'*, because we are Beings of light, made up of filaments of Light, and our hearts are incredible magnets of love, the vibration of which is incredibly powerful. In my work I focus on 'connection'. Once we have a strong connection with our Selves, the fundament of all Being, the way will be opened up to connect with others that bring us true love and light, and enhance our lives in beautiful ways.

Our Beings of Light do get clouded by all of the conditionings that we receive in life: namely shame, guilt and blame, which are not actually emotions, but impressions of society- inevitably covering our true emotions, and then especially that of anger and rage, which are significantly repressed in women, and distorted in men. Manifestation is inevitably pronounced when our channels of light are clear of these conditionings; old beliefs that do not serve us, and only serve to attract fearful circumstances into our lives, and emotions that are heavy- the energy of which make deep energetic imprints on our Being and recreate situations, over and over again, so that our lives can end up looking like circular patterns. This is why I give the gift of tools to clear our channels of Light.

I studied the Journey method, and learnt how all of our emotions, and even our memories, are held in our bodies, and in the cells and DNA of our bodies. When we use simple methods, to connect with our subconscious, we can connect with this world of emotions and memories, and also deep-seated beliefs that want to pour out of and be freed from our cells, when the time is right. In this way, we are prevented from developing physical disease and disorder in our bodies, and it keeps our energy completely in flow and ease.

I employ the use of art therapy, journaling, shaking, visualization techniques, NLP techniques, meditation techniques and Osho techniques to shake up the conscious psyche and tap into the wonderful world of the inner Being. We all have our own modes of resonance, depending on our 'type'. Are we a visual person, kinaesthetic or auditory. This can also impact how well we work with different methods for healing our bodies and psyches.

Deep visualization tools will allow access to our subconscious psyches and enable us to change the old patterns and the old story. Our psyches are 95% made up of the subconscious mind, so that tells you what a great impression the subconscious holds over our Beings. If you have a sense of curiosity and playfulness, mixed with a willingness to be vulnerable, you can 100% shift and transform your Subconscious mind. This will heal old trauma wounds, PTSD, stress & deep anxiety.

Our greatest challenges in life are discovered as our greatest gifts, and when we go and explore these challenges, explore the emotional density that they are made up of, we find that these hold the greatest potential for growth and healing in our lives.

Then, we have the awareness of what facets we have to release, let go of or transform in order to heal from this energy, and we step into a new, up leveled energy, where we notice that we are no longer triggered by the old energy patterns.

Because we no longer get triggered by these energies, this is the space in which we can positively impact others, and share with them how they too can shift these energies.

We thus step into a higher awareness.

The awareness of the heavier density of the old experience, mixed with the heightened awareness of the new experience, gives us a great vantage point and a great understanding.

The compassion for ourselves and for others, is birthed from this experience, and thus we receive incredible gifts from this experience.

I want to share how I first manifested a wonderful thing in my life: my apartment, and how this manifestation impacted my future visioning for Humanity.

I lived for 6 months in Sweden, in a beautiful community aimed at conscious living and celebrating one's true self. This was a vibrant community, which provided all my basic needs- food, shelter, connection and communication with other Souls. In this place I found and felt the potential to 'self-actualize'- to step into my own inner potential and to feel what gifts I am inclined to offer the world. This encompassed offering Spiritual meditations: Osho Active meditations, which use the power of movement to stimulate and release the emotions, and to activate the life force energy. By offering these sessions each morning at 7am, and having the freedom and space to do this, I felt incredibly light and aligned with my inner purpose. Each day, around 4 people from the community would join me to energize and align their inner channels. From this space I met an elder from the Maori tribe of New Zealand, who shared with us the location of the two 'Mother Trees' in the forest.

These trees provide nutrition to other trees through the root system, and create a unified network under the earth that supports all surrounding trees, whether or not they are the same species.

I prayed to this Mother tree whilst I was in Sweden, and I felt the impact of my prayers, as I wished for an apartment in the Netherlands, with 30 very specific points. I made this out as a gratitude list, titled 'Thank you for', and then I listed all of the following points on an A4 sheet. I took this over to the Mother Tree, and prayed consistently, whilst taking the physical action to search for a new apartment. After just two searches, I found an agency and a listing of an apartment with all the points on the paper, except for one thing: a bath. (Baths are not common in the Netherlands) I signed up for the apartment with a motivation letter and I was accepted. Next thing I knew, I was arriving in the Netherlands with my one suitcase, and I received a key to an apartment I had never even seen before in real life! This was an epitome of trust for me and of going with the flow. And, it was the most perfect decision I made: all because I felt safe and in alignment at the community; to let myself be carried by life.

For this reason, I desire to inevitably manifest the realization of communities throughout the world. It is my true belief that living in this way, is the most natural and aligned way to live; where all of your needs can be met in a moment, where there is a natural overflow of abundance: of resources, of time and of energy, and where your self-potential can truly be realized.

Connectedness and Beingness are the truth, and in this remembering, we will also heal the Natural World. We must remember that we are a tribe, and we are intimately connected to our Earth.

The reason I also mentioned the Mother Tree, is that I truly felt in tune with her, and I felt that she gifted me the connectivity to the Universe, to manifest my greatest dreams and desires. The natural world listens to us and hears us, and so when we welcome the presence of the trees, plants, bees and butterflies, and actively communicate with them, they in turn communicate with the Spirit world and send electromagnetic waves through the Universe to pulsate our desires into manifestation.

It is all vibration. It is all frequency.

And for this reason, it is poignant, that human beings move out of the sense of individuality that hurts us and only enhances our Egos and our personalities, and move more deeply towards the sense of groundedness, that reminds us of how interconnected we all truly are. Out of 'knowing', and towards 'intuition'.

By stepping into the path of alignment with my own inner channel of Light, and living in my truth, aligning with my Soul, I can sense that I am becoming a guide and mentor for other women, who are also ready to live in their Truth, and to clear away the barriers, the conditionings and the energies that are stopping them from doing that.

I have guided many women in one-to-one sessions, to clear away this cloak of untruth and invisibility, that has clouded them in their lives. My intention is to work with women who decide to step into their Soul Truth, and away from the conditionings of their society that hold them back from their true purpose in life. I have also stepped into many communities, and activated my assertiveness to create power and potential in group settings. When I speak up and out about the shifts that I can already envision taking place, I can see the changes begin to happen and the energies begin to alter. Sometimes a fire needs to be started in order to purify and cleanse the energies that are there.

The greatest impact I currently feel is my massive sense of intention and the visions I have for humanity. To make these real, I intend to produce films that support my vision fully and make it manifested. Workshops, weekend events and community projects are being initiated and are coming into form.

I also envision coming together in group workshops and online sessions: opening the portals of Light in the magnetic framework around the world, and welcoming the Spirit Beings onto earth that can enhance our true knowledge of our DNA strands- remembering the power that we truly have, and encouraging us to activate that further.

My impact in the world:

I have inspired women to step into their power.

In my local community I have inspired women and men to step into their Leadership potential and live in their Light.

I have actively encouraged tree planting, and connection with the natural world by organizing tree planting events, and I have inspired further action and collaborations.

I initiated Red Tent Tilburg- a women's circle in my local area.

I am starting an organization, Red Roots, that teaches women how to plant and manage tree growth, and to take a stand for the Earth, which we are intimately a part of.

My business The Liberation Sanctuary is being activated online.

I am carrying out group workshops for healing, and individual coaching to step into your Power and your Light.

I have learnt to not take myself too seriously, and if something comes up for me, I know that it is for my greatest learning and growth. I can be objective with my triggers and take them with a pinch of salt. I would say: Follow your hunches and your intuition. It knows best. Step into the fear and the fire and you will transform yourself and others.

Step into YOUR EMOTIONS and feel them fully!!

That is the greatest lesson in life.

When I discovered my purpose, it felt very satisfying, yet also bewildering, because I did not know how I would fulfill this mission. I just had to keep my greatest Vision in mind, and follow the smaller breadcrumbs in life, to take me to the grand picture, which required some time and patience.

I do regular exercise and I prioritize being in nature, and swimming in the outdoor lakes to cleanse my Spirit. I love to feel free to wander in nature wherever I am called. Planting wildflower seeds and trees brings me great nourishment.

I hope my story inspires others to feel the importance of their time here on earth now, and to not be afraid to step into the fire of transformation and into their Truth.

My advice to others is: Remember the three steps to manifestation: Awareness, Intention and Action. Journal! And write down your insights about your own struggles with a sense of objectivity and compassion. Do the Inner Work!

'A butterflies' wings can cause a tornado on the other side of the world...'

Edward Norton Lorenz: The Chaos Theory

Just remember how powerful you are, and when you have an inspired Vision, have no doubt that it is meant for you. Even if it takes another 20 years to get there, taking small steps will give you so much satisfaction and peace on your path in this life. I believe that we are all meant for a great destiny on this Earth. So, live your most inspired and greatest Truth, and actively remove all of the obstacles that are stopping you from getting there!

Namasté

Claire Libré

The Liberation Sanctuary

Bio

Claire Libré: The Liberation Sanctuary

Claire Libré is CEO of The Liberation Sanctuary, an organization that endeavours to heal your inner world via Emotional attunement, in order to create great transformations in your outer reality. Claire holds coaching sessions to guide women on a path of true Soul Purpose, by clearing away blocks that no longer serve you in your life. She holds workshops to invite women to step from Fear into Power, to stimulate the inner fire that enables us to take true heart centered action in the world. Her Vision is to activate greater inner connection, that enables for community living in harmony.

www.theliberationsanctuary.com

Soochen low-

The Next Wave- Creating Value-ABLE leaders in our next generation

As I sit here, at the 48th year juncture of my life experience, contemplating how best to share the insights, wisdom and clarity I gained; it is fascinating to me that my life purpose and legacy became clear to me at the most chaotic and tumultuous phase of my life. A time Dr. Wayne Dyer defined as the 6pm of your life, the turning point where most 'die' in the face of a major crisis whilst others discover their higher self and become aligned to what they are destined to create in this lifetime.

The old me did die; my life imploded and exploded; shattering my ideals, identity and place in this world. When I thought that was the end and could only see a perpetual void ahead of me; a new me was born and rose from the smithereens. I saw with acute clarity this "awful wrong thing that should not have happened to me" happened *for* me, for a greater purpose, to prepare me for the contribution I was destined and uniquely designed to create in this life and world.

It is now approaching 3 years after I walked out of a 10 year abusive marriage. In this time, I've had to process and heal from the trauma, grieve the death of a significant relationship, navigate a challenging divorce and settlement process that triggers a painful past, let go of the life I knew, release ideas of how my life should have turned out, deal with practical challenges like where to live, what to do about money, whilst bearing witness to the delicious and miraculous new life experience I fashioned as the more evolved, intentional and powerful creator that I am.

In the quiet and solitude, I found myself confronted by several questions that wanted answers-

How did I get here? Who's to blame? What do I do now? Where to from here? and Who do I choose to be from now on?

The Universe gifted me answers through the blessing of children. On my 46th birthday, 1 week after I left my marriage, I received a call from a potential client that catapulted my finances from negative to a 6 figure yearly revenue, established my new company and became the start of my legacy project unfolding. It was the answer to *"What do I do now?"* and *"Where to from here?"*

It was an opportunity to travel and work closely with primary and high school students in metropolitan Sydney and country regions of Australia, activating their creative power through hands-on problem solving in mathematics and numeracy. I have now worked with 60,000 students impressing on them the creative power of a positive and growth mindset, values and collaborative team work. In return, I received priceless gifts that healed and inspired a battered spirit who was bone tired, heart weary, and though spiritually resilient was displaced by the chaotic circumstances in my life.

The Gift of Motherhood

I have always loved children and thought I would have my own family when I got married. Children and I have a common language because I remember vividly the pain and struggles I went through as a child, teenager and young adult. I see, feel, hear and know where they are at. As a result, they gravitate towards my loving and trusting energy, often coming to hug or talk to me. Many times they ask if I have children. and when I answer, "No", they always say, "I think you make a good Mum."

When I walked out of my abusive marriage to save myself, it meant an end to having children. When I was gifted the joy and privilege to work with at least 500 children a week, I knew the Universe had granted my wish in a better and grander way than I could ever have imagined. Even though I had to forgo the experience of having children go **through** me, the significance of being surrounded and working so closely with them in such great numbers daily was not lost on me. It was Universe's knock on my door. The call is to be of service to children as a role model or catalyst. Someone who honors their inherent creative power and uniqueness; guides them to fulfill their potential by being the example of how to live that out in everyday life.

The Gift of Presence

I love children's ability to be fully immersed in the present moment. This is why they can laugh one minute, cry the next and go back to laughing again. Being with children helped me forget my pain and let go of 'what's going to happen next' and 'will I be all right'? Their laughter and freedom inspired me to laugh and be free as I looked down upon my life seeing that all is well and everything is unfolding for my highest good. In this energy where we are most connected to our true creative power and the Universe, problems become opportunities for growth.

The Gift of Authenticity

Before they evolve to teenagers, children are at their most authentic. They care less about what people think or what they should or should not say. They are totally comfortable with who they are and express that fully. I welcomed their refreshing honesty; it contained a sincere wish to learn the truth without shame of 'not knowing'. What others may consider rude, I saw them expressing their uniqueness unapologetically. As a veteran people-pleaser who thought I needed to earn love and approval from everyone until my abusive marriage taught me otherwise, I celebrated this value children had. It helped me continue to practice claiming and owning my right to be the unique me, totally loveable and superawesome no matter what. If others did not agree, it did not change the inherent worth I knew was my birthright.

The Gift of Creativity

Children love to play. Using their imagination comes naturally to them and they are always finding new ways to have fun, explore and create. I observed that even when they are unable to read what they are asked to do at specific activities, they are able to form their own level of understanding. Even if it may not be 'correct', they start interacting with the pieces and jump right into enjoying what is in front of them. When you show them exactly what the activity asks them to do, they respond with an excited, "Ahhhh!!" and quickly continue playing. They do not stop to justify or defend why they got it 'wrong' or they 'didn't know'. Their optimism and openness to infinite possibility reminded me of when I was 4 years old and the idea of 'never ending fun' delighted me with great anticipation. It is interesting that things that seemed like 'fun' when we were younger and couldn't wait to experience eventually became burdens, worries and fears that as adults have to struggle with through life. This inspired memory reminded me to approach my life as a curious creator instead of a defeated victim.

The Gift of Goodness

From ages 4 through to 16, the common thread I observed across the varying faiths, cultural, economic and family backgrounds, was children's inherent goodness- the willingness to do good and be the best they can be. They are like eager sponges, always ready to learn and change in their desire to be helpful, respectful, loving, kind and *good*. In their presence, I saw that I too have always tried my best to be helpful, respectful, loving, kind and good in all the varying roles I played throughout my life. Whilst I was gratified by this realization, it also triggered the question- "If I have truly been respectful, kind, loving, and good, then why did this awful bad thing happen to me? **How did I get here?**

The Gift of Vulnerability

When children first come into this world, they are innocent, blank canvases. They come with a predestined trust they will always be provided for. They are open to receive love, food, shelter and everything they need to foster their growth and development. Their unrestrained vulnerability calls us to protect and help these defenseless beings navigate the ways of this world. Paradoxically, this same vulnerability exposes them to potential manipulation, harm and abuse. Even though my intuition had warned me when I first met my ex-husband, I was too young to understand the message. Instead I trusted people are inherently good and can change when showered by love and kindness. This kept me working on my abusive marriage for 10 years, leaving no stone unturned. When I realized no matter what I did, how I did it, or how much I gave was not going to change him or our marriage, it gave me clarity to leave.

The problem is not in my kindness, love and goodness; it is in his **choice** to manipulate and abuse instead of honoring it. I got here because I chose to be good, kind and loving anyway, to live as the authentic me; *not* to prevent 'bad' things from happening. As a child, I trusted my goodness would keep me safe. As an adult, I learnt my goodness led me to recognise those who sincerely honor it.

The Gift of Compassion

The vast majority of my 60,000 experiences have been very enjoyable; a credit to the parents and teachers who passed on their wisdom and modeled the values and behaviors that serve children as they grow up as members of society. I have also worked with children who are disrespectful to their peers, teachers and equipment, bossy, selfish, impatient, aggressive, easily defeated, reliant, clingy, entitled, unkind, and disengaged.

As isolated behaviors, they may seem insignificant, after all, 'kids are kids' but when they amass in critical numbers of 60, 70, 80 in 60 min sessions, up to 400 students a day, these 'insignificant' behaviors quickly gather into an exhausting and draining force. During those moments, it would be easy for me to direct my frustrations at the children. However, I realized they are walking reflections of what they have been soaking up from the people in their lives and environments. Until the age of 7, children haven't the ability to accept or reject what comes into their consciousness. Through osmosis, they adopt it all through their parents, family, siblings, teachers, friends and all whom they are connected to, including social media. This can be a positive if we as adults, elders, or leaders desire to see and know exactly what we are impressing on our next generation. Conversely, this truth can be confronting and humbling when we understand exactly how much power and influence we truly have. As my heart goes out to the innocent children, I also feel for us adults, who are doing the best we can to get on with life whilst learning to overcome the hurt from our childhood. Despite this, we still have underlying intentions to improve what we've been taught so others can avoid the pain we may have suffered.

On days when my past visited me through nightmares, sleepless nights and unexplainable fear, my instinct was to blame someone for my suffering and find where it all started. First, I made peace with myself. Next, my ex-husband. Then, my parents. I discovered I learnt people-pleasing from my parents which spread to how I interacted with the world including my life partner. My abusive marriage played out the familiar yet debilitating patterns I learnt. Blaming Mum and Dad did not release my anger or resentment. Instead, I felt the noose tighten as I relinquished my power over to them.

Through the gift of compassion, I recognised my parents also learnt to earn love and approval from their parents; and my grandparents did too from my great-grandparents. This is a common thread of injustice that spans generations across cultures. What ultimately freed me was that 'Hurt people hurt people'. Seen from this light, I appreciated that my parents were also hurt by the conditions imposed by their parents to earn love and acceptance. Despite their hurt, they got on with life, tried to change or improve what their parents did so I would not suffer as they did. Honestly, what they did missed the mark in many ways. But when I put myself in their position and asked, "If I was still hurt from my past and trying to do better, knowing only what I knew *then*, surrounded by the cultural conditioning of that time, could *I* have done better?" My answer was, "No". My parents left me with wounds I needed to heal from, but also gifted me values of kindness, love, patience, resilience, generosity, perseverance, commitment, dedication and purpose which enabled me to navigate my married years with hope and courage; rise from the fallout and ultimately heal and triumph.

So, "Who's to blame?"

Not my parents, my ex-husband or me.

To be clear, I am not condoning out of integrity behavior. I became more skilled at understanding my intuition and developed an intolerance for anything that remotely smells of manipulation or misalignment. I also have a heightened level of discernment to know who is responsible for the dark behavior and no longer hesitate to call it out when I feel its presence. Identifying the source is clarity and wisdom. Blaming it, instead of choosing what new experience I wish to create fueled by the new found clarity is giving permission for it to continue puppeteering my life, forever at its mercy.

It is said our life lessons are delivered through our traumas, wounds, pain and suffering; a Divine plan for us to lead *extraordinary*, not comfortable or easy lives. To master and triumph over them, we are also gifted with tools, skills, talents and resources.

Life is not a perfect science. We make mistakes; we learn, grow, evolve and do the best we can from what we know until the next moment.

As adults, we now have the opportunity to curate the life experience we feel is aligned to our authentic self by having agency of the old programming we received and only accept what that supports us as unique creators of our life and destiny.

When we take our power back from what or who limits us, see the 'good' as supporters, 'bad' as catalysts sent to facilitate our growth and expansion, we evolve from the child within and emerge as adult victors of our new stories.

The Shift

Along with the gifts, I observed an interesting yet disturbing shift. I saw the authenticity, presence, creativity, vulnerability, and goodness I celebrated in children begin to contain traces of fear, scarcity and comparison in their mindsets, and interactions with each other from ages 10-11 and through to 16. They are signs that children are departing from their authentic selves as they grow. They run into detours that potentially derail them from their inherent unique creative power.

The Trap of Mistakes

"If I don't try, then I can't fail."

Where students younger than 10 years old view mistakes as 'how we learn and grow' and 'everybody makes mistakes, you can try again', high school students appear burdened by mistakes.

Where primary school students continue to be resilient, persistent, imaginative, open to try, explore and make mistakes when problem solving, the same activities see high school students walking away without even trying. They are reluctant to read questions with lengthy text and want answers spoonfed. They second guess themselves and are afraid of being seen as who they are and judged as 'too smart', 'too slow', 'too stupid'... According to teachers, the price of trying and failing is too high so it's better if they don't try at all. This way, no one is around to witness their weaknesses or 'failures'.

They copy answers from their friends instead of solving it for themselves. They go for activities that look easy and avoid those that appear hard. Some could argue this is due to laziness or lack of interest in the subject but I would suggest that if children are inherently curious, creative, open to explore and have fun, perhaps there has been a shift in their conditioning where they now view their mistakes as failures and consequently define themselves as failures. As the purpose of life is to learn, grow and evolve, life will be full of 'mistakes'. If our young people already believe they are failures because they make mistakes and mistakes confirm they are failures, they give up before they even start. Life then becomes a never ending cycle of pain and despair where they are unable to create fulfilling and meaningful lives on their own terms.

The Trap of Unworthiness

"You are a waste of life."

In my introduction to students, I shared with them the difference between positive and negative communication in teamwork and their impact on the creative problem solving process. To illustrate an example of negative communication, I asked, "If your teammate made a mistake when solving the question, what is something negative you would say?"

When a student answered, "You are a waste of life"; we all winced as the harshness cuts us at the core. I was shocked and saddened that he had to hear this so early on in his experience. Whether it came from a friend, an adult or social media, it had already taken root far and deep in his consciousness to apply it to a different context from which he may have heard originally. His peers did not seem surprised at his comment confirming they too are exposed to similar messages. In this scenario, high school students now equate mistakes to a life wasted and a waste of existence. Specifically, our teenagers think they are unworthy. Instead of being excited about life's adventures, eager to rise to challenges with enthusiasm, trusting they will always triumph whilst showcasing the best of who they are as they learn and grow; I grieve how discouraged, disengaged and hopeless they feel as every 'failed' attempt from poor grades, not getting a job or dysfunctional relationships later in life constantly reminds and mocks their unworthiness. As young people trudge through life carrying the badge of "Unworthy", this phenomenon has reached critical mass where recent statistics reveal that already high percentages of youth suicides, violence, alcohol and drug abuse, depression, bullying etc are on the rise, not only in Australia but globally. Unless a more powerful and positive force is in place to mitigate and turn the tide, their limited mindsets will continue to grow as they grow to adulthood, creating a generation of leaders who feel unworthy at their core.

The Trap of 'Not Enough'

"My mom defines me by the marks I get"

During the 5-10 min debrief with students at the end of the problem solving session, I ask, "What is one positive thing you learned about yourself today?" One student said she learnt her friend is 'actually really smart at Maths'. My response was, "Well, for you to see that in your friend means you are very smart too."

I was surprised when she came to me after the other students had left and confessed, "Miss, I am not smart at all. I'm very dumb at Math. I failed Math, I got less than 50% on my exam."

I replied, "Do not let your marks define how smart you are. She answered, "Yes I know, but my Mum defines me by the marks I get in Maths."

This exchange illustrates how we as adults have modeled defining our value through external labels. In our achievement oriented society, different benchmarks determine how successful a person is. Grades define how smart we are, age defines how valuable we are, money defines how rich we are, career defines how successful we are and number of followers on social media define how popular we are. When our youth observe us abandoning our dreams, values and purpose in order to live up to these external labels, they learn there's no room for their uniqueness; they are 'not enough" and need to earn love and approval to fit in and survive. Over time, they forget their authentic compass, give up on fulfilling their dreams and live out their lives without purpose or direction.

The Trap of Money, Fame & Power

"I don't need to know Math. When I become rich, I'll hire an accountant."

In a discussion with students, I shared why Math or numeracy is relevant to everyday life. A student raised his hand and said, "Miss, when I'm rich, I'll hire an accountant so I won't need to know Math. He'll do it for me."

I replied, "Yes, he will but you still need some understanding of numbers so you know he's managing your accounts correctly."

This conversation indicates our young people have learnt that money, synonymous with fame and power, helps you bypass what you like or don't like to do. It is a shortcut and fast track to a great life without the 'hard' work. As a business owner, I agree that money is a powerful resource and an impactful enabler. However, when seen as the 'magic pill' that can buy you friends, love and acceptance, worthiness and 'make all your problems go away', it is a misleading picture we have painted for our youth. Instead of placing importance on how kind and resilient a person is, they are more focused on how 'cool' someone is, how many Instagram followers they have and how rich they are. Many successful people who reached the pinnacle of wealth, fame and power often discover the peace, joy and love they thought they would find out of reach.

When our young people see attaining large sums of money, fame and power as the goal, learning and self-growth along with values like resilience, perseverance, kindness, commitment and courage become unnecessary and inconvenient. As they chase after the illusions that money, fame and power promises, their authentic value and moral compass gradually erodes as they become potential instigators or victims to unethical business practices, corrupt and coercive management, domestic violence, and crimes in order to fill the insatiable void within.

"Who do I choose to be from now on?"

After I reflected on the observations I've shared with you thus far; I revisited my abusive marriage, this time seeing my ex-husband and I as who we inherently were- 2 children. We were born in different parts of the world, had different parents model for us what life was all about according to their culture and faiths, we each learned who we needed to be and what to do to get on with life, we carried with us our unique life lessons, traumas, skills, strengths and weaknesses as we grew until the moment our paths merged and decided to create a life together. With the power of what I know now, what would I like to tell my 5 year old self?

I'll say to her,

"You are unique, special, powerful and loveable exactly the way you are. No matter what anyone else says or what happens in life, remember this Truth. You do not _ever_ need to be someone else to have what you want. Keep learning to find out how and why you are unique, special, powerful and loveable exactly the way you are. When you know, keep growing to be more of that, all the time, for your entire life- this is your superpower."

To him, I'd say, "You are good and kind, so you deserve goodness and kindness in your life. It is safe for you to enjoy and treasure them with all your heart. This is how they will stay with you forever."

What would you like to say to your 5 year old self now that you are clearer and wiser? What lessons or wisdom would you like to share with your child, children in your care or young people in your life to help them create fulfilling and meaningful lives?

As a Creative Power Business Alchemist and Sovereign Leadership Catalyst in my business coaching practice, a major part of my 'Monetise your Creative Power' methodology involves helping my female clients like entrepreneurs, coaches, healers, and personal transformation experts release the darkness from their childhood, extract the wisdom to own their unique creative power and grow their businesses to consistent $10K months. It means understanding why and how they no longer need to be trapped by old limiting stories of failure, not enoughness, unworthiness, competition and having to earn love and approval and ultimately be in sovereign leadership of their income, life and destiny. These are the same traps that high school students are already falling into as they grow into adults. To stop this cycle from repeating itself, **now** is my time to share my insights, life lessons and wisdom with children in ways that nurtures their authenticity, presence, vulnerability, creativity and goodness whilst encouraging their uniqueness to flourish. I choose to be someone who puts an end to disempowering cycles and guides them to fulfill their unlimited potential as intentional creators of their lives and destinies. In turn, they can then lead the change for their next generations.

Creating Intergenerational Change- 'Potentia Regina'

Latin for 'Queen Power' or Sovereignty, **Potentia Regina** is an action research project I created inviting parents/caregivers- leaders at home, teachers/educators and our young people to engage in a collaborative conversation where we establish a new set of standards from which we create value-ABLE leaders in our next generation. These leaders become of service and *add value* to their communities and society by expressing and sharing their inherent creative power whilst being grounded by their *embodied values*. Grounded by Eastern values until 9 years old, then matured into adolescence and adulthood supported by Western values of individuality, freedom and creativity; I've enjoyed the best of both worlds and have come to discover a beautiful balance. To veer too much to the West is like a wild horse; whilst too much to the East can be breaking its spirit and turning it into a workhorse. The powerful middle is like the horse whisperer who honors its free spirit whilst harnessing its creative power to heal. The same can be said for children. When their inherent creative power is stifled by limiting social conditioning, they are unable to express their unlimited potential. Without grounding forces to provide structure for their free spirits, they do not know how best to apply their power and can become vulnerable to distractions and manipulation. Values are supportive yet expansive structures that serve as their North star whilst holding space for them to create purposefully.

For real, sustainable and intergenerational change, this movement needs the support of leaders at home, leaders in schools and leaders in society to model the values that we as a collective decide are critical to creating value-ABLE leaders in our next generation. Together, we can then develop practical tools and resources designed to help them develop value-ABLE skills and create their unique, fulfilling and meaningful education, career and life pathways.

If you've ever been a child, a parent, teacher or leader in society, I know you have invaluable life lessons and wisdom to share. I am not talking about the knowledge that comes from textbooks but the gold you've gained firsthand through life's ups and downs. They are the answers to questions like, "Should I still respect someone rich and powerful when they put me down? Who should I listen to- everyone or my heart? How do I know who I can really trust in life? How to tell the difference between someone who is truly kind from someone who looks kind? If something were to happen to you tomorrow and you are not here anymore, how do I know I will be OK?'

223

I'd love to see a world where leaders know they are unique, worthy, powerful and loved. They lead from embodied values of love, kindness, compassion, generosity, resilience and courage to create fulfilling and impactful lives full of love, joy, peace, wealth and abundance.

If you share this vision, I invite you to share your insights and wisdom by joining us in this collaborative conversation and movement. Together, let's create a deep and enriching fountain of wisdom from which our next generations can draw from. Let's come together and make fear, scarcity, violence and abuse be a thing of the past, superseded by the value-ABLE leaders that we curate together.

Bio

Creative Power Business Alchemist & *Sovereign Leadership Catalyst* Soochen Low is CEO of Happy.Positive.Successful, Founder of *'Potentia Regina'*, 2X International #1 Bestselling Author and International Keynote Speaker.

With 30 years experience in the coaching, hospitality, fashion & haircare industries, she helps creative female coaches and entrepreneurs grow their businesses to consistent $10K months without struggle, people-pleasing, or having to prove themselves, by harnessing their creativity to build expansive business structures, customized to their genius, so they can own their unique power and be in sovereign leadership of their income, life and destiny.

With a BDesign with First Class Honours in Fashion Design, MBA from University of Technology specialising in Management & Managing for Sustainability, she is an inspiring speaker and teacher. She has changed the lives of millions of Chinese listeners through her Business Alchemy methodology and is a regular guest on summits and podcasts.

Women and children are Soochen's passions. She's a STAND for their sovereignty and is testament of the magic and abundance that flows into your life when you own, harness and unleash your unique creative power.

Connect with Soochen: www.happypositivesuccessful.com

Book your FREE Monetize your Creative Power Soul-Strategy call https://ed.gr/durs8

Freebie: '1 Magic Ingredient to grow your biz to $10K months' Masterclass https://forms.aweber.com/form/09/294265009.htm

Linktree: https://linktr.ee/soochenlow

Rebecca Engle-

Your Trip is Uniquely Yours

I am Rebecca Engle, a 22 year-old educator on the verge of completing my master's degree. My passion for teaching is deeply rooted in my personal experiences growing up with special needs, navigating the public school system, and overcoming developmental delays. At four, I was non-verbal, prone to tantrums, and struggled with motor skills. My parents were given a grim prognosis from doctors who doubted I would ever speak or progress beyond basic tasks. One even suggested my mother use school hours to focus on hobbies, implying my potential was limited. However, my parents refused to accept this, embarking on a journey of research, therapy, and dietary changes that unlocked my voice, personality, and abilities. By the end of fifth grade, I no longer required an Individualized Education Plan (IEP), having made significant strides. My achievements were made possible by the unwavering support of my family and educators who believed in my potential.

My experiences highlighted the need for special education reform. The traditional system often fails to support students with neurodivergent conditions, which are too frequently viewed as limitations. Autism and other developmental differences are not deficits but variations that should be understood and embraced. My journey is a testament to perseverance and the power of supportive communities. I aim to inspire others to see the potential in every student and advocate for an inclusive education system.

My mission extends beyond the classroom. I am driven by personal experiences that shaped my understanding of what it means to be both a student and teacher in a system that often overlooks those who are different. Early on, I struggled with the label of being "different." Despite the low expectations placed on me, I eventually spoke my first words, defying the experts' predictions. This pivotal moment fueled my desire to help other children find their voices, both literally and metaphorically. My purpose became clear: to advocate for every child, particularly those who are misunderstood or misjudged.

The turning point in my career came when I observed a special education classroom in high school. The challenges these students faced, combined with systemic injustices, reinforced my commitment to make a difference in their lives. I am not just focused on academic instruction but on creating environments where every child feels valued and capable of greatness.

The bullying and exclusion I faced throughout my schooling, including relentless teasing and even physical aggression and cyberbullying, taught me resilience and the importance of

self-worth. Middle school also introduced another harsh reality—sexual harassment—further fueling my desire to stand up for myself and others. Seclusion, often used as a misguided form of behavior management in schools, isolated me in damaging ways, reinforcing the need for reform in how we approach special education.

These experiences led me to advocacy work, where I share my story and raise awareness about the challenges students with special needs face. I began volunteering in special education classrooms and became involved in advocacy organizations, deepening my understanding of the importance of support and inclusion. I am committed to fostering classrooms where every student feels seen, heard, and valued.

Throughout my life, I've learned the power of perseverance, creativity, and service. I turned to poetry to process my emotions and engaged in volunteer work, which earned me both

district-wide and presidential recognition. Despite the challenges I faced, a strong support network of family, mentors, and friends helped me cultivate a growth mindset. This allowed me to skip 11th grade and graduate high school early, marking a significant milestone in my journey of giving back and making a difference.

My story is about overcoming challenges, embracing differences, and advocating for an inclusive future. I hope to inspire others to see the unique potential in every child and join me in creating a more inclusive and supportive educational system.

Finding My Voice

My journey to finding my voice began with various forms of self-expression, beginning with my business during the COVID-19 pandemic. After high school, I turned knitting into a business, which provided me with not only a creative outlet but also a supportive community. This entrepreneurial endeavor allowed me to connect with others who appreciated my work, giving me confidence in sharing my creative pursuits.

As my business grew, so did my willingness to share my poetry, which had always been a deeply personal form of expression. I began submitting poems to publications, and seeing my work published gave me a sense of validation and reinforced my desire to keep writing. This recognition helped me reach a broader audience, allowing me to connect with people who resonated with my experiences and ideas.

Public speaking became a powerful avenue for self-expression. Speaking at schools and events allowed me to challenge stereotypes, share my story, and promote empathy. These combined efforts helped me find my voice and use it to inspire others to embrace their strengths and advocate for positive change.

Building a Support Network

Throughout my journey, building a strong support system has been critical to my personal and professional growth. My business friends, boyfriend, and best friend and family have each played vital roles in shaping my success. My business friends have offered mentorship and guidance, helping me navigate challenges and open doors to new opportunities. Their belief in my vision has encouraged me to take risks and expand my reach.

My boyfriend and family have been a steadfast source of encouragement, offering emotional and practical support. Their unwavering belief in my abilities has helped me stay grounded and confident, especially during moments of self-doubt. Their presence has been a constant reminder that I am not alone in my journey.

Equally important, my best friend has provided emotional support and friendship, always ready to listen and celebrate my achievements. Their understanding and encouragement have been a driving force behind my continued growth. With their support, I've been able to push beyond my comfort zone and pursue my goals with a renewed sense of purpose.

Together, these relationships have created a foundation of trust, belief, and collaboration that continues to sustain me as I navigate the challenges and triumphs in both my personal and professional life.

Key Milestones

My journey has been filled with significant milestones that have profoundly shaped my personal and academic growth. One of my earliest accomplishments was skipping the 11th grade, which marked the beginning of a series of transformative experiences. Transitioning off my Individualized Education Plan (IEP) by the 5th grade was another pivotal milestone that reflected my resilience. While this transition was a source of pride, it also introduced challenges, as I encountered moments where I lost points on assignments due to speech-related difficulties. Despite the frustrations, I learned the importance of self-advocacy, developing skills to communicate my needs effectively.

Graduating high school early with honors was a moment of immense pride and reflection, symbolizing years of hard work, determination, and resilience. This accomplishment motivated me to pursue higher education, where I immersed myself in learning opportunities that expanded my horizons. My time in college was not just about academic achievement; it was also a period of personal growth and exploration. During this time, I was recognized with several awards for my academic excellence and contributions to my community. These accolades underscored my commitment to making a positive impact and fueled my passion for education.

One of the most transformative experiences during my college journey was becoming the youngest elected woman in Texas at the age of 19. This achievement was a testament to my dedication to advocacy and community engagement. It was a remarkable opportunity to represent my peers and contribute to meaningful discussions on issues affecting our community. This role deepened my understanding of civic responsibility and further solidified my desire to create inclusive environments for all individuals.

In addition to my political involvement, I had the honor of being featured in various magazines and tv outlets, highlighting my achievements and perspectives as a young leader. These features provided a platform to share my story and inspire others, emphasizing the importance of resilience and the power of community. Sharing my journey with a broader audience reinforced my belief in the importance of representation and the impact that diverse voices can have in shaping our society.

As I pursue my master's degree in Educational Policy and Leadership, I am committed to deepening my expertise in areas that promote equitable education for all students, particularly those with diverse needs. This journey is not merely about academic advancement; it's about preparing myself to advocate for change and make a meaningful impact within the education system. I am excited about the potential to contribute to innovative practices that enhance learning experiences and outcomes for all students.

Each milestone in my life has taught me valuable lessons about resilience, advocacy, and the importance of community. My journey reflects a commitment to personal and professional growth, ready to embrace new challenges and opportunities that lie ahead. I look forward to continuing to make a difference, using my experiences and insights to empower others and advocate for positive change.

Challenges and Triumphs

Throughout my journey, I encountered numerous obstacles that tested my resolve, and one of the most painful was the discrimination I faced in college, particularly regarding my abilities as an aspiring educator. Despite excelling in my coursework and demonstrating my capabilities in the classroom, several professors openly questioned my capabilities for teaching due to my disabilities. Without directly bringing them up

They doubted whether I could manage a classroom or effectively communicate with students, even though I had proven my skills time and again.

What made this discrimination especially difficult was the fact that these professors were fully aware of my background, yet they chose to focus on their biases rather than my achievements. During observations and practical teaching experiences, they scrutinized me more harshly than my peers, frequently questioning my methods and abilities in ways that felt rooted in doubt about my disability rather than legitimate critiques of my teaching practices. This created an environment where I was not only expected to meet the high standards set for all student teachers but also to overcome their preconceived notions about what I could and could not do.

One professor even implied that I might not be suited for a career in education, not because of any shortcomings in my performance but because they believed my disability in my communication skills would prevent me from being an effective teacher. These comments were not only disheartening but also unjust, as they disregarded the dedication, passion, and success I had shown in both my studies and my fieldwork.

Despite the adversity, I remained determined to prove them wrong. I pushed forward, excelling in my teaching alternative cert program and earning praise from the students and staff I worked with. Graduating with honors was not just a personal accomplishment—it was a victory over the biases and discrimination that could have undermined my confidence and derailed my career path. Each challenge I faced reinforced my belief in my abilities and fueled my passion for creating inclusive, supportive learning environments for students of all abilities.

This experience further strengthened my resolve to advocate for myself and others in similar situations. I am deeply committed to ensuring that future educators, especially those with disabilities, are not subjected to the same unfair treatment and that our schools foster environments where diversity is valued and celebrated.

Giving Back

As a board member for multiple non-profits, I'm deeply involved in shaping and supporting initiatives that address various community needs. My roles encompass strategizing on program development, fundraising, and community outreach efforts. By leveraging my skills and experiences, I help drive meaningful change, ensuring these organizations can effectively achieve their missions.

Beyond my professional responsibilities, I actively engage in numerous projects and events organized by these non-profits. I help plan community events, mentor emerging leaders, and advocate for critical issues affecting our communities. For instance, I have participated in initiatives aimed at enhancing accessibility and inclusivity for individuals with disabilities, striving to create environments where everyone can thrive. My contributions are always centered around enhancing the impact of these organizations, fostering collaboration, and building lasting relationships with community members.

In recognition of my dedication and the positive impact of my efforts, I have received several presidential awards, which serve as a testament to my commitment to service and leadership. These accolades highlight my ability to mobilize resources and inspire others to join in our mission to uplift underserved populations. The recognition is not just an honor; it is a reminder of the importance of community service and the collective effort required to drive social change.

Through these experiences, I have learned invaluable lessons in leadership and collaboration. Working alongside passionate individuals who share a common goal has reinforced my belief in the power of collective effort. I have witnessed firsthand the difference that dedicated individuals can make in their communities, and I am continuously inspired by the resilience and determination of those I work with.

My journey has also underscored the importance of giving back. By actively engaging in community service, I not only contribute to meaningful projects but also cultivate a deeper understanding of the challenges faced by others. This empathy drives me to advocate for positive change and empowers me to support initiatives that make a tangible difference in people's lives. Each interaction and experience has enriched my perspective and fueled my commitment to promoting social justice and equity. Ultimately, I believe that through collective action and compassion, we can build stronger, more inclusive communities for all.

Impact on Others

Reflecting on my journey, I've seen how my actions and initiatives have positively affected others in several meaningful ways. As a special education teacher, I've strived to create an inclusive environment that caters to students with diverse needs. My commitment to implementing individualized learning plans has empowered many students to achieve academic milestones that once seemed out of reach. I take great pride in witnessing their growth, and I'm grateful for the feedback I receive from parents and colleagues, who often highlight the supportive and effective learning atmosphere that my approach fosters. By focusing on each student's unique strengths and challenges, I aim to cultivate a classroom where every learner feels valued and capable.

Beyond my teaching role, my involvement with non-profits has been another avenue through which I can make a significant impact. Participating in fundraising events and community outreach efforts has allowed me to support crucial resources for underserved populations. I have seen firsthand how access to education, mentorship, and basic necessities can transform lives. Feedback from community leaders and beneficiaries underscores the difference these efforts have made, reinforcing my belief in the power of collective action. It is inspiring to see how these initiatives have provided individuals with opportunities that can change the trajectory of their lives.

Additionally, my roles in volunteering and board membership have provided me with the opportunity to mentor emerging leaders. I find immense joy in guiding individuals as they navigate their own paths, offering support and sharing the lessons I've learned along the way. The testimonials from those I've mentored reflect the positive influence I've had on their careers and personal development, reminding me of the ripple effect that one person's commitment to uplift others can have.

Each of these experiences confirms the meaningful impact of my contributions and the positive changes they have brought about. I believe that every interaction, every effort to support someone else, and every initiative to foster inclusivity adds up to create a larger movement toward equity and opportunity. As I continue my journey, I remain dedicated to championing the causes that matter most, knowing that the work I do today can help shape a brighter future for others. This commitment fuels my passion for education and advocacy, driving me to make a lasting difference in my community and beyond.

Personal Growth and Development

Throughout my life, I have embarked on a profound journey of personal growth that has shaped my identity and aspirations. Resilience and adaptability stand out as cornerstones of my character, honed through various challenges and experiences. Growing up as an autistic individual, I faced unique hurdles, particularly being non-verbal until the age of fou. This experience instilled in me a deep understanding of communication's complexities and the diverse ways people express themselves. It has also fostered a profound sense of empathy for others facing similar challenges.

Navigating the education system as a student with learning disabilities required me to develop strong advocacy skills early on. I learned to articulate my needs, whether through meetings or classroom discussions, ensuring that my voice was heard. This experience laid the groundwork for my future role as a special education teacher. My journey in education, filled with ups and downs, allowed me to embrace my authentic self and realize the importance of supporting others in their unique paths.

As a special education teacher, I have cultivated a supportive and inclusive environment in my classroom. This role has challenged me to think critically about the diverse needs of my students, fostering my creativity in developing teaching strategies that resonate with various learning styles. I draw from my own experiences to inspire my students, emphasizing that challenges can be stepping stones to success. Each day, I strive to instill a sense of empowerment in my students, encouraging them to embrace their identities and pursue their goals.

Serving on nonprofit boards has further enriched my skill set and broadened my perspective. Collaborating with like-minded individuals has enhanced my leadership capabilities and deepened my understanding of community needs. Through these experiences, I have developed strategic thinking and problem-solving skills that enable me to contribute meaningfully to our collective mission. My passion for advocacy has grown, as I recognize the power of collective action in driving positive change.

Inspirational Moments

Several pivotal moments have inspired me and propelled my journey forward. Launching my business was a dream realized, representing not only my passion but also my commitment to making a meaningful impact in the lives of others. The process of turning my ideas into reality was filled with challenges, yet each obstacle became an opportunity for growth. From securing my first client to expanding my services, each milestone reinforced my belief in my abilities and the value I bring to the table. Witnessing the positive impact of my work has been incredibly fulfilling, motivating me to continue pursuing my mission.

Another transformative moment in my life was obtaining my teacher certification. This achievement was the culmination of years of hard work, dedication, and self-discovery. It validated my skills and knowledge, opening doors to new opportunities to make a difference in the classroom. I vividly recall the emotions I felt on that day—pride, excitement, and a renewed commitment to education. The journey leading to this achievement deepened my passion for teaching and reinforced my belief in the importance of supporting students from diverse backgrounds, particularly those with learning disabilities.

Additionally, volunteering in various capacities has provided countless inspirational moments. Engaging with community members and witnessing their resilience and determination has profoundly influenced my perspective on challenges. Their stories of overcoming adversity serve as a constant reminder of the strength inherent in each individual. These experiences have not only inspired me but also reinforced my commitment to being an advocate for those who may not have a voice.

Overcoming Doubts

Despite these successes, I have faced periods of self-doubt and imposter syndrome, particularly during significant transitions like starting my business and pursuing my teacher certification. The pressure to meet high expectations, both from myself and others, often loomed large, leading to moments of uncertainty about my capabilities.

To combat these feelings, I developed a multifaceted approach. First and foremost, I engaged in self-reflection, reminding myself of my accomplishments and the hard work that led me to this point.

Reflecting on milestones like successfully launching my business and earning my teacher certification allowed me to acknowledge my capabilities and reaffirm my self-worth.

Seeking support from mentors and peers has also been crucial. I actively reached out to trusted individuals, engaging in conversations about my doubts and seeking their perspectives. Their encouragement and constructive feedback provided the reassurance I needed, allowing me to regain focus and confidence. I realized that everyone experiences doubt, and sharing these feelings with others fosters connection and support.

Setting small, achievable goals has been another effective strategy. By breaking down larger objectives into manageable steps, I could celebrate each success, reinforcing my confidence and motivation. This incremental approach allowed me to build momentum, gradually diminishing the weight of self-doubt.

Vision for the Future

As I look ahead, my vision is centered on deepening my impact both professionally and personally. In my teaching career, I aspire to develop innovative programs and strategies that enhance learning outcomes and provide even greater support for my students' diverse needs. I envision collaborating with fellow educators and institutions to share best practices and create inclusive environments where every student can thrive.

My business will continue to evolve as I refine my services and explore new opportunities to reach a broader audience. I am committed to seeking partnerships that align with my mission, amplifying the positive impact of my work. By collaborating with organizations and individuals who share my values, I hope to create a network of support that fosters growth and innovation.

In my role as a non-profit board member, I will focus on strengthening our initiatives and exploring new avenues to address community needs. Expanding our reach and forging meaningful partnerships will enhance our effectiveness, enabling us to make a more significant difference in the lives of those we serve.

My vision for the future extends beyond professional goals. I aim to continue my personal growth journey, seeking opportunities for learning and self-improvement. This includes ongoing education and development in areas that align with my passion for advocacy and support for individuals with disabilities. I hope to leverage my experiences to inspire others, sharing my journey and the lessons I've learned along the way.

Lessons Learned

The experiences and challenges I have encountered throughout my life have imparted several invaluable lessons that shape my identity. Embracing resilience and adaptability has taught me to navigate challenges with grace, turning obstacles into opportunities for growth. I have learned the importance of self-advocacy and confidence, empowering me to pursue my goals despite the ever-present specter of self-doubt.

The power of collaboration has been another significant lesson. Engaging with mentors, colleagues, and community members has enriched my personal and professional endeavors, providing diverse perspectives and valuable feedback. I have come to appreciate that collective action amplifies our impact, allowing us to drive positive change in meaningful ways.

Commitment to continuous learning and self-reflection has been essential for my growth. Regularly assessing my progress, celebrating achievements, and remaining open to feedback have been cornerstones of my development. I recognize that personal and professional growth is a lifelong journey, one that requires patience, dedication, and a willingness to embrace new challenges.

Collaboration and Networking

Collaboration has been instrumental in my success and growth, shaping the trajectory of my professional journey. Engaging with colleagues, mentors, and community members has provided diverse perspectives, valuable feedback, and support, enriching my experiences. For example, collaborating with fellow educators has led to innovative teaching strategies and a more inclusive learning environment. The exchange of ideas and experiences fosters creativity and allows us to develop solutions that address the complex needs of our students.

Building a strong network involves several key strategies. Actively engaging with others in my field through events, professional organizations, and online communities has been essential. By connecting with like-minded individuals, I have built meaningful relationships that provide support and inspiration. I prioritize reciprocal relationships, offering assistance and encouragement to others while seeking their guidance in return.

Maintaining these connections is crucial. I make a conscious effort to stay in touch with my network, providing value through updates, resources, and collaborative opportunities. This ongoing engagement fosters a sense of community and support, creating a network that can help navigate challenges and achieve shared goals.

Balance and Self-Care

Maintaining balance between my mission and personal life is essential for sustaining my energy and passion. I prioritize self-care and set clear boundaries between work and personal time.

Scheduling moments for relaxation and joy is vital for my well-being. Whether it's enjoying my hobbies, such as knitting or writing, or spending quality time with loved ones, these activities allow me to recharge and remain focused on my professional endeavors.

I also practice mindfulness and reflection as part of my self-care routine. Taking time to assess my thoughts and feelings helps me stay grounded and aware of my emotional well-being. This practice enhances my resilience, allowing me to navigate challenges with a clearer perspective

The Power of Community

Being part of a community has been a source of empowerment and motivation throughout my journey. The support and encouragement from those around me have provided validation and motivation, helping me stay focused on my goals. The sense of belonging and shared purpose within my community drives my personal and professional growth.

Collective action amplifies our impact. Whether collaborating with colleagues, serving on non-profit boards, or participating in community initiatives, our combined efforts towards common goals have led to more substantial outcomes. This collaborative spirit fosters a sense of solidarity and shared achievement, reinforcing the idea that we can accomplish more together than alone.

Through my community involvement, I have learned the value of diverse perspectives. Engaging with individuals from various backgrounds and experiences has broadened my understanding of the challenges others face, deepening my empathy and commitment to advocacy. I recognize that by lifting others, we create a stronger, more inclusive community that benefits everyone.

Advocacy for Mental Health Awareness

Recognizing the significance of mental health, I have developed a strong passion for advocating for mental health awareness, particularly within educational settings. Understanding that mental health plays a crucial role in a student's overall well-being and academic success, I strive to create a supportive environment where students feel safe discussing their mental health challenges.

I have initiated conversations about mental health in my classroom, encouraging open dialogue and reducing stigma. By integrating mindfulness practices and self-care discussions into my curriculum, I aim to equip my students with tools to manage stress and navigate their emotional well-being. I believe that fostering a culture of mental health awareness not only benefits my students but also contributes to a more compassionate and understanding school community.

Final Thoughts

As I reflect on my journey, I want to leave readers with a message of perseverance and empowerment, much like the insights one might gain from solving a Rubik's Cube. Each challenge I faced, and every milestone I achieved reminds me of the words, "The cube is a puzzle, and solving it is a journey." Overcoming obstacles and achieving goals is akin to twisting and turning the cube until you find the right solution.

Remember the quote, "Success is not the end, failure is not fatal: It is the courage to continue that counts." My experiences have taught me that with resilience, a supportive community, and a commitment to continuous growth, you can navigate the complexities of your journey and make a meaningful impact.

My story inspires you to approach your challenges with the patience and determination to solve a Rubik's Cube. Embrace your journey with confidence and trust in your abilities, and remember that each twist and turn brings you closer to your goals. Your trip is uniquely yours, and with perseverance, you can find the solution and make a lasting difference.

Bio

Rebecca Engle is a dedicated educator and author with a strong background in special education. She holds a Bachelor's Degree in Interdisciplinary Studies from Incarnate Word and is pursuing a master's in Educational Policy and Leadership at Texas Tech. With a passion for creating inclusive learning environments, Rebecca is committed to supporting her students' growth and development. Outside the classroom, she enjoys knitting, writing, and volunteering. Rebecca is also an active board member for several non-profit organizations.

Athena Menelaou-

Why did I become a teacher?

My journey as a teacher began before I was born. I was born in Limassol, Cyprus, an island in the Eastern Mediterranean Sea.

A note about Cyprus's history: The Ottomans conquered Cyprus in 1571 until 1878.

In 1878, the island of Cyprus in the Eastern Mediterranean Sea came under British control. Its population is both Greek and Turkish Cypriots. The Greek Cypriot majority desired the removal of British rule and union with Greece, known as Enosis. In 1955, the campaign for Enosis led by the president, Archbishop Makarios of the Cyprus Orthodox Church and by Colonel George Grivas, Head of- National Organisation of Cypriot Fighters (EOKA). They aimed to achieve Enosis by attacking government and military installations and personnel and mobilizing the civilian population to demonstrate against the British presence. EOKA launched its campaign on 1 April 1955 with a series of bombing attacks against government offices in the island's capital Nicosia. The island's governor, Lord Harding, declared a state of emergency in November 1955. The British Government started looking for a political solution to this problem.

In March 1956, president Makarios, is exiled to the island of Seychelles. Many British reinforcements continued to arrive and began operations against EOKA. Gradually, British tactics began to have an effect and by 1957, most of the EOKA's leaders were either killed or captured. EOKA continued to organize riots by using students and schoolchildren. These attacks continued throughout 1958, even after Makarios had abandoned his initial demand for Enosis. An agreement was reached in London and finally things ended in February 1959. Cyprus was to become an independent republic.

Britain would retain two sovereign base areas on the island at Akrotiri and Dhekeila.

In August 1960, Cyprus became a republic, but in the following decades, it was plagued with violence between the Greek and Turkish communities. In 1974, a Greek military coup, which aimed to unite the island with mainland Greece, led to a Turkish invasion and the division of the island between Turkish Northern Cyprus and the Greek Cypriot Republic of Cyprus. Cyprus remains divided to this day. That is the some history of Cyprus, there is more….many cultures since ancient times have invaded Cyprus because of its location.

Now for my parents, George and Afendra Menelaou had a unique journey to education.

Their views of school were very different. My mom was the youngest of six siblings and disliked school, because of her teachers. They would yell at her and some even would hit her. Finally, she had enough and at grade, three she dropped out. Her mom would drag her to school and she would always run away. Her mom had enough and left her alone.

My mom learned the school of life, how to cook and sew. The priest's wife taught some girls in the village how to sew without a pattern by using a newspaper. She also learned to cook from her sisters. Mom was ready for her role as a wife when the time came. Her husband would take care of all her needs. Mom took her time to get married. She was about 27 years old when she got married. Most of her friends were married by 16 years old.

Mom at this time was living in the city of Limassol; her brother moved the whole family there when she was young for a better life. A neigh borough introduced my parents and after one year of courtship, they got married. My dad told my mom that he always wanted to leave Cyprus for a better future and mom agreed but the children needed to be born in Cyprus she told him. They had three children, two girls and one boy.

Mom was my first teacher and taught us all to read before we attended school. My dad bought my mom a beginner's reader to reading. We were ready for grade one, thanks to mom.

Coming to Canada, she took care of us and then she began to focus on herself. She would attend all night vigils with her friends but she could not read the prayers very well. She wanted to pray to Virgin Mary properly but did not know all the words. She set out to learn by repeatedly saying her prayers and asking dad for his help on some of the words that she did not know. She set out her goal to read and did it. She was very proud of her achievements. Today you see her carrying her pray book everywhere she goes. She would sometimes say to me, "These prayers helped me to read." She felt so accomplished and happy.

My father's story is different. His father, Menelaos Philipou, wanted my dad to get education. My grandfather was a poor shepherd man and he greatly valued education. He would often tell my dad, "Son, get educated. Do not remain stupid like me. Life unfortunately, had other plans for my dad. His father suddenly died early, leaving behind four children to fend for themselves and their mom.

My dad been the eldest had to support his family and he dropped out of school to get a job. He could not take care of the sheep and some of the villagers even began to steal from him. The family sold the sheep and my dad went to the city of Limassol to look for a job. He found a job as a mechanic and then rest of the family joined him. Grandma and dad worked while the younger kids attended school. Grandma was not afraid of work. She even worked in construction making roads by carrying rocks. Over the years, she found a better job by working with my dad at the British armed basis as a housekeeper. She would make toast and tea for the British nurses. My dad taught her some Basic English words; toast, cheese, jam, butter and she did great. She understood the nurses and took care of their breakfast.

My father's passion for learning was ongoing and did not stop by him dropping out of school. He would read Greek newspapers to improve his Greek; he read books on different languages like Italian and British English. He already knew Turkish from his village. He also loved history and read many books on that topic. On his spare time, he would draw, paint, or make things with his hands.

My parents had three children and my oldest sister started school. My brother and I would wait anxiously for her return. My mom gave her money and she would buy us candy. I was anxious to tell me what she learned at school

That day. She would pretend she was the teacher and would teach me the lesson.

My turn came to go to school in grade one and I was excited.

In Cyprus, everyone wore uniforms. My mom sewed us the white and black checkered dress with two pockets in the front. We wore white ankle socks with black shoes and a band on our hair. If your hair was long, then you had to braid it. In the morning, we all lined up in our lines according to our grades and waited for our teacher to arrive; the inspection began and they would check if our shoes and nails were clean, and if they were not, the teacher would sent you home to clean up. Our school was only two minutes away.

We all sat in rows in our class, and raised our hands to talk. My teacher was kind and I liked him very much.

At school, every class had a garden where we would plant things like beans, cucumbers, and flowers. It was a beautiful garden and every class would take care of their garden.

We had concerts, and all the parents and kids from the neighborhood would come to watch us sing. In grade three, the school had home education, and the first they taught us was how to make Greek/Turkish coffee. I was looking forward to making coffee for my mom and relatives. It was also the beginning of learning how to speak British English. Now, I can have conversations with my dad and his friends when they come over the house. School is fun and exciting!

My father one day informed us that we were leaving from Cyprus to go to Canada. He applied for his work visa to work in Canada and it finally arrived after waiting for three years. He had chosen Canada because someone from our neighborhood was living there. Dad wrote him a letter about Canada. His friend Mr. Andreas told my dad, that Canada was great and it was 1970s.

Dad was wondering what countries to go to, Argentina,Canada or England? He finally picked Canada. (I have not asked him why he did not go to England since he worked for the British armed forces and Cyprus was near England.)

My dad came first by ship and landed in Halifax, Nova Scotia. (Years later when we visited Nova Scotia, he would show us where the ship landed and what happened later. He then took a train to Toronto with three other men he met on the ship. One of them had a sister living in Toronto, and they asked him if they could live with her and pay rent to her. She agreed and they all lived in the basement. The rent included a light breakfast.)

He needed to find a full time job and an apartment for his family. He finally did and on October 4th, 1970 he sent for his kids. We flew for the first time in an airplane. I do not remember been scared, I was happy to see my dad. I recalled that I kept asking the flight attendants for things with the little English I learned in school, like coke and cookies. My sister was too shy to ask and my brother was too young.

We finally landed, and it was great to see my dad. He really missed us. Dad found a job in Mississauga and an apartment for us until we bought a house in the city.

I was in grade 3 now, and school was a challenge because of the language. I did not know how to read or speak much English. The difficulty began when I needed to go to the washroom. I would put glue on my hands, show the teacher, and run to the bathroom. I get my clothes all sticky. I did this several times, and my teacher started frowning. I knew I had to change my way, and I finally asked my dad to write on a piece of the word washroom so I could show it to my teacher. He did, I showed it to her, and she was smiling. She tried to help me by getting students to read with me. One day, it was a boy. I was so shy that I kept moving away from him while he was moving closer to me; we went all the way around the table, and I had to stop because there was no more space. The teacher next time would put a girl to read with me.

On picture day, I wore the warm pants that my mother had made, and the photographer placed me in the front center row. All the other girls wore dresses. I was the only one with pants. Years later, I noticed it; I thought I was special because he placed me in the middle. My sister and I made a few friends but I still missed my friends and relatives back home.

The weather in this new country was horrible and very cold. One windy day, we were going to school, and the wind threw us into puddle even though we were all holding unto a pole.

The couch in the living room was our bedroom and bed. Mom even put plastic over the couch to preserve it because we were not going to buy another one for a long time.

We had that couch for 40 years, and she moved it into the basement of the house. Finally, I had enough and with my brother, we threw it away without telling her. We bought her another one in its place. She was upset at first then she was fine.

My parents brought money with them to buy a house in Toronto, and after a year living in the outskirts, we were ready for the city. We bought a in the Greek area known as the Danforth (Danforth was the area for new immigrants of Greeks and Italians). My location and neighborhood were primarily Italian. The Greek area began from Pape to Broadview. I grew up with Italian bakeries, Italian shoe stores, and beautiful Italian boutiques. Hearing Italian in our streets, I began to pick the Italian language.

I worked as a salesperson at a clothing store on Saturdays and the Italian words came in handy with the Italian women. They even thought I was Italian.

Life in the 70s was a great time to be in Canada. Life was very affordable, and many things were free. For instance, the neighborhood community center had many free programs. I learned to play the guitar at 12 years old, exercise at the gym with mom; she would sometimes come with my friends and me. We had Greek and English movie theatres that were affordable on Saturdays with deals at noontime tickets.

Great shoe stores and boutiques. Great Greek restaurants and bakeries. One Greek bakery would make awesome sculptures out of chocolate and he would display them at his front window. He won many awards and he was always in the newspaper. I loved looking at his window to see his creations. We had it all in that neighborhood.

Life moved on. We had a house, went to Greek school and Sunday school. Sunday was special day where we attended church and then to the movies (years later, dad told me that in Cyprus he would go to the movies on Sunday because they played a double feature with one ticket. His favorite movies were westerns and they still are.)

Eventually, my parents met other Cypriot families, and we all would gather to celebrate anything and everything: birthdays, name days, getting a job, anniversaries….just a reason to get together to laugh, tell stories and dance. That central location was where Dad used to live when he first came to Toronto, Mrs.

Veroni's and Mr. Sotiris's house. I remembered the dancing and lots of laughter. Those were good days, and people took the time to meet. I always looked forward to those house parties. We created many friendships, and we went to different parks for picnics, visited Niagara Falls, and visited cottages near Lake Simcoe and the park at Jackson Point. Jackson Point was near Toronto and many Greeks and other nationalities would go to escape the city.

School now, things changed when I moved to my new school in Toronto called Wilkinson. They put me back a year because I could not communicate in English well. My ESL teacher was very mean to me and made me feel dumb and dirty. I would not answer her simple questions, pretending I did not understand. One day she asked me, how long I was in Canada, and I told her I did not know. (I was only in Canada for a year, but I did not want to answer her.) Every day I had to go to endure going to her class for one hour to practice English. I am in grade four; I hate my ESL teacher and school. She managed to make me feel stupid and I believed her lies.

Years later, I learned the truth about her, from a VP that was at Wilkinson. I approached him for help with interview questions and he helped me out. The conversation came by and he wanted to know why I wanted to be a teacher. I then told him my ESL experience and I never want to see a child go through school feeling as I did. He revealed that he know that teacher and she had issues. Finally, I learned the truth all these years.

School for me was a place that I went to see my friends, and not to learn anything because I was dumb. The ESL teacher damaged me and I believed her. My parents taught me to respect your elders and teachers. I would put my head down when I went to my ESL class because I did not want to look at her in the face. I did not make an effort to improve and I believed her lies that I was stupid and could not learn. I am in grade four and I hate school.

The years went on and in grade five, I would get in trouble for talking because I was so bored. I started to doodle so I would not speak and would not listen to the nonsense that he was saying that I came from apes. I do not believe in that. It was a theory, so why were they teaching it like the truth? I thought that God made me. I would go home and talk with my dad about what they taught us in school. He said, do not cause trouble; listen and learn the language. We believe in God, not apes. My dad was my support system, and we had great conversations. He would tell me stories back home of how life was, and they were exciting. Life for him was difficult, and he wanted a better life for us. He knew education was the only way out of poverty.

Grade 6 was excellent, with a wonderful teacher, but the feeling of being stupid never left me, and no one knew about it. I do not know why I never shared my ESL story with him. I felt he had many things to worry about, mortgage, his work, and providing food for us.

My sister would come to my rescue and help me with my schoolwork. I was a hyperactive child and could not focus. I did not have the patience to sit and read like my sister.

She would summarize the important things, I would memorize them and I would write the tests. (One time, my Greek schoolteacher thought I cheated and I said, no my sister helped me to study.)

I discovered in high school that I needed glasses. The optometrist said that I did not need them. I finally tested my eyes again in University and the optometrist said; I should have gotten them in high school. Well, it is never too late.

Years later I learned from my second cousin about a school that would place new immigrant's students, teach them to get to their level then put them in the grade that they belonged. She never failed. That school was near our house and I never understood why we never attended that school? I guess we were three children and that meant money for the school.

School experiences continue…..

One teacher I had in grade eight left an impression on me. My grade eight, homeroom teacher who drank from a Coke can filled with alcohol and ate chocolate by touching his mustache so we could not smell his breath. He did all that in front of me. I was just laughing inside of me. He was an alcoholic and I am surprised the other teachers did not say anything to him. My best friend and I would ask him to go to the library, and he said yes. I spent the whole year in the library and I did not learn anything that year. That cost me in grade nine because I did not learn anything in grade eight.

High school years was a place where I went to socialize, skip classes like gym, and go to the cafeteria dances every month with Kathy.

We had many great teachers in Riverdale Collegiate. I took chemistry, did well because my teacher was funny, and tried to make the lessons enjoyable. I noticed that if I liked the teacher than I did better at the course.

One of my gym teacher was mean and thought I was a lesbian because I did not have a boyfriend in high school. She did not know my dad or the Greek culture. My dad was very strict about things like that; he wanted me to focus on school. One finishes school, then your parents find, you a suitable mate. You have a choice to say no.

One year for my prom, I brought my best friend Jim. When the gym teacher saw me, her jaw fell open. She could not believe it.

I had many male friends in high school, but I would not date them. My dad was right; males want one thing from a girl. I thought, why tease my male friends? I could not give them what they wanted, so I kept them at a distance and were friends. Many males liked me, as they later told me and I told them, I had no clue.

My first job,I had to beg my dad to keep my job and he said as long as you keep up your grades in school.

I finally bought my first skinny Calvin Klein jeans, and I loved them. I wore them until I got holes, and my mom finally threw them away. I was able to help my siblings by giving part of my money to them. My dad would give us some money but he had a mortgage to pay off.

I started shopping with my best friend Kathy; we would take the subway downtown, find designer stores and then find her parents to give us a ride back home. We found beautiful designer stores and clothes. Dressing well was very important for me back then.

My sister was too shy to work and was not encouraged to work. My brother once he was older started looking for a part time job.

My best friend Kathy, and her brother had a band, and they would practice in her basement. I often went to her home to see the people in the band. His band performed at our school, and then to other venues. We were so proud of them. Her brother moved on to become a professor for University of Toronto.

Most of our friends in high school were Greek and we had so much fun speaking our language. Some teachers though did not like. We were careful to watch out for them and we would speak when they were not around.

In my last year of high school, I was so confused about my future and I did not want to go to University. I attended college and took general courses, which prepared me for university.

I then applied to university which I received my Bachelor of Arts. While there, I studied British literature and drama. I really enjoyed my acting classes that I was serious about getting into acting, but I read a book that changed my mind about acting. The book mentioned that it was very competitive and unstable job. (Later years, I did a background performer for films, I saw what it entails, and it was long hours. Glad for the summer experience but it was not for me.)

After my B.A. I applied for my Bachelor of Education in Edmonton, Alberta. I had my Early Childhood Education and it helped me when I needed to communicate with parents as an elementary teacher.

After two years, I finished teachers college. TDSB (Toronto District School Board of Education) hired me as a full time special education teacher. I also took extra courses in drama.

I taught many different grades, kindergarten to grade eight and I learned many things from my students.

As a first year teacher at my first school, I had many help from parents, coaches and other teachers. One of my parents would help me every morning with group of students working on their high frequency words. That really helped them increase their reading levels.

I would ask consultants to help me with some of my behavioral students. The consultant would come to my class, observe the class, and offer suggestions. She suggested one of my behavior students to go on the computer as soon as she came in the morning then I could focus on the rest of the class.

My assistant had many years' experience as a special education. She gave me great suggestions of how to teach special education students in math and other subjects. I had a lot of respect for her.

We had a lot of respect for each other. She was had difficulties with walking up and down the stairs, so I would photocopy things that I needed. I would never send her. That is respect and cooperation. It was important to have respect with the people I worked with.

I wanted to be the best teacher for my students and I attended many workshops after school to learn as much as I could.

If I knew a teacher was great in math, I asked them if they could help me. Math was always my weakness. One of our teachers would come to my class on his prep time and did a math lesson while I took notes. He pointed out that one of my grade 4 students was bored in my class but he could manage grade 6 math. I often sent him to the grade 6 teacher to do math and he loved it. I am glad that this teacher noticed my student he was happy going to do grade six math.

When I was teaching grade two, I decided to do something different with my students. I would give each student a week's outline of what needed to complete for that week. The students would choose what subject they wanted to begin that day, say art and begin with that. On this schedule, they needed to complete language arts, math, art, science, and social studies. They loved it. It was more work for me, but I felt they needed to be excited about school. They should choose what they want to learn.

I was not afraid to ask for help from other teachers. I wanted to be the best teacher for my students; I did not want them to be bored like I was in school.

I would always try different things, such as experiments or field trips. Anything to make learning engaging for my students.

I taught different grades, but the ones I loved the most were grade 4 and drama. One of my principals recognized how much I liked drama and gave me that position. I taught drama as a prep teacher and I would go on and put on plays for the whole school. I would plan performances with different classes to highlight every month. This was much more work for me, but that is not how I saw it. I felt the arts were essential in the education system. Students needed an outlet to express themselves, and the arts did exactly that.

One year while I was doing some research on great schools, I found a video on an elementary school in New York where the students were failing. They introduced art in their entire curriculum, and the scores increased. Students wanted to attend and were on a waiting list to attend that school.

Education needs to change. We need to find ways to reach to all our students.

I wanted to be a teacher to make a change in the lives of my students and treat them with respect

Sadly, our present education system is failing our students. The government has taken money out of the education system and reduced the consultants, assistants, and resources.

Special needs students are placed in large classes and are having a difficult time.

One year, I had a kindergarten student who exhibited signs of autism. He was nonverbal; he ran out of the classroom and covered his ears when the national anthem came on. My new principal did not assist me with this child. I took matters in my own hands. Thank God, his father and I worked together. He brought him in in the mornings, for a bit until he got used to full day. I changed the setting, and placed him near me. He liked books and bubbles. I put different animals in his bubble tray and he would play. I often consulted with the diagnostic kindergarten assistant and she gave me great ideas to try. I finally brought him up to the school team, and we discussed the child with the father, who was present. He agreed, with our suggestions and we placed him in the diagnostic kindergarten program, which we had at our school where he thrived.

Some of my students liked to set up clubs, and they would lead them. I supported them by giving up my lunch and classroom. I watched with amazement as they accomplished what they did, and I was very proud of them!

At the board level, I was able to join many different committees. I started with the social and ended with the ARESJ (anti-racist committee). One of the events I helped organize with the other members was teaching grade 7 and 8 students how to be a teacher

My stories are many! I was not afraid to advocate for my students. My students deserve the best education. Many returned and told me what they did with their lives: engineers, business people, teachers…..I was very proud of them!

I did my best. I worked hard on my lesson plans, researched new teaching methods, decorated my classroom, and spent many sleepless nights wondering about my students.

I greatly valued education because of my father and his father, two generations that valued education.

Education comes in different forms as long as we learn, grow, and contribute to society for the greater good.

Bio

I wanted to share my experience of how I went from disliking school to becoming a teacher. I had the support of my family, my colleagues, my parents and my consultants.

It takes a village to raise and educate a child.

I am still teaching but I changed the big city life to a remote northern community in Manitoba. I am teaching in a small community where I teach grade one to four.

It is a great experience and the students are very loving!

Dr. Sherine Brown-

Trials to Triumph

My name is Dr. Sherine Brown, and I graduated from Walden University. My research focused on church leaders' perceptions of their role in deterring juvenile reincarceration. I obtained a bachelor's degree in counseling and an associate degree in Family Life Education. I also obtained a master's in philosophy from the university. I am a member of the National Society of Leadership and Success, the Golden Key International Honor Society, and the Tau Alpha Chi Honor Society.

In May 2016, I started my PhD program at Walden University. Throughout this period, I worked three jobs. One might wonder why I had three jobs. I needed financial stability, especially as an international student. Despite facing skepticism and concerns about managing three jobs alongside my studies, I was resolute in my determination to make it work.

My chapter will be about how, as a woman from humble beginnings, I endured and overcame trials and became victorious from being raised by my grandmother (deceased in 2023) and single parent to find a light at the end of the tunnel. Keep pressing on! We can make it despite the odds. My purpose and my why, and now graduating with a PhD. I aim to use this story to show that I have been through challenging times and never gave up in a small community in Clarendon.

Sowing the Seed

Growing up in Jamaica, in a small community in Clarendon, I always wanted to have influence in the lives of others. I grew up watching my grandparents provide support to others in the community. My grandfather always referred to me as his giant' Words are powerful and can determine one's destiny. I held on to the scriptures and motivation I received to press on. My favorite scripture is I can do all things through Christ who strengthens me." (Philippians 4:13). I am a firstborn, and my goal was to set an example for my siblings and make a difference in the world. I have taken up the mantle, I have sown the seed, and it is my goal that others will learn and benefit from my actions. I have also planted a seed in my youngest sister, who resides in Jamaica. I wanted to ensure that she could gain an education, so I encouraged her to enroll in college, and this year, I can say that she has completed her degree in Business Administration. It all starts by sowing a seed and helping others to believe in themselves. I was encouraged to press and complete this journey by sowing a seed. I also live by this philosophical thought: "Whatever it is you want, plant it, sow it, give it, and it shall be given unto you." Adrian Rogers

Trials that make me strong

In 2021, I received prospectus approval. As I began Chapter 2, I decided to gain motivation while helping others by facilitating a support group held every Sunday via Zoom. We learned a lot in the group and offered support to each other. It took me a few years to complete Chapter 2, "The Elephant." I was faced with many setbacks, including having back pain, which was unbearable at times, and I could not write.

The year 2023 was indeed one of significant challenges. Although I focused my time, energy, and heart on helping others, the same people hurt me. I will continue to do good no matter what because I have a genuine heart. I also suffered an eye injury that prevented me from being able to see clearly for a few weeks. I have faced many obstacles, such as the onset of intense back pain that led me to seek medical attention and frequent visits to the chiropractor. I woke up one day to realize I could not walk. Consequently, I went to the doctor to find out that I had sustained a minor chip on my ankle some time ago. My mobility was compromised without a crutch.

In 2022, I changed jobs and spent the time learning about my new job while continuing to write chapters 2 and 3. I gained approval for the proposal, and finally, I did it. I completed my oral presentation. I gained IRB approval a few weeks later. The next step was indeed the phase I was most excited about: the data collection phase. I encountered a few challenges while completing this phase, which took me about eight weeks to gather all my participants for my study. Just when I thought I had faced some significant challenges.

My grandmother (my best friend) passed away two weeks after my birthday. I was torn apart, and I could not and still do not believe what had happened. On the day I heard the news about my grandmother's passing, I had an interview scheduled with a research participant. Instead of canceling, I kept the appointment since my grandmother would encourage me to continue. I had to take time off to travel home to make plans and attend the funeral. I decided to take unpaid leave for a month to be there for my family after the funeral to support and help with family-related activities. Upon returning a few weeks later, I found out that my grand aunt (my grandmother's sister) passed away. I was again broken and could not fathom the news. I had a mentor who encouraged me, my grandfather, who has been a tower of strength, and my mom, who has always prayed for me.

Without support, encouragement, and prayer, where would I be? I later gained the motivation to keep pressing on! Through it all, I learn to trust in Jesus; I learn to trust in God. I also always try to remember my Why."

Faith, Hope and Self-Care

When I embarked on the journey to completing my Ph.D., I was still determining how to finance my education since I always paid my way through college without a loan. The search to find a school that would offer me a scholarship to complete my PhD was long and tedious. I decided to start the takeout loan and start the program by faith. I was reminded of the scripture, For I know the plans I have for you declares the Lord, plans to prosper you and not to harm you, plans to give you hope and a future. (Jeremiah 29:11).

Through this reassurance, I always believe that God will see me through. I often listen to motivational speakers like Les Brown, Jim Rohn, and others. I often read motivational quotes such as we rise by life, others up" by Robert Ingersoll. With this understanding, we also help lift ourselves when we lift each other. I also created a group called PhD Motivation and Wellness to provide motivation and help others understand the importance of ensuring that they are engaging in self-care activities while on this journey. I aim to plan a retreat for PhD students to provide them with an opportunity. I often engage in self-care activities every week. My self-care activities range from taking a nature walk to traveling to a new location (trying new food and learning a new language. Self-Care Tips: Take time each week to engage in self-care activities. Try to refuel and Recharge yourself.

The Outcome

I completed the data collection phase and wrote chapters 4 and 5. I began writing Chapter 4 and finished it in record time. I was motivated to finish it; I stayed up late and woke up early to finish the paper. I submitted chapter 4 and received things great feedback. I quickly completed Chapter 4 and began writing Chapter 5. I was so excited to receive such positive feedback. I was reminded that hard work and diligence bring success. The feeling of graduating with my PhD in Human Services Concentration in Criminal Justice became a reality when I walked across the stage on July 19, 2024.

Bio

My goal is to impact the lives of others positively. I plan to use my research to help effect positive social change. It was a transformational journey, and I look forward to guiding and encouraging others to do the same. I also have a Facebook page called Ph.D. Motivation and Wellness. Although 2023 has been incredibly challenging, 2024 will mark a significant turning point. I am happy that I have come to this point to make my family proud! In closing, I will reflect on one of my favorite scriptures states, Delight yourself in the Lord, and he will give you the desires of your heart." Psalm 37:4

Debra Ebel-

The Divine Whisper: Following the call

A child born of purpose, a little being shaped by a powerful force of destiny. Even as a tiny vessel, I carried the weight of something bigger, a feeling in my bones that God had a plan for me, even if my young shoulders struggled under the load. There was always a whisper . . . the voice that kept me moving forward. A nudge, a promise, a hope in tomorrow. It's almost poetic that it took me sixty years to unwrap the gift of purpose. I've always been a little late. I just had to learn patience and time's role in shaping the best things in life.

From my earliest memories, I thought that plan meant a life of conformity, with a backdrop in a high place high nestled in the mountains, surrounded by the silent echoes of stone walls. I started to dread my nightly prayers, because I couldn't imagine a life of solitude and an overriding pull to follow Gods plan. For a while I avoided the nightly conversations with God. The irony of it all my fear wasn't even religiously aligned. In retrospect, perhaps an early lesson that fear weaves a lie into our mind dimming the light of what's possible.

Thank goodness, faith has always triumphed over fear. My journey to a purpose-driven life persevered, like a compass constantly pointing me towards true north, even when I felt lost. So often, I thought I'd gone astray, buried under the weight of responsibilities and challenges. Life's hardships- caregiving, parenting, and career climbing- it all felt like it was dragging me further from my dreams. At times my life was the furthest from being purpose driven. I sought solace in the unhealthiest ways and found myself fading- becoming a stranger to my own self, disconnected from the essence of who I was. Isn't that life though? It's our journey through the wilderness losing and finding our way.

Until one day everything crystalized. The whys, the anguish, life lessons and desire to be more all had meaning. My purposeful guiding star became my beacon of hope. It transformed my past and turned my lessons into wisdom and promised me that my journey was not in vain. I dared to listen to the whispers of my child to open my heart, embrace the process and in doing so I found my way back. My purpose was my redemption, my transformation and the bridge between who I was, and I am destined to be.

To truly understand the enormity of the journey, let's start at the beginning. My childhood wasn't filled with the warmth of trust, the safety of security, or the innocence of unicorns and rainbows. It was a time marked by struggles that no child should ever face. I remember all too well the violent fights, the terrifying suicide attempts, and the countless times I packed my bags, desperate to escape the madness. That chaos became my version of normal.

My mother battled with an undiagnosed and untreated bipolar disorder. Yet, despite everything, I loved her unquestionably and my family fiercely. The thought of losing them was my deepest fear, and I would have gone to any lengths to keep us together, no matter the cost.

Through all the pain, my life became the forge where resilience was hammered into my very being. My soul, though scarred, was strengthened, and those early years shaped me into the person I am today In the fires of adversity, I found a strength that has carried me through time.

I'm the firstborn child of three raised in small towns where family ties ran deep. My Grandparents, part of the Oklahoma land rush, were farmers – the embodiment of grit, faith and resilience. It's from them that I inherited my optimism and determination. Family was everything, yet ours was a tapestry woven with secrets, double lives and confusion of daily life.

My parents never had high expectations for me. Being a girl born in the 50s, my future according to them was marriage and children. Secretly I thought there should be more. I barely graduated high school and moved on to the expected next step – marriage then children. My past distorted my ideas of relationships and family. Unresolved issues continued to surface. I married a very powerful narcissist politician just to remind me that I had a lot of personal work to do. A life pattern that continued to surface, "unhealed wounds have a way of surfacing, repeating their lessons until we finally face them and set ourselves free". Past traumas, hidden memories, and untold secrets were bubbling up. I clinched my jaw and carried on. At twenty-five with two boys, I had to grow up; now!! I believe that ending my marriage was the beginning of my healing. While the need to care for my children was an overriding factor, there was an underlying current of my own desires. I had to dig deep because my future seemed bleak. No child support, navigating his threats and abuse, fearing for our safety, a job that wouldn't support us and no education to fall back on. However, this young optimist would not go down without a fight. I found my courage and decided I had to go back to school. I enrolled in every government program to support my little family, humiliating but invigorating. I was free to become. For the first time in my life, I felt smart, powerful, and hopeful. This naive girl that almost flunked out of high school would graduate from college with highest honors.

As my belief in myself grew, my life improved. I married a man that God gave to heal me and my little family. As I reflect on my life, God was always providing. When we don't even know what's best for ourselves, He's orchestrating. Hubby and I were raising a family, building a life and I had stars in my eyes of what I could create in the business world. This small-town girl was embarking on a big life. Yes, the girl that everyone expected so little from was building a name in the business world. All the early struggles gave me resilience in corporate America. I found my creativity– I was a visionary. Guided by my higher power; I wasn't going to a monastery - I was going to build an empire. I had the good fortune to live in an area with national corporations. Brands with which I could really create something. I built a merchandise line for one of the top non-profit organizations in the world. Hundreds of products were put into the marketplace that could impact people's lives. This was my first introduction into the health arena, and I felt a sense of purpose. I was doing something that was greater than my individual talents. I was creating a worldly difference. I was exposed to brilliant people, thriving. I was responsible for a library of publications, healthy food products, kid's health programs, which generated millions of dollars to support research and awareness for heart health.

My career was just beginning. I moved onto a children's entertainment company where I rebuilt the brand with new creative and world class partnerships. When you are working with corporate giants like Random House Publishing, Viacom, Warner Brothers, Marriott, Mattel and Fisher Price, you know you have arrived. I started traveling the world, Asia, Europe and all over the US to create award winning products.

But all the underlying dysfunction was still deep within my soul. I had not unpacked my rucksack of pain. Surfacing again, the pattern of buried issues was at the front door knocking. I can remember despite my accomplishments, I was still the little girl, full of doubts, still facing sexual harassment in the workplace, eating her unresolved feelings from the past. Sure, I was stressed. These were big jobs. But there was an uncertainty deep in my soul. It was much deeper than work pressure. Little did I realize I was on a collision course with my past. I know now, those heartbreaking valleys are our chance to heal. That chasm was one of hope. A chance to forgive, hold my pain close to my heart, and learn that I would soon be a circuit breaker in abuse. One day very soon, I would be a difference maker.

Healing requires digging deep into our pain. This valley is not serenity. The valley is rock bottom. A place where you are not certain of survival. Despite the risk, there's growth in what's yet to be.

I was at the peak of my corporate career. I had broken so many glass ceilings - accomplished what I thought was even possible. I was negotiating with celebrities, creating products that were loved by millions, and considered a brand building architect. Sure. I still had dreams, but I felt I was on the glide path of life. Our kids were grown. My marriage was intact.

My little internal voice said, don't get comfortable. God's coming to shake things up. He's not going to let you carry this trauma burden the rest of your life. Change is coming. My emotional baggage was about to intersect with my mother's mental disease. Her undiagnosed bipolar condition was getting worse. Honestly, at times I thought she might take her life. In her early years she had tried so many times. Living with that fear of losing your mom to suicide is the worst agony.

All my accomplishments, my corporate climb, my financial stability was about to come crashing down. Her mental health secrets couldn't be hidden anymore. The diagnosis was aphasia – a form of Alzheimer's coupled with her Bi-polar condition. This type of illness will destroy a family, and my dad was declining quickly.

I still remember the call; my dad was being care flighted to a major heart hospital in the city He was in kidney and heart failure. A million thoughts were running thru my head. In the time I reached the hospital he had coded. Decisions had to be made. Thoughts you never want to face. But here I was. We placed him in a drug induced coma to see if we could save his life. My fear circled– it wasn't time. Who would care for my mom? He still had life to live. I'm not ready to say goodbye. For two long, excruciating weeks we tried everything.

How do you take your dad off life support? I assure you, there are no answers for these questions. Perhaps the doctors' assurances, "he would not suffer -is more important than hanging on. But the last twenty-four hours were full of pain and agony. My Dad gained consciousness before his death. His last words haunt me today. "OH CRAP!!!" Those words hung in the air with such heaviness. Words of regret. A life not complete. The hope of more. Gone. Little did I realize at that moment; those two words would shape my purpose. The cry of regret lodged in my brain.

There was no time to grieve. My mother was seriously ill. The next years were defining. She needed constant care. I realized early on how dire this was. Her thoughts were tormented – she lost everything, her home, husband, friends, memories – her mind. I could no longer keep up the pace with my career. The transition from corporate executive to my mother's caregiver was a steep hill – but required.

In the beginning she was volatile, bitter, psychotic. All the fear I experienced as a child came rushing back. As the disease progressed, the hostility diminished. My mother was loving, as she was always intended to be. God gave us five years of peace, harmony and love despite the disease ravaging her mind and body.

As she lost her ability to speak, I knew her thoughts. I read her eyes, reassured of her love as we hugged. I was able to forgive her of all the years of mental abuse and accept that she did the best she could. Her anger, suicide attempts, and depression were the results of her bi-polar condition; not the deep love she always carried for me. What irony, Alzheimer's, a disease so horrific, brought us healing.

But amid caring for my family, I lost myself; I sacrificed all. I no longer recognized that woman in the mirror. I was 100 pounds overweight - depressed and sad. Who was this woman and where was this girl with purpose?

Emptiness. Uncertain of tomorrow. I was broken. My health was a crises of high blood pressure, fatty liver disease, both knees blown and insomnia . . . a physical train wreck. Life had taken a toll. In my resignation as only a caregiver I had forgotten about myself. The piper came calling standing in the ER, rushing me onto a gurney attaching electrodes – was I coding like my dad? Defining moments with my plea to God. Was this my "Oh Crap?" "Oh God, throw me a life preserver. I promise to change everything." Wasn't I chosen? Had I used all my chances?

God had sent so many interrupters in my path, but I was so busy controlling everyone else's health and safety, I wasn't listening. I did it all in the belief that I was the savior for my family. Obviously, the only person I could save was myself. But I had failed at that as well. God knew I needed an intervention, and he was just warming up – the real work was ahead.

In life's rearview mirror, you realize that every human connection is purposeful, made by God to save us from our own mistakes. It's not by accident that the right person comes into your life with an answer. My angel was a health coach. I started another diet. We've all tried a million of them and most are failures; eighty percent of us fail on weight loss programs. Within a week however, I had lost twelve pounds. This was impossible but here I was staring down at the scales screaming. In thirty days, I had lost twenty-one pounds. Perhaps I could do this. I was healing, focusing on myself for the first time in years. This was so much more than a diet- it was my rescue net.

My sis and I were still grieving over the loss of our mother and the next call was unthinkable. "I have cancer, Deb," cried my sister. I can still hear her voice. The fear. Life came rushing back in again. And you proclaim immediately it's a mistake. They cure cancer all the time, and it's all a bad dream.

I packed my bags and swore I would stay true to my health plan while considering stopping at every Dairy Queen from Texas to Oklahoma to soothe the uncertainty of tomorrow. The next weeks were a blur. With each turn the news was worse. Triple negative breast cancer, and the grade of cancer was off the chart. We had a battle ahead. Every step I assured my sister, that she would not face this alone. This was all too familiar – I was once again the caregiver.

I promised, this would be different. I would take care of myself as I cared for her. We would heal together. The intent was there, but I struggled as we all do. The next three years were the hardest of my life. Every test a disappointment. Double mastectomy with complications. Metastasized to her lungs. Then to her brain and chest wall. At this point I practically lived with my sis. She had taken nine different chemo's, 3 surgeries, radiation, immunotherapy and we were losing. My heart was broken, but God was still whispering – still guiding. Through this entire journey, he held me close. I had lost over 100lbs. I started coaching others to regain their health. I was helping others as I held my sister's hand. Believe it or not, it was my respite from the cancer. I started to believe that if I could help someone find their health, perhaps there would be enough stars in the heavens that my sis could have her miracle.

I started going to church again. I went to prayer groups. I learned to pray. It's not that there's a class on how to pray. Or a right and wrong way to talk to God. I never prayed publicly, only whispers in the dark. Broken pleas where I begged for help, I gained faith in my conversations with God, and he was holding me in preparation of the miracle.

Our miracles are not always the ones we pray for. I could see in my sister's eyes that her journey was at a conclusion. She was in liver and kidney failure. The cancer had not come calling but the chemo wrecked her body. I desperately clung to hope. I held her every night- hoping I could keep her from leaving me. If I didn't let go, she wouldn't leave. Together we prayed often. In one of her more lucid moments as I prayed, she squeezed my hand and smiled. She asked me if I heard the bells and birds of heaven. She was close to the gates of paradise. I had one hand, and God had the other. I was going to have to do the impossible. The inevitable was here. I remember her last look into my eyes. Her last breath. Would I ever be ok again?

For the next six months the grief was overwhelming. I had counseling, church, community, exercise, depression meds. . . lots of them. My eating was horrible again, but I was in survival. I started looking into alternative health treatments- nothing traditional was working. Honestly, my death would be a blessing compared to this agony.

In my life, God had a habit of sending miracles. An angel that I only met online, spoke of natural healing. She believed in energy, super foods and nootropics. What did I have to lose? Within thirty minutes of my first dose of this magic elixir everything changed. After six months of hell, the world didn't seem so dark. Was that joy I felt? I didn't feel the pain so deep from inside your bones as if you no longer could hold yourself up. I've read that is defined as anguish. Yet, almost in the flash of an eye, there was a light in the tunnel. I felt a glimmer of hope.

For the next thirty days, all my cracks and fractures started to mend. Like the traditional Japanese art of Kintsukuroi, something once so broken repaired with gold. The fractures filled with beauty; the imperfection of the pain would be even more resilient. The vessel would be stronger than before.

I never was angry; not like others described. I never felt betrayed, or resentful that we didn't get our miracle. But It took me being grateful, for me to receive again. Can you imagine being grateful for a loss so great. I had to reframe my thoughts. The moment I prayed to God and thanked him for saving Terri, I knew I was healing. You see, she finally beat cancer. God gave her the miracle. Finally pain free. And she had gone on ahead of me to care for me, this time.

The loss of my family was so great. Surely all of this had to be of some purpose. These lives lost had to mean something. Undoubtedly it was more than a diet. God had so diligently made the fire so great to forge something special. A big plan. So many days of soul searching but all I had to do was be still and know.

According to the universe, my plan was written, I just had to endure. All these years He was shaping me. Creating a heart so soft. A soul so passionate. A purpose so great. You see, my purpose from the very beginning made sure that I had the right experiences – as difficult and exuberant as they were. All the heart-breaking moments lead me to this place. This very moment. My perfect time.

Here I was, over sixty, rightfully ready for retirement, but ready to take on my biggest role of a lifetime. Through all this learning, growing and self-improvement my insight occurred with age.

I was the perfect age to advocate for everyone who has entered the "golden years" of life. In the final quarter of our life, we face our biggest challenges and hurdles. This should be our time of possibility. But aging is associated with pain, decline, sadness. Why are we resigning from life, settling for something less? Is this self-imposed our societal norms?

We've worked tirelessly, held families together, raised children to be the next generation of leaders, and ushered our parents through their final years. We have financially and socially contributed to the world. This is not the tragic swan song– this is our time to shine, to be celebrated for all we've done and all we continue to be.

But what is the reality of old age? Today's sixty-five-year-old can expect to live another twenty years, although for the first time in decades our life expectancy is declining. Our overall health is even worse than our parents. We have multiple diseases. Seventy percent of the population is obese. Forty-seven million older American households are facing financial uncertainties – many unable to take care of themselves; financially, medically and basic living. Long term care is not covered by Medicare and there is a shortage of medical staff. Social isolation and loneliness are taking a heavy toll and almost 7 million are affected by depression. Our most cherished elders no longer have a purpose.

We live in the wealthiest country and have the best medical care, but our seniors are suffering. Many must make decisions about eating or buying medicine, where they can live or who will take care of them. Is this really the last chapter of our life; the retirement we dreamt of? A life alone, lacking in care, and equipped with only a panic button.

Seniors need government help, but the burden can't rest just on hand-outs. Regretfully, in our early years, we lived a life of overindulgence, high stress, and bad food choices. Our lifestyle consisted of fast food, processed grocery items, portions to indulge our hard work and emotional imbalances, sugary coffee and soft drinks versus water, insomnia from poor work schedules, anxiety and overeating. We've zoned out on Netflix, social media and excessive snacking. We feel a deep isolation and loneliness from long work hours, Facebook, and a lack of community. We are entering our golden years in the worst health condition ever. As my father said, "OH CRAP!"

I embraced a mission starting with myself. What better way to serve aging society than to have lived thru the transformation. To be a hope dealer, shedding light that we can reinvent aging – truly our golden years.

B.Wonder.Full was founded with a clear purpose, to empower people to realize that age should never limit the quality of life. We are fully capable of living vibrant, fulfilling lives, no matter our age. We owe it to ourselves to be healthy, happy and productive throughout our lifespan. It all begins with the right mindset- believing that we are responsible for our own well-being through proper nutrition, regular movement, and the renewal of our mental strength. I call it, Empowered Health – where we accept that "We are the Medicine", An individual accountability.

A world where communities build strong connection, fostering friendships and nurturing our spiritual well-being are equally essential. Continuous learning, living with purpose, and giving back are key to maintaining good mental health and ensuring that we live life to the fullest every day.

The landscape of healthcare is evolving with alternative and holistic treatments gaining recognition and popularity. On the forefront are integrative approaches that combine traditional medicine with practices such as acupuncture, yoga and strength training. Advances in nutritional science highlight the power of superfoods, vitamins, and minerals in disease prevention and overall health. Frequency treatments and mindful practices are being embraced for their therapeutic benefits. This holistic approach addresses not only the physical aspects of health but also the emotional and spiritual offering a more comprehensive and personalized path to wellness.

My journey has included trainings and certifications in weight management, nutrition, behavior modifications, alternative treatments with vitamins nutrients, super foods as well as frequencies. I'm studying the impact of deep breath work and physical motion. The practice of grounding, affirmations, cold treatments, and gratitude can self-regulate the body.

Can you imagine the possibilities? To fully care for ourselves up until end of life. Not having to rely on our kids or long-term care facilities. To be contributors in the world after retirement. To help redefine aging. Transforming our bodies beyond our chronological age. Truly creating a health span vs. a lifespan. To B. Wonder.Full! Always learning, growing.

The ripple effect of health empowerment is palpable. I've helped 1000s regain their lives. Transcend disease thru healthy practices. Just by embracing healthy lifestyles were able to reduce blood pressure, sleep without machines, reverse type two diabetes, improve moods, regain confidence, and thrive despite worn out joints and inflammation. Going from not being able to lift yourself off the floor to thriving in Pilates, biking, hiking and weightlifting. Eating to fuel your body versus soothe your emotions. Healing from the inside out.

But there's so much yet to do. All these practices and education should be available and affordable to our aging population. We must create awareness and inspire hope that regardless of our current plight or the season of our life we can improve. God made our body magnificently capable of healing. As more and more embrace a new way of medicine we can create hope dealers, health evangelists, trainers and coaches to reach more and more of our population. The self-healing creates evangelists for change, which leads to personal purpose.

This is my mission: to educate, inspire, recruit, and empower with empathy and a deep sense of commitment. My goal is to encourage people to confidently explore alternative treatment options, to actively participate in their own personal care, and to recognize that true healing goes beyond surgeries and pharmaceuticals. It's about reclaiming our lives and achieving health through better lifestyle choices

This year I am dedicating myself to offering self-help courses, group and individual coaching and the "Go and grow" series of events. These immersive retreats are designed to help us grow- spiritually, physically and vibrantly while experiencing the beauty of the world around us.

I'm building communities where we can inspire each other, hold ourselves accountable, and for some, pass the torch to continue this important work. I believe the best way to expand this mission is through a grassroots approach, leveraging network marketing to build teams that are united in purpose but diverse in strength. Each person will have the opportunity to create their own thriving business all while contributing to a collective effort that raises awareness with our government and communities.

It's time to modernize the way we approach healthy again and elevate individual responsibility to a new level. Together we can create a movement that empowers each of us to live our best and most vibrant life. Sounds grandiose, overambitious and perhaps overwhelming?

But here's what I've learned. All our life events have pulled us in a direction of purpose. Each one of us is uniquely qualified for a specific role because of our life experiences. Our challenges that we felt were overwhelming, unattainable, gut wrenching; yet we survived and overcame. It's those triumphs that are stories waiting to be told. They give us passion, determination and grit. We have a reason to follow our pursuits because they are deeply personal. They almost haunt our thoughts, and the worldly need is begging us to step in. We are groomed for this moment. Our life challenges are shared; to share, teach and make a difference. In this scenario, age is the difference.

This is where my faith plays such a role in my direction. He places the dream, the quest, the knowing in your heart. And every contact, life challenge, and opportunity are leading you to that cause. According to Ryan Holiday, 'the obstacle is the way." We turn our adversity into our advantage. But it takes such courage and tenacity. But isn't it true, God does not call the most qualified. The story of David and Goliath illustrates that overcoming great challenges does not always require the most obvious or traditionally qualified individuals. In this biblical account, a young shepherd boy, David defeats the giant warrior Goliath not with brute strength or advanced weaponry, but with courage, faith and a simple slingshot. This narrative highlight that true capability often lies in uncongenial qualities like ingenuity, determination and belief in oneself, rather than solely in conventual qualification or experience. It teaches us that anyone, regardless of their perceived status or strength can rise to the occasion and triumph against seemingly insurmountable odds.

Ten years ago, I was "David." The most unqualified to defeat the giant. Morbidly obese facing insurmountable health issues. I was depressed and at a loss on how to fix my circumstances. Insecurities, buried wounds, and life's challenges left me weak. God reminded me all my life experiences were my 'slingshot' of purpose. Because I watched my family die prematurely from preventable diseases, my desire to redefine health and aging is my battle cry.

I have no idea how big my crusade will become. And honestly, it doesn't matter. If I can make a difference in just one more life – that's enough. Because someone reached back for me. I know how magnificent this challenge is and what my work could mean for millions. So, I will continue to tell my story, educate, make connections, provide solutions until God tells me, "The race is done, you finished well." And perhaps that place in the mountains that I dreamt were my purpose, is the palace in heaven where I will join my beautiful sister. I think she will be proud.

Bio

Debra Ebel is a trailblazing entrepreneur, writer, speaker and life coach with over two decades of experience in the health and wellness industry. As the founder of *B.Wonder.Full*, a brand dedicated to holistic health and wellbeing, Debra is transforming the way people approach aging and living through self-care and mental wellness.

Her groundbreaking approach blends behavioral mindset improvements, nutrition, movement and strength training, and frequency charged nootropics and minerals. She firmly believes that true health is a harmonious balance of mind, body, and spirit. A key part of her philosophy is the importance of continuous learning and living with purpose.

Debra's journey began in a small farming town, where she developed a deep passion for health through a farm to table mentality. There is nothing more powerful from a healing standpoint than naturally grown foods.

Debra's unwavering dedication stems from the deep heartache of losing many family members too soon. all to diseases that could have been prevented with healthier choices. This painful reality ignited her passion and commitment to transformation lives through wellness.

After spending thirty years building brands and merchandise in the corporate world, Debra launched her own company in 2020. She tirelessly researched products and programs to offer easy, effective, and solution based.

Her entrepreneurial success is deeply rooted in her unwavering belief in the power of purpose driven business. She is a strong advocate for using network marketing to foster grassroots growth and build diversified teams.

Debra is a devoted mother of two and grandmother of four. Together with her husband, they create curated bespoke travel experiences that offer immersive learning in diverse locations. Their spiritual growth and making a positive impact in the fields of health, wellbeing and aging is their cornerstone business.

Michelle Padgett-

From Victim to Victorious

Where should I begin to discuss the ups and downs of this roller coaster that we call life?

Maybe for you, life has also been full of challenges where you have been unsure of your purpose. Perhaps your experience in life has been that of a victim and now you are ready to live victorious.

Hi, My name is Michelle Padgett aka 'Victorious Michelle'.

I want to share with you my journey which I believe can change the trajectory of your story. So Together, You and I can weave a tapestry of hope, transformation and victory.

My goal is that when you look in the mirror from this day forth that you will begin to define yourself as victorious too!

So here is a little about me.

I grew up in a very small town of 125 people where everyone knew everyone and keeping up with the Jones's was your typical lifestyle.

From the surface level, everything looked like a peaceful little American town: there were beautiful trees, hills,and the sound of the rushing creek. You would see and hear children of all ages out in the grassy fields or on the streets laughing, playing and riding bicycles until the sun went down.

When the street lights came on you would hear the sound of our father's loud whistle which meant it was time to return home.

However, If the main street or the alleys of that little village could talk,

It would tell a whole different story.

One that would expose a lot of hidden secrets of rejection, hurt, disappointment and many victims cries.

As it is all across North America and the globe, when dark deeds are done the victims are not heard and their stories are left untold. It is this silence and secrecy that has kept these various cycles of abuse and trauma continuing, leaving victims internally bleeding while on the outside everything remains to look 'put together' and perfect.

Perhaps you or somebody you know were one of those who was told to keep quiet or you might still be carrying those deep dark secrets.

Here is your safe space and I invite you to be vulnerable and transparent too.

It's time to let go of the pain and give yourself permission to step into the freedom of the light.

It was there in that small town that I have so many memories. Our childhood home, family owned businesses, neighbors whom I loved and adored, the local activities that I participated or led and crowns that I had the honor to wear and represent, but it was also the place where some of my deepest wounds were created.

Upon graduation, I left this little town of horrors and tried my best to run away as far as I could from there.

When I ran, I found myself taking all the heavy secrets that weighed down my attempted escape.

I never wanted to return or ever go back and face the truth or the perpetrators ever again.

I would suppress the past problems so I could start all over with a clean slate and live a productive and fulfilling life.

However, It did not turn out the way that I expected it to.

Just like any other victim, From the compounding years of trauma that haunted me, along with the emotional scars that were left on my wounded soul, I became paralyzed by FEAR, self-rejection, self-hatred and hatred towards all white men.

I wish I could say that I could wave a magic wand and I was miraculously healed overnight, but the truth be told - it has taken me years of emotional struggles, and a whole lot of fight to arrive at the finish line of victory.

In this chapter, I want to share with you my good and bad experiences as I navigated the rocky terrain of discovering how to get past the point of no return.

I was so lost because I didn't know how to unconditionally love myself or properly love others.

Like many victims, I went looking for love in all the wrong way. Because it was white men who first abused me, I thought I would find love in men from other ethnicities and nationalities, but because my wounds were open and bleeding, it really didn't matter what color the man was the cycle went on and on where I was always met with rejection, abuse, and even more trauma.

Let me tell you how I failed forward so that you can be empowered to have grace, self-love, so my trials and pitfalls shall become what gives you courage in your own journey.

Do not make the same HORRIBLE mistakes I did. LOL) I have more than enough failures for you to learn from. As well as share with you the victories I have had in Christ.

This will avail you the opportunity to be able to see the light at the end of the tunnel and feel and know that *Christ's light and presence is with you.*

By identifying and exposing the core problems and events of your life that have vexxed you, You can now remove the thorn and start the restoration process and thus be able to **step into your dreams and purpose much faster.**

While my introduction to darkness and unnecessary evil started in childhood, I was also aware of the fact that I was embraced and led by the power of love. I had very many supernatural experiences with God, not the god of religion and judgment, that you may know or believe. Unfortunately much of society and even many churches today only preach and teach about a little g, god that rule through through fear and anger instead of love, justice and freedom. These false doctrines are fear based and cause people to have a skewed life perception that causes its very own form of deep seated roots of trauma. Some of you may have experienced victimization from religious abuse where spiritual authorities figures used their power and position to control and influence you.

As a leader, I want to apologize to you on their behalf and I want to let you know that you are accepted and there is hope for your full healing too.

My first encounter with Jesus happened in 1974 when I was 4 ½ years old and full of adventure.

I ran out to the swingset barefoot, my little pigtails flapping in the slight breeze as I ran with excitement and leaped with joy onto the new swing set. This was my safe place - where all my fears and worries disappeared and I could get lost in innocent childhood imaginations.

On that day while I was pumping my legs with all my might, swinging and singing away, a man came close to me. It was in my adulthood that I discovered this man was Jesus. I had no fear in his presence, yet I was more comfortable than I had ever been in my life. He stretched out his arms wide and I could see holes in hands. I felt a love that I had never felt before. This love felt like a warm blanket on a very cold winter day and it was directed right at me. It wasn't just a general love - it was a very encompassing and personal love.

As I swung up to get closer to him, he had a great big smile on his face and his eyes twinkled. He spoke to me with a gentle and soft voice. He looked me straight in the eyes and said, **'My child, you are called to change the world. I have called you to be a world changer.'**

As quickly as he had come to me - he then disappeared.

However, the words that he spoke have reverberated in my soul forever and echoing off the chambers of my heart. It was those words that were spoken to me that allowed a deep firm roots of a calling on me which was the catalyst that would eventually lead me into my mission.

After this supernatural encounter on my swing-set that day,

I ran and told my mom about the experience I just had. At school, I also would talk about draw pictures of changing the world with 'the man'.

My mom was not surprised because from a young child on I was very sensitive to the spirit real and all things pertaining to God. When I told her all the details of my encounter, She was a little startled but she and others knew by my intensity and passion for the subject that I had a real divine experience.

You see, My mom and I always had a very unique and special bond because of the difficult pregnancy that she experienced with me.

When I became an adult, my mom and I would have deep conversations where she got very transparent with me, sharing about some of her life struggles. She confided in me that at times she battled with manic depression, fear, rejection and even suicidal tendencies.

After one particular incident, She explained to me that she asked God for a sign that everything would be alright.

Well, Truthfully, You can't get any more clear sign than what happened next …

After a very traumatic incident - that could have ended tragically - both my mother's life and my life were spared. Mom stated,she knew from this point on there was something very special about the child she was carrying, who happened to be me.

There is no coincidence that the name that my mom gave me has great significance:

"Michelle which means One who is made in the likeness and the image of God"

Many years ago mom passed on to glory, many years ago, but not one day goes by that I wish I could call her on the phone and have some more of these very intimate mother/daughter "life" talks together.

Through this chapter in this book, I am inviting you to have an intimate conversation with yourself.

Have you ever had a trauma from your childhood follow you into your adulthood? Have you ever had those destructive cycles that keep repeating itself from the filthy bloodstains and gaping wounds from sexual abuse, abandonment or rejection that never seemed to close up or be healed?

You are not alone and together, WE CAN STOP THESE CYCLES!

You, my friend, you are the one to stop the cycles of destruction and break every family curse!

For me, It became obvious as I watched the unhealthy patterns repeat itself, over and over again.

I was that little hamster on the wheel, running and running faster, while getting nowhere.

Year after year, and one relationship to a situationship, as I would attempt to build and then instead it would backfire and I would lose it all.

Until one day, I was forced to stop running and to look at myself in the mirror.

I did not like what was peering back at me.

I saw a lonely, fragmented and hopeless woman, I saw that little child whose innocence was stolen at such a young age, and nothing but utter brokenness..

It was at this very moment, then I knew the only person who was responsible for changing the future of my life- it was me who needed to change.

I was the only one who could take the steering wheel and drive my life in a different direction.

So you might be asking, how did you get off the hamster wheel and become victorious?

Or you may identify as that scared little caged hamster too, seeking answers to your personal problems.

Michelle, I am so exhausted and tired from running around in circles and I feel stuck because of my past. I need answers on how to fulfill my desires to pursue my God given purpose or childhood dreams.

It's not a mistake that you are reading this book right now!!!

You are chosen to be the light of the world and no matter what circumstances have surrounded you - now is your time to shine brighter than you ever have before!

The Power f Forgiveness

Forgiveness is our golden key to getting off of the wheel. When you forgive, you are now able to live free from your own prison. Often we have layers of unforgiveness, bitterness and hatred we must peel back through the power of grace and mercy. Healing ourselves means asking and receiving forgiveness from ourselves, others, and God. Change this back to original

Forgiveness is a choice, it is not a feeling.

Even though at times it was an internal struggle and a fight, I had to be willing to choose to forgive until the sting from the traumatic memory disappeared.

In my own personal life,

I had to willingly choose to forgive so many. my childhood perpetrators the person who is my children's father who abused me and tried for years to take my very life and destroyed the family.the christian ministers who used and abused me for my spiritual gifts, talents and skills for their own benefit. the narcissistic Pastor, who claimed to be a Man of God who sexually violated me the two perverts that molested my daughters, and some people that I chose to share my life with called "friend/ or best friend's, whom I trusted that betrayed me and stabbed me in the back. and the list could go on

Next, I had to choose to forgive myself

I had to choose to forgive myself for all the wrong things and unhealthy choices I made throughout my life, for choosing to have an abortion when it was totally against my human morals and beliefs, my parental failures as a mom, financial and business poor choices that made me bankrupt and for not loving others, myself, or God, the way that I should have and a pretty long list of injustices.

Then finally, the greatest forgiveness action of all, I had to ask God to forgive me for all of my past mistakes of not trusting Him with my whole life or believing that He would lead me, guide me and direct me in the right direction.

One of the greatest learning lessons I had to come to the understanding of, God is the almighty Judge and you nor I ever have to seek revenge or try and get back at someone for their wrongdoing or betrayals.

I was given a very clear global assignment.

Yes to some, It might seem like a simple yet unobtainable goal.

As you can see from my story,

To get to this place where I am learning to walk in complete forgiveness and love towards the "unlovable" in my life hasn't been easy but I will say it's worth it.

I lived, laughed and loved and now I continue to press on to fulfill the mandate in my life.

The most beautiful part of maturing is that I gained so much knowledge and wisdom through it all: the good, bad and even the ugly. I gained my power back as a Victorious woman and you can too when you choose to take your power back through walking out forgiveness and learn to break through all of your trials, tragedies and failures into another level of love.

Now, I want you to take some time and compose your list of all the people and traumatic situations that have kept you as a prisoner in your soul and in your mind and search your heart and ask God to reveal to you where you may need to go through that heart transformation process

So that you can experience and receive your ah-ha moments of breakthroughs in your personal journey.

A Little Bit Of Love Goes A Long Way

The older I get, the wiser I have become, and tend to think first before making decisions and honor this precious gift called time.

After going through the many years of trials and triumphs,

I began to reprioritize and concentrate on what brings me joy, giving, showing, and modeling what I believe is love to those around me wherever I am and whoever is strategically placed into the path of my life:

whether this is feeding and clothing the homeless in streets of America, guiding and being a positive role for my little ones at my job, ministering to the broken and lost of the nations, or walking the streets of Mexico giving hugs to and speaking into the hearts of prostitutes, pimps and orphans.

Choosing to take a different route to reach my goals of unconditional love has brought me healing, joy, and freedom.

When you choose to love daily - you too will find peace and a meaningful direction.

"To make a difference in someone's life, You don't have to be brilliant, rich or perfect, All you need to do is show love by showing you care."

VictoriousMichelle

Creating Room For Holistic Healing:

There was a season where I just focused on helping people heal from toxic relationships by focusing on relationship skills.

However, I soon realized that people healing from toxic relationships didn't only need to learn to communicate better, however they also needed holistic healing and freedom.

They needed to learn about how to create wealth and prosperity, take better care of their bodies, and shift their mindsets. So I started coaching and counseling people how to have whole life transformation.

So what does this look like for single people, Coaching them to become the very best version of themselves so that they can attract the Perfect mate.

For married couples, I love to help them improve their communication and conflict resolution skills, learn each other's love language, work together to improve their intimate relationship, teach them about financial matters, how to walk in the power of forgiveness, and so much more.

It is extremely rewarding to me when I can use my expertise to help couples in crisis to save their marriage.

Time to experience healing, freedom, good relationships, a sense of purpose and wealth

No matter what pain, darkness, or secrets you have lived through - I have created a community of light, love, hope, healing and opportunity for you.

This is a safe community for you to be your True self,

To be open, honest and real.

Come share the struggles you have been through or the challenges you are currently experiencing.

It's where you will feel empowered to launch into your full potential, develop personally and grow in every area of your life.

And most of all,

It is right here that you and your successes will always be celebrated.

Having A Servant's Heart

I want to serve **those who are seeking total transformation!**

Are you ready to get real, raw and honest with yourself as you step out of victimhood and into your victory?

The time is "now'"to put YOU first.

Do the work, show up, and believe in yourself.

If this is you, Let's connect so you can get on my waitlist for our upcoming live virtual events on freedom, fullness and living victorious.

Here is the link to my website and my fb page.

VictoriousMichelle.com

https://www.facebook.com/mchllpdgtt?mibextid=LQQJ4d

In closing. Here are some daily affirmations for you to speak over yourself that will help you recreate and form the "new" improved YOU!

Daily Goals & Affirmations

Read and speak these positive affirmations over yourself for the next 21 days and begin to see how your perception, self-confidence relationships and everything around you will evolve for the best.

Warning: Expect Miracles of Healing in your heart, mind, body, and soul.

POSITIVE SELF AFFIRMATIONS

I AM FORGIVEN

I AM BEAUTIFUL

I AM CONFIDENT

I RESPECT MYSELF

I WILL ESTABLISH HEALTHY BOUNDARIES IN ALL MY RELATIONSHIPS

I AM NOT MY PAST MISTAKES

I WAS CREATED FOR GREATNESS

I AM WORTHY OF LOVE, HONOR AND RESPECT

I WILL PROSPER IN ALL THINGS

I AM MADE TO BE EXCEPTIONAL

THIS IS MY TIME TO SHINE

I AM CHOSEN TO BE A LIGHT TO THE WORLD

I WILL PROSPER IN ALL THAT I DO

I CHOOSE TO NO LONGER IDENTIFY AS A VICTIM, BECAUSE I AM VICTORIOUS.

Bio

As the CEO of Miraculous Breakthrough Academy and a seasoned Life and Relationship Expert with over two decades of experience, I focus on personal growth, emotional healing from trauma, and career development. My approach as a Social Justice Reformer involves combining empathetic listening with practical strategies to help individuals discover their life purpose and maximize their potential.

Clients have described my sessions as eye-opening, inspirational, and transformative, fostering deep healing and life-altering changes. My heart and life goal is to guide individuals in discovering their true potential, serving as their chief motivator and supporter on their journey of self-improvement and dream fulfillment, ultimately becoming the best version of themselves.

Because You My Friend Are Chosen To Live "VICTORIOUS"!

Traci Everett-

Diagnosis to Determination: Navigating Challenges and Embracing Change

The lab results were back. I had officially gone from "prediabetic" to diabetic. The doctor offered to prescribe medication that would both lower my blood sugar levels and help me to lose weight. While this was tempting, I realized that I knew there were a lot of things I could do that would help me with those two goals.

My doctor supported my decision to implement lifestyle changes before starting medication. I found a nutrition coach who was able to help me learn some things about how blood sugar spikes work. She encouraged me to have high-fiber foods before eating protein or carbs. She also taught me about the importance of protein and that I don't need to feel deprived of the foods I love. I can eat some of my favorite foods in smarter ways. I added "adrenal cocktails" to my daily routines—coconut water with lemon juice and high-quality sea salt. I began to be more aware of the things I was eating and when I was eating them. These changes didn't feel radical or overwhelming, and with the support of my coach, I was able to stay on track and enjoy the process.

Because social media seems to be aware of all the things going on in our lives, it wasn't long before my newsfeed was sprinkled with ads for Constant Glucose Monitors (CGM). I contacted one of the companies and filled out their online questions. It took a bit, but my insurance and doctor agreed that being able to see in real-time how different foods, activities, and stress impacted my blood sugar would be helpful.

This was revolutionary for me. I could take the things I was discussing with my nutrition coach and then see for myself that, yes, in fact, having some cauliflower before the pasta kept it from spiking. Knowing it to be true from reading and listening to my coach was great, but confirming it with my own numbers was even better. I also learned from the online community that everyone is different. For example, I can eat popcorn with no problem at all, but for some people who are diabetic, that is not the case.

I felt like the support of my doctor, the work with my coach, and having a CGM was a trifecta for my health! I had tried to make lifestyle changes in the past on my own, but this time was very different. I was prepared and supported, as well as being motivated. My family has a significant history of diabetes. I had seen firsthand how this disease impacts lives.

The changes didn't happen suddenly, of course. Slowly, though, I realized that changes were happening. My clothes started to fit differently. I had more energy. And I could see that CGM data showing my blood sugar in range more and more of the time. The number on the scale also began to drop, although that wasn't my main goal. I knew that the blood sugar spikes were causing harm even if I was at a "perfect" weight. The number on the scale wasn't the bottom line problem. It was more about changing my metabolism so that my body is better able to manage glucose.

It was pretty amazing, though, to see all the numbers when I went for my 9-month follow-up appointment! My A1C, which is how diabetes is diagnosed, was below the pre-diabetic level for the first time in more than 5 years. Other lab numbers were also trending in the right direction. It was clear that the lifestyle changes I had implemented were having an impact. Knowing that nothing about it had been "painful" or felt like deprivation made it obvious that I could continue on this path for the rest of my life, continuing to make the changes that will make sense for me over time.

During this same timeframe, there was a different scenario playing out with my adult son, David. He was diagnosed with ADHD. My initial reaction was, "How did I miss that all those years???" But when I was honest with myself, I realized that I had always known that he struggled with executive functioning challenges, but when he was growing up, we didn't really have a clear understanding of how those challenges were connected to ADHD. So, yes, it makes sense for sure.

David was offered medication to help him focus. As soon as he started taking it, he felt like it was miraculous! He was able to focus in meetings at work like never before. He felt like a new man. The transformation was immediate.

This transformation, though, was incomplete. He was offered no opportunity to learn new strategies that would help him to really overcome the challenges that his ADHD causes. He just had the meds to help take the edge off.

And then, there was a shortage of the medication. He was suddenly expected to manage his life without medication after just a short time of seeing how amazing it was to be able to focus well.

Honestly, it was more than an issue with the shortage of medication. Even when he was able to access meds, he realized that they were having other impacts on his life. He needed to take them early enough during the day or they interrupted his sleep. And, importantly, he still didn't know how to manage some of the other symptoms, because ADHD is more than having difficulty focusing. He struggles to stay organized. He tends to process his thoughts out loud, which isn't always a problem, but in some circumstances, thinking through things before speaking is advantageous. Also, he may be more able to focus but he doesn't always focus on the right things.

These and other issues have led him to see that, while the medication is absolutely useful in his life and he will likely continue to take it, he needs other support as well.

Thinking about our two situations, it became clear to me that when we attempt to manage complicated issues in our lives with a simple quick fix, it is likely not going to be enough.

Finding ways to incorporate real lifestyle changes along with, or even before, the quick fix is worth investigating.

For me, changing my eating habits and adding more activity to my life has proven not only helpful in my journey toward better health but also quite fulfilling. I feel really good about myself as I see the lab work numbers trending the right way. I rather enjoy the challenge of figuring out ways to add a little fiber to my diet before having protein and carbs. And I still enjoy desserts fairly often.

It's not perfect and it's not always easy. For example, I had cereal for breakfast pretty much every day for decades, and it was my go-to meal in the evenings when I couldn't decide what else to have. But using the CGM helped me see that every cereal on the market caused a significant spike in my blood sugar—even oatmeal which is good for so many things. If I have cereal, I need to make sure to have a salad beforehand and I don't usually want a salad before cereal at 7 o'clock in the morning. This has been harder for me than other diet changes, but I see the benefits and choose to have long-term health over a box of Frosted Mini-Wheats.

Being able to manage my diabetes without medication for as long as possible is important to me. I know that genetics play a large role in my personal health but I also see that I have more control than I had once thought. The medications that are available do wondrous things and there is no doubt that they save lives. Still, they all come with side effects, especially if used for long periods of time. I have a great uncle, for instance, who has been on a standard diabetes drug for more than 40 years. He's in his 90s and still drives himself wherever he wants to go. He's active and healthy by most anyone's standards, except that he has a permanent catheter because the medication deteriorated his bladder over all those years. He feels it's a small price to pay. I understand that but also believe that since we know more about how diabetes works and the lifestyle changes that can really make a difference, I would like to avoid those drugs as long as possible, and forever if I can.

My real point, though, is not just about avoiding medication that seems to be a quick fix. It's about possibility. It is possible to make significant lifestyle changes. I didn't know when I started this journey a year ago, but I am now convinced. I started small. I gathered support from my doctor, my nutrition coach, and my family. I gathered data using a constant glucose monitor. And I'm enjoying the journey! I feel good about the progress I'm making and I'm empowered from knowing that I did this without medication. I made changes to the foods I eat and the order in which I eat them. I am adding more physical activity to my days. I'm also using mindfulness and gratitude to keep me on track.

As an ADHD Life Coach, I also see my clients making real lifestyle changes. They don't need to have a salad before their Wheaties, but they do need to make lifestyle changes, and they can! Even though they may believe that they can't change those things about them that contribute to the challenges of ADHD, with support and data, they can.

We start by clearly identifying their goals. What is important to them? What do they want to accomplish— personally, professionally, in their relationships, and in other areas of their lives?

Then we start the journey together. What is the next small step they can take? How can we break down the goal into the smallest of tasks? How can they succeed in these small tasks, even though they have been trying, maybe for years?

One of the goals that many of my clients have shared with me is maintaining a tidier space. Rather than considering the whole house, we start by looking at a particular room, or even a particular part of one room. With one client, it was literally the dining room table that had been a catch-all space for years.

We set aside time for her to clean off the table and to put things where they actually belonged. When we initially completed the task, it had felt both overwhelming and a bit nonsensical. She had bigger tasks to accomplish. She has ideas about how to make this world a better place and yet I was encouraging her to just put the odds and ends from the table in their proper places.

But here's what happened: she completed that task. The dining room table was finally spotless. And we celebrated that win. It was a small win, and yet it was also a really big deal for her. She had resigned herself to just always having a messy table, but she saw how great she felt when she accomplished this task.

We have used the momentum she built from that win to create more and more wins for her. She is building a lifestyle that allows her to accomplish the things she has dreamed about for years. It started with cleaning off the dining room table.

While I wholeheartedly believe that people who have ADHD can find success and fulfill their dreams, I also know that having a neurospicy brain does make life more challenging. I spent more than thirty years in the field of education and I saw it firsthand. When a student has ADHD, it is difficult for them to jump through the required hoops of our school system. When I first started teaching, ADHD was almost exclusively diagnosed in little boys who bounced around the classroom. They were constantly in trouble and had a hard time with boring and repetitive tasks. As they grew older, they were the ones arguing the loudest about not wanting to show their work on math problems. They often forgot their homework at home or in their locker. They sometimes even forgot they had homework, or that tests were coming up, or that they needed to start writing that big research paper weeks in advance instead of the night before it was due. Teachers, and sometimes even parents, called them "lazy" and they bought into this story. This narrative of being in trouble and being called lazy day after day, year after year, often led to serious self-esteem issues. They also were frequently the kids who would completely ace standardized tests which was baffling for the adults. How could he know so much if he never even does his homework, and he never pays attention in class? It always seemed like a mystery, but I discovered that the ADHD brain can be highly capable and quite intriguing.

Then, I started seeing something else about ADHD. There were other students who had a very different experience. They were the daydreamers. They were compliant and frequently even perfectionistic. Very often they made it much further in their educational journey before needing support. Even though they had hidden their challenges, they were struggling and eventually hit a wall. Over the years, the scientific community began to see that these students also had ADHD. The more people studied the brain and how people learn, the more we began to see the neurospicy brain as just "different" and not wrong or broken or less than the neurotypical brain. With appropriate accommodations, students who learn differently can demonstrate their knowledge. Instead of seeing them as lazy, we began to see them as avoiding things that were boring, but quite capable and often ingenious in various aspects of life.

Whichever type of ADHD my students displayed, I saw over and over that many of them had unique and extraordinary abilities. They were often passionate about a particular thing, whether it was hockey or the environment or poetry or whatever else. They have brilliant ideas - some of them have so very many brilliant ideas! Their passion and their creativity can bring about so much good in this world. But first, they needed to graduate from high school.

I was able to spend the last several years of my educational career working directly with these kinds of students. They were so capable but also struggled so much. When we put structures in place and showed them how to manage those tricky aspects of school like time management and organization, they were able to do well. I was even able to help many parents and teachers reframe their thinking about what was happening. ADHD is not a character flaw. It is a neurological difference and rather than trying to change the students who don't fit our schools, we need to change our schools so that all students can learn and feel good about themselves. Each one of them has something wonderful to bring to this world that only they can offer. Why stifle them when we could instead encourage them?

I will admit that I can be a bit overly optimistic at times. Never in my life was this more evident than in early 2020. I remember so clearly thinking that the necessity to go to remote teaching would give educators the incentive they needed to implement the universal design strategies that we know work well for students. We could use the opportunity to rethink how we do things, based on the research about the brain and how people learn. Never have I been more wrong. The fiasco that followed led me to, instead, rethink my own life. While I have loved every job I have had (or at least certain aspects of all of the jobs I've had), I knew I could no longer be a part of such a catastrophically broken system. I believe that I can make a bigger impact on the world by working directly with students, families, and adults who have ADHD than continuing to work in a school setting. I was able to complete a training program for coaching clients who have ADHD. I absolutely believe in the value of coaching and I am also absolutely convinced that people who have neurospicy brains can change the world. This is the perfect fit for me and I'm thrilled to be able to spend the next several years doing what I love.

Interestingly, during my long career in education I said that I supported people who are neurodivergent but that I was neurotypical. Then, I left the structure of school. The bell no longer rang to tell me when it was time for a break or to have lunch or to begin or end my day. There was no clear plan for what I was supposed to do with my days. All those traits of the day-dreamy ADHDers that I had spent years supporting started showing up in my own life. I haven't yet gone through the process of getting a formal diagnosis but if it walks like a duck and quacks like a duck, a duck seems highly likely.

I have been putting into place lifestyle changes that allow me to accomplish the things I want and need to do. As is true for many women, I have struggled to prioritize my personal life since leaving education. It is easy to let myself work all the time. It took several months to even make myself take a day off each week. I'm learning.

One thing I believe as I've begun putting all these thoughts together is that coaching is such an important and valuable resource. I need the accountability of a coach in my life. I need the support a coach provides and to spend time regularly considering what I want and need and how to bring those things to life.

Meaningful lifestyle change is possible. Whether it's about getting physically healthier or attaining those dreams you've had for years, you can accomplish the things that are important to you. Having the support of medication for health issues may absolutely be necessary, but looking for that quick fix without also implementing changes that will support your goals will likely lead to less than stellar results. Looking within yourself and finding experts and a community that will support you is much better than just going for the quick fix.

Bio

Meet Traci Everett, a vibrant life and business coach who passionately supports individuals with neurodivergent tendencies, especially those with ADHD. With her engaging and relatable approach, Traci connects with hundreds of ADHDers and their supporters across various platforms, offering practical advice on overcoming procrastination, time management, and organization. Her strategies are tailored to help you make the most of your precious time and find mindfulness techniques that calm and focus your wonderfully neurospicy brain.

Known for celebrating every win, big or small, Traci believes that success breeds success. As a TEDx speaker, she has delivered impactful presentations on the impact of ADHD, mental health, and valuing neurodivergence, further establishing her as a thought leader in these areas. Her talks have inspired and educated diverse audiences, shedding light on the unique strengths and challenges faced by those with ADHD and advocating for greater understanding and acceptance.

Traci has also shared her insights as a guest on numerous podcasts and international stages, helping those facing mental health challenges discover real solutions for thriving in all areas of life.

When she's not coaching, Traci loves spending time with her husband of 35 years and their adorable dogs, a Shih-poo and an Irish Doodle. She cherishes visits with her friends, family, and seven grandchildren as well as exploring the world. Traci's hobbies include cooking, reading, hiking, and cheering for the New York Rangers. Her zest for life and dedication to helping others shine through in everything she does

Traci Everett: Champion of Neurodivergent Success

Traci Everett is a dynamic Life Coach and ADHD Coach based in New York, dedicated to empowering individuals with ADHD, neurodivergent entrepreneurs, and those aged 55 and older. With her innovative framework, IMOVE (Intuition, Marketing, Operations, Velocity, Execution), Traci has transformed the lives of countless clients by helping them unlock their potential and achieve their personal and professional goals.

Author of the "Strategic Connections ADHD Toolkit," Traci combines her extensive expertise with a deep passion for advocacy, ensuring her clients thrive in every aspect of their lives. Her approach is holistic, compassionate, and tailored to the unique needs of each individual, making her a beacon of support and inspiration in the ADHD and neurodivergent communities.

Through her programs, such as the "Neurodivergent Women's Business Collective," Traci continues to break barriers and create inclusive spaces where everyone can flourish. Her commitment to fostering understanding and providing practical strategies has solidified her reputation as a leading voice in the field of neurodiversity.

Kellie Haehnel-

The Lighthouse in the Storm - Illuminating the Path

Every life is marked by its share of storms—those moments of hardship and challenges that test our resolve and character. These storms came in many forms: personal losses, health challenges, and professional setbacks. Yet, each storm also brought growth, self-discovery, and transformation opportunities. By embracing these challenges, I found strength I never knew I had and discovered the resilience within me.

Through my journey, I learned invaluable lessons that have shaped who I am today. I knew the importance of perseverance and the power of a positive mindset. I discovered that setbacks are not failures but rather stepping stones to success. I understood that vulnerability is not a weakness but a source of strength, allowing us to connect more deeply with ourselves and others. Each lesson was a light that guided me through the storm, illuminating the path ahead.

In the darkest moments, finding the light within myself was crucial. Fueled by hope and determination, this inner light became my guiding force. I could navigate the most challenging times by focusing on my goals and maintaining a hopeful outlook and believing in my capabilities. ..This inner light not only guided me but, I believe, also became a beacon for others, showing that it is possible to emerge stronger and wiser from life's storms

By sharing my story, I offer guidance, hope, and encouragement to those experiencing their own storms. My journey is a testament to the power of resilience and the importance of never giving up. Through my experiences, I aim to empower other women to find their inner strength, embrace their challenges, and illuminate their paths.

May my story be a beacon of inspiration and empowerment for other women. I hope it serves as a transformative light, guiding you through your storms and helping you discover the immense power within you. Remember, no matter how fierce the storm, there is always a light to guide you through—sometimes it's within you, and other times it's found in the stories of those who have walked similar paths.

I invite you to join me on this journey in the following pages. Let my experiences, lessons, and reflections be a source of light and hope for you. Together, let's navigate through the storms of life, illuminate our paths, and become beacons of light for ourselves and others.

Welcome to "The Lighthouse in the Storm - Illuminating the Path."

I was raised by a family who instilled an unwavering belief in the power of mutual support and the importance of operating with integrity. In our household, we were taught from a young age that the strength of our family bond was rooted in how we lifted each other during times of need and celebrated each other's successes with genuine joy. Honesty and ethical behavior were not merely encouraged but expected, forming the bedrock of our interactions within our family and the outside world. This upbringing created a foundation of trust and reliability, shaping our characters and guiding our actions throughout life. We knew that no matter our challenges, we could rely on each other for support and that maintaining our integrity was paramount, even when no one was watching.

This belief was ingrained in both sides of my family. On my father's side, family and community were highly regarded pillars in our lives. My grandfather was a highly respected farmer. His reputation as a hard-working, honest man extended throughout the community, and his farm became a central gathering place for our large family. We spent many weekends at the farm, engaging in various chores. One of my fondest memories is picking raspberries, where it was common practice to place one in the basket and eat two or more with each picking! Cleaning corn for family gatherings was another cherished activity, highlighting the close-knit nature of our family.

Even though only two of my uncles from the original twelve siblings remain, our family continues to honor the tradition of gathering each year for a family picnic. This event is deeply valued not only by my generation but also by my children and grandchildren. It's a testament to the enduring legacy of togetherness and support passed down through the years.

On my mother's side, weekends were often spent with relatives, and our home was usually the hub of activity. My dad would fire up the grill, making chicken (his staple dish), turning our backyard into a lively and joyous space. My mother was the linchpin of her siblings, embodying the principle that family is always there to support you through life's challenges. Her dedication to her family was unwavering, and she set a powerful example for us all.

My father was a truck driver whose integrity and supportive nature earned him great respect among his coworkers and friends. His reputation was built on hard work and ethical behavior, which he passed on to his children.

This sense of family and community support was never more evident than when, on January 16, 1978, we received the devastating news that my father was killed in a trucking accident. I was just 15 years old at the time, and the shock and grief were overwhelming. In those dark days, both sides of my family came together in a remarkable display of unity and support that underscored the values they had always lived by.

My father's untimely death left a gaping hole in our lives. He was known for his integrity and dedication, but he was suddenly gone, leaving my mother and us children to navigate a world without his steady presence. The pain of his loss was profound, but the response from our family was immediate and unwavering.

Despite the immense grief, there were moments of profound connection and even joy as stories of my father's life were shared and his legacy was honored. The family picnics continued, though they were tinged with a sense of loss. These gatherings became an essential part of our healing process, a testament to the enduring strength of our family ties.

The unity and resilience demonstrated by both sides of my family during this tragic time left an indelible mark on me. It reinforced the lessons we had been taught about the importance of family and community. It showed us that even amid unimaginable loss, family bonds could provide a foundation of strength and hope.

In the years that followed, these values continued to guide us. We honored my father's memory through annual family picnics and how we lived our lives—supporting one another, acting with integrity and cherishing the precious bonds that hold us together.

2001, I experienced a series of life events that I never dreamt I would face. Within a week, my life was turned upside down. I lost my job, filed for divorce, and temporarily took my two young daughters to move in with my sister. With no money and an uncertain future; I found myself at one of the lowest points in my life. This drastic change was another test of the tenacity and support that my family had always exemplified.

The loss of my job was the first blow, stripping away not only my income but also my sense of stability and purpose. Shortly after that, the dissolution of my marriage added an emotional toll that was almost unbearable. Faced with caring for my daughters amidst such turmoil, I felt overwhelmed and adrift.

In this moment of crisis, my sister opened her home and heart to us without hesitation. Moving in with her provided a semblance of security and a foundation to rebuild. Despite the cramped quarters and the challenges of suddenly merging two households, my sister's unwavering support became a lifeline. She helped care for my daughters, providing them with the needed stability while I navigated our new reality's emotional and logistical challenges.

The rest of my family rallied around us as well. My mother was a constant source of strength and comfort. She reminded me of the resilience that our family had always shown in the face of adversity. Her words and actions echoed the principles she had lived by, demonstrating that the family would always support and uplift each other no matter how dire the situation was.

Despite the hardships, there were moments of grace and gratitude. My daughters, though young, displayed remarkable resilience, buoyed by the love and attention from our family. The laughter and joy they brought into our lives were daily reminders of what we were fighting for.

Gradually, with the unwavering support of my family, I began to find my footing. I secured a new job, could reclaim my home, and started rebuilding our lives. The experience, though harrowing, reinforced the lessons of resilience and unity that had been a constant theme throughout my upbringing.

This chapter of my life, marked by unexpected challenges, became a testament to the strength and solidarity of my family. Their support helped me survive and thrive in the face of adversity. It underscored the deep-seated belief that no matter what life throws at us, we can endure and overcome with the love and support of those we hold dear.

As the initial shock of my life upheaval began to wear off, I soon discovered that I was surviving, not thriving. Though my family's support had been crucial in helping me navigate the immediate crisis, I realized that I needed more than just stability; I needed to rediscover myself and find a more profound sense of purpose and fulfillment. This period of introspection led me to embark on a transformative journey toward my authentic self.

During this time, I was introduced to Reiki, a form of energy healing that promised to align the mind, body, and spirit. Skeptical yet curious, I attended my first Reiki session, not knowing it would begin a profound change in my life. The experience was nothing short of enlightening. I felt a sense of peace and connection that I had not felt in years, and this newfound sense of calm allowed me to begin healing from the   inside   out.

Reiki opened the door to a broader exploration of holistic health and wellness. I started to delve into practices such as meditation and mindfulness, each contributing to a deeper understanding of my inner self. These practices became integral to my daily routine, providing me with tools to cope with stress, build resilience, and maintain a positive outlook.

Through these explorations, I began to peel back the layers of my former self, uncovering passions and aspirations that had long been buried beneath the weight of life's responsibilities and hardships. I discovered a deep-seated desire to help others heal and find their paths to wellness. This realization guided me towards training in Reiki and other healing modalities, aiming to share the benefits I had experienced with others.

As I embraced this new path, I transformed from the inside out. My relationships with my daughters deepened as I became more present and centered. I reconnected with old friends and formed new, meaningful connections with people who shared my interests and values. My professional life flourished as I integrated my newfound sense of purpose into my work as an HR Executive, transformational Life Coach, and Energy/Sound Healer through counseling, mindfulness, and healing practices.

Living my purpose brought me personal fulfillment and allowed me to give back to the community that had supported me through my darkest times. I began offering Reiki sessions and workshops, empowering others to embark on their journeys of self-discovery and healing. The gratitude and positive feedback I received reinforced that I was on the right path, living authentically and contributing to the well-being of those around me.

Though born out of adversity, this chapter of my life became a powerful testament to the resilience of the human spirit and the transformative power of self-discovery. By embracing my authentic self and living my purpose, I found a way to thrive and created a ripple effect of healing and positivity in my community. My journey taught me that there is always a path to growth, fulfillment, and true happiness, even in life's most significant challenges.

As life progressed, I faced another significant challenge: a diagnosis of thyroid cancer. It all began during my annual check-up when I asked my doctor why I hadn't started menopause at the age of 55. She ran some blood tests and discovered that I had hyperthyroidism.

Reluctantly, I started medication to manage the condition. However, with a combination of the -prescribed medicine and my dedication to energy-healing practices, I managed to regulate my thyroid levels within 30 days, much to my doctor's surprise.

Despite this initial success, my health took a concerning turn. At my six-month follow-up, I told my doctor I was feeling exhausted. She recommended an ultrasound of my thyroid, which led to a biopsy. The results were alarming: I was diagnosed with stage 4 cancer of the thyroid and one of my parathyroid glands. Surgery was immediately recommended, followed by a high dose of radiation.

The news was devastating, but my family's unwavering support and my commitment to holistic healing gave me the strength to face this new battle. The surgery was intense, and the subsequent radiation therapy took a toll on my body. One of the most troubling side effects was frequent, severe nosebleeds caused by the radiation.

However, my recovery once again defied expectations. My surgeon was astonished by the speed at which I was healing. During one of my follow-up visits, he inquired about the product I was using to treat my nosebleeds. I told him about Skin Food, a natural remedy that healed the lining of my nose. Impressed by its effectiveness, he even mentioned recommending it to his other patients.

Throughout this journey, I leaned heavily on the practices that had become central to my life. Reiki and other energy-healing techniques played a crucial role in managing my stress and aiding my recovery. The support of my family, who had always been there through thick and thin, was invaluable. Their love and encouragement gave me the strength to keep fighting, even when the odds seemed insurmountable.

My battle with thyroid cancer was a harsh reminder of life's unpredictability. Still, it also showcased the incredible potential for recovery and healing when holistic practices complement conventional medicine. This journey tested my physical endurance and deepened my understanding of wellness, further solidifying my commitment to living authentically and helping others find their paths to healing.

Today, I am incredibly blessed and filled with gratitude. After navigating numerous challenges and life-changing events, I find myself in a place of profound fulfillment and contentment. My career as an HR Executive is thriving, allowing me to utilize my skills and experience to make a meaningful impact within my organization. Additionally, my coaching and energy healing practice is growing, allowing me to help others discover their authentic selves and achieve their own healing.

This sense of fulfillment didn't come quickly; it was forged through years of perseverance, resilience, and unwavering support from my family. The trials I faced—from losing my father and enduring a painful divorce to battling thyroid cancer—have only strengthened my resolve and deepened my appreciation for life. These experiences have taught me to cherish every moment and approach each day with gratitude.

In my role as an HR Executive, I draw on my diverse life experiences to foster a positive, inclusive workplace. I advocate for employee well-being, championing initiatives that promote work-life balance and mental health. My journey has equipped me with a unique perspective, enabling me to empathize with colleagues facing their own challenges.

My coaching and energy healing practice has flourished parallel to my corporate career. What began as a personal journey of self-discovery and healing has evolved into a mission to guide others toward their paths of wellness and authenticity. Through energy healing, mindfulness practices, and personalized coaching, I help clients unlock their potential and overcome obstacles. Witnessing their transformations is incredibly rewarding and reaffirms my belief in the power of holistic healing.

The blend of my professional achievements and my passion for healing creates a harmonious balance in my life. It allows me to be a source of strength and inspiration for others while continuously growing and learning. My grown daughters have watched my journey and understood the importance of resilience, integrity, and pursuing one's true purpose. Their pride in my achievements is one of my most significant sources of joy.

Reflecting on my journey, I am profoundly grateful for the support and love surrounding me. My family's unwavering belief in me, the wisdom imparted by my parents, and the healing power of holistic practices have all contributed to the person I am today. This gratitude fuels my desire to give back, to help others find their strength, and to live authentically.

As I look to the future, I am excited about what lies ahead. My goals include expanding my coaching and energy healing practice, positively impacting the corporate world, and cherishing the moments I share with my family. Life's journey is unpredictable, but with resilience, support, and a focus on wellness, I am confident I can navigate whatever comes my way. I embrace every opportunity with an open heart and a spirit of gratitude. I am committed to living my purpose, helping others heal, and creating a legacy of love, strength, and authenticity.

The Power of Compassion in Leadership:

As an HR Executive, I have always believed in maintaining compassion when balancing company policy with individual behavior. Approaching each situation with empathy and a non-judgmental attitude has often been critical to resolving conflicts and fostering growth within the workplace. One particularly challenging incident underscored this belief and left a lasting impact on me and an employee I worked closely with.

An employee's work ethic and performance had become a significant concern. The situation demanded strong counsel and intervention. It was not an easy conversation, and the initial response was defensiveness and frustration. However, I knew the approach needed to be firm yet compassionate for real improvement. I provided ongoing coaching, clear expectations, and continuous encouragement.

Each interaction was an opportunity to listen, understand, and guide the employee towards better performance. It wasn't just about enforcing company policy; it was about helping her see her potential and supporting her in achieving it. Over time, I noticed gradual improvements, and her attitude toward work began to shift. However, before seeing the entire outcome of our efforts, I left that workplace to pursue another opportunity.

Approximately five years later, I returned for a visit. To my surprise and delight, that same employee sought me out. She thanked me profusely for the valuable coaching and compassion I had shown her during those difficult times. She proudly informed me that she had become a department supervisor, attributing much of her success to the experience and guidance she received. She explained that the challenges she faced and the support I provided had equipped her with the skills and confidence to be an effective manager.

This encounter was incredibly humbling and affirming. It reinforced my belief in the power of compassionate leadership. By taking the time to understand and support individuals, we can foster better performance and personal and professional growth. The transformation of that employee from someone struggling with work ethics to a confident supervisor highlighted the lasting impact that empathy and encouragement can have.

As I continue my journey in HR and beyond, I carry the lessons learned from this and many other experiences. They serve as a testament to the fact that compassionate leadership can genuinely change lives and foster a culture of growth and respect within any organization. By sharing these stories, I hope others will be inspired to lead with empathy, understanding, and an unwavering commitment to supporting their colleagues and employees.

Coaching: Redefining Purpose and Reconnecting with Self

Throughout my career and personal journey, I have been blessed with the opportunity to accompany individuals on their path toward redefining their purpose and reconnecting with themselves. Each encounter has been a profound reminder of the transformative power of self-discovery and the importance of guiding others toward a deeper understanding of their true selves.

One of the most memorable journeys I witnessed was that of a woman who, like me, had faced her fair share of challenges. She was navigating the complexities of a divorce, recovering from breast cancer, and grappling with unemployment. Despite her resilience, she questioned her self-worth personally and professionally. However, through our work together, she embarked on a journey of self-discovery and transformation that ultimately led her to embrace her inner light and manifest her true purpose.

As we delved into her story and aspirations, she expressed a deep-seated desire to become a massage therapist specializing in treating women with cancer. This calling resonated deeply with her own experiences and struggles. However, she felt daunted by the prospect of starting anew, uncertain of her worthiness and ability to succeed.

Her initial hurdles were finding a place to perform massages and attract clientele. I encouraged her to share her vision with others, believing that the universe can align opportunities with our intentions. Soon enough, a friend offered her a free space to offer massages—a fortunate turn of events that bolstered her confidence and affirmed her path.

Despite this initial breakthrough, she still grappled with insecurity and doubt. I encouraged her to keep track of her practice sessions, logging the clients she treated for free and envisioning what she would charge them if she were. This exercise helped her meet the required hours for graduation and planted the seeds for her future success.

Upon graduating, she wasted no time in setting up her massage practice. Armed with newfound confidence and clarity of purpose, she began attracting clients and building a reputation for her healing touch. Before long, her appointment book was filled with eager clients seeking her specialized services.

She discovered her inner light through her journey and unearthed a sense of purpose that had long eluded her. By embracing her authenticity and following her heart, she manifested the massage practice she had envisioned, transforming her struggles into triumphs.

This story is a powerful reminder of the transformative power of self-belief and perseverance. In supporting her journey, I witnessed firsthand the remarkable resilience of the human spirit and the profound impact that belief in oneself can have on achieving one's dreams.

As I continue to guide and inspire others on their paths of self-discovery and transformation, I carry the lessons learned from her journey. It is a testament to our inherent potential to overcome obstacles, embrace our true selves, and manifest our deepest desires.

Healing the Mind and Body:

An attorney contacted me seeking relief from the daily stress and sleeplessness that had become all too familiar in her demanding profession. As we embarked on her energy healing session, her initial apprehension gradually faded, replaced by a sense of calm and relaxation. It was a profound moment when she drifted into a deep and restful sleep—a testament to the power of energy healing to soothe both mind and body.

When she awoke at the end of the session, her amazement was palpable. She expressed disbelief at how quickly she had fallen asleep and marveled at the peace and tranquility now enveloped her. Witnessing the tangible impact of energy healing on her well-being was a humbling experience.

During the session, I noticed some subtle energetic imbalances around her liver. While I hesitated to overstep the bounds of my expertise, I felt compelled to share my observations with her and encouraged her to consult with her natural path doctor. She took my advice to heart and later reached out to inform me that her doctor had indeed expressed concern about her liver health and recommended a cleanse.

This experience poignantly reminded her of the interconnectedness of mind, body, and spirit. While energy healing provided immediate relief from her stress and insomnia, it also revealed underlying imbalances that needed attention. By addressing these issues holistically, she could take proactive steps toward restoring balance and vitality to her body.

As a healer, it is a privilege and a responsibility to support others on their journey towards holistic well-being. This encounter reaffirmed my belief in the transformative power of energy healing and the importance of listening to the body's subtle messages. By nurturing the mind-body connection and fostering a sense of inner harmony, we can unlock the body's innate capacity for healing and vitality.

These stories, and many others like them, are potent reminders of the profound impact we can have on each other's lives. By guiding others toward self-discovery and helping them reconnect with their authentic selves, we can empower them to live with purpose, passion, and fulfillment.

As I continue my journey as a coach and healer, I am deeply grateful for the opportunity to walk alongside individuals as they redefine their purpose and reconnect with themselves. Each encounter is a sacred reminder of the beauty and resilience of the human spirit, and I am honored to be a part of their transformative journeys.

As I reflect on my journey, I am reminded of the profound interconnectedness of all beings—the intricate threads that weave together the tapestry of life. Through my experiences and challenges, I have discovered a deep-seated passion for inspiring and supporting others on their journeys of self-discovery and healing. Like a lighthouse guiding ships through stormy seas, I am committed to being a beacon of light for those navigating the turbulent waters of life.

Each person's journey is unique, yet we are all bound by a shared humanity—a universal longing to find meaning, purpose, and connection. Through my work as a healer, coach, and mentor, I strive to create a safe harbor where individuals can find refuge amidst life's storms. Here, they can take a moment to catch their breath, redefine their purpose, and reconnect with themselves profoundly.

Central to my philosophy is the belief that true healing begins from within—that by embracing our inner light and honoring our authentic selves, we can navigate life's challenges with grace and resilience. My role is not to provide all the answers but to empower others to discover their truth and wisdom. Together, we uncover the innate gifts and strengths that lie dormant within, igniting a spark of inspiration and possibility.

I encourage those I work with to put themselves first—to prioritize self-care, self-love, and self-discovery. Only when we nourish our souls can we shine our light brightly into the world. Through compassionate guidance and unwavering support, I help individuals recognize their worth, embrace their uniqueness, and step into their power confidently and gracefully.

The journey of self-discovery can be challenging. It requires courage, vulnerability, and a willingness to face the shadows within. But as we journey together, I am reminded of the incredible resilience and beauty of the human spirit. Each breakthrough, each moment of clarity, is a testament to the transformative power of self-love and self-awareness.

My message to all those I have the honor of guiding is simple yet profound: the world needs YOU. Your unique gifts, authentic voice, and shining light are invaluable contributions to the tapestry of life. By embracing your authentic essence and sharing your gifts with the world, you become a beacon of hope and inspiration for others. Together, we illuminate the darkness, celebrate the light, and weave a tapestry of love and connection across time and space. Ultimately, our shared humanity and interconnectedness remind us of the beauty and potential inherent in every soul.

Be a beacon of light in a world that sometimes feels dim, for even the slightest flicker can illuminate the darkest paths.

Bio

Kellie Haehnel, the compassionate owner of The Spirit Wellness Center and International Best-Selling Author, believes in the profound influence of touch, considering it the most potent of our senses. She dedicates herself to assisting individuals on their journey to wellness, encouraging them to transcend the ordinary and connect with their true, authentic selves. Kellie's mission is to serve as a guiding light, providing support and nurturing through heart-centered alternative modalities that promote mind, body, and spirit harmony. Kellie inspires others to wholeheartedly embrace their authentic lives with abundant love and joy, making her a dedicated advocate for holistic well-being.

Are you ready to dive into your inspiration? Check out our exclusive eBook, packed with valuable insights and tips.

www.thespiritwellnesscenter.com

Claudia Brushke-

Finding Purpose: The Transformative Journey to Self-Discovery and Inner Clarity

Claudia is a dedicated transformation and empowerment coach with a rich background in humanitarian work. As the founder of Within The Bigger Picture Coaching and a partner at the non-profit BaRuls e.V., she draws on over 20 years of international experience to drive impactful change.

Claudia collaborates with global organizations and corporations to foster resilience and connection within communities and teams. Her work empowers leaders to build inner strength and self-efficacy, creating a ripple effect that extends beyond individual success to uplift entire communities. Claudia's approach emphasizes social impact and the importance of meaningful, transformative leadership.

www.claudiabruschke.com

"Your purpose in life is to find your purpose and give your whole heart and soul to it." — **Buddha.**

Discovery My Purpose: The Start of My Journey

I'm Claudia, and my journey is seeking purpose, losing it, and rediscovering it with a deeper understanding of who I am and what truly drives me. I initially found my purpose early on, with a clear vision of making a difference and helping others. However, as life progressed, doubt and confusion gradually clouded my sense of direction, leading me to question and lose sight of my purpose.

In this chapter, I invite you to join me as I reflect on this transformative journey. I'll share how I initially enthusiastically embraced my purpose, only to face challenges that made me question my path. Through a relentless pursuit of meaning and a journey of self-discovery, I eventually found my purpose again, now with a richer and more profound understanding.

Today, I'm dedicated to empowering others as an empowerment and transformation coach and through my work with our non-profit organization in Kenya. I focus on helping communities and organizations build resilience, foster connection, and navigate challenges with compassionate and mindful leadership. I hope my story inspires you to explore your journey of self-discovery and find the purpose that resonates deeply with you.

Stepping into the Unknown: How Exploring the World Shaped My Path

From an early age, I was driven by a sense of adventure and a deep desire to make a meaningful impact. I couldn't wait to leave after graduation, even though I had never done anything like this before. While still a student, I knew I wanted to explore the world—to travel and help make a difference. This sense of purpose was clear to me, even though I didn't know what that would look like.

After much searching, I found volunteer opportunities and felt that was a good start. So, right after graduation, I packed my backpack and jumped on a plane to Thailand, a world so different from my own. It wasn't my first time away from home, but there wasn't a host family or familiar culture to guide me this time. Thailand would throw me into the deep end, and I had to learn to swim quickly—finding my way around places that felt strange, navigating conversations without knowing the language, and adjusting to a completely different way of life.

My family was highly supportive, which gave me the confidence to take this leap. Growing up in East Germany, my parents didn't have the same opportunities to travel the world, but they understood the value of broadening one's horizons and experiencing different cultures. Their encouragement, combined with my adventurous spirit, helped me feel fearless. I was doing it on my own, but not alone. Knowing they had my back gave me the wings to explore with confidence.

From Immersion to Insight: The Transformative Lessons from Exploring New Worlds

When I landed in Thailand, I felt like I was coming alive. I'll never forget those first few nights in a small bamboo-walled hostel in Bangkok. Despite the heat, humidity, and noise from the bustling streets, I felt an incredible sense of arrival. I knew this was the beginning of something unique and life-changing. And that's precisely what happened. The following 14 months in Thailand and Kenya would forever change my life.

In Thailand, I worked with a safe house for children from the slums, helping those escaping poverty, addiction, and abuse. I also engaged in a cultural exchange program with local youth, focusing on sharing our cultures and realities to foster mutual understanding. In Kenya, I supported programs for AIDS orphans and helped raise awareness about HIV/AIDS. These experiences allowed me to see these communities' beauty and harsh realities far beyond the typical tourist perspective.

Living with the locals in both countries, I quickly adapted to the often primitive living conditions. I didn't mind staying in makeshift huts in Phuket with water dripping through the roof or in mud houses in Kenya without electricity or running water. What made it so easy for me was the warm welcome I received from the locals and the people I worked with, who shared their lives and culture with me. Through them, I learned the true meaning of resilience, community, and strength.

This journey was more than just an adventure; it was a profound learning experience that solidified my purpose. I realized that exploring the world and working with others was the best way to understand and connect with different cultures and communities. It fueled my passion for empowering others and making a meaningful difference.

Inspired by this experience, I returned to Germany and studied Applied African Studies at university. I wanted to deepen my understanding of development cooperation and learn how to create positive change in communities that lacked access to basic needs like clean water, education, and healthcare, among many other challenges. My studies shaped my approach to working with communities worldwide, but early on, even during my studies, I began to question if I was indeed on the right path.

When Doubt Creeps in Facing Challenges and Confusion

In the early stages of my journey, I felt a deep sense of purpose guiding me. I was passionate about creating positive change and empowering others, believing that my work in development would make a meaningful impact. However, as I pursued this path, subtle cracks began to appear. These cracks represented doubts that grew into more significant questions: Was I making a difference? Was my work truly empowering others, or was it inadvertently creating more dependency and need? The system I grew up in, which often placed value on numbers, titles, and external validations, further fueled my doubts. I began to question how these metrics could genuinely define a person's worth or a project's success. These doubts weren't immediately obvious but slowly shaped my thoughts and perceptions.

Despite these emerging uncertainties, I continued to follow the path I had set for myself, exploring various roles and approaches. But there was always a persistent, nagging sense that something was missing—a feeling that I wasn't fully aligned with the system or the work I was doing. This feeling wasn't something I could easily define at the time. It was more like an undercurrent of unease, a subtle sense that, despite my best efforts, I wasn't where I was supposed to be.

Part of the struggle was that we were not taught how to recognize or understand when something didn't feel right. We aren't given the tools to ask the right questions or to navigate these feelings. Instead, we are conditioned to fit into the systems and structures around us. And when we don't fit, our instinct is to question ourselves rather than the system. This self-doubt can erode confidence and self-belief, making us feel lost and disconnected from our true purpose.

Bridging the Gap: Understanding What Was Missing in My Journey

I did the same. I looked for answers and solutions on the outside, trying to find ways to make the system work for me. I tried different jobs, different approaches, and different roles, hoping that one of them would provide the clarity I was seeking. But the feeling that something was missing persisted, growing stronger with time. It was frustrating because I genuinely wanted to find the right path for myself, decide, and move forward. But I felt stuck, unable to identify what wasn't right and what I truly wanted.

Looking back, I can see more clearly now what some of the reasons were for my feelings of misalignment. The first conflict I started to feel was with the work itself. On the one hand, I sincerely believed in the importance of development and community work. I had seen firsthand how it could create positive change and empower communities. But I also saw how often it fails and sometimes causes more dependency rather than fostering true empowerment. This was particularly true in international development, where I worked on various projects worldwide.

Additionally, the broader societal system—where grades, titles, and salaries often measure worth—felt increasingly misaligned with my values. I struggled with the idea that my value could be reduced to a resume or credentials. My most meaningful experiences came from working directly with communities where no external markers mattered. My commitment, compassion, and support defined my worth in those settings. I felt seen and valued for my identity, not my titles. This is precisely what I wanted to achieve with my work: for people truly to feel valued for who they are and empowered in what they can do.

In the corporate world, my value was determined by numbers and achievements, not by the impact I was making or the relationships I was building. This disconnect was particularly challenging in organizations that had a mission to create a better world. I saw burnout, stress, and internal conflict even in these environments. It became clear that creating positive change on a larger scale required change starting from within, with self-care, support, and a foundation of mutual respect and understanding.

However, I took time to see and understand these things more clearly.

Embracing the Uncertainty: The Journey of Transforming Doubt into Purpose

The more I searched for answers, the stronger my determination became to find out what I truly wanted. Yet, this determination was often met with frustration and a sense of hopelessness. It felt like I was holding a map with countless trails, but without knowing my destination, I was stuck—unsure which path to take. I missed having clarity and direction. I wasn't indecisive by nature, but the lack of a clear path made me feel paralyzed, unable to make meaningful progress. The frustration of not knowing what I truly wanted made change feel impossible.

Looking back on those moments when I felt lost, I now realize how crucial they were in shaping my journey. For over a decade, I struggled to find my true purpose, constantly searching for answers and trying different paths. It was frustrating, and I often felt like I was drifting further from the clarity I sought. Yet, I never gave up. Even when I didn't have the right tools or questions, I listened to that inner voice that told me something was missing, urging me to persist in finding solutions and true meaning beyond the confusion.

Through this struggle, I learned that finding clarity and aligning with one's true purpose is a process—one that demands time, patience, and deep self-reflection. It requires recognizing the discomfort of misalignment, questioning the systems we live within, and challenging our own beliefs and expectations. Ultimately, it's a journey that involves looking within rather than seeking answers solely on the outside.

The Breakthrough: Rediscovering Clarity

The turning point that reconnected me with my true self and purpose came in 2018, in a moment of undeniable clarity. After years of frustration, confusion, and struggling to understand what I truly wanted from life, this profound shift transformed my life forever. It came unexpectedly during a casual conversation with a friend who was unhappy with his job and life circumstances. I encouraged him to take action, pointing out that remaining in an unsatisfying situation was far worse than making a change.

It wasn't until days later that the irony hit me—I had been giving him the very advice I needed to follow. This realization was the catalyst I had been waiting for, sparking the change I so desperately sought and setting me on a new path of self-discovery and purpose.

I remember that moment vividly. It was a cold, rainy evening in November, and I sat on the carpet in front of my fireplace, the darkness outside reflecting the uncertainty I felt inside. But as I sat there, something shifted. It was as if a light suddenly turned on, revealing a path that had been hidden for years. In that moment, I experienced an overwhelming sense of clarity—a stark realization that I had been avoiding change by waiting for the perfect solution. The breakthrough didn't come from finding the right answers; it came from understanding that I needed to take decisive action, even if I couldn't see the entire path ahead. I still remember the suffocating feeling of seeing myself in the same place and situation five years into the future. That night, I made the first decision: I would quit my job. I didn't know what would come next, but I was convinced that by creating space in my life, something new and meaningful would find its way in.

That decision set everything into motion. I left my job, gave up my apartment, sold my car, and got rid of most of my belongings. I took time off and embarked on a long-distance hike along the Continental Divide Trail, stretching from Mexico to Canada through the Rocky Mountains. Although I had some experience with hiking and camping, this adventure was on a completely different scale—challenging, uncertain, and exhilarating all at once. But that clarity I had gained gave me the confidence to embrace the unknown.

The Trail to Self-Discovery: How Solitude and Nature Revealed My True Self

As I hiked through the wilderness, I reconnected with myself in ways I had never imagined. The solitude, physical challenges, and the raw beauty of nature forced me to slow down and be present. Each day on the trail taught me to listen to my body, mind, and inner voice. Without distractions, I could reflect on my life, choices, and beliefs. The experience taught me that real change doesn't come from trying to fit into an external system or searching for solutions outside myself. True transformation begins within.

That hike was a turning point when I fully embraced and embodied the changes I needed to reconnect with my true self. I learned that clarity comes from within and, with it, the ability to understand why we react to situations the way we do. I began to see how our beliefs, behaviors, and habits shape our reality and how much power we have in choosing how we respond to life's challenges. This understanding of inner strength and grounding became the foundation for my personal growth.

Finding My Missing Piece: The Transformative Power of Mindset and Inner Change

My journey through uncertainty and self-discovery has ignited a deep passion for personal development and transformation. After this turning point and my time on the trails, I realized that the missing piece in my life was understanding and embodying the principles of mindset and inner change. This revelation was like finding the final puzzle piece that brought my purpose into focus. For so long, I struggled to see how to genuinely align with my purpose of making a difference and empowering others. I knew my goal was to help others discover their own strength, but but I wasn't sure how to fully live and reflect this in my own life and work. Now, I feel deeply aligned with my purpose and a renewed sense of clarity about how to achieve it. My approach to personal development has evolved into a central focus of my professional life.

Since that transformative moment, I have immersed myself in personal development, investing significant time and effort into understanding and mastering mindset and inner change. I've attended workshops, participated in seminars, and earned a coaching certification, all of which have not only accelerated my own growth but have also become the foundation of my professional approach. These experiences have profoundly reshaped my methods in coaching and community empowerment, giving me the tools to guide others toward their own transformation.

The Strength of Community: How Connection and Support Build Resilience and Purpose

A key lesson from my journey has been the profound value of support and community in building resilience and purpose. While my parents provided a strong foundation for my resilience, it was my work with diverse communities abroad that truly revealed the power of collective strength. I learned that genuine resilience isn't just about personal toughness—it comes from forward-thinking, adaptability, and, most importantly, the ability to unite and support each other through challenges.

Furthermore, finding my tribe of like-minded individuals made a significant difference. Sharing my story with others on similar paths gave me clarity, direction, and encouragement I needed. I realized that true strength isn't found in isolation, but in the connections we foster and the stories we exchange.

Today, these insights shape both my personal life and professional work. As an empowerment and transformation coach, I guide individuals and communities to develop the right mindset, behaviors, and beliefs necessary to build resilience and foster deeper connections.

My mission is to equip others with the tools to navigate challenges and align with their true purpose. By cultivating supportive and compassionate communities, I strive to create lasting impact and empower others to make a broader difference in the world.

From Setback to Strength: The Ripple Effect of Inner Transformation on Community Impact

A vivid example of my transformation can be seen in my work in Kenya. Initially, my focus was on implementing and managing community projects—tasks that, while important, only scratched the surface of true empowerment. As my perspective shifted toward fostering inner strength and resilience, so did my approach. This shift proved especially critical when we encountered a major challenge: a project leader misappropriated significant funds, breaching the trust of the entire team. In the past, such a setback would have led to widespread frustration and hopelessness, with many resigning to the belief that such breaches were inevitable. But this time, I approached the crisis with a new understanding.

Drawing on my deeper insights into resilience and inner strength, I guided the team through the crisis with a focus on maintaining clarity and staying grounded. One key strategy was using a visualization technique, where I encouraged the team to imagine a protective barrier, helping them remain calm and focused despite the deceit they faced. This not only allowed me to handle the situation more effectively but also set a powerful example for other project leaders on how to stay centered and resilient in moments of adversity.

Beyond managing my own response, I worked closely with the leaders to help them rebuild trust within their teams and reinforce the foundation of our collective vision. We shifted the focus toward open and compassionate communication, encouraging leaders to support each other and foster a sense of unity. By aligning with our shared vision and maintaining a strong sense of purpose, we turned what could have been a devastating setback into an opportunity for growth.

The leaders not only addressed the immediate crisis but also learned to build stronger, more resilient teams capable of tackling future challenges. They developed skills in compassionate communication, mutual support, and keeping their focus on their vision. As a result, the entire community grew stronger. The transformation has been remarkable—project leaders now face challenges with confidence and self-efficacy. They apply the lessons from past difficulties with a proactive, positive mindset, leading to improved project outcomes and a culture of continuous learning.

Witnessing this transformation has been incredibly rewarding. It reinforces the power of personal development and its far-reaching impact on individuals and communities. Seeing leaders approach challenges with resilience and pass those lessons on to others is the essence of empowerment. This experience highlights that fostering inner strength and compassion can lead to lasting positive change.

My personal journey has equipped me with the tools and insights to support others in their growth. The lessons I've learned and the strategies I've adopted are now central to my work as a coach, allowing me to facilitate meaningful transformations. Helping individuals and communities build resilience and align with their shared purpose has brought me clarity and fulfillment, affirming that true empowerment starts from within and radiates outward.

Insights for Your Journey: Valuable Advice for Navigating Uncertainty and Finding Purpose

As you begin your journey to discover your purpose or make a meaningful impact, remember that the path is often winding and uncertain—yet that's perfectly okay. The first, most essential step is to tune into your inner voice, the one that knows you're meant for something greater. Trust that intuition, even when the way forward seems unclear.

In my experience, I've learned that the answers you're looking for are already within you. It's easy to seek solutions outside yourself, but the reality is we have little control over external circumstances. What we can control is our mindset, beliefs, and behaviors. By aligning with your inner self, you can navigate your path with confidence, creating solutions even in the face of challenges. This internal clarity becomes your compass, guiding you through uncertainty and keeping you grounded in your purpose.

One powerful way to find that clarity is through reflection. When you're feeling overwhelmed or unsure, taking a step back can offer the perspective you need to move forward with renewed energy. Engage in activities that make you feel alive and reconnected with your core self. These moments of self-care are crucial - they help you to recharge and refocus, allowing you to return to your path with fresh energy and insight.

Another vital lesson is the importance of taking decisive action. Often, the hardest step is releasing what no longer serves you. Holding onto what drains your energy can be consuming, leaving little room for growth. Trust that any change, even when uncomfortable, opens the door for better opportunities. Every experience, whether positive or challenging, contributes to your growth. When faced with numerous options, take time to evaluate them carefully. Choose the one that resonates with your inner truth. Even if it's not the "perfect" choice, taking action will reveal more about your desires and needs, fueling your growth and self-discovery.

Resilience will be one of your greatest allies on this journey. As you gain clarity and align with your inner self, challenges will continue to arise—but a clear vision will serve as your anchor, keeping you focused and determined. Resilience allows you to adapt and thrive, even when the path gets tough. Knowing where you're headed empowers you to make decisions confidently, free from external pressures. It helps you build the inner strength necessary to stay committed to your purpose, no matter what obstacles you encounter.

To support this process, develop practices that nurture your inner clarity and resilience, such as mindfulness, journaling, or visualization. Mindfulness keeps you grounded and calm in times of chaos. Journaling helps you process your thoughts and emotions, providing deeper insights into your desires and fears. Visualization creates a mental blueprint of your goals and the steps needed to achieve them, reinforcing your focus and commitment.

Remember, your purpose doesn't need to be grand or perfectly defined right away. It evolves as you do. Begin by taking small, meaningful steps that align with your feelings. Each step will bring you closer to the clarity you seek. Don't be afraid to experiment or make mistakes—they are essential to your growth.

Surround yourself with a supportive community. Seek out mentors, peers, or groups that understand your journey and can offer guidance and encouragement. Collaboration and connection are critical—none of us succeed alone. Being part of a community that shares your values and goals provides you with the support, inspiration, and motivation to keep moving forward.

Finally, approach your journey with compassion—for both yourself and others. Growth and self-discovery are processes, not destinations. Be patient, celebrate your progress, and stay dedicated to your vision. Your unique strengths and experiences have the power to create meaningful change—not only in your life but in the lives of those around you. By aligning with your true purpose and building the resilience to face challenges, you can make a lasting, positive impact on the world.

Creating a Ripple Effect: Future Goals for Empowerment and Sustainable Impact

Looking ahead, my future goals are grounded in deepening my impact and expanding the reach of the work I am most passionate about. As a woman driven by purpose, I am dedicated to continuing to empower individuals and communities by sharing the knowledge and tools that have been transformative in my own journey. My focus is on creating more opportunities for personal growth, resilience-building, and leadership development, particularly for women and marginalized groups who face the greatest obstacles.

I am creating and already working with workshops and online programs that provide accessible and practical resources for cultivating inner strength and aligning with one's true purpose. Additionally, I continue to collaborate with global organizations to implement sustainable community projects that prioritize economic development as well as emotional and mental well-being.

My vision is to create a ripple effect, where those I support go on to inspire and uplift others, ultimately building stronger, more compassionate communities across the world. As I continue on my journey, I will keep learning, growing, and adapting—staying true to my vision while remaining open to new possibilities. My journey is far from over, and I am committed to evolving alongside the people and communities I serve, making a lasting, positive impact on the world.

Final Reflections: Embracing Your Journey and Purpose

Reflecting on my journey, I see how every step—a triumph or a challenge—has shaped me into who I am today. The moments of uncertainty, frustration, and breakthrough have all been essential in helping me understand my deeper purpose and develop resilience. Through these experiences, I've learned that true empowerment comes from within and that aligning with our inner selves is the key to unlocking our potential and making a meaningful impact in the world.

The heart of my story is simple: we all possess the power to create lasting change, but it begins by tuning in to that quiet inner voice that knows our true purpose. It's about cultivating resilience, staying connected to our vision, and taking bold steps forward, even when the path seems unclear. One of the most profound lessons I've gained is that we don't need to wait for the perfect moment or ideal circumstances. The clarity we seek is already within us, waiting to be discovered.

So, here's what I leave you with: Trust your journey. Embrace challenges as opportunities for growth, and never underestimate the impact you are capable of. Whether your purpose feels grand or modest, it is uniquely yours, and the world needs the contribution that only you can offer. Now is the time to step forward, align with your purpose, and create the difference you were born to make.

"All our dreams can come true if we have the courage to pursue them."

— **Walt Disney.**

Bio

Finding Purpose: The Transformative Journey to Self-Discovery and Inner Clarity

Claudia is a dedicated transformation and empowerment coach with a rich background in humanitarian work. As the founder of Within The Bigger Picture Coaching and a partner at the non-profit BaRuIs e.V., she draws on over 20 years of international experience to drive impactful change.

Claudia collaborates with global organizations and corporations to foster resilience and connection within communities and teams. Her work empowers leaders to build inner strength and self-efficacy, creating a ripple effect that extends beyond individual success to uplift entire communities. Claudia's approach emphasizes social impact and the importance of meaningful, transformative leadership.

www.claudiabruschke.com

Julia Michasiewicz-

Unlocking your Sales: The powerful synergy of effective Marketing Strategies and Energy Work

I am an artist at heart. This fact plays a significant act in the story I am about to tell you. Beauty, in any form, has always been an instrument that transcends my soul. I grew up in a Slavic family—Polish, to be precise—as you can tell by my surname. Born and raised in a country of art and sophistication, namely France, I took immense pride in my culture. Polish culture's vibrant, colourful traits mixed beautifully with the French chic. I loved considering myself a quirky, chicky, and the world's noisy young lady.

Growing up, I had big dreams. I wanted to travel the world, but most importantly, I wanted to make a difference! That was until I was shut down by my own self-doubts, insecurities, and the noise of the world. "You have to grow up," they said. "Find a serious job!" After all, who was I to think I could make a difference in the world? I didn't have a specific talent or anything.

My fears made me crave security. I wanted to appear successful more than I wanted to be successful. Most importantly, I wanted to choose the path that seemed the safest! I chose the stability of a 9-to-5 job in finance, specifically in audit. Don't get me wrong; I was fortunate. I found a job in the public sector that matched perfectly with my love for volunteering and traveling. I travelled to places I would have never visited and met incredible people— all in the safe bubble of my secure job, hiding my true potential behind a computer and a few Excel sheets.

But there was a catch: I felt I was meant for more, deep inside. The sterile environment of numbers and reports stifled my artistic spirit, and I became increasingly empty inside. For years, I tried to bury this feeling deep within me!

All I wanted was a 'normal' happy life—a good 9-to-5, a good man, kids, and a friendly, happy family.

I was convinced that art and creativity couldn't be part of the equation and that to sustain my life, I needed money; I needed to be serious!

Until I realized that the price I was paying for this seemingly happy life was way too high. True fulfilment isn't found in living the life you're "supposed" to live. I needed to start my own game and play by my own rules.

Awakening: The Journey to Self-Discovery

What drives me is my quest for authenticity and fulfilment in life. This journey has required immense introspection and courage, particularly when I was torn between societal expectations and my true desires.

On the surface of what seemed to be a successful life, I felt deeply that I was meant for more. No matter how hard I tried to ignore this feeling, it always came back to haunt me. I knew my soul came to this life with a purpose that transcended the comfort of the life I had built.

I greatly admire those who realize their chosen path is not for them and can change direction just like that, even after years of hard work and sacrifice! It takes being brave!

I spent years fighting this feeling. I thought if I could just find someone, have kids, and build a seemingly happy family, everything would be just right!

But the universe— (aka. my soul)—had other plans.

My purpose was much bigger, and resisting it only made that voice louder. No matter how hard I tried, my relationships constantly failed, and I felt like I was merely surviving, never truly thriving, until I hit rock bottom. One more failed relationship and all my hopes and dreams of this perfectly successful facade life were dead once I couldn't fake the strong woman I always claimed to be anymore; I had no choice but to surrender.

I lost my connection with the universe and with it any meaningful sense of direction.

That was one of the darkest moments of my life, but it was also one of the most transcendental. It illuminated my need for genuine self-discovery and the courage to embrace change. I learned that true happiness lies not in the external validation of others but in aligning my passions with my purpose.

I was committed to pursuing my life purpose, yet I had no idea what that purpose was. All I knew was that I needed to find out quickly. The dissonance between my current life and my inner calling became unbearable.

In search of clarity, I embarked on a scary but transformative journey to the Amazon rainforest for an Ayahuasca retreat. This decision began a compelling week in my quest for a deeper understanding of the universe and my unique role within it.

As I immersed myself in the rituals and reflective practices, I faced many challenges, primarily confronting the fears and doubts that had plagued me for years. During the ceremonies, I battled emotional resistance and vulnerability, exposing the layers of my psyche. The experience was enlightening and frightening, forcing me to confront the reality of my existence and the impact I wished to make in the world. Even though I ended the week with probably more questions than answers, I knew this connection to my feminine energy, which is divine feminine, was the key.

I started the quest to reconnect to my feminine energy, which was the start of my extraordinary life!

The Epiphany: Reconnecting to my divine feminine

For years, I operated from a place of masculine energy, relentlessly pursuing a life defined by hustle and grind. This mindset left me feeling exhausted and unfulfilled. My life was shaped by the limiting beliefs that I had to choose between happiness and financial stability. Nothing could be further from the truth! As a matter of fact, fulfilment leads to abundance, but more on that later.

Each day, I adhered to a belief system that suggested financial success required sacrifice at the expense of my joy and well-being.

But I was completely mistaken. The truth is that not only do you not have to choose between happiness and success, but fulfilment is exactly what leads to success. The two most obvious reasons are that when you do what you love, you do it with more passion, and naturally, you will be brilliant at it. The second reason, which you will have to trust based on the miracles I and many other have witnessed and experienced pursuing their Purpose, is that when we are on the right path, we do get help from the other side. It doesn't mean it will be easy, but here's the thing: there is no easy journey, so we might as well choose the most meaningful journey.

Reconnecting to my divine feminine energy led to extraordinary results. Slowly, I was able to reconnect with my intuition and emotional intelligence, transforming my approach to life and work, allowing me to create a reality that felt more aligned and authentic. It opened my eyes to the world we live in.

This led me to realise that I wasn't the only one who had chosen a life that wasn't truly mine.

The world is shaped by very toxic beliefs such as "life is hard," "money doesn't grow on trees," and "we can't make money out of what we love." I already know that some of you will be reading these lines thinking, *"Yes, I work X hours per day to barely feed my family. Yes, life is hard."* If this is you, I know this might be hard to read, but your beliefs have shaped your reality. The world is a whole of possibilities; the ones that were available to your perspective were the ones that aligned with your beliefs.

As women, especially in the corporate world, we tend to believe that to fit in, we need to operate from our very masculine energy, completely disconnecting from our divine feminine. We do not realise we are leaving our most significant power on the table—the power to create miracles.

We don't need to work hard, be consistent, or be disciplined to achieve success. Digging the wrong hole doesn't matter how consistently you dig; you will never reach the treasure. Using the power of intuition and simply asking the Universe is the simplest, most efficient way to dig in the right place. My life mission became clear: to rebalance the feminine and masculine energies and help women create the life and abundance they genuinely deserve with ease and joy.

From Whisper to Roar: Embracing My Authenticity

We live in an incredible world where I can begin sharing my truth online and spreading the message about the amazing power within. I was so excited and hopeful; however, I quickly discovered that expressing this mission effectively was a different challenge altogether.

Initially, I shared my insights through social media platforms like Instagram and Facebook to connect with my audience. However, I realised that crafting a message that truly resonates is an art form in itself.

I became obsessed with learning about copywriting, messaging, and personal branding for my own needs at first. I needed to figure out how to spread my message.

Quickly, I realised that there are countless extremely talented people online who are struggling with promoting and selling their offers. Overcoming these limitations is crucial to building a prosperous business and attracting clients consistently.

I became obsessed with learning about copywriting, the art of effective communication, messaging, and personal branding for my own needs at first. I needed to figure out how to spread my message.

I noticed that many women worked diligently to generate leads but often met with disappointing results, blaming the strategies and shifting the approach, only to generate similar results, which is extremely frustrating.

Overcoming these limitations is crucial to building a prosperous business and consistently attracting clients while promoting.

The secret lies in powerful messaging, falling in love with selling your offer, and aligning your marketing strategy with your energy.

My epiphany was that we could harness our divine feminine energy to enhance our marketing efforts, just as we do in other areas of life. By combining this powerful energy with effective strategies, extraordinary growth becomes possible.

Thus, I discovered that energetic marketing is the key to unlocking the potential of our efforts, allowing us to transform passion into a successful business. This realisation not only guided my own journey but inspired me to empower others to embrace their unique voices.

Stronger Together: The Transformative Power of Building a Support Network

I quickly understood that nobody succeeds alone. I have been fortunate to manifest the exact people at the perfect time to support the growth of my business.

These key supporters shared their wisdom and guided me in developing essential skills. Initially, I believed my spiritual path was meant to lead me to empower other women in business, only to realise that my spiritual evolution truly began as I immersed myself in the business world.

Entering the business world makes us face our deepest fears. Overcoming these fears leads to the purest form of freedom, but having the right people to provide you with the right tools and skills on this journey is crucial on your path to success.

I truly understood that having a solid network was an absolute game changer in my journey. I had a strong desire to create a strong community of women empowering women.

While online coaching offers flexibility and accessibility, nothing compares to the energy generated in face-to-face interactions.

This realisation inspired me to organise free in-person events designed to gather inspiring women and foster a climate of collaboration and empowerment.

At these events, women come together to share experiences, build meaningful connections, and uplift one another. The energy in the room is palpable, igniting new ideas and motivation. Additionally, my program includes a business retreat—a vital experience that accelerates growth and elevates participants' businesses over just one weekend.

Ultimately, it is the combined strength of my mentors and the vibrant community I have cultivated that propels my journey forward. This network supports individual growth and ensures that we all rise together, embracing a shared vision of empowerment and success.

One of the most significant milestones in my journey was organising my first retreat in France last summer. This experience was not just an event; it became a transformative moment that solidified my belief in the power of womanhood.

As gathered diverse women from various backgrounds working on their entrepreneurial journeys, I witnessed firsthand the magic that unfolds when women support each other. The energy in the room was just amazing, filled with laughter, shared stories, and mutual encouragement.

It was a celebration of strength and resilience, and in those moments, words felt inadequate to express the profound connection we shared.

Building a community where women could feel safe, heard, and empowered is the most beautiful feeling I've ever experienced. Through workshops and discussions, we uncovered our true potential, learning from one another and igniting passions that had long been dormant. The success of this event has shaped my trajectory, reinforcing my commitment to creating spaces where women can uplift one another. It inspired me to pursue more opportunities for collaboration and connection, solidifying my role as a facilitator in this empowering journey.

Ultimately, this milestone taught me that together, we can achieve what seems impossible, and it ignited a stronger desire within me to champion women's voices and experiences as a pivotal part of my mission moving forward.

The courage to Believe: How connecting to my Life Purpose helped me rise beyond doubts.

Starting a business is undeniably a challenging journey, marked by a slow, often frustrating process that demands immense resilience and patience. Each step forward is intertwined with feelings of fear and doubt. I vividly remember the anxiety I felt when posting my first video—the fear of judgment, the fear of being ridiculed publicly. Similarly, my first sales call was extremely scary; I was sweating, overwhelmed by insecurity, and secretly wishing that the person wouldn't show up. Many women embarking on entrepreneurial paths can relate to these initial struggles. However, as I navigated these challenges, something transformative occurred. The deeper I delved into my entrepreneurial journey, the more I connected with my life purpose.

This profound connection created a powerful shift in perspective. When you align with your purpose, the weight of doubt and fear begins to lift. Suddenly, self-doubt and fears become irrelevant in the face of the greater mission; it isn't about me anymore.

Embracing this purpose ignited an extraordinary sense of freedom within me. It's as though the barriers that once felt insurmountable faded away, replaced by an unwavering commitment to my vision. Throughout my personal and professional growth journey, I've been driven by a deep desire to give back to my community and the world. As I developed my business and gained confidence, I recognised the importance of uplifting others, particularly women, in their pursuit of fulfilling their life purpose. This realization sparked my initiative to organize free in-person events to inspire women to embrace the potential of living a life they love while being generously rewarded for their passions. In these events, I share the teachings of the Feminine Alchemy Academy, fostering a supportive environment where women can connect, learn, and thrive. It's not just about individual success; it's about creating a ripple effect that empowers others to chase their dreams. I strongly believe in the philosophy that giving back makes a virtuous circle: the more we contribute to others' lives, the more we receive; the more we receive, the more we can give, both personally and professionally. Through mentorship, workshops, and community outreach, I aim to spread knowledge and resources that uplift women globally. By fostering an atmosphere of cooperation and encouragement, I strive to ensure that more women are aware of their potential and the possibilities available to them.

Ultimately, my contributions are not just initiatives but a commitment to cultivating a sense of community where each woman feels valued, inspired, and capable of creating her own success story. Together, we can shape a brighter future, one event and one woman at a time.

Reflecting on the impact is the most incredible feeling of fulfilment. I've guided women in building their businesses through my coaching, which is a great privilege. My mentees recently shared, "Thanks for your support and advice! I never thought I could achieve this level of success." Hearing such testimonials motivates me to continue pushing forward. Additionally, my work organising workshops on unlocking the power within has significantly benefited participants, which is the greatest reward for my efforts. Each story and testimonial fuels my passion, reminding me that positive change is always within reach.

Starting a business has been the most beautiful spiritual journey of my life, revealing my deepest fears and limiting beliefs. I developed resilience, adaptability, and self-awareness—essential equational growth, transforming my mindset and skillset.

By implementing my simple four-step process for reprogramming the mind, I discovered an effective tool to confront and overcome my inner obstacles. This process not only catalysed the growth of my business but also facilitated significant changes within myself, fostering greater peace, freedom, and trust in my life.

Ultimately, my contributions are not just initiatives but a commitment to cultivating a sense of community where each woman feels valued, inspired, and capable of creating her own success story. Together, we can shape a brighter future, one event and one woman at a time.

I learned to embrace uncertainty and view setbacks as stepping stones rather than roadblocks. This shift in perspective has empowered me to approach problem-solving with a positive mindset and a strategic outlook. Moreover, feeling guided by the universe—and sensing support from a higher power—has added vibrancy to my life. I now navigate my journey with an open heart, grateful for the lessons that every experience brings.

Each challenge became an opportunity for learning, allowing me to cultivate a deeper connection with my intuition and the universe.

The personal growth I've gained through this entrepreneurial journey has been transformative. I'm not just building a business; I'm evolving as a person, continually learning and expanding my horizons while fostering a more profound sense of purpose in everything I do.

Self-doubt and imposter syndrome used to be my constant companions throughout my journey, yet I discovered that connecting deeply with my purpose significantly diminishes these feelings. Embracing a mission greater than myself has been a freeing experience, making all my doubts and fears irrelevant.

While fear still exists in my life, I no longer let them control my actions anymore. When I decided to book a room for an in-person event, I was highly fearful, regardless of the outcome. I worried that no one would attend; that would have been brutal—all that energy and money invested for nothing! But believe it or not, I also feared the opposite—that people would come! Then, I would have to deliver the best possible workshop and ensure they gained so much value from this day! What if I was not able to do it? What if I wasn't good enough? What if they didn't enjoy it? These thoughts rushed into my head, creating a whirlwind of anxiety. My deepest fear use to be the fear of being seen, and I let it lead my life for a long time. Choosing a career where I could hide behind my computer was not a coincidence—organising a full-day workshop was a huge deal!

However, I leaned into the most straightforward and effective four-step process that powerfully guided me through this journey. This framework is designed to rely on your Higher Self to show you the most. Higher Self whispered the idea of organizing my first in-person workshop, and my Higher Self whispered shop in the first place, as I use it every single day now..

This framework reassured me that I was making the right choice and that I had the capability to succeed. With each step, I felt my confidence building, and I reminded myself of the potential impact my event could have on others. Being guided by the Universe is a game changer; I knew I could not go wrong as this was the guidance I received.

The more I embrace this lifestyle, the fewer doubts I have because I simply because I don't give them any Power anymore.

That is the beauty of being guided by the Universe. Of course, I had to fulfil my part of the contract to make this event successful; I still had to do the marketing, prepare the whole workshop, take public speaking classes, and manage many more logistics, but I knew it was right!

Connecting to my purpose empowers me to face self-doubt head-on, reminding me that the outcome of my efforts holds far more significance than my temporary fears.

Beyond boundaries: Crafting a new era of Possibility

I envision the Feminine Alchemy Academy evolving into a global movement that significantly influences humanity's consciousness. As part of this transformative change, we are in the process of elevating energy and consciousness in the World and the Feminine Alchemy Academy stands as a part of this transformative change. My primary goal is to redefine conventional success, moving away from the relentless hustle and grind that often leads to burnout and dissatisfaction. Instead, I aim to promote a philosophy rooted in self-love and empowerment that leads to extraordinary growth. By integrating the Feminine Alchemy Academy practices, which encourages inner exploration and personal development, we can foster an environment where individuals tap into their innate potential and create a life of abundance and passion. This approach enhances individual well-being and cultivates community, collaboration, and support among participants. Moving forward, my plans involve expanding our reach through workshops, online courses, and community events that resonate with talented, conscious women entrepreneurs, spreading the principles of Feminine Alchemy. Furthermore, I envision partnerships with like-minded organizations and thought leaders to amplify our message. Through these collaborations, we can create a holistic network that empowers individuals to embrace their unique journeys, nurturing a collective shift toward compassion, creativity, and authenticity. Ultimately, the Feminine Alchemy Academy is not just a program; it is a movement dedicated to transforming lives through self-love and conscious living, making a meaningful impact on the world, and inspiring future generations.

If there is one thing, I want the world to remember from my story, it is that if deep inside you feel that you are meant for a bigger life, believe it! Don't wait; act on it now!

The journey toward realising your dreams requires courage and determination, but it begins with that one step. Don't wait for the perfect moment or the perfect plan; take the step that feels best right now. Sometimes, this might mean simply exploring your interests or reaching out to others who share your passions. Another crucial takeaway is the importance of seeking support. Whether from mentors, friends, or family, support can propel you toward your dreams much faster than you could have ever imagined. Surrounding yourself with a network of encouraging individuals can provide guidance, ideas, and motivation. Don't hesitate to ask for help or share your ambitions; you might be surprised by the assistance and resources available.

Lastly, remember that failure is part of the journey. Every setback offers valuable lessons that can shape your path forward. Embrace these moments and use them as stepping stones rather than roadblocks. Trust in your abilities and remain resilient. Keep your vision clear and believe that you deserve a fulfilling life. Follow your intuition and take action; you can achieve more than you know!

Opportunities have never been as abundant as they are today. Social media offers a great platform to do so; use it to create the life you deserve.

If there is one thing I've learned through my journey as an entrepreneur, it's that there are more opportunities than ever to pursue what you love and be generously rewarded for it. In today's world, the barriers to entry for starting a business have significantly lowered, allowing passionate individuals to turn their dreams into reality.

However, it requires a clear strategy for success and mastery of clear communication skills. Combining powerful personal branding—including effective messaging and marketing—with energy work is the most effective way to stand out in this overcrowded market. Building and marketing your business online has now become more accessible than ever.

Collaboration plays a crucial role in driving success and innovation. It allows individuals and businesses to combine their strengths, share resources, and expand their reach in ways that would be challenging to achieve independently. Throughout my experiences, partnerships have fostered growth and enhanced visibility in the marketplace.

Collaborations have not only fueled my creativity but also provided fresh perspectives and insights that inspire new ideas. By engaging with others, I have accessed diverse skill sets and knowledge that have enriched my projects.

Moreover, collaborations enhance authority in the market. When businesses align with reputable partners, they create a more substantial brand presence, leveraging each other's credibility to establish customer trust. This synergy encourages a culture of shared learning, which ultimately drives innovation. To build a strong network, be open to new opportunities, and actively seek out potential partners who share your vision and values. Attend industry events, engage on social media, and participate in collaborative projects. It's essential to cultivate relationships based on mutual respect and support. Regular communication is vital; maintaining connections with your network can lead to unforeseen opportunities in the future.

Balance and Self-Care

Maintaining a balance between my mission and personal life is vital for my well-being and success. As I delve into the importance of feminine energy, self-care emerges as a crucial priority. It creates harmony between my feminine and masculine energies, allowing me to welcome miracles.

Starting my business has been one of the busiest periods of my life. Juggling that with a full-time job forced me to evaluate my priorities and make sacrifices. Surprisingly, this experience became a blessing, sharpening my focus on what truly matters. I found myself saying no to activities like nights out and drinking alcohol, realising they added little value to my life, to say the least. It hit me that in the past, I had engaged in these activities to "fit in," but they were never genuinely fulfilling to me.

I had to completely reevaluate what has value and what doesn't in my life. It was clear that preserving time for the gym and practicing self-care was a priority. These practices not only boost my physical health but also nurture my mental and emotional well-being.

Embracing self-care allows me to maintain the balance I seek, ensuring I can passionately pursue my mission while nurturing my personal life.

By prioritising myself, I cultivate resilience and clarity, paving the way for progress and joy on this journey.

The Power of Community

Being part of a community has profoundly empowered me, catalysing personal growth and purpose. Choosing consciously and carefully whom I let into my life has been a game changer. When I began to embody my life purpose, I sought connections that aligned with my values. This led me to an incredible community of like-minded women with similar aspirations and challenges. Their support and encouragement became a powerful blessing.

In this nurturing environment, I discovered the importance of collective action. We uplifted each other through shared experiences, creating a safe space to express our dreams and fears. Collaboratively, we embarked on projects that advanced our individual goals and contributed positively to our broader community. Through this journey, I've learned that community empowers individuals and amplifies their impact on the world.

Conclusion and Final Thoughts

As I conclude my story, I want to leave you with a heartfelt message: pursue your passions and make a difference. Life is filled with opportunities waiting to be seized, yet often, we find ourselves hesitating, confined by fear or doubt. My journey has taught me that the most rewarding experiences arise from stepping outside our comfort zones and embracing what truly ignites our spirits. When you follow your heart, you unlock your potential and inspire those around you to do the same. I hope my story resonates with you, encouraging you to take that leap of faith toward your dreams. Whether starting your business, advocating for a cause you believe in, or daring to try something new, remember that your actions can create ripples of change. In a world that often prioritizes conformity, be a beacon of authenticity Share your unique gifts, and don't hesitate to make an impact, no matter how small. We can cultivate a landscape of passion, creativity, and meaningful change. So, go forth and pursue what fills your heart; the world needs your light.

Alana Corpuz-

Female Contractor Creating Spaces and Transforming the Outdoor Environment

So, I have a dream to reverse the 100 years plus of destruction humans have caused to the planet. Ever since I was a little girl, I have made choices with a carbon footprint. I have built a successful business that honors my values, continues to educate others, and attunes the human eye's awareness of the beauty of the natural world. I have a dream that my children's children will not be worried about the accelerating natural disasters, the economic despair across the globe, that they will have the privilege of drinking fresh water, breathing clean air without artificial filtration, and consuming organic foods that have not been modified or sprayed with chemicals to make them grow.

This dream is not too much to ask for. It is about integration. It is about giving back. It is about respecting the very thing that supports our existence: the Earth. Do you know right now the majority of villages in the Amazon that do not have access to fresh water? These are the very areas where we originally extracted medicines to cure infections to create antibiotics in Western society to cure centuries of pain and disease. This is where natural petroleum is extracted to fuel jets that bomb countries, fuel wars that tear cultures to shreds, fuel a trucking industry that feeds modern-day consumerism, and fuel our entire global economy that capitalism is built upon.

Yet, the very people who live in these natural environments, who depend on the natural resources of their environment, cannot drink fresh water; their rivers are contaminated with trash and oil streaks so visible

324

you can see it in a cup of water. What I know is that with the advance of technology, the collective intelligence of the human mind and science, the development and integration of AI, and the genuine movement of humans rising to their highest potential, we have the capacity and all the tools to heal our earth, not continue to extract from it. And all it takes is consistent micro actions from everyone.

I dream that for every 1 million dollars, any company makes a mandatory donation of 1% back to environmental protection for natural legacy. But how can we claim generational wealth if we are not taking action to protect this earth that our children will be struggling to live in? Just this summer or 2024 alone, the heat has hit records, people in Texas, Las Vegas, Ecuador, China, and Mexico. In Ecuador, people died walking out on the streets, and others were physically not able to go outside because of the heat. It is too hot to be out in the world. "As heat waves get higher and longer and more frequent due to the climate crisis" (CNN Laura Paddison), it is essential to understand the stress it is causing to human bodies and the animals that live in the environment. During June 2024, 14.5% of the world's surface had a record-high June tab and monitored the miles of long beaches at temperature, exceeding the previous June record set in 2023 by 7.4%.

While these numbers combine many factors, I believe there is a direct correlation between modern human life on land; I am listening to "Creating General Wealth" and "Creating Your Legacy" on social media while our race is becoming increasingly detached from the actual Earth we live on. Yes, I am talking about the dirt in the soil, the food we eat, the water we drink, and the air we breathe.

I have been passionate about protecting this Earth since I was a little girl. I grew up on the Big Island of Hawaii and since the age of 8 was participating in the "Keep Our Oceans Blue" movement, protecting sea turtles, creating signs in school classrooms that showed instructions on how to cut the plastic loops around soda cans, and tourist education about the dangers of trash and litter in our oceans. I remember one year, in second grade, after a New Year's Eve firework celebration, waking up before dawn, looking outside and grabbing my mom's broom from the kitchen, walking down the driveway, and at the early hours of the morning, voluntarily sweeping the left-over debris, and eventually getting other neighbors to pitch in on the cleanup. This is one of the thousands of micro-actions I have made for my community and this planet.

When I was 19, I was selected as one of the youngest interns to live and work in a national botanical garden. The national botanical garden, called "The Botan," is located on a small island in the Netherlands, Antilles, one of the southernmost islands in the Caribbean, called St Eustatius. During the internship, every day, we woke at 7 am to tend to the native gardens during the cool hours of the morning. When night came, we took shifts walking and looking for signs of the leatherback sea turtle's presence on the long dark beaches. Often we found them laying eggs or helped new baby hatchlings make their waddling way from the underground sand nest to the ocean. In my early 20s, I developed programs and co-founded an urban community garden in San Francisco, California, named Esperanza. We hosted educational programs for the community and taught high school garden programs, providing classes about permaculture, native horticulture, and medicinal plants, arboriculture, cob/natural building, and even flower bouquets. We converted one empty lot into a community city garden with 25 fruit trees, a cob pizza oven, and rows of organic lettuce that we sold to a local restaurant in the neighborhood. Every action in these community gardens was done with the intention to bring people closer, celebrate life, connect to the earth, touch the soil, and participate in small acts of gratitude. We were part of a "free farmers market," where all walks of life from the unhoused to college students stood in line and filled their grocery bags with free local, organic fruits and vegetables.

This personal drive to protect the Earth and reconnect people's hearts to the natural world began in elementary school and has continued into my adulthood. I am almost 40 years old and have made a career by creating beautiful outdoor spaces.

About 15 years ago, before my now 13-year-old daughter was born, I remember I had a job as a tree arborist, working for the Parks and Recreation in the City of Albany, East Bay Area. As an arborist, I was responsible for tending to all the city trees- assessing disease, pruning, chain sawing, amending, treating, and replanting. Most days, I walked on the sidewalks or led community gardening days. Because I was out in the community, homeowners started asking me if I could select plants for their gardens, which eventually turned into landscape design. I had no formal design education then, but I knew how to draw. So, on the weekends, I would show up at the client's house, sketch out my ideas, select the plants, stones, and hardscape materials, and install these small habitat gardens. I soon learned that I needed more skills in this realm. I had already completed undergrad for a BA in Communications, but I knew I was developing a deep passion for landscape design. So, I went back to school to study landscape architecture. Leaning into my passion and being humble to develop new and useful skills was the beginning to success. Success is not always about the accomplishments, but about the subtle awareness and ability to stop and lean into the opportunities placed right in front of you.

Around the same time, I had begun my partnership with my daughter's dad, Alexis Massol Jr, son of Alexis Massol, an international Goldman environmental prize winner and creator of Casa Pueblo, a 100% solar-powered community-run eco, arts, science, and history center that in 2002 was entrusted by the United Nations to manage and protect the entire mountain ranges and ecosystem of southern Puerto Rico. Honestly, if you want to learn about the environmental "lucha" of Puerto Rico for the past 40 years, I highly recommend visiting Casa Pueblo in Adjuntas, PR; famous musicians and professors from all over the world visit, study, and contribute to the organization. Its grassroots history and story are remarkable and worth the visit just for the inspiration of all acts of natural forest.

I was so inspired by his history, I decided to have my first-born child, Eva Massol Corpuz' birth in the Adjuntan mountains, in the same home, mountains, and jungle where her father had grown up. It was a wild dream, but we made it a reality. At the time, her father and I lived in San Francisco, working and doing everything one does when living in a busy city. However, after growing up in Hawaii and understanding the beauty of Puerto Rico, I knew I did not want my daughter's first breath of life to be in the cold city air. I wanted for her, what I long for all children, for her to enter the world embraced by fresh, cool air, the orchestra of rushing rivers and ocean waves, the chorus of birds, crickets and frogs echoing off of the mountain's walls, surrounded by family, parranda holiday music, rivers and lush tropical forest botany.

Why do I share this intimate personal history? I share all of this because, in reflection, each life decision was created by my deep desire to create spaces. As I have experimented and worked with the earth, I have learned there is a symbiotic relationship with humans who tend to nature; by creating habitat for birds, bees, hidden invertebrates, and the mycelium web in the soil, we then receive the benefits from the trees around us, receiving shade that cools us, oxygen that allows our lungs to breathe and wide canopies for us together and come together in celebration who does not love the shade of tree on hot day, or the sweeping view from a distance of the forest. The more we understand we are part of this earth, the more abundant we feel, the more confident, grounded, at ease, our anxiety begins to melt away, and we settle into our truth.

After my daughter was born, we moved back to San Francisco to continue our life and work. I continued with my studies and landscape projects. I began my career working for other design and construction companies. I knew my limitations when it came to large-scale projects and construction, and for years, I worked and learned from others who had been in the industry for decades. Even after receiving my degree in Landscape Architecture, I took a part-time job for $17/hour. I knew that access to knowledge, and the opportunity to work on large projects would eventually pay off. In 2019, I officially went full-time into my own business. I created the ART GARDEN DESIGN firm to unite men and women from multiple disciples and treat and pay everyone fairly. Since then, it has been a roller coaster; there have been blood and tears shed, beautiful moments, and trivial times, and to this day, I am still learning, transforming, and growing each day.

I remember, before my daughter was born when I ran the community garden projects, there was a blatant crossroads in front of me. It was the spring of 2009, and I was very involved in the dance world; I had been a ballerina and modern dancer since I was five years old and all through college. I was taking five dance classes a week and working as a tree arborist for the city of Albany. I remember toying with the idea: Should I go on the landscape path or should I follow my love for dance? It is so clear, as if it happened yesterday; I was standing in the waiting room at the dance studio in San Francisco, observing the people as I packed up my bag after class. Off in the corner, I saw this girl leaning against the wall; there she was, with her perfect bun, wrapped ballet sweater, and on her cell phone. I looked at the walls and ceilings of the space and the cool air conditioning blowing in and felt at that moment the dance was too linear, too constrained for me.

I could feel all four walls closing in on me. Then, I looked at my hands and began to see landscaping and its vast options and career directions, the opportunity to work in urban planning, private residences, gardens, or public outdoor spaces. At that moment, my heart expanded at the possibility I would never be bored or confined because there were so many different avenues to try. I chose a career as a landscape designer, and I have never stopped since.

What I love about choosing the landscape path over dance is that I did not make a sacrifice. Since dance was and is still a big part of me, I have incorporated my love of dance into my designs. A dominate element in my designs is, movement through space, in more technical terms, paths of travel. It is how all occupants are going to move through the space, the areas you want them to slow down in and the areas you want them to move faster, sit, stand, dance, socialize, and so on. In landscape design, it is crucial to curate a space that does not have pinch points, making sure doorways and walkways are not blocked off or cluttered, creating enough room to move around a fire pit, an outdoor kitchen, or table, yet still keeping it intimate and proportion it, placing meandering paths that slow you down and other areas that are more linear to get from ease to the front or back door, not having trip hazards for older family members, or dangerous drop-offs for little ones and envisioning how the homeowner will move through the space and access the garden, creating ease and desire to pick a fruit from the tree or smell a scented flower.

Creating flow through space is a core element in my design style. The fun part is that every space, person, and project is unique, so the layout is molded and customizable.

My company, ART GARDEN DESIGN, was incorporated in March 2020, a few weeks before the

COVID-19 pandemic shut down. I had all my ducks in a row; I had my degree in landscape architecture, I had my contractor license, all the paperwork, liability insurance, business license, and contract templates, and I was ready with the team to start on the largest project of my career, an entire landscape exterior gut and rebuild from front to back. Guess what happened? We got shut down.

Instantly, my brain went into overdrive; I was like, "Oh hell, no, I have gone this far; I am not going to fail!" A previous client, a doctor, had called me a couple of days after the mandated stay-at-home alert and asked if we could build him some vegetable boxes. He was asking for a "Victory Garden." We built three custom Redwood planter boxes lined with protective gopher wire, hooked up irrigation, backfilled with organic soil, and planted with vegetables. I think, not including the cost of vegetables and irrigation, labor and materials, and overhead, it costs about $2,500 for each planter box. We made about $9,000 installing his vegetable garden.

And I was like, hey, this is a good idea. I pulled out my phone and began calling all past clients, parents from daughters' schools, and anyone I knew who had their number or email. I called and said, "We are now installing Victory Gardens." We built vegetable gardens for two or three months while the world was quiet and tucked safely at home, collecting government checks and wearing masks and gloves at grocery market shopping. It was so simple, yet so profound. After a couple of months, I got that call from my client, and my "big job" was back on schedule; we began the construction and never looked back. For a time reference, this project was in the middle of construction when we had that crazy day in California, where there was so much smoke from the fire, the sun did not show for an entire day. Many people stayed home and inside because this was 2020, not us, we were out in the dark in the middle of the day.

And it has been non-stop for the past 4-5 years. It is a crazy, non-stop rollercoaster that I still am on every day of the week. When you are an entrepreneur, you may take breaks, but there is no such thing as a "weekend off." Before going too further, I want to take a moment to clarify the "landscape construction" piece of this journey. I got into landscape construction because of my love for growing edible foods and medicinal plants. However, I knew if I wanted to have a more significant impact, to reach more people and be heard, I needed to provide more than plant knowledge and garden skills. I wanted to be able to offer everything: demolition, civil grading, engineered walls, drainage, the direction of water from home downspouts and storms, creating leveled and raised areas for gathering and interest, sculpting the landform, designing hardscape and how different materials molded together, understanding the architecture and how to mirror its details in the landscape, build sculptures, and honor other architects, I set out to get my contractor licenses, flowers, and habitat could exist. I wanted to be looked at as an expert in the field, I wanted to be treated with respect, I wanted to share knowledge and experience and insight. And I knew the only way to get there was by going through it, making all the mistakes, asking all the questions, doing all the work, and then finding the answers and continuing to build on the accumulation of knowledge and experience.

While working at the design firm, I set out to get my contractor license. I want to remind you that I was working full-time, doing my design and installation projects on the side, and raising an elementary school child as a single mother. I remember calling my dear friend and saying, I will pay for dinners if you can watch my daughter two nights a week while I go to this night class to get my contractor license. This was another friend of mine who had three children and offered to help for two months while I attended night school to pass my contractor license exam. I cannot believe I did all of this during this time, but I had a goal, a vision, and a purpose, and I knew getting this license was one of the keys to accomplishing my dreams.

I got extremely organized with child care, meal planning, work expectations, client expectations, and put aside summer trips and weekend outings. I am pleased to say, I passed my contractor license test. This certificate gave me legitimacy in California, the ability to create actual contracts, charge higher prices, take on more completed projects, apply for permits, and feel like a bad-ass boss lady. This was only five years ago, and I cannot imagine today going through all that hard work. It is a great reminder that the sooner you push aside instant gratification and focus your energy on the work needed to achieve the long term goal, the smoother the rest of the ride becomes once you make it to the other side.

When my daughter was in elementary school, she used to go to an after-school program, and I would pick her up at 6 pm, drive home, make dinner, get ready for bed, work for a few hours at night, and then start all over again the next day. Today, I will work hard and sometimes long days, but some days of the week, I pick her up at 1:30 pm, go out to a park or pick up a snack, come home, maybe do some work, and then ease into my evening routine. I would say the work I have to do now, 5 years later is more intense, but because I put the hard work in early on, I can condense my work sessions into 2 hour increments and then support my mom, daughter, or community as needed throughout the week. To be clear, I work fewer hours now and make way more than 5 years ago because of the goals and visions I set forth years ago. Those night classes compounded with a whole work week were worth it to have more free time now.

Today, I run a thriving landscape construction company, ART GARDEN DESIGN INC. My most significant accomplishment for this year was collaborating with a local non-profit to provide design and construction services for creating open green spaces in 8 public schools. This is not just a small garden, although those are very important; this is the process of removing 10s of thousands of square feet of asphalt, layers of concrete, and base rock, and then building up the soil and creating an organic infrastructure of large shade trees that have been calculated to be the highest carbon reducing species for that area.

Working with local arborists and nurseries to procure the best quality trees for the installation and then creating days centered around planting understory native plants or spreading mulch layers with the kids from these schools.

The other day, I was putting signs up for our current project; the sign reads, "School Yard Greening and Hands-On Learning WCCUSD $3.5 Million Grant for WCCUSD. The design and installation for 8 green schoolyards is brought to you by ART.GARDEN.DESIGN.INC, the garden education for school programs by GROWING TOGETHER BAY AREA, and the projects funded by CALFIRE." As I hung the signs to the fencing outside one of the schools we were working at, a woman biking stopped to ask me questions. She was a school teacher for 20 years and learned about a large federally funded project for creating safe bike trails for the city. Yet, she had no idea who to talk to, how to facilitate the work, and how to piece everything together. I took about thirty minutes speaking to her on the sidewalk in the shade of some street trees as cars passed on this boulevard.

I explained to her the network I was building; how we could streamline the work by partnering with different companies and non-profits with specific niches. My company provides design and construction services. We can push projects faster through permitting and approval boards because we will install the work. There is less paperwork for details that must be combed through, securitized, and reviewed. We know the most effective and long-lasting way to install the work and can make quick edits in-house to provide the stakeholders with whatever information they request. I have been using this word in all my conversations and speeches lately. "We need to look at all projects from a holistic perspective." Once we see the whole picture, for example, the purpose of the project, who it is to serve, the tasks at hand, the specific funding, the timeline, and other local requirements, once we have a solid and clear understanding of this, we are the right specialist to facilitate the differable to find an environmental education non-profit, and local government facilities and create large demolition companies, other landscape companies, an environmental education non-profit, and local government facilities and creating an ecosystem to streamline any public work project. This has been in process for the past two years: learning, studying, making mistakes, asking many questions, pushing back and seeing how much we can go back, being compliant with the necessary rules, and at all times, being flexible.

The process has been challenging, but I would expect nothing less from life. I would instead push, expand, learn, and grow, make some friends, inspire others, and create natural beauty everyday rather than sit on the beach drinking Piña Coladas y Mai Thai's until the sunset. Don't get me wrong, I love an excellent tropical vacation, but after two days, I'm like, how can I contribute, how can I use my skills to be this world, how can I be humble enough to ask the most straightforward questions that I am genuinely curious about, how can I better understand a situation better, a person's story, a culture. Life is not all about leisure and gratification, it is about creation, innovations, and the opportunity to challenge and expand ourselves, break through ancestral blocks and carve a little history in our contribution.

I cannot reiterate this enough: we need to be our own social archeologists, Digging deep into the human story, into the human emotion, asking "why" do you do the thing you do, "what" makes you get up in the morning, and "where" you resource. I will tell you where I get my infinite source of energy. It is from nature, grandfather Redwood and grandmother Elderberry tree, from sister river and Brother Eagle soaring above. It is when I am entirely silent and consumed by the orchestras of nature, the forest, the ocean, and the beautiful Mother Earth.

I don't care if you live in the densest city or the more rural desert; nature is all around us; we have to seek it out and make an effort to connect; once you arrive, it is there waiting for you to embrace you, teach you, and listen to you. I said earlier that my daughter is my greatest teacher, but nature is my sanctuary, source, and protector, always there waiting for me when I need the most guidance, support, and love.

There is not a day that goes by that I get scared, have self doubt or worry if I am making the wrong decision. When I go deep into my internal think box, my mediation, my intuition and pull out that fear with the strong belief that this is possible. It is possible to create the life you want, to uplift others along your way to success, to honor your skill sets and hard work along the way and become whatever you put your heart into. It is a journey, and it is not over until the very last breath.

Bio

My name is Alana Corpuz, and first and foremost I identify as a mother. I am a mother to a beautiful 13-year-old girl named Eva Massol. She is my compass, my queen, and why I am so driven each day.

Being a mother has forced me to awaken and begin to heal my deepest wounds, it has made me an advocate for the future generations, and given me a purpose outside myself, another life to live for, and a planet Earth to fight for.

As for me, I was born and raised on the island of Hawaii, have been a long-time resident of Oakland, California, and love bringing people together through community gardening projects or just talking about plants and how to heal ourselves through natural remedies. When I am not facilitating my mom duties, I am owner and CEO of ART GARDEN DESIGN INC, a full-service landscape design and construction company that transforms both private and public outdoor spaces. The work we are currently doing is making an impact on the individuals we serve and creating green spaces for human and wildlife habitat.

An Outro Message from Shyla Day

As you turn the final page of this book, I want to thank you from the depths of my heart for joining us on this transformative journey. The stories you've just read are not just words on paper—they are the legacies of powerful women who, like you, are committed to making the world a better place.

You've absorbed their wisdom, shared in their triumphs, and felt the weight of their struggles. I hope you see that every chapter you've read is a mirror of the potential within you. Each of us has the power to create ripples of change, and it begins with taking action, no matter how small.

The journey toward impact is ongoing. Your story is still unfolding, and this book is a testament to the fact that when women rise together, we are unstoppable. Whether you're called to lead, to serve, or to inspire, know that you have a community of women standing beside you, lifting you up.

Let these stories fuel your fire, guide your steps, and remind you that you, too, are a woman of purpose. Keep pushing boundaries, keep breaking barriers, and remember that your unique contribution to this world is more than enough.

Together, we can create the change we wish to see. Let's keep moving forward with grace, strength, and unwavering purpose.

Any part of this book may have been made with the help of AI. No infringement intended.

2024 Women of Purpose

www.Women-of-Purpose.org

About Women of Purpose

Women of Purpose was founded with a single, powerful vision: to create a community where women from all backgrounds, professions, and walks of life can come together to amplify their voices and drive meaningful change. It's more than just a project—it's a movement. Women of Purpose is a platform designed to highlight, empower, and inspire women to live purposefully, to lift one another up, and to challenge the status quo. Every woman has a unique story, a message to share, and a purpose to fulfill, and Women of Purpose exists to celebrate and support that journey.

Through collaborative book projects, global events, workshops, and mentorship, we've built a network where women encourage each other to be bold, resilient, and impactful. By sharing our individual and collective experiences, we're creating a ripple effect that reaches far beyond these pages. Women of Purpose believes that when women come together with aligned values and a commitment to uplift each other, we become a force for positive transformation across industries, cultures, and communities.

In Women of Purpose: Creating a Better World, we honor the visionaries, trailblazers, and compassionate leaders who have contributed their stories to this work. Each of them is a testament to the power of purpose-driven lives. Whether you're an entrepreneur, an artist, a humanitarian, a teacher, or anything in between, Women of Purpose is a space where your story matters. This community is built on the belief that when we support one another, we rise together—and together, we can create a better, more inclusive, and more equitable world.

Let's take a moment to recognize the remarkable impact that each of us is here to make, individually and together. Women of Purpose: Creating a Better World isn't just a book; it's a testament to the power, resilience, and endless possibilities of women across the globe. Each chapter, each story, and each word reflects the courage of women who refuse to be defined by limitations or societal expectations. These are women who have stepped into their purpose, who are lighting the way for others, and who are committed to building a world where voices are heard, achievements are celebrated, and lives are uplifted.

Through this journey, we've learned that no hardship, challenge, or injustice we face as women can diminish our collective strength. As a global community, we understand the unique struggles we encounter and the incredible courage required to overcome them. These are experiences that only we can truly understand, challenges that only we can rise to meet, and triumphs that only we can create. Our shared path isn't always easy, and the obstacles before us are often great—but it is precisely because of these shared challenges that we are uniquely equipped to lift each other up, to inspire resilience, and to create lasting change.

In every corner of the world, women are quietly—and sometimes boldly—changing lives through their skillsets, talents, platforms, businesses, passions, and more. We see women breaking barriers in industries where doors were once closed, leading families and communities with unwavering dedication, speaking truths that challenge systems, and using their voices to inspire change on every level. It's through these diverse and powerful contributions that we create a ripple effect, one that grows with each passing day. Every woman in this movement is a spark of possibility, and together, we are a blazing force for good.

Let this book be a reminder of what we're capable of when we come together with a shared mission to create a better world. Let it inspire you to continue pursuing your purpose, to empower others, and to remain steadfast in the belief that our combined impact can—and will—reshape the future. We are each carrying forward a legacy of strength, courage, and compassion, and by supporting each other, we honor this legacy in a way that's timeless and transformative.

May this book, this movement, and this community serve as a beacon for women everywhere—encouraging each of us to take up space, to embrace our purpose, and to know that we are never alone. We are bound by a sisterhood that transcends borders, and together, we are unstoppable.

Dedication:

This book is dedicated to the women around the world who are still fighting for women's rights and equality. To those who refuse to be silenced, to those who continue to break barriers, and to those who dare to envision a world where every woman has the freedom to live, lead, and thrive. You are seen, you are celebrated, and you are the inspiration behind every word on these pages.

Let's continue to create, to uplift, and to build a better world—together.

Printed in Great Britain
by Amazon